Bookvan

Bookvan

The
Dictionary
Wars

The Dictionary Wars

The American Fight over the English Language

PETER MARTIN

Princeton University Press
Princeton and Oxford

Requests for permission to reproduce material from this work
should be sent to permissions@press.princeton.edu

Published by Princeton University Press
41 William Street, Princeton, New Jersey 08540
6 Oxford Street, Woodstock, Oxfordshire OX20 1TR

press.princeton.edu

Library of Congress Control Number 2019931238

ISBN 978-0-691-18891-1

British Library Cataloging-in-Publication Data is available

Editorial: Anne Savarese and Thalia Leaf

Production Editorial: Ali Parrington

Jacket/Cover Credit: 1. Illustration from a pamphlet on the evolution of the American flag,
c. 1945–50, color lithograph / Bridgeman. 2. Paper stock / Shutterstock

Production: Jacqueline Poirier

Publicity: Jodi Price, Katie Lewis, and Alyssa Sanford

Copyeditor: Beth Gianfagna

This book has been composed in Minion Pro

Printed on acid-free paper. ∞

Printed in the United States of America

10 9 8 7 6 5 4 3 2 1

For Maureen

Scarce any can hear with impartiality a comparison between the writers of his own and another country; and though it cannot, I think, be charged equally on all nations, that they are blinded with this literary patriotism, yet there are none that do not look upon their authors with the fondness of affinity, and esteem them as well for the place of their birth, as for their knowledge or their wit.
—Samuel Johnson, *Rambler*, no. 93 (February 1751)

We can scarcely conceive of a more valuable contribution to the literature of a country, than a good dictionary of its language. He who prepares such a work is . . . identified with the preservation of the language in its beauty and vigor, and its transmission as a correct vehicle of thought, from age to age.
—*New Englander*, January 1848

The War of the Dictionaries threatens to become as celebrated in the annals of literary controversy as [Jonathan Swift's] famous Battle of the Books.
—*New York Times*, May 26, 1860

Contents

Preface

This book is about the turbulent birth pangs of the American language and the American dictionary. The word *wars* in its title spotlights the militancy that characterized the development of the English language in America, the contests for dictionary supremacy between American lexicographers in the nineteenth century, and the keen international rivalry between Britain and America that soiled relations between the two countries regarding the use of the English language during the early years of American nationhood.

The dictionary battlefields in these "wars" were mainly in the United States, where after the American Revolution, the English language was fought over with bitterness scarcely imaginable or understood in Britain. These wars not only pitted lexicographers against each other but also drew into the conflict America's earliest internationally known authors, its first colleges, state legislatures, newspapers, publishers, libraries, and individual citizens all over the rapidly expanding nation. It was a civil war over words that illuminates America's search to identify and know itself. It was about a defining hunger for knowledge of the language and how to use it, about English linguistic heritage and domination and the way that Americans, restless to come out from its shadows, dealt with it. It was also a war between American reformers versus American traditionalists, between the growth of populist democracy and the defenders of traditional values and manners associated with elegance and refinement. It is also about the private war that America's dictionary idol, Noah Webster, waged with himself, arguing himself in and out of self-confidence, attacking people in a way that he knew would be damaging to himself, constantly feeling insecure about his vocation and role in the new nation. America's progress and struggle with the English language, mediated by the country's ongoing dictionary controversies, amounts to a conflicting, acrimonious heritage that helps account for what America is today.

Pronouncements about the language and the publication of new dictionaries, or new editions of dictionaries, made national news and were taken up by pundits who had to weigh in about the niceties of every detail. Everyone, it seemed—the young and the old; people from differing social and economic classes; scholars and leading authors, educators, librarians, and journalists—was looking in different ways at how the language should be managed—or if it should be managed at all. The goalposts for dictionaries were constantly being moved. And overlying that was the ever-present theme of how patriotism should play its part.

This book is also about the personalities and passions vying with each other for a voice in the debates, eager to be heard regarding the English language. And at the center of those disputes were the lexicographers and editors working mostly alone for years on end, struggling to get their books out amid the din of language battles. Their desperation and agonies, triumphs and failures, praise and mockery, seemed to them sometimes not to be worth the lives they feared they were wasting in their studies. It was their fate, wrote the literary "colossus" Samuel Johnson, "to be disgraced by miscarriage, or punished for neglect, where success would have been without applause, and diligence without reward."

Note to readers: Original spelling in quoted sources is preserved throughout. For the sake of clarity, in some instances the modern equivalent is provided in brackets. The reader also may consult the glossary of publishing terms in appendix C, which includes explanations of frequently mentioned book sizes and other aspects of publishing. For currency equivalents of the American dollar between the early nineteenth century and the present, I have used the consumer price index (CPI) provided by the United States Bureau of Labor Statistics: on that basis, $1 during that period is equivalent to about $25 today.

PART ONE

NOAH WEBSTER'S BATTLES

1

British Mockery and American Disdain

"We see with other eyes, we hear with other ears; and think with other thoughts than those we formerly used," wrote Thomas Paine, author of *Common Sense* (1791) and *The Rights of Man* (1792). One of the most persuasive spokesmen for American independence, he championed the clearing away of British "cobwebs, poison and dust" from American society. American independence, he argued, could never be complete without that.

Many Americans thought the same way: that apart from economic stability and success, what they needed almost more than anything else after political independence was intellectual and cultural independence, free from the stifling influence of British arts, letters, and manners. They resented their cultural subservience, which had not disappeared with the signing of the Declaration of Independence. Yet for more than a century after the Revolution, the majority of literate and cultured Americans did not want to turn their backs on British culture, "their ancient heritage"—especially its literature and the historical traditions of its language. About seventy long years after Paine's statement, the popular English novelist Anthony Trollope elegantly expressed this powerful, persistent, and apparently inescapable linkage: "An American will perhaps consider himself to be as little like an Englishman as he is like a Frenchman. But he reads Shakespeare through the medium of his own vernacular, and has to undergo the penance of a foreign tongue before he can understand Molière. He separates himself from England in politics and perhaps in affection; but he cannot separate himself from England in mental culture." Janus-like, and often at less than a fully conscious level,

Americans knew that their "mental culture," whether they liked it or not, was linked to Britain's, and they had little taste for parting with it.[1]

2

America's lingering literary and linguistic attachment to England is nowhere so evident as in the nation's pervasive ambivalence toward Samuel Johnson and his great dictionary, published in 1755, which many call the first major dictionary of the language. He was the great sage of English literature, brilliant essayist, moralist, poet, lexicographer, and biographer, the "Colossus of Literature" and "Literary Dictator" of the second half of eighteenth-century England, a figure thoroughly synonymous with Englishness. Throughout his career as an author, Johnson advertised his multilayered and complicated dislike of America and Americans. In 1756, the year after he published his famous dictionary, he coined the term "American dialect" to mean "a tract [trace] of corruption to which every language widely diffused must always be exposed." He had in mind an undisciplined and barbarous uncouthness of speech. With typical hyperbole on the subject of Americans, he once remarked, "I am willing to love all mankind, *except an American* . . . rascals—robbers—pirates."[2]

Yet Americans could not get enough of him. They devoured his books, which libraries held in great numbers. His influence on American thought and language was vast. Thomas Jefferson recognized this as a grave problem: he wanted to get Johnson off the backs of Americans. In a letter in 1813 to his friend the grammarian John Waldo, he took note of Johnson's *Dictionary* as a specific drag on the country's cultural growth: "employing its [own] materials," America could rise to literary and linguistic preeminence, but "not indeed by holding fast to Johnson's Dictionary; not by raising a hue and cry against every word he has not licensed; but by encouraging and welcoming new compositions of its elements." And yet, as one historian writes, "It was to prove more difficult to declare independence from Johnson than it had been to reject George III." The weight of Johnson's authority on culture in America was a legacy, both positive and negative, that would loom large in the American psyche far into the nineteenth century. Several of the leading American authors at the time actually fed the appetite for Johnson rather than attempted to dampen it.[3]

One of them, Nathaniel Hawthorne, revered Johnson. Although he complained in *Mosses from an Old Manse* (1845), "How slowly our [own] literature grows up," for him Johnson could do no wrong. In London during the 1850s on government business, he recorded in his *English Note-Books* walking in Johnson's footsteps—taking a meal at Johnson's favorite London tavern, the Mitre; traveling up to Lichfield in Staffordshire to pay homage to the great man's birthplace; and exploring Johnson's rooms at No. 1 Inner Temple Lane in London, where his imagination luxuriated in the sense of place: "I not only looked in, but went up the first flight, of some broad, well-worn stairs, passing my hand over a heavy, ancient, broken balustrade, on which, no doubt, Johnson's hand had often rested. . . . Before lunch, I had gone into Bolt Court, where he died."[4] As for James Fenimore Cooper, he was liberally using Johnson's dictionary as his principal authority on the language, even after America's first large (unabridged) dictionary was published by Noah Webster.

This type of American adulation of Johnson persisted into the second half of the century. Herman Melville, in *Moby-Dick* (1851), the novel he dedicated to Hawthorne, has his narrator, Ishmael, remark that in his telling of the story he had "invariably used a huge quarto edition of Johnson [his dictionary], expressly purchased for that purpose; because that famous lexicographer's uncommon personal bulk more fitted him to compile a lexicon to be used by a whale author like me." Louisa May Alcott, in her American classic *Little Women* (1868–69), features Johnson's *Rasselas* and his book of essays, *The Rambler*, in a memorable scene or two. Mark Twain (Samuel Langhorne Clemens), however, was not so positive about Johnson, bearing witness to this Johnsonian obsession even as he debunked it. He had a go at Johnson at the expense of American Johnson lovers when he toured London only a few years before the outbreak of World War I. One day at the Cheshire Cheese tavern, near which Johnson had lived and where, legend has had it, he spent a good deal of time, Twain was enjoying some refreshment in the "Doctor Johnson room" with Bram Stoker, author of *Dracula*, and the American journalist Eugene Field, when he burst out: "Look at those fools going to pieces over old Doc Johnson—call themselves Americans and lick-spittle the toady who grabbed a pension from the German King of England that hated Americans, tried to flog us into obedience and called George Washington traitor and scoundrel." One could understand the adulation of Johnson by the English, he continued, "but of our own people, coming to the Cheese, ninety-nine per cent do so because they don't know the man, and the others because they feel tickled to honor a writer a hundred and fifty years or so after he is good and rotten." For the rest of his time at the inn, in protest against his fellow Americans, he kept up his "slaughter of Johnson." As for himself, he boasted he never read Johnson, "never a written word."[5]

3

Cultural ambivalence was one thing. The persistent burden of cultural inferiority was another, at the center of which were the language and a national literature. There was little leisure, inclination, or confidence in the tempo of the nation's early history to turn to literature and language in order to express and give meaning to the "new circumstances" of nationhood. Jefferson felt particularly strongly about this. A liberal advocate for linguistic reform and "lexical and orthographical innovation" in America as a sensible and natural way of promoting a stronger national identity and confidence, he lamented this weakness. Literary activity in the country was flat, he wrote in his letter to John Waldo, and there was no springboard for it: "[W]e have no distinct class of literati in our country. Every man is engaged in some industrious pursuit. . . . Few therefore, of those who are qualified, have leisure to write." That was regrettable, yet at the same time in order to compensate for the barrenness of the American literary landscape—and revealing his own ambivalence over the British-American cultural imbalance—he encouraged the study of English authors, "the example of good writers, the approbation of men of letters," and "the judgement of sound critics," by means of which the English of Americans could be improved.[6]

Jefferson came in for some English criticism of his use of Americanisms in his only book, *Notes on Virginia*, in 1787. His use of the word *belittle* (a perfectly good word today, of course) in it inspired this piece of mockery in the *European Magazine and London Review*:

> *Belittle!*—What an expression!—It may be an elegant one in Virginia, and even perfectly intelligible; but for our part, all we can do is, to *guess* at its meaning.—For shame, Mr. Jefferson! Why, after trampling upon the honour of our country, and representing it as little better than a land of barbarism—why, we say, perpetually trample also upon the very grammar of our language? . . . Freely, good sir, will we forgive all your attacks, impotent as they are illiberal, upon our *national character*; but for the future, spare—O spare, we beseech you, our *mother-tongue!*[7]

It is noteworthy, incidentally, that Jefferson has been credited with coining about 110 words included in the *Oxford English Dictionary*, and with some 400 quotations providing the earliest record of meanings of specific words. That he felt keenly the importance of freeing American English from English restraints and conventions is as clear as a bell tolling American independence. Americans are different, he pointed out to John Waldo: "The new circumstances under which we are placed, call for new words, new phrases, and for the transfer of old words to new objects. An American dialect will therefore be formed." There was no need to be ashamed of that.

Beware the abuse of such British editors, Jefferson advised Waldo, especially those of the influential *Edinburgh Review*, "the ablest critics of the age," which in Jefferson's view were spewing out retrogressive nonsense about how the Americans had been misusing the language. The best thing for Americans was to nourish their freedom and "separate it [American English] in name as well as in power, from the mother-tongue." Jefferson dreamed of what the American language would become "in strength, beauty, variety, and every circumstance which gives perfection to language, were it permitted freely to draw from all its legitimate sources." That meant using without embarrassment the new American words springing up across the land—Jefferson coined the word *neologize* to describe them—even if "in this process of sound neologisation, our trans-Atlantic brethren shall not chuse [choose] to accompany us, we may furnish, after the Ionians, a second example of a colonial dialect improving on its primitive."[8]

As for dictionaries, whatever you do, avoid looking back to Johnson, Jefferson implored John Adams—although elsewhere he singled out Johnson's *Dictionary* as essential reading for Americans, one of the books he said would "fix us [Americans] in the principles and practices of virtue." In that comment he was remarking on Johnson's *Dictionary* for its moral value, not as a guide to how Americans should use the language. He did not need the authority of any dictionary to sanction the legitimacy of new American words: dictionaries are but the "depositories of words already legitimated by usage. . . . When an individual uses a new word, if ill-formed, it is rejected in society, if well-formed, adopted, and after due time, laid up in the depository of dictionaries." In another letter to William S. Cardell, Jefferson stressed the extreme importance of this subject: "[T]he improvement & enlargement of the scope of our language is of first importance. . . . Judicious neology can alone give strength & copiousness to language and enable it to be the vehicle of new ideas."[9]

John Adams managed to sound even more combative and visionary than Jefferson on the subject of the American language. Notwithstanding the fulminations of British reviewers, he waxed prophetic in a letter to Edmund Jenings in 1780: "I am not altogether, in jest. I see a general encreasing Inclination after English in France, Spain, and Holland, and it may extend throughout Europe. The Population and Commerce of America will Force their Language into general Use." "English will be the most respectable language in the world," he added later.[10]

There was one prominent contemporary of Jefferson's, however, who did not see this matter as did Jefferson and Adams and was greatly troubled by what he observed was happening to the American language. Although he had great admiration for America and Americans, the Scottish churchman John Witherspoon, a signer of the Declaration of Independence and member of Congress, as well as president of the College of New Jersey (renamed Princeton University in 1896) from 1768 until his death in 1794, was one of America's important political figures and intellectuals awkwardly caught in the crossfire of the Anglo-American battle of the languages. Witherspoon understood and appreciated Jefferson's celebration of neologisms and other types of vocabulary expansion as natural parts of language development, but he had no taste for the extreme forms of language he heard cropping up in all walks of life in the country. He deplored American slang and indiscriminate, undisciplined looseness of expression on the part of the better educated, including members of Congress, lawyers, and clergymen: "vulgarisms," "common [grammatical] blunders arising from ignorance," "cant phrases," "personal blunders," and "tautology." "I have heard in this country," he wrote in 1781, "in the senate, at the bar, and from the pulpit, and see daily in dissertations from the press, errors in grammar, improprieties and vulgarisms which hardly any person of the same class in point of rank and literature would have fallen into in Great Britain." Among the *Americanisms* that he said he heard everywhere—he claimed he was the first to use that term to describe differences between British and American English—were the following: the use of *every* instead of *every one*, *contrive it* for *carry it*, *mad* for *angry*, *I thinks* for *I think*, *he had fell down* instead of *fallen* down, *I had wrote* instead of *had written*, had *spoke* instead of had *spoken*, and *drownded* instead of *drowned*. Witherspoon also took note of prolific contractions such as *an't, can't, could'nt, don't, han't, should'nt, would'nt*. He particularly disliked *this here* or *that there*. He did concede that many departures from British English in the higher reaches of American society did not arise from ignorance or "inelegance" and therefore were authentically and therefore legitimately American. That, however, did not make them any more palatable to him. A malapropism was a malapropism, a "personal blunder," in whichever country it occurred, although he said he heard them more often in the United States than in Britain.[11]

4

An avalanche of British attacks on American society and culture in general and language and literature in particular in the early nineteenth century did not improve American self-confidence. While such British offensives did not exist in isolation from larger political events at the time that contributed to a hostility between the two countries, which eventually ignited in the War of 1812, that larger context fails to account for the harshness and frequency with which British writers insulted American life and manners. Many British travelers' attacks in books and the British press were simply outrageous and in poor taste, ill-informed or not informed at all, aiming to appeal sensationally to a portion of the British reading public that was either ignorant of America and prepared to think the worst of it, or welcomed such attacks as exotic and improbable adventure stories.

Fanny Trollope, mother of the novelist Anthony Trollope, wrote a sensational best seller, *Domestic Manners of the Americans* (1832), based on her months of traveling all over the country. An engaging but also wounding account, often insightful and sometimes appreciative, it is marred by a recurring strain of anti-Americanism. As she sees it, the abuse of the language was no small part of Americans' lack of discipline and bad taste and manners. She shudders over what she saw and heard as the vulgarity of American manners and language, appalled at the "strange uncouth phrases and pronunciation." She is short on examples, but in an appendix she added to the fifth edition of her book seven years later in 1839, she records some family conversation in an unspecified part of the country. It contains this specimen of a father's pride in the chickens the family is about to serve up for guests: "Bean't they little beauties? hardly bigger than humming birds; a dollar seventy five for they. Three fips for the hominy, a levy for the squash, and a quarter for the limes; inyons a fip, carolines a levy, green cobs ditto." She links the speech she heard to the prevalent lack of refinement resulting from the low esteem in which women were held. If America was ever going to rescue itself from this revolting social malaise, she writes, it would have to be through the refinements of the arts: "Let America give a fair portion of her attention to the arts and the graces that embellish life, and I will make her another visit, and write another book as unlike this as possible."[12]

In those early years of nationhood, Americans only occasionally protested. If you feel insecure, you are not apt boldly to fire back at your critics. The now forgotten Philadelphia scholar and diplomat Robert Walsh, whom Jefferson once described as "one of the two best writers in America," did protest in "An Appeal from the Judgements of Great Britain Respecting the United States of America" (1818), but he managed simply to reinforce the persistent British belief that Americans were vain and supersensitive to criticism, "cherishing imaginary wrongs." The shocks to American confidence and self-respect, however, being dished out by these British travelers, commentators, reviewers, and authors eventually proved to be too much for Washington Irving. They drove him to write a nine-page essay, "English Writers on America" (1819), in which he aims to stir up Americans to believe in themselves:

> I shall not . . . dwell on this irksome and hackneyed topic; nor should I have adverted to it, but for the undue interest apparently taken in it by my countrymen, and certain injurious effects which I apprehended it might produce upon the national feeling. We attach too much consequence to these attacks. They cannot do us any essential injury. The tissue of misrepresentations attempted to be woven around us, are like cobwebs woven around the limbs of an infant giant. Our country continually outgrows them. One falsehood after another falls off of itself. We have but to live on, and every day we live a whole volume of refutation.

If the English persist with their "prejudicial accounts," they will succeed only in "instilling anger and resentment within the bosom of a youthful nation."[13]

Looking back at a century of such British mockery, the historian Allan Nevins in 1923 conveyed the seriousness of the threat relentless British mockery posed to the American psyche in the first quarter of the nineteenth century and the anxiety it stirred up in the young country: "The nervous interest of Americans in the impressions formed of them by visiting Europeans and their sensitiveness to British criticism in especial, were long regarded as constituting a salient national trait." Henry Cabot Lodge, US senator from Massachusetts, was appalled by the effect on American authors: "The first step of an American entering upon a literary career was to pretend to be an Englishman in order that he might win the approval, not of Englishmen, but of his own countrymen." American poet, journalist, and commentator H. L. Mencken, in his linguistically patriotic book *The American Language* (first published in 1919), provides another retrospective in sections titled "The English Attack" and "American Barbarisms." He describes the clash as "hair-raising," an "unholy war" of words. Captain Thomas Hamilton, a Scot, mentions a few of the prevalent barbarisms: "The word *does* is split into two syllables, and pronounced *do-es. Where*, for some incomprehensible reason, is converted into *whare, there* into *thare*; and I remember, on mentioning to an acquaintance that I had called on a gentleman of taste in the arts, he asked, 'Whether he *shew* (showed) me his pictures.' Such words as oratory and dilatory, are pronounced with the penult syllable, long and accented; missionary becomes *missionairy*, angel, *ângel*, danger, *dânger*, &c."[14]

5

With considerable zeal, the British assault on American values, manners, and achievements also turned to the state of literature in the republic. In 1810, the *Edinburgh Review* was severe: "Liberty and competition have as yet done nothing to stimulate literary genius in these republican states. . . . In short, federal America has done nothing, either to extend, diversify, or embellish the sphere of human knowledge." Again in the *Edinburgh Review*, Sydney Smith, founder and first editor of that magazine, whose brilliant and witty essays and reviews particularly injured American pride, mischievously asked in 1820, "[W]hy should the Americans write books, when a six week's passage brings them in our own tongue, our sense, science and genius, in bales and hogsheads?" Harriet Martineau, while pleased by America's lack of "aristocratic insolence," wrote bitingly in *Society in America* after her travels in America in 1836, "If the national mind of America be judged of by its legislation, it is of a very high order," but "if the American nation be judged by its literature, it may be pronounced to have no mind at all."[15]

The American literati chimed in with vigor. John Pickering, the Harvard-educated diplomat and American jurist and linguist (more about him later), admitted in 1816, "in this country we can hardly be said to have any authors by profession." In his book *The Importance and Means of a National Literature* (1830), William Ellery Channing, the famous Unitarian minister and early Transcendentalist, declared that what he meant by a national literature was "the expression of a nation's mind in writing," and he called for America's literary mind to awaken. America needed "a high intellectual culture" that paid more attention to the spirit than to material aggrandizement: "There is among us much superficial knowledge. . . . There is nowhere . . . an accumulation of literary atmosphere." More than half a century after independence, America still relied "for intellectual excitement and enjoyment on foreign minds, nor is our mind felt abroad."[16]

American literature did rise, however, sooner perhaps than Jefferson and Adams had envisioned. James Fenimore Cooper, Washington Irving, William Cullen Bryant, Nathaniel Hawthorne, Oliver Wendell Holmes, and Ralph Waldo Emerson, to mention but a few writers, all made names for themselves by the 1840s and 1850s as creative artists to be reckoned with not only in America but also in England and throughout the Continent.[17] Emerson, the prophet-poet who strove "to extract the tape-worm of Europe from America's body," knew the American "renaissance" was dawning. "We have listened too long to the courtly muses of Europe," he declares in his pamphlet *The American Scholar* (1837), which was delivered and first published under the title *An Oration, Delivered before the Phi Beta Kappa Society, at Cambridge, August 31, 1837*. In his essay "Nature" (1836), he writes, "The foregoing generations beheld God and nature face to face; we, through their eyes. Why should not we also enjoy an original relation to the universe? Why should not we have a poetry and philosophy of insight and not of tradition, and a religion by revelation to us and not the history of theirs?" The speech secured Emerson's fame.[18]

6

Hand-in-hand with their trashing of American literature and intellectual life, British bashing of the American language in the press was a particularly vitriolic and crowded sport. It was the British attacks in this sphere that, more than any other, reinforced Americans' sense of cultural insecurity in relation to the British throughout the nineteenth century. The British press, "the Reviewers and magazine-men" whom Walter Savage Landor in England once described as "the linkboys and scavengers of literature," gave no quarter to the ways American authors were using the language. American writing offered them ripe opportunities to exercise their wit and appeal to the prejudices of their readers. "Their pens have been dipped in gall" with "a mixture of malevolence and falsehood," scoffed the president of Yale University, Timothy Dwight. At the root of much of this was a bias against how Americans presumed to "possess" the ancient English tongue and, as the British saw it, mangle it to such an extent that it was either vulgar and offensive or often simply incomprehensible. It was a disgrace to the venerable tradition of English letters. One day, the critics warned, if this mauling continued, the British would need a glossary to understand American writing; nor would the great works of English literature any longer be intelligible to the Americans.[19]

"Poor Dr. Johnson," wrote the Scottish antiquarian and engineer John Mactaggart after three years in Canada in the 1820s and obligatory travels in America. Had Johnson known what the Americans would be doing with the language, surely he would have led the charge in his dictionary against the invasiveness of Americanisms: "The great Dr. Johnson, when he was arranging his noble national Dictionary, did not seem to be aware that he had so many mortal enemies at his door. . . . Here then is the *ruination* of our classic English language already begun. It is nonsense to imagine that our authors will there live immortal in their native strains."[20]

Jonathan Boucher, an English clergyman who lived for decades in Maryland and Virginia and was one of the most eloquent and controversial preachers of his day—a friend of George Washington, no less, in spite of his loyalty to Britain—took a hostile interest in the American language in his *Glossary of Archaic and Provincial Words*. A distinguished historian and philologist, Boucher was only one of a legion of British prophets of doom late in the eighteenth century who imagined the day would come when Englishmen would be unable to understand Americans: "[T]heir language will become as independent of England, as they themselves are; and altogether as unlike English, as the Dutch or Flemish is unlike German, or the Norwegian unlike the Danish, or the Portuguese unlike Spanish." That sentiment was a commonplace in England by the 1830s. If that were to be the fate of American speech, Captain Hamilton writes, so be it: "Unless the present progress of

change be arrested, by an increase of taste and judgment in the more educated classes, there can be no doubt that, in another century, the dialect of the
Americans will become utterly unintelligible to an Englishman, and that the
nation will be cut off from the advantages arising from their participation in
British literature." Alluding to Noah Webster, already famous by then for his
"American" dictionary, he predicts the result would be "as novel and peculiar
as the most patriotic American linguist can desire."[21]

In one of his many illuminating essays on early American speech, the
twentieth-century American historian of early American English, Allen
Walker Read, attempts to demystify what he describes as misguided notions of the American language from the late eighteenth century right up
to Mencken and later. It was the British reviewers of American books, he
suggests, who should have known better, not the impressionable British travelers. While many travelers certainly cringed when they heard American accents, coinages, "vulgarisms," and (to their minds) misuse of perfectly good
English words, or noticed the continued use of words and phrases that long
ago had become archaic in England, they were on the whole more generous
and approving than the professional reviewers and commentators. They were
able at least to discover firsthand, for example, and acknowledge, the existence of relatively little regional dialect in America. Recalling her travels in
America in 1834, the otherwise critical Harriet Martineau, who apparently
was hard of hearing and needed an ear horn, rejoices over how clearly (without an accent) the Americans spoke: "I shall have no bad tales to tell in England about the peculiarities of American speech; for the truth is, it is quite
a holiday treat to an unready ear like mine to meet with intelligible English
all over this great country, after being perplexed with the provincialisms with
which one is assailed as often as one takes a journey in England."[22]

7

What were the unbridled Americanisms and other offenses that set so many
British and several American commentators' teeth on edge? One of the most
prolific examples was the epidemic and unlicensed use of nouns as verbs, such
as *beat, dump, interview, notice, process, progress, scalp,* and so on. Contractions
and sloppy pronunciation became widespread, as did other "vulgarities" of
language such as *gents, pants,* and *thanks* and informal and essentially private
terms of endearment between spouses that (it was felt) should be kept private

and not be heard across a room in public. Racy language and low expressions were other lamented features. Such usage for many was insulting, careless, undisciplined, idiomatically imprecise and illogical, and disrespectful.

There was no want of other examples of what British observers classified as "degradation" and "debasement." To begin with, accounts invariably mentioned the unbearable volubility of Americans, who prided themselves on being "born orators," but their speech was blemished with uncouth vulgarity in vocabulary, profanity, runaway "innovation," flaccid inaccuracy and imprecision, grandiloquence, high-flown rhetoric, and lazy or shortcut pronunciation. In New England, some took note of a "whining cadence" and twang that Nicholas Cresswell, a visitor from Derbyshire earlier in the 1770s, found was quite beyond his powers of description, although elsewhere in the country he did not notice any dialect. Cresswell, who nevertheless wished to move to America from Derbyshire, participated so completely in American ways of speaking that he began to talk and throw his weight around like an American, one morning almost getting into a gunfight with a man who "threatened to scalp and tomahawk me."[23]

Thousands of popular words and expressions, what could be called American provincialisms as well as Americanisms, infiltrated the speech of even the most educated Americans who did not normally use them in their writing—individuals who, in the words of a Yale graduate in 1855, "in half a dozen [spoken] sentences, use at least as many words that cannot fail to strike the inexperienced Englishman who hears them for the first time." "Fail to strike" only feebly describes the English loathing of the mushrooming of Americanisms. With deepening resentment, the English deplored them as vulgar and incomprehensible. On the other hand, Daniel Boorstin (historian and Librarian of Congress) follows Mencken's line of defense by applauding the "brash vitality" of the burgeoning "tall talk" and flamboyant American speech. He illustrates the "flood of racy and unprecedented words and phrases" with his own sample list: *to affiliate, to Americanize, down-and-out, down-town, to engineer, to enthuse, flat-footed, to funeralize, highfalutin, to hornswoggle, hunkydory, to itemize, to lynch, non-committal, on-the-fence, plumb crazy, rambunctious, to resurrect, scalawag, scrumptious, shebang, to skedaddle, slambang, splendiferous, true-blue, under-the-weather.* "The new riches of an American language," Boorstin writes, "were not found in the pages of an American Shakespeare or Milton but on the tongues of Western boatmen, town boosters, fur traders, explorers, Indian-fighters, and sod-busters. While the greatness of British English could be viewed in a library, the greatness of American English had to be heard to be appreciated. America had no powerful literary aristocracy, no single cultural capital, no London. And the new nation gave the language back to the people. No American achievement was more distinctive or less predictable."[24]

8

Apart from conservative "traditionalists" among them, many literate Americans were not willing to endure silently this British disrespect. Across the country, Americans believed that, no thanks to the British, clarity and unity in both written and spoken English, not to mention elegance, were what they wanted and were certain they had already achieved. One of the most insightful and commanding American voices to protest the British criticism of the way Americans used the language was the eminent Edward Everett. A distinguished Harvard professor of Greek literature by the age of twenty-one, a universally admired orator, editor of the influential *North American Review*, US secretary of state, ambassador to Britain, and president of Harvard from 1846 to 1849 (he disliked the job), Everett had a brilliant pedigree. He was a highly respected authority and leader in American cultural thought, and he plays a significant, though minor, role in the dictionary history told in these pages. "I know nobody else in the country," wrote one critic, "who holds such a pen. He is the American Junius." At Harvard and for many years afterward, he was accorded heroic status by Emerson, who heard him preach as Unitarian minister at Brattle Street Church in Cambridge and concluded that his voice "of such rich tones, such precise and perfect utterance, that although slightly nasal . . . was the most mellow, and beautiful, and correct of all instruments of the time." He had the honor of speaking for nearly two hours at the dedication of the Gettysburg National Cemetery before Abraham Lincoln got around to delivering his brief, eloquent, and legendary address on November 19, 1863, the day after which he graciously wrote to Lincoln, "I should be glad, if I could flatter myself that I came as near to the central idea of the occasion, in two hours, as you did in two minutes."[25]

After several visits to England, Everett felt he could speak out with "reasoned patriotism" and authority about the comparative state of the language in England and America: "[W]e submit it fearlessly to any person, who has had the means of making the comparison, and is at all qualified to do it, whether one might not rather suppose that America were the native country of the language, and England a remote colony, exposed to all the chances of corruption, so villainously is the language spoken in all the provinces of the latter country, so wholly distorted in a score of rustic jargons, that do not deserve the name of dialects." The British critics were hardly justified in "stigmatizing as a corruption" all American neologisms. By whatever authority, whether dictionaries, "good company," or "good writers," "more provincialisms, more good words in false acceptations, and more newly coined words" are to be found in respectable English writers than in equally respectable American writers and society, he claimed.[26]

Finding himself in a coach en route to Cambridge, England, in 1818, Everett was shocked to discover that the five others in the coach "spoke worse English, than any five well dressed people that one would be apt to meet in any part of America, with which I am acquainted." Indeed, throughout his travels in England, Everett was appalled by the level of English ignorance and dogmatism regarding American English: "[W]e ought neither to be *reviewed* out of the right of coining any words which the peculiarity of our situation requires, nor browbeaten into the belief, that in respect to new words we speak and write the language more corruptly than we do." The English had best concentrate on saving their own language from corruption instead of "ringing insipid changes on the 'American language,' wrestling with the puritanical Christian names of our writers, and waging a quixotic warfare against barbarism never approved, and denounced already here."[27]

Belonging to the wealthy, educated, patrician class in Boston society, George Ticknor was a close friend of Everett's, a brilliant Spanish and French scholar at Harvard, and author of the monumental three-volume *History of Spanish Literature* (1849). It would never have occurred to him that he spoke anything but the best English. It amazed him, therefore, when a visiting Englishman in 1815 "expressed to me his surprise that I spoke so good English, and spoke it, too, without an accent, so that he should not have known me from an Englishman." "This is the first instance I have yet met of this kind of ignorance," Ticknor noted in his journal. "He is himself a cockney." Another priceless American riposte later in the century shocked a sprightly, young, upper-class New England woman who was not exactly swept off her feet when a young officer in the English army told her that her English was excellent and asked if she was unusual in that respect for an American woman. "Oh, yes," she replied, "but then I had unusual advantages. There was an English missionary stationed near my tribe." One other impatient American woman more testily replied in 1839 to an Englishman who had asked her, "Why do you drawl out your words in that way?" that she would "drawl all the way from Maine to Georgia, rather than *clip* my words as you English people do." The London *Literary Gazette* in 1839 regaled its readers with a host of other examples of what must have seemed to them like chatter from some sort of underworld American conspiracy against England's noble language. A couple of specimens here will suffice to convey the tenor of the dialect and "twisting" of the meaning of words that English people felt was afflicting America: "The old phrase of 'straining at a gnat, and swallowing a camel,' is, in the Eastern States, rendered 'straining at a gate, and swallow a saw-mill'"; another concerned the words *nasty* and *nice*: "one of the strangest perversions of the meaning of a word which I ever heard of is in Kentucky, where sometimes the word *nasty* is used for *nice*. For instance: at a rustic dance in that State a Kentuckian said to an acquaintance of mine, in reply to his asking the name of a very fine girl, 'That's my sister, stranger; and I flatter myself that she shews the nastiest ankle in all Kentuck.'"[28]

James Fenimore Cooper tried bravely to have it both ways. While he thought that Americans had gone overboard with their reforms, he nonetheless declared they had "an equal right" to the language. He predicted that soon America would blossom with a literature "felt with a force, a directness, and a common sense in its application, that has never yet been known." "Twenty millions of people not only can make a word, but they can make a language, if it be needed," he wrote at the end of a footnote defending Americanisms in his novel *Satanstoe* (1845). Waxing prophetic and audacious at the same time, he predicted in *The American Democrat* a bright future for American English but doubted English attitudes would soften anytime soon:

In *fine*, we speak our language, as a nation, better than any other people speak their language. When one reflects on the immense surface of country that we occupy, the general accuracy, in pronunciation and in the use of words, is quite astonishing. . . . We do amend, and each year introduces a better and purer English into our country. . . . [I]n another generation or two, far more reasonable English will be used in this country than exists here now. How far this melioration or purifi-cation of our language will affect the mother country, is another ques-tion. It is, perhaps, twenty years too soon to expect that England will very complacently submit to receive opinions or fashions very directly from America.[29]

9

The Scottish critic and folklorist Andrew Lang, looking back in 1895 on a century of Anglo-American wrangling over language, adopted a laissez-faire attitude. He asserted the rights of Americans to use the language the way they wanted to, but he could not bear to contemplate, as did Cooper, American influences on British English: "I, for one, have never been able to see why Americans should not use Americanisms. It is a free country, and has a right to develop its own language in its own way. . . . As long as they bud and blos-som in America only, they are of mere philological interest to us; but when they begin to invade our language, like the American weed in our waters, surely we may, inoffensively, try to check their profusion? Or is this rude and offensive?" He added, "Only time and usage can sanction new words and phrases: the fittest survive."[30]

Nevertheless, the fight was still on, as the prominent English essayist John Ruskin demonstrated in 1873 with this surprisingly impertinent remark: "[T]his dying England taught the Americans all they have of speech, or thought, hitherto. What thoughts they have not learned from England are foolish thoughts; what words they have not learned from England, unseemly words; the vile among them not being able even to be humorous parrots, but only obscene mocking-birds." One could hardly be more insulting than that. The intellectual and social derailment the language wars generated infected even brilliant philosophers and critics like Ruskin. By the third decade of the nineteenth century, informed and fair-minded people—and even the unin-formed and biased—on both sides of the Atlantic were beginning to fear that if this transatlantic linguistic boxing match went on much longer, "the last drops of goodwill toward England that exist in the United States" would be turned into irreversible bitterness.[31]

Americans had repaid the British handsomely for their sneers, but they were nevertheless confronted by the embarrassing and increasingly incon-venient fact that they were, as we shall see, still relying on English-language authorities like Samuel Johnson and his irrepressible dictionary. An English journalist ill-naturedly had warned as early as 1787 that the American language was already so different from the English that English dictionaries in the future might as well ignore Americanisms: "If this is true, let us leave the inventors of this motley gibberish to make a Dictionary for themselves." That is exactly what Americans would do. The American language was rushing into the future, following its own course and needs, and the majority of Americans were little disposed to let English attitudes and prejudices, and dictionaries, keep it back. Only a truly comprehensive American dictionary, recording what the American language had become, could keep pace with the rapid changes in American society and the new words, meanings, and pronunciations pouring into it. When it came, it surely would, once and for all, set the seal on their declaration of linguistic independence from the mother country.[32]

2

Noah Webster

"The Wildest Innovator"

As an independent nation, our honor requires us to have a system of our own, in language as well as government. Great Britain, whose children we are, and whose language we speak, should no longer be *our* standard; for the taste of her writers is already corrupted, and her language on the decline. . . . However they [the Americans] may boast of Independence, and the freedom of their government, yet their *opinions* are not sufficiently independent; an astonishing respect for the arts and literature of their parent country, and a blind imitation of its manners, are still prevalent among the Americans. . . . *Now* is the time, and *this* the country. . . . Let us then *seize* the present moment, and establish a *national language* as well as a national government. . . . Delay, in the plan here proposed, may be fatal.
—*Noah Webster*

That is what Noah Webster wrote in 1789 at the age of thirty-one, long before he had compiled the nation's first major dictionary.[1] It is a clarion call for American linguistic unity and independence in his *Dissertations on the English Language*—a 409-page treatise remarkable for its boldness and length as much as for its sweeping generalized history of the language. John Adams had said much the same thing in 1780: "England will never have any more honor, excepting now and then that of imitating the Americans." Webster, however, was echoing his own lecture delivered in Boston in 1786, combatively titled "Some Differences between the English and Americans Considered. Corruption of Language in England. Reasons Why the English Should Not Be Our Standard, Either in Language or Manners." These are intensely patriotic words from a young man caught up in a wave of nationalism in the early years of independence. He never really outgrew them. With such language he moved on to denigrate England and especially Samuel Johnson, whom he regarded as the most popular (and therefore damaging) embodiment of the corruption, as he put it, of the English language from which he wished America, before it was too late, to declare its independence. The English language in England was in a progressive state of decay, he announced. Although his militantly missionary brand of language reform won him few friends, his extraordinary persistence, resilience, confidence, stubbornness, and industry led him early in his career to publishing success with his spelling reforms and, later on, to international fame with his much-debated and embattled dictionary. He became known as the "savior" of the American language, the "schoolmaster" of the country.[2]

The defiant Webster was not alone among Americans in attacking British English. Johnson (and his dictionary) came in for a licking also from critics who accused him of an exclusive, pompous, artificial, and formal regularity of style. They preferred instead a natural form of democratic expression more in keeping with the surging American romantic spirit of freedom, simplicity, and individuality in a revolutionary society. "The English language has not been as well written in England since the time of that literary dunce, Samuel Johnson, who was totally destitute of taste for the *vrai naturelle*, or simplicity of nature," wrote Hugh Henry Brackenridge, author and Pennsylvania Supreme Court justice, in 1792. Those were strong words but not as revolutionary as those before 1786 (though not published until 1832) of Joseph Brown Ladd, an impatient, aspiring poet who was killed in a duel at the age of twenty-two: "Dr. Johnson was a writer of rather more genius, and a greater share of popularity. He was on that account the most dangerous; . . . of all modern perversions of taste, the works of Johnson have done the greatest mischief." The emulation of Johnson's style and language would divide America, not unify it as Webster proclaimed "Federal English" would do—that is, the English of the common "yeoman" of his native state of Connecticut, for example. There were no American dictionaries that might stop the insidious flow of Johnson's influence, but Brackenridge argued that a book urging an American style to match American life "might do more to effect so desirable an end, than can be accomplished by all the dictionaries and institutes, that were ever made."[3]

2

Judging from the remarks of several contemporary witnesses, Webster made his progress through life more difficult and tempestuous than it might have been had he not been so cranky, irritable, and arrogant, unloading in print his politically and linguistically charged opinions, whipping himself up into polemical frenzies, and refusing to temper his language when dealing with people who disagreed with him or with whom he disagreed. He was not an easy man to like. Annoyed by the American provincialism of such preaching, Thomas Jefferson, who had an aversion to Webster's Federalist politics and the "Federal English" he championed, disliked the man, once describing him in a letter to President James Madison as a political "busybody" and nuisance: "I view Webster as a mere pedagogue of very limited understanding and very strong prejudices and party passions."[4] John Pickering, a contemporary of Webster's, well-known to him, who wrote a book on the contentious subject of the American vocabulary, called him "a pusillanimous, half-begotten, self-dubbed patriot." Jill Lepore has put not too fine a point on it, calling him "a failed schoolmaster, a passionate flutist . . . an intriguing essayist, an inexhaustible lobbyist, a shrill editor, a pompous lecturer"; "an arrogant, self-promoting pedagogue"; and "a tight-lipped, supercilious, embittered patriarch." Nevertheless, Webster was the sort of truculent man whom many of his contemporaries may well not have liked but had to admire for his pugnacity, perseverance, seemingly boundless energy and courage— and thick skin.[5]

Webster was born in 1758 into a relatively poor farming family in a small agricultural hamlet (now known as West Hartford) on the outskirts of Hartford, Connecticut. Seeing young Noah around the farm with a book in his hands far more often than a pitchfork, his father realized there were other than agricultural currents stirring in his son's mind, but the son's college ambitions posed difficult problems for the father. There was little money in the family for anything except the necessities for keeping the farm going, especially during troubled times when the colonies seemed on the verge of revolution. The father hesitated to comply but finally consented. As Noah's daughter, Eliza, put it many years later, "When my Father was a boy of fourteen he showed a decided love for study and books. . . . My Grandfather was a wise man, and, finding Noah stretched on the grass forgetful of his tasks, he decided to permit him to follow his inclinations. . . . The father was deeply interested in his son's career, for he mortgaged the farm to pay his college expenses. . . ." With that money in hand, the boy, not quite sixteen, entered Yale College in September 1774.[6]

In some respects it was an unfortunate time to attend Yale, or any college in the American colonies, for with the outbreak of the Revolution during Webster's freshman year, campus life was disrupted and remained so the entire time he was there. Because of food shortages in the impoverished countryside, Yale had insufficient provisions for students and was forced to close briefly in December 1776. When the students returned in January 1777 from Christmas recess they found there was still not enough to eat; there was also little wood, and they had to burn straw in their fireplaces. Then the fear of a British invasion of New Haven Harbor forced the college to close briefly in March. When it reopened, classes were resumed in Glastonbury, Connecticut, well away from endangered New Haven. That summer of 1777, Noah and his two brothers even joined a small militia commanded by their father, "shouldered a musket," and marched two days to the Hudson River to join the resistance to General Burgoyne's advance into southern New England. News of Burgoyne's defeat spared them from any fighting, however, and they returned home safely, physically exhausted and emotionally drained.

Yale was then a small campus with 150 students; two professors (one of whom was the President Naphtali Daggett); and three tutors, including Timothy Dwight, later president of Yale, who remained a lifelong friend of Webster's. For a young man with a keen curiosity and quick intellect, it was a good place to be. Students were made to feel they could and should do much to ameliorate society's problems: "Remember that you are to act for the empire of America," Dwight stirringly told the 1776 graduating class: "You should by no means consider yourselves as members of a small neighborhood, town, or colony only, but as being concerned in laying the foundations of American greatness. Your wishes, your designs, your labors, are not to be confined by the narrow bounds of the present age, but are to comprehend succeeding generations, and be pointed to immortality." They debated current social and political issues, wrote papers on them, and formed intense friendships shaped by the common conviction that a new age of promise and hope was dawning in America. Webster kept company at Yale with fellow students who went on to distinguish themselves nationally in politics, diplomacy, the legal world, literature, education, and religion. Among them were Joel Barlow (later ambassador at the Court of St. Cloud in France), Oliver Wolcott (who became secretary of the treasury under President John Adams and whose father was one of the signers of the Declaration of Independence), and Zephaniah Swift (who would rise to become chief justice of the Supreme Court of Connecticut).[7]

Webster ended the last weeks of his undergraduate career on a few sour notes when his already well-known capacity for reckless outspokenness and indiscreet activism showed itself. One such incident involved his tutor Rev. Joseph Buckminster, with whom for some reason he fell out just before his graduation in September 1778. In a letter to Webster about a year later, Buckminster regretted his former student's overly strident "independent spirit" and predicted that unless it was tamed, it would in the future expose him dangerously to "errors and mortifications." "Had you listened to the advice of one who had from his first acquaintance studied your interest," he wrote, "I am persuaded you would have closed your academic studies with . . . reputation. . . . [Y]ou must endeavor not to be forward in applying . . . to persons with whom you have but a slight acquaintance, nor be too frank in opening your heart to them. Such is the perverseness of human nature [that] they will be disposed to ridicule you and perhaps set you down among those who have too high an opinion of their own importance." Buckminster was prophetic, envisaging all too clearly that in his life Webster would often find he had dealt "treacherously" with himself.[8]

When Webster returned to his farming home with his degree, he hoped to be able to study law, but there was little family money for that. Nor did he have any prospects of a job. He wrote of being "cast out upon the world, at the age of twenty, without patrons, in the midst of a war which had disturbed all occupation, had impoverished the country; and the termination of which could not be foreseen." He fell into a depression out of which he tried to lift himself by keeping to his room and reading. Considering how much and how soon he would disparage Samuel Johnson's dictionary, it is surprising that the work he says rescued him from his melancholia was Johnson's famous *Rambler* moral essays. Thirty years later, in the middle of a life-changing religious conversion in 1808, he remembered how Johnson had helped him through those dark days: "Being set afloat in the world at the inexperienced age of twenty, without a father's aid which had before supported me, my mind was . . . overwhelmed with gloomy apprehensions. In this situation I read Johnson's *Rambler*, with unusual interest and with a visible effect upon my moral opinions, for when I closed the last volume, I formed a firm resolution to pursue a course of virtue through life, and to perform all moral and social duties with a scrupulous exactness." Until the end of his life he remained grateful to Johnson for this lifeline, while attacking him relentlessly for the damage he said his dictionary was wreaking on the English language, especially (but not exclusively) in America.[9]

After a period of private study, he managed to pass his bar exams in Hartford in April 1781 but found he could not make a living by practicing law. Over the next few years, he took to teaching, twice starting his own schools, both of which failed. It was during this period that, exasperated by the schoolbooks available for children in America, he made the bold decision to write two "small elementary books for the teaching of the English language."[10]

3

He sat down in his rented rooms to write a spelling book that might replace the persistent imposition of spelling and grammar books from England, chiefly Rev. Thomas Dilworth's elementary grammar, *A New Guide to the English Tongue* (1740), which had reigned supreme in American schoolrooms since the mid-eighteenth century: editions were published in America and continued to be used there well into the nineteenth century. Writing of Dilworth's book that "one half of the work is totally useless, and the other half defective and erroneous," Webster mainly objected to it because it was English. Dilworth's prescriptive *Short Introduction to English Grammar* in 1762 ignited outbursts of Webster's inflammatory words of anti-British abuse. His friend Joel Barlow cautioned him: "You know our country is prejudiced in favor of old Dilworth, the nurse of us all, and it will be difficult to turn their attention from it; you know, too, that the printers make large impressions of it and afford it very cheap." Ignoring such warnings, Webster went on to complete the first draft of the speller in the summer of 1782, which was published the following year as *The First Part of the Grammatical Institute of the English Language*. In a revised edition in 1786, he changed the title of the speller to *The American Spelling Book*, more in keeping (he thought) with the simplicity of his method. It became known thereafter as the "Blue Back Speller" because of its distinctive blue paper cover.[11]

By the time he completed the speller, he had decided on a more ambitious, three-part plan: a speller, a grammar, and a reader, which at that point he was calling *The American Instructor* but later, at the suggestion of his mentor Ezra Stiles at Yale, he awkwardly renamed *A Grammatical Institute, of the English Language, Comprising, an Easy, Concise, and Systematic Method of Education, Designed for the Use of English Schools in America.* His scheme was to replace Dilworth's difficult (for children) British explanations and illustrations of spelling, pronunciation, and grammar with a more accessible, distinctly American "local" approach—although, puzzlingly, he admits he has based his spelling on Johnson's dictionary. Under the existing system of education, he asks, "How would a child or a foreigner learn the different sound of *o* in these words, *rove, move, dove,* or of *oo* in *poor, door*? Or that *a, ai, ei,* and *e* have precisely the same sound in these words, *bare, laid, vein, there*? Yet these and fifty other irregularities have passed unnoticed by authors of Spelling Books and Dictionaries." He took pity on children and foreigners by arranging his word lists into subjects and orders that smoothly and practically took them from the easy to the more difficult. The book was also illustrated with coarse woodcuts of stories from Aesop's fables and such scenes as a rude boy who stole apples and a country maid with her milk pail. He replaced Dilworth's British references, of which few American children could ever have been expected to make much or any sense, with American proper names, geography, and history. His book, he wrote in the introduction, was a "mite [thrown] into the common treasure of patriotic exertions." It was the first step in his life-long journey toward fostering an American language. The book also scorned what he called "those odious distinctions of provincial dialects" in American speech, and he cautioned boys and girls against slovenly and provincial pronunciation.[12] To that end, he composed short dialogues that students, depending on their age, were asked to read aloud, as well as tables of graduated lessons, inviting students to repeat vertical columns of words such as this one:

glade	snake	tract	clank	clamp	black
grade	glaze	pact	crank	champ	crack
shave	craze	plant	shank	cramp	match
wave	prate	sang	plank	spasm	patch
quake	slate	fang	clump	splash	fetch
stage	shape	rang	thump	crash	vetch[13]

Webster was never modest. His spelling book, he maintained rather grandly, "does more to form the language of a nation than all other books," and he hoped it would "promote the interest of literature and the harmony of the United States" by "purifying" its language. The word "purifying" played up Webster's obsession that there was an urgent need both to unify pronunciation seamlessly across the nation and reject England's "corruption" of the language. He bore down on this "corruption" in an essay, "English Corruption of the American Language," which was later printed in his *Collection of Essays and Fugitiv Writings* (1790). One wonders how he came to such defiant observations never having been to England nor having had much of an opportunity by then to converse with the classes of English people he cites. What jumps out in the following passage is its resolute linguistic patriotism rather than any close study of England's speech habits:

> Our language was spoken in purity about eighty years ago; since which time, great numbers of faults have crept into practice about the theater and court of London. An affected erroneous pronunciation has in many instances taken place of the true; and new words or modes of speech have succeeded the ancient correct English phrases.
>
> Thus we have, in the modern English pronunciation, their "natshures," "conjunctshures," "constitshutions," and "tshumultshous legislatshures;" and a long catalogue of fashionable improprieties. These . . . offend the ear, and embarrass the language.[14]

As he set about writing his school grammar books teaching spelling, syntax, and pronunciation, he realized the formidable competition he faced with the well-established eighteenth-century British grammar books that had taken root in the American classroom. It almost overwhelmed him. In addition to Dilworth, Webster excoriated another highly influential author of an English grammar textbook, Robert Lowth. Lowth was the bishop of London and a professor of poetry at Oxford. His *Short Introduction to English Grammar* (1762) was among those most maligned by Webster. Other less popular grammars, like James Buchanan's *The British Grammar* (1760) and Joseph Priestley's *The Rudiments of English Grammar* (1761), found their way onto the schoolroom desks of American children. They were soon followed by more general works on language, such as George Campbell's *The Philosophy of Rhetoric* (1776) and Hugh Blair's *Lectures on Rhetoric and Belles Lettres*

(1783), which remained popular in America until the late nineteenth century. It has been estimated that in the last forty years of the eighteenth century in Britain some 157 different grammars were in circulation.[15]

Webster, however, had tapped into a market for homegrown American grammars and spellers that was about to swell beyond anyone's expectations. A British journalist and grammarian, Samuel Kirkham, who lectured on grammar across America for some thirty years in the early nineteenth century and published his own *English Grammar in Familiar Lessons* (1829), explained the social importance grammar had assumed in America by 1820: "As grammar opens the door to every department of learning, a knowledge of it is indispensable; and should you not aspire at distinction in the republick of letters, this knowledge cannot fail of being serviceable to you, even if you are destined to pass through the humblest walks of life."[16]

Two popular American grammars that followed Webster's were Caleb Bingham's *The Young Ladies' Accidence: Or, a Short and Easy Introduction to English Grammar* (1785) and Caleb Alexander's *A Grammatical System of the English Language* (1814). Alexander also published one of the earliest dictionaries in America, the *Columbian Dictionary* (1800). Between 1820 and 1850, schoolbooks available in America, mostly grammars, grew from 30 to 44 percent of all copies of books published in the country. According to one estimate, some 250 separate American grammars were published in the first half of the nineteenth century. Kirkham himself was selling some sixty thousand copies of his *English Grammar* every year in the 1830s. Nonetheless, the British competition was fierce and actually grew instead of diminished. The most famous grammar book to become a close companion of American life, published near the end of the eighteenth century, was Lindley Murray's *English Grammar, Adapted to Different Classes of Learners* (1795). It was far more popular in America than any American rival, with more than three hundred editions published before 1850. By then, more copies of it had been sold than any of Webster's schoolbooks except his speller. Murray's book stayed in print until the 1880s, selling in the millions. For all social classes, it was thought to be, and was used as, a lifeline to success and an improved social status.[17]

In his preface to the speller, Webster styles himself from the start as "the prophet of language to the American people." His combative language is surprising for someone only twenty-four, so self-defining in its stridency.

Americans, he maintains, now see England's vices "with abhorrence, their errors with pity, and their follies with contempt." How could Americans tolerate British educational methods any longer when "Europe is grown old in folly, corruption and tyranny"? In an early example of the doctrine of American exceptionalism, he writes: "In that country laws are perverted, manners are licentious, literature is declining and human nature debased. For America in her infancy to adopt the present maxims of the old world would be to stamp the wrinkles of decrepid age upon the bloom of youth and to plant the seeds of decay in a vigorous constitution."[18]

By the time he finished writing his speller in 1782, Webster knew it was perfectly suited to exploit the rush of rising patriotic fervor in the nation. But there was the problem of how to get it published. He also worried about literary piracy in a nation where there was neither national copyright law nor copyright laws for any of the individual states.

4

Copyright law had existed in England since 1710 ("The Statute of Anne") to protect British authors, as well as Americans who had either published previously in Britain or resided there. That law, the first copyright statute in the world, protected authors for fourteen years, with an optional renewal of another fourteen years. But in America there was no such protection. As Webster's friend Joel Barlow put it in an imploring letter to Congress in 1783, "the rights of authors should be secured by law. . . . We are not to expect any works of considerable magnitude . . . offered to the public till such security be given."[19]

Young Webster, like any other author, craved to be able to protect his exclusive right to publish and sell his book in every state. Over the next five years, he dedicated himself to achieving this goal with whatever money he could scrape together from teaching and loans from friends. In the autumn of 1782, he mounted a horse and set off on an ambitious journey to curry support for his book, promote the idea of copyright legislation with influential people and state legislatures, and find a publisher. He traveled, manuscript in hand, to Philadelphia, Princeton, New Jersey, and New York State; wrote letters to authorities in other states; persisted with his more personal contacts in Hartford; and took his cause to some state legislatures. After he returned from his circuit of advertising and petitioning in behalf of his speller, he composed a letter on October 24, "To the General Assembly of Connecticut," urging legislators in his own state to pass a law granting to him "the exclusive right of printing, publishing, and vending" of his speller (which he was then calling *The American Instructor*) "for the term of thirteen years." At first, legislators shied away from meddling with the status quo because there existed few books by Americans who had a personal stake in the copyright issue. Another impediment was the republican insistence on the unregulated, unhampered circulation of books as a democratic right. Webster managed to obtain a testimonial here and there, though, such as one in September 1782 from Samuel Stanhope Smith, professor of moral philosophy and future president of the College of New Jersey (now Princeton University), to whom he personally showed the manuscript and who judged that the book was "very proper for young persons in the country. . . . And it is my opinion that it can be of no evil consequence to the state, and may be of benefit to it, to vest, by a law, the sole right of publishing and vending such works in the authors of them." Congress at last, in May 1783, recommended that the individual states grant copyrights to authors of new books in their states for at least fourteen years. After that, Connecticut, New York, Massachusetts, New Jersey, New Hampshire, and Rhode Island promptly passed such legislation. After his speller was published in October 1783, Webster rode off again, this time to "middle and southern states," to promote his book in Charleston, Baltimore, Delaware, and Richmond, Virginia, and to urge copyright legislation as well. Congress took bolder action in 1790, finally passing a Copyright Act, the first federal copyright law, virtually a duplicate of the British Act of 1710, which had never applied to the United States, granting authors copyright for fourteen years with a further fourteen if the author survived the first period.[20]

Some sixty years later (1843), as Webster rounded up a few of his fugitive papers for publication before he died, he published "Origin of the Copy-right Laws in the United States," in which he made a case for himself as the driving force behind those regulations. As David Micklethwait, however, makes clear in his book, *Noah Webster and the American Dictionary*, these early copyright efforts by Webster in 1782 were aimed at protecting only his speller and any other schoolbooks he might write; he was not then motivated chiefly to promote copyright law to protect all authors. While it is therefore a bit of a stretch to call Webster "the father of copyright legislation in America," as his biographer Harry Warfel has done, Webster certainly played his part, along with Barlow and others, to raise the consciousness of legislators in individual states about the need for some sort of copyright law.[21]

5

As for getting his speller published, Webster claimed it met with "general approbation" from those he asked to read it, but it ran into stiff opposition because of its staunch rejection of Dilworth and its "visionary" reforms of American pronunciation and spelling. In a letter to a friend in January 1783, Webster complained of a "popular prejudice" for Dilworth and that "people are apt to slumber in the opinion that he is incapable of improvement." Appealing to patriotism, his overarching theme was the vital need to break free of Europe's "mouldering pillars of antiquity." Still, initially no printer or bookseller he approached would answer the call and touch his manuscript— there were no publishers as we know them today—unless Webster was willing to pay for the labor, ink, and paper. Friends came to his aid, however, and the first part of the *Grammatical Institute* was finally published in October 1783 by Barzillai Hudson and George Goodwin, the printers of the *Connecticut Courant* in Hartford. Webster's contract with his publishers stipulated that he sign over to them all publishing rights for new editions, which turned out to be a horrible mistake.[22]

The speller had 120 pages and was small, only three and a half by six and a quarter inches; it quickly became an astonishing success. Five thousand copies were printed and quickly sold. By January 1785, the book was selling at the rate of five hundred to one thousand per week, and the printers planned to print twenty thousand to thirty thousand more. By 1804, more than one million copies of the 1787 edition had been printed, most of them in Hartford and Boston. From 1804 to 1818, more than three million were licensed for sale; and between 1818 and 1832, an estimated three million more were printed. This success story did not end there: almost four million copies of Webster's *Elementary Spelling Book, Being an Improvement on the American Spelling Book*, published in 1829 to counteract the falling sales of *The American Spelling Book*, were licensed for sale between 1829 and 1843. The little book continued to sell well throughout the nineteenth century, making it one of the best sellers in American publishing history.

In 1784 and 1785, Webster published parts 2 and 3 of his three-part scheme, the "grammar" and "reader." Not for the last time, unfortunately, his reformist zeal led him astray. He made wild claims for American prose at a time when it was generally acknowledged to be unspectacular: "The people are right. . . . I have been attentive to the political interests of America. I consider it as a capital fault in all our schools, that the books generally used contain subjects wholly uninteresting to our youth; while the writings that marked the Revolution . . . are perhaps not inferior to the orations of Cicero and Demosthenes." "I have begun a reformation in the Language, and my plan is but yet in embryo," he told Timothy Pickering in 1785, with not a little exaggeration.[23]

Predictably, the *Grammatical Institute* ran into a torrent of scorn from critics because of the appendix Webster attached to the speller titled, "An Essay on the Necessity, Advantages and Practicability of Reforming the Mode of Spelling, and of Rendering the Orthography of Words Correspondent to the Pronunciation." In that short piece he boldly (and recklessly) proposed reforms of English orthography so as "to render the orthography sufficiently regular and easy." He was not advocating a fine-tuning of spelling to reflect, for example, American pronunciation, but nothing less than a major revolution. His and other reformers' (including Benjamin Franklin) idea was to make spelling more phonetic and logically analogous with related forms. But Webster's overhaul of orthography was so idiosyncratic and extreme that it tended to make spelling more, not less, complicated, multiplying possible spellings so much that they were difficult to grasp and follow. Much of the public ridiculed him and continued to do so for the rest of his life.

Ridiculed or not, several of his reforms caught on, while others did not. Modern readers can identify easily which of the following examples had no future at all. He proposed the "omission of all superfluous or silent letters," such as *a* in *bread*; therefore, henceforth *bread, breast, built, friend, give, head, meant*, and *realm* would be spelled instead as *bred, brest, bilt, frend, giv, hed, ment*, and *relm*. He would substitute "a character that has a certain definite sound for one that is more vague and indeterminate," so that *grieve, mean, near, speak*, and *zeal* would become *greev, meen, neer, speek*, and *zeel*; and *believe, blood, daughter, draught, grief, key, laugh*, and *tough* would become *beleev, blud, dawter, draft, greef, kee, laf*, and *tuf*. In addition, *ch* should become *k*, making *architecture, character, cholic*, and *chorus* become *arkitecture, karacter, kolic*, and *korus*; and *ch* should also be changed to *sh* in *chaise, chevalier*, and *machine*, making *shaze, shevaleer*, and *masheen*. He also dictated in the speller itself that numerous other silent letters had to be banished: for example, the *s* in *island*, and *b* in *thumb*; one of the double consonants in the likes of *jeweller, traveller, waggon*; the *u* in *colour, endeavour, odour*; and the final *k* in such as *frolick* and *publick*. The *re* in words like *calibre, centre*, and *theatre* also had to be changed to *er*; and the *c* in *defence, offence, pretence*, and so on would be spelled with an *s—defense, offense, pretense*. And there was a long list of sundry other radical proposals that never got off the ground, such as *acre* to *aker, crowd* to *croud, soot* to *sut, woe* to *wo*, and *women* to *wimmen*. Others, like *gaol* to *jail* and *plough* to *plow*, did stand the test of time.[24]

It would not be long before Webster laid out at length the principles and philosophy behind these and other linguistic reforms. But for the time being, in spite of the radical nature of his reforms, he was still guided by the same rationale in the teaching of spelling that had impelled it since the sixteenth century: the reason behind it was the more important goal of teaching a pupil how to read. As Jennifer Monaghan puts it in her book *A Common Heritage*, "a spelling book presupposed that reading involved pronouncing and that reading was therefore oral, not silent. The purpose of a speller was to teach children how to pronounce hundreds of words, most of which were not already in their oral vocabulary. The question of comprehension was deferred for other texts. . . . [T]o teach children to read was in some sense to teach them to speak."[25]

6

For the next several years, Webster continued to travel from one state to another, visiting politicians and college presidents, trying to win endorsements for his schoolbooks and continuing to push for copyright protection. In 1785, he ventured into politics with his *Sketches of American Policy*, advocating as a Federalist a much stronger central government to exist side-by-side with (but able to control) personal freedoms. He gave copies of it to George Washington when he visited Mount Vernon in November 1785, who in turn passed it on approvingly to James Madison in Philadelphia. He made a point of visiting Benjamin Franklin, Thomas Paine, Aaron Burr, and virtually all the presidents of the leading American colleges in his travels, pushing his opinions on politics and language and promoting himself in a series of lectures in Baltimore, Wilmington (Delaware), Annapolis, and Philadelphia in 1786. Not everyone approved of his ideas or his ardor, as in the case of Rev. John Ewing, president of the University of the State of Pennsylvania (now the

University of Pennsylvania), who was suspicious, calling him a "retailer of nouns and pronouns" and "fomenter of rebellion."[26]

In November 1787, he moved to New York City to start a monthly literary periodical that he called the *American Magazine*. To finance it, he agreed with his publisher that in exchange for a quick bulk payment he would sacrifice royalties in New York State for five years—the second huge financial mistake that he made in behalf of his speller. The magazine failed while sales of the speller in New York soared.

It is no surprise that he began to feel like a failure. In spite of his tireless, some might say frenetic, correspondence with friends and men of influence in behalf of "the gospel of nationalism in language and politics," he felt neglected by people of influence and power. He was also taking a beating from anti-Federalists. Lonely and dejected, he took stock of himself. "I sometimes think of retiring from society and devoting myself to reading and contemplation, for I labor incessantly and reap very little fruit from my toils," he complained to his fiancée, Rebecca Greenleaf (whom he called Becca), a vivacious young woman from a prosperous Boston family with whom he fell hopelessly in love in 1787. "I suspect I am not formed for society. . . ." Perhaps he should moderate his behavior, he thought: "I suspect that I have elevated my views too high, that I have mistaken my own character and ought to contract my wishes to a smaller compass." That was a more realistic and sober self-assessment than what he wrote to Rebecca a few days later: "The eyes of America are upon me. . . ." They were indeed, at least in certain circles, but not always in the way he imagined or hoped for.[27]

John Pickering, who several years later would be on the receiving end of Webster's artillery over the current status of the American language, spread it around that Webster had too high an opinion of himself. That, at least, is what he told his nephew: "[W]ith a competent share of good sense, he possessed a *quantum sufficit* of vanity, so that he really overrated his own talents." Ebenezer Hazard, postmaster general of the United States, on March 5, 1788, described Webster to the clergyman and historian Jeremy Belknap, one of the overseers of Harvard College: "He certainly does not want understanding, and yet there is a mixture of self-sufficiency, all-sufficiency, and at the same time a degree of insufficiency about him, which is (to me) intolerable." Hazard called him a "literary puppy." Between themselves they referred to him deprecatingly as "the Monarch."[28]

At thirty-one, tired of bachelorhood and eager to "be known as an established resident and citizen," Webster married twenty-three-year-old Rebecca in October 1789 and retreated to his hometown of Hartford, where he was confident he could make a living as a lawyer. Endlessly patient and enduring, Rebecca turned out to be a huge comfort and stabilizing influence for him. Although he was happy enough in his family life—over the next eighteen years, he and his wife would have six daughters and two sons (one son died within a few months of birth)—pangs of alienation continued. He could make no headway as a lawyer. In any case, he did not really like the law. He involved himself in local civic life and was elected to the Hartford Common Council, but his overwhelming passion was still for American language reform. With only a small income from his schoolbooks, because he had negotiated himself out of most of his royalties, he turned to writing a treatise that he must have known would rouse a storm of protest against him.[29]

When Webster published his *Dissertations on the English Language* in 1789, he dedicated it to Benjamin Franklin, for a while a kindred spirit on the matter of spelling reform—"a great Philosopher and a warm Patriot," Webster writes, who never assumed a "dictatorial authority." But the book's main argument goes something like this: there is to be no elite in America, no linguistic differentiation between classes and regions. He might as well be preaching from a pulpit: "*Now* is the time. . . . Delay, in the plan here proposed, may be fatal." The note of urgency in these phrases is an example of Websterian hyperbole, but for him a national language was as vital as a national government, and new nationhood provided unique opportunities for reform of the language. These were opportunities that would fade quickly, he warns, if not grabbed before America's language, like Britain's, deteriorated owing to homegrown "corruptions" such as regional dialects, affectation, nostalgia for English manners and customs, class divisions, and innumerable other evils. At least America did not have to cope with the deleterious effects of "superfluous ornament" in prose like Edward Gibbon's and Samuel Johnson's, the language of nobility and the British Court, and "the influence of men, learned in Greek and Latin, but ignorant of their own tongue; who have laboured to reject much good English, because they have not understood the original construction of the language." Johnson is his prime target. He is "mischievous," "stupid," the dispenser of "erroneous opinion," and the promulgator of "pedantic orthography"; he had done more with his dictionary to damage the language than anyone else. His "principles would in time destroy all agreement between the spelling and pronunciation of words." Webster had begun sounding off in this way about Johnson in the 1780s and was still at it when he died more than half a century later.[30]

The *Dissertations* illustrates, at a young age, Webster's copious memory and tireless and detailed attention to what would become self-defining themes in his efforts to reform the profile of the English language in America: hundreds of sounds and numerous examples of classes of letters and words that complicate English pronunciation, orthography that confounds consistent pronunciation, irregularity of orthography that bedevils young people and adults alike, and etymology to which few people paid much attention but would, if handled his way, clarify and help solve a good many problems in the way the language is learned and used. The sheer effort is impressive. The most distinctive character of the *Dissertations*, however, relates to his assessment of flaws in American culture; his antipathy toward foreign influences; his strident plea for the banishment of local dialect and pronunciation; the establishment of a national "standard" of language; his assertions that all languages descend from "a common stock"; his elaborate scheme to reform spelling in America; and, especially, a distrust of a variety of so-called authorities in matters of language usage that, if unchecked, he is adamant would threaten national unity. His tone of urgency often comes across as "overturn, overturn." If, as he says in his dedication, Benjamin Franklin never assumed "dictatorial authority," it is less clear that he himself avoids it. Here are a few examples:

> when a particular set of men, in exalted stations, undertake to say "we are the standards of propriety and elegance, and if all men do not conform to our practice, they shall be accounted vulgar and ignorant," they take a very great liberty with the rules of the language and the rights of civility.

> if language must vary, like fashions, at the caprice of a court, we must have our standard dictionaries republished, with the fashionable pronunciation, at least once in five years; otherwise a gentleman in the country will become intolerably vulgar. . . . [These are] generally corruptions.

The two points . . . which I conceive to be the basis of a standard in speaking, are these; *universal undisputed practice*, and the *principle of analogy*.

As a nation, we have a very great interest in opposing the introduction of an plan of uniformity with the British language.

Customs, habits, and *language*, as well as government should be national. America should have her *own* distinct from all the world.[31]

In his *Collection of Essays and Fugitiv Writings* (he spells *fugitive* provokingly without the *e*) published the following year, Webster exhibits his proposals with an ardor that became the butt of jokes for years to come. He was mocked, for example, for parading his spelling reforms in his preface with a warning to his readers that amounts to a self-parody: "In the essays, ritten within the last yeer, a considerable change in spelling iz introduced by way of experiment. This liberty waz taken by the writers before the age of queen Elizabeth, and to this we are indeted for the preference of modern spelling over that of [John] Gower and [Geoffrey] Chaucer. . . . There iz no alternativ. Every possible reezon that could ever be offered for altering the spelling of wurds, stil exists in full force. . . ." Getting into the swing of it and explaining why he concealed his name in many of his early essays, he continues: "MOST of thoze peeces, which hav appeered before in periodical papers and Magazeens, were published with fictitious signatures; for I very erly discuvered, that altho the name of an old and respectable karacter givs credit and consequence to hiz ritings, yet the name of a yung man iz often prejudicial to hiz performances. By conceeling my name, the opinions of men hav been prezerved from an undu bias arizing from personal prejudices, the faults of the ritings hav been detected, and their merit in public estimation ascertained."[32]

He lost a good $400 (about $10,000 today) from the *Dissertations*, which added to his money worries. More than anything else, he wanted to write, but he thought he might try the business world, perhaps as a book merchant in Boston: "To renounce all my literary pursuits, which are now very congenial with my habits, would not . . . make me unhappy." He decided instead to take up an offer to edit and write a new Federalist newspaper, the *American Minerva*, in New York, which failed after five exhausting years. He had succeeded mainly in making enemies. William Cobbett, the successful editor of *Porcupine's Gazette* in Philadelphia, who had endured just about enough of what he regarded as Webster's self-proclaimed and bombastic authority, called him "a most gross calumniator," "a great fool," and a "bare-faced liar." Many others also taunted Webster in print.[33]

Embittered and deeply in debt, Webster mourned that America had begun to "crumble," that mankind was innately perverse and selfish: "From the date of Adam, to this moment," he ranted in the July 12, 1797, issue of the *Minerva*, "no country was ever so infested with corrupt and wicked men, as the United States. . . . [B]ankrupt speculators, rich bankrupts, 'patriotic' Atheists . . . are spread over the United States . . . deceiving the people with lies. . . . We see in our new Republic, the *decrepitude* of Vice, and a free government hastening to ruin, with a rapidity without example."[34]

Webster was certainly not alone with his Jeremiah-like lamentations. There was widespread dismay among Americans, including the Founders, that they were quickly losing the plot, that the social and intellectual foundations of the new nation had been corrupted by the lack of unifying authority in an undisciplined democracy, whether in politics, social customs and manners, religion, or language. What set Webster apart from most others was that he took to writing and lecturing prolifically and angrily about this apparent slide into "barbarism." In his essay *Revolution in France* (1794), he urges his readers again to believe that mankind is inherently depraved and evil. It must be saved from itself. He writes: "If the word *aristocracy* is applicable to anything, it is to that *personal influence* which men derive from . . . age, talents, wealth, education, virtue"—in other words, an elite. Natural aristocracy exists "universally among men," but society has to ensure that its influence flourishes. The nation's early years, however, had shown him that it was failing to do that.[35]

The "natural aristocracy," however, in which Webster and others placed their hopes displayed an altogether different sort of gentility from the British aristocratic class he scorned for corrupting the English language. He blamed the British ruling classes for most of the problems he identified in early American childhood education and the American language. He regarded this as part of the malaise of a new nation that was failing to declare its cultural independence from Britain. In Webster's mind, the heart and soul of this problem was linguistic subservience. It turned him into what some have called the nation's first language strategist. Having read essays by German philosophers on how a national language could determine the moral behavior of a country's populace, he became convinced that a national language could be an integral part of a comprehensive American cultural revolution. Such a revolution would ensure the preservation of a distinctly American republican culture with far-reaching effects on the country's institutions as well as on the moral standards and behavior of its citizens. Webster's revolution was just beginning.[36]

3

Webster's First Dictionary

The *Minerva* had all but extinguished Webster's hopes of a literary career—but not quite, as he explained to the prominent journalist and man of letters Joseph Dennie in 1796: "I once intended to have devoted my life to literary pursuits. The cold hand of poverty *chilled* my hopes, but has not wholly *blasted* them. . . . My plan of education is but barely begun. When I shall complete it is uncertain." By "education" he meant mostly the linguistic education of Americans and promotion of a distinctly American language.[1]

He needed to get out of New York. With income still trickling in from his spelling book, he decided to move his family to New Haven, where he imagined he could return to his "literary" life, meaning books of one kind or another on language. Dragging his considerable debts behind him, he and his family made the move in 1798. His "literary" plan was something of a fantasy, but he was desperate.

In his writing about language, he had demonstrated credentials to take on the task of writing an American dictionary. New Haven would be a good place to attempt it. Rev. Elizur Goodrich, soon to become a professor of law at Yale, was the first, back in 1787, to propose that Webster should write a dictionary. It was initially a vague and, to Webster, seemingly impossible idea that the young schoolteacher was ill-prepared to pursue, as he stated in 1828: Goodrich had "suggested to me, the propriety and expediency of my compiling a dictionary, which should complete a system for the instruction of the citizens of this country in the language. At that time, I could not indulge the thought, much less the hope, of undertaking such a work; as I was neither qualified by research, nor had I the means of support, during the execution of the work, had I been disposed to undertake it." For years afterward people kept telling him he should consider writing a dictionary. "Sir, we must . . . have a Dictionary, and to YOU we must look for this necessary work," wrote an admirer in 1790. "I hope this work is already begun—I wish it were finished."[2]

He felt hounded, exhausted, and relieved. It was like coming home. Settling in for what turned out to be almost fifteen years, he rented the forfeited two-story Georgian house built by Benedict Arnold, which he purchased not long after. It enjoyed a commanding view of Long Island Sound, with a well-planted garden where he could indulge his emerging enthusiasm for horticulture, and generally promised all the virtues of a retreat for a man still determined to reform America but now more retiringly, from the sanctuary of his study. To signal his determination and new sense of purpose, he ensured his study would remain shielded from the "madding crowd" by lining its walls with sand to keep out entirely the sounds of his growing and boisterous family.[3]

Before getting down to work on a dictionary, there were still a few sentiments he felt compelled to get off his chest. In an aggressive circular "Letter" to American colleges and other "seminaries of learning" he sought to "awaken" his readers to the egregious errors and "extreme ignorance" of "foreign" grammarians. "I have long since laid aside the study of language, and been a silent spectator," he writes, but he cannot remain silent any longer. He asserts that his main theme will be that "language is not only formed but must arrive to a tolerable state of perfection before a grammar of that language can be constructed. Languages are not formed by philosophers but by ignorant barbarians. . . . Men *speak* before they *write*. . . . Grammars are made to show the student what a language *is*, not how it *ought to be*." He dresses his argument in extravagant nationalistic language. Mentioning the sins of Johnson and Lowth, who "had no idea of the true principles on which the language is built," he sets the stage for the brand of patriotic lexicography on which he was about to embark: "Where shall we rest if we are to be led from change to change by the caprice of any foreign stage player who chooses to be singular or any compiler of a dictionary or grammar who sets his own opinions in opposition to the established practice of a nation?"[4]

One could conclude from these general remarks that Webster was advertising himself as an opponent of linguistic prescriptivism of any kind, grammars (especially British) and dictionaries included, and that when he got into dictionary-making he was going to preach that dictionaries must simply confine themselves to recording the way people use the language. This issue, however, is complex and has never been clear-cut in lexicography, either before or after Webster, and we shall see that, if anything, Webster turned out to be quite prescriptive—more so, certainly, than Johnson. One reason was that Webster believed grammar and lexicography should be moral agents, shielding the public by omitting language that was morally repugnant and offensive and providing definitions that were morally instructive. He could not abide what he called the rude or vulgar words that Johnson had included in his dictionary, such as *sucked, fornication*, and *whore*, and he would therefore studiously avoid drawing on "old" plays, especially by Shakespeare, to illustrate the meaning of words. He profoundly mistrusted the English stage. In October 1807, he would tell David Ramsay, a physician from Charleston, South Carolina, one of the first major historians of the American Revolution and the first biographer of George Washington, that from plays such rude words "pass into other books—yes, into standard authorities; and national language as well as morals are corrupted and debased by the influence of the stage!" In a later chapter, I shall return to this issue of prescriptivism, what the scholar Jack Lynch has called the "lexicographer's dilemma."[5]

Webster's mission in 1798 was to settle down to work on a dictionary that would adjust the balance in favor of American English in the United States, even if anglophiles in New York and Boston, annoyed by his animadversions on England's language and culture, were ganging up on him: "The English are determined to ruin my influence, if possible, for no reason unless that I do not love England better than my own country: for I aver I never have treated their nation with disrespect. But I will not long submit to be thus abused by the subjects of foreign nations." These are fighting words. He seemed to be warming up for the main event: a dictionary that would wage his private war against British language usage and settle the question of American linguistic sovereignty with the voice of authority that a dictionary would give him. He now believed he was eminently qualified to write the kind of dictionaries he was convinced the country needed. On June 4, 1800, he announced in the New Haven newspapers that he was proceeding with his plans to write not one but three dictionaries: one for schools, one for the countinghouse (a place where commercial business is transacted), and one for "men of science"—not what we think of as a "scientific dictionary" but one for the learned generally. His dictionary, above all, would be an American dictionary, "long since projected": "The differences in the language of the two countries will continue to multiply, and render it necessary that we should have *Dictionaries* of the *American Language*."[6]

His public notice that he was about to write a dictionary, especially an American or "Columbian" one, once again stirred up a hornet's nest against him. Warren Dutton was chief editor of the *New England Palladium* and an arch conservative in matters of language. In two harsh articles in 1801, he argued that Webster's declared intention to write a dictionary that would use as his model New England spoken English would corrupt the language. He explained the danger of enthroning such provincialisms in a dictionary:

> A language, arrived at its zenith, like ours, and copious and expressive in the extreme, requires no introduction of new words. . . . Colloquial barbarisms abound in all countries, but among no civilized peoples are they admitted with impunity into books. . . . Now, in what can a Columbian dictionary differ from an English one, but in these barbarisms? Who are the Columbian authors who do not write in the English language and spell in the English manner, except Noah Webster, Junior, Esq.? The embryo dictionary then must either be a dictionary of pure English words, and in that case superfluous, as we already possess the admirable lexicon of Johnson, or else must contain vulgar, provincial words, unauthorized by good writers, and in this case, must surely be the just object of ridicule and censure. . . . If the Connecticut lexicographer considers the retaining of the English language as a badge of slavery, let him not give us a Babylonish dialect in its stead, but adopt at once the language of the *aborigines*. . . . If he will persist, in spite of common sense, to furnish us with a dictionary, which we do not want, . . . I will furnish him with a title for it. Let, then, the projected volume of foul and unclean things bear his own Christian name, and be called "NOAH'S ARK."

"I do not like my name, Noah," Webster once ruefully admitted; now he had reason to like it even less.[7]

He replied curtly in a letter, "To the New England Palladium," on November 10, 1801, "It would be as difficult for *me* to *corrupt* and *debase* the language as it is for *him* [Dutton] to *improve* it." Reminding the public of Webster's "absurd orthographical doctrines," Dutton had the last word: "Sometimes vanity appears among us in the shape of a new spelling-book, which, ornamented with a wooden engraving of its author, fondly hopes, together with its own merits, to transmit his features to posterity. Sometimes it appears in proposals for publishing a *Columbian* dictionary, in which the vulgar provincialisms of uneducated *Americans* are to be quoted as authorities for language."[8]

Other scurrilous attacks had appeared just a few days after Webster's announcement. One appeared in the *Philadelphia Aurora* newspaper. It called him a ridiculous "oddity of literature," set on making money "by a scheme which ought to be and will be discountenanced by every man who admires the classic English writers, who has sense enough to see the confusion which must arise from such a silly project—and the incapacity of a man who thus undertakes a work which, if it were at all necessary or eligible, would require the labor of a number of learned and competent men to accomplish it." Another attack was an offering by Joseph Dennie, the exasperated, sardonic, and highly influential editor of the Philadelphia *Port Folio*, a magazine constantly on the hunt for American excesses and eager to expose them. He hoped Webster's dictionary, if it ever appeared, would "meet the contempt it deserves from all the friends of literature." Dennie compared Webster to "a maniac gardener, who, instead of endeavoring to clear his garden of weeds, in opposing to reason, entwines them with his flowers!"[9]

2

The United States was not languishing in a lexicographical desert when Webster decided to become a lexicographer. There was always Johnson's dictionary in addition to the numerous pronouncing and spelling dictionary imports from England. School dictionaries, particularly, had long been recognized as vital for American schools into which there was a steady flow of immigrants and others with little or no ability with the language. As early as 1751, Benjamin Franklin wrote in his pamphlet *Idea of an English School*, "Each Boy should have an English Dictionary to help him over Difficulties"—he never specified which one, although it would have had to be British. There was nothing else to choose from. In 1771, a teacher in an English grammar school in New York made it clear that everybody in his class "will have Johnson's Dictionary"—he does not say which edition. Added to English imports, dictionaries printed or written in America were also available: an edition of William Perry's *Royal Standard Dictionary* issued by Isaiah Thomas of

Worcester, Massachusetts, in 1788; Thomas Sheridan's *General Dictionary of the English Language* published in Philadelphia in 1780; the clergyman Caleb Alexander's *The Columbian Dictionary of the English Language* in 1800; and a couple for schools produced by residents of Connecticut.[10]

One of the latter, *A School Dictionary, Being a Compendium of the Latest and Most Improved Dictionaries* (1797–98), was compiled by Dr. Johnson's namesake, Samuel Johnson Jr. (no relation), born a year before Webster, who was teaching just a few miles down the road in Guildford, Connecticut, and living in New Haven. He published his dictionary in 1798, the very year Webster moved to New Haven. Containing 4,300 words in two hundred pages, small enough for a schoolboy to fit into his pocket, it was the first dictionary of English compiled by an American, copies of which today are difficult to find, although there is one in the British Library and one at Yale. Unlike Webster, Johnson Jr. had no idea of revising or reforming Johnson but instead in his abridgment attempted to Americanize the Scot William Perry's *Royal Standard English Dictionary* (published in London in 1775 and in America ten years later). Johnson Jr.'s lexicographical effort, surprisingly, sold out in a few months, prompting him to pick up with a neighbor in East Guildford, a pastor named John Elliott, producing a revised version, *A Selected, Pronouncing and Accented Dictionary*, printed in Suffield, Connecticut in 1800. Containing five thousand more words than Johnson Jr.'s earlier edition, it included more Americanisms and deliberately set out to "purify" the language by excluding "vulgar" words, which appealed to Webster. Apparently learning of Webster's nearby presence in New Haven, Elliott sent him a copy of the manuscript (containing an introduction praising "the ingenious Mr. Webster") for his thoughts. He then inserted Webster's positive response as part of his preface: "I have not time to examine every sheet of your manuscript but have read many sheets in different parts of it: your general plan and execution I approve of, and can sincerely wish you success in your labours." That was perfunctory, to be sure, but apparently useful enough to Elliott, since by then Webster's name was well known, chiefly owing to his spelling book.[11]

Caleb Alexander's 550-page dictionary was far more successful. It announced on its title page that it contained "many new words peculiar to the United States." As Webster had been and would be again, Alexander was roasted by conservative American critics for that innovation because, as we shall see, the concept of a dictionary of American English was in many people's mind of quite a different and threatening order than a dictionary that was merely printed in America and faithfully recorded British English. Because of its Americanisms such as *caucus, chipmunk, lengthy, moccasin,* and *wigwam,* one reviewer called Alexander's book a "disgusting collection" dragged in from "the boors of each local jurisdiction in the United States."

3

When he got down to it, Webster grabbed an edition of Johnson's dictionary and began to make notes in its margins. By June 1805, he was confiding to Mathew Carey, a Philadelphia bookseller and friend of Benjamin Franklin's, that he "had been engaged for some time in preparing to give an improved dictionary of the language and, as a preliminary step, have been learning the Anglo-Saxon, the mother tongue of the present English." He also intimated to another bookseller in August that he was already "compiling a larger work," a dictionary, that he was confident would banish Johnson for good. He had finally chosen the path that would determine the rest of his life.[12]

In February 1806, he came out with *A Compendious Dictionary of the English Language,* published in New Haven by Hudson and Goodwin. By *compendious,* Webster meant *concise,* intended for the general public, not for schools. It contains a lexicon of 355 pages; 53 pages of tables, charts, and statistics at the end; and 40,600 entry words, all except 5,000 of them plucked out of John Entick's spelling dictionary of 1764. It was succeeded the following year by his abridged school edition, "omitting obsolete and technical terms, and reducing it to a dollar book," from the profits of which he hoped to finance his work on a "complete dictionary" that he was then telling himself he could finish in three to five years. In his preface to the *Compendious Dictionary,* Webster speaks unapologetically to the public directly, much of which he knew was hostile to the entire idea of an "American" dictionary: "Men who take pains to find . . . proofs of our national inferiority in talents and acquirements, are certainly not destined to decide the ultimate fate of [this] performance." He was determined "to make one effort to dissolve the charm of veneration for foreign authors which fascinates the mind of men in this country, and holds them in the chains of illusion."

He makes sure to devote a large part of this preface to explaining the mistakes he claims Dr. Johnson and other British lexicographers had made in orthography, pronunciation, definitions, and etymology. He asserts that his dictionary is innovative, with a lexicon containing more than five thousand entry words not in Johnson—and its rejection of many words that Johnson had included and that Webster maintained either were not part of the functioning language (written or spoken) or were inadmissible (such as *fart, turd*, and sexual terms) because they were "vulgar" (i.e., "low," "mean," "common") and "offensive" to moral sensibilities. It also includes several American tables and lists "for the benefit of the merchant, the student, and the traveller." Such tables had long been a staple feature of several English dictionaries since the seventeenth and eighteenth centuries, but in the more elaborate and detailed way Webster introduced them, they represented what became a new and distinctly American contribution to the history of dictionaries of English. The tables enabled a dictionary to function as a comprehensive reference source regarding money and currency, proper names, poetic fictions, classical mythology, geographical information such as capitals of states and countries, weights and measures, and biblical information, to name but a few categories.[13]

Most of all, Webster's preface broadcasts that his *Compendious Dictionary* is a bold push to Americanize lexicography. Several thousand entry words, he claims, were drawn from American life: jargon; provincialisms and Native American loanwords (e.g., *skunk, snowshoe, tomahawk, wampum*); the language of law and government (*advocate, congressional, constitutionality, departmental, docket, irrepealability, presidency*); industry and commerce (*cent, customable, dime, dollar, dutiable, irredeemable*); technology and science (*aeriform, alkaline, electrometer, gazometer, platina, pyrometer*); medicine (*vaccination*); agriculture (*rattoons*, verbs such as *to gin, to girdle*); geography; proper names; and, generally, the details of American culture. But in the face of the hostility and mockery he had encountered, he hoped that much of his readership would understand that he had backed off somewhat from his proposed spelling reforms for America. (Actually, he only slightly moderated them, retaining such innovations as *aker* for *acre* and *wimmen*, which he describes as "the primitive and correct orthography" for the plural of *woman*). Regarding orthography, he now concedes, "No great changes should ever be made at once," but he insists that his reforms must proceed with "such gradual changes, as shall accommodate the written to the spoken language . . . especially when they purify words from corruptions, improve the regular analogies of a language, and illustrate etymology."[14]

Webster's readers did notice a variety of inconsistencies in his banishment of certain letters in words, such as double letters in polysyllabic words and the final *k* in words like *logick*. These were early days in his journey into lexicography, however. He had firm ideas about the language, as he stated in his *Dissertations*, but he was not able to execute them consistently as a lexicographer. Compounding this was the reality that the spelling of some individual words, and classes of words, were in a transitional stage in both Britain and America. As a result, from place to place in his works, and from time to time, he might simply have tried to accommodate variant spellings. In his monumental book *The English Language in America* (1925), George Philip Krapp pointed out that inconsistency was a major flaw in Webster's system of reforms: many of them were based on nothing more than his personal opinion, and he changed his mind from one part of the dictionary to another. "One may question," he writes, "the advisability of making an elementary dictionary, or in fact a dictionary of any kind, the exponent of theories of reform in spelling, but if this is done, the reforms ought to be carried through systematically and formally, not merely suggested here and there as preferences of the compilers. In this book Webster wrought mainly as an educator, not as an unbiased recorder of words, and he seems to have introduced his reforms more or less casually with the intent of showing what he thought American spelling ought to be, not what it was."[15] Webster stated that although Benjamin Franklin had asked him "to prosecute his [Franklin's] scheme of a reformed alphabet, and offered me his [printing] types for the purpose," he had "declined his offer, on a full conviction of the utter impracticality as well as inutility of the scheme." Krapp's take on this was that "Webster was above all a practical, not a theoretical reformer. Even while he was toying with the idea of a phonetic alphabet, he was engaged in preparing and advertising for the public his elementary books of instruction for which no sale could have been expected, had they made use of an invented phonetic alphabet."[16]

Nor did Webster appear any longer to value a fixed, unifying standard of pronunciation for an entire nation that he championed in his *Dissertations*, to be achieved through new rules that would purge it completely of dialect and what he called "barbaric" regional variations. With both British and American patterns of pronunciation in mind, he continues in the dictionary's preface: "the rules of lexicographers and the practice of poets are utterly disregarded by the bulk of the nation; who regulate and will forever regulate, their practice by a decided preference of sounds—that is, by what may be termed the *natural accent*. To oppose this popular preference of a natural, easy, English accent, is as fruitless, as it is destructive of the uniformity of pronunciation and the beauties of speaking." That last sentence, however, is vague and depends on what he means by a "popular" "natural accent." It looks as if he is thinking of dialect there, "a decided preference for sounds"; if so, opposing it, of course, would not tend to destroy "uniformity of pronunciation." On the contrary, according to his earlier *Dissertations*, opposing local accents would tend to support the notion of uniformity. Webster systematically runs through Johnson and the pronunciation of most of the other British lexicographers—William Kenrick, John Walker, Sir William Jones, Robert Nares, John Entick, Thomas Sheridan—to illustrate where each of them has gone astray and how they disagree with each other, contributing to a virtual Babel of mixed sounds. To demonstrate how misleading it is to rely on any of them as a guide, he includes a table showing their varying pronunciations of several words. He instead takes comfort in his notion that "the common unadulterated pronunciation of the New England gentleman"—his own pronunciation, in fact—was how most English people spoke before the likes of Sheridan, Walker, and Jones had corrupted that aspect of the harmonious uniformity and stability of the English language.[17]

In short, Webster found himself in a sea of inconsistencies and shifting currents in the language, within both Britain and America, and between them. He was still ready to chastise his British lexicographical forerunners but with a diminishing sense of his role, and ability, to control and direct the language. He was on more secure ground with his definitions, which are brief and simple, for example, *cant*: "corrupt or whining talk, a turn"; *caucus*: "cant name of secret meetings"; *constitutional*: "the state of being agreeable to the constitution, or of affecting the constitution"; *electrician*: "one versed in electricity"; *foliage*: "pertaining to or growing from a leaf"; *hickory*: "a tree, a species of walnut"; *slang*: "vulgar language, cant phrases"; *woman* (verb): "to make pliant like a woman." Unlike what lies ahead in Webster's dictionaries, the definitions contain little in the way of personal, moral, religious, political, and social themes; nor is there any etymology included in the definitions, although he speaks of it in general terms in his preface.

Five months after publication of the *Compendious Dictionary*, Josiah Quincy, who later became president of Harvard, told Webster he would be well advised not to seek reviews, not at least "until it has gotten into more hands, which it will in a short period I think, gradually. Some man of sarcastic temperature may thereby be stimulated to exercise himself upon it and thus give it a temporary unpopularity." There were not many reviews, in fact, but Quincy was too late anyway: negative ones had already appeared by the time he warned Webster. One in the newspaper in July 1806 took him to task severely, with "malignity," Webster thought, for his spellings. His sympathetic brother-in-law Thomas Dawes (married to Rebecca's sister), later chief justice of the Massachusetts Supreme Court, recommended "a middle path" between him and his critics, confessing some irritation of his own at Webster's spellings: "*Chooseday* for *Tuesday* I cannot bear, and as to *keind* [for *kind*], it sits worse on my stomach than Indian Root." Webster had asked for support from John Quincy Adams, then Boylston Professor of Rhetoric at Harvard and later the sixth president of the United States, but Adams sent him back a personal but cool assessment in November after reading another harsh review in the *Albany Sentinel* that censured Webster's spelling, pronunciation, and inclusion of "vulgar words." Adams thought Webster was far too radical: "A patriotic spirit will from a sense of duty encourage domestic manufactures, but to prescribe their use by LAW, and to prohibit the introduction of them from Great Britain, is at least of more questionable policy, and perhaps not quite so practicable. . . . Alterations of spelling or of pronunciation upon the *authority* of a single writer have an inevitable tendency to introduce confusion into a language." Adams was worried: "I am apprehensive that your example and authority may produce a similar inconvenience to the writers and speakers of English. . . . I would neither adopt or reject a mode of spelling or pronunciation either from deference or resistance to the English Court or Stage." He advised Webster to "shun all controversy on the subject." As for Webster's nationalistic lexicography, Adams did not "deem it proper to engage national prejudices or passions in the Cause," especially directed against Britain; and he was definitely against "hunting up" regional vocabulary and words with a short lifespan for inclusion in a dictionary of "classical English." "Between vulgarism and propriety of speech some line must be drawn. . . ." That pretty much said it all. Adams was not ready to recommend that Harvard "pledge its support" to his "system" of spelling and pronunciation and the "departure from the English language." Harvard did not support Webster, in fact, until more than half a century later. There would, however, be more fertile ground in New Haven.[18]

By November 1807, Webster was reeling from the wounds inflicted by reviews. It was not a good place to be, he admitted, to have most of the newspaper and magazine editors against him. "We have, to oppose us," he informed Barlow, with whom he had been corresponding about orthography and neologisms in the American language, "the publishers of most of the popular periodical works in our large towns," all of whom "repose implicit confidence in Johnson's opinions" and are "arrayed against *me* and my *designs*." One of the most important reviews appeared in the *Monthly Anthology and Boston Review* in October 1809, delayed more than three years partly because the editors did not want to be drawn into the middle of the furor of Webster's making. It is harsh. "In fifty, or perhaps a hundred of our village schools," it begins, "this *Compendious Dictionary* of Mr. Webster is insinuating suspicions of the definitions of Johnson, justifying ridiculous violations of grammar, and spreading hurtful innovations in orthography." It goes on from there to refer to Webster's "twenty years warfare" over orthography and calls him "the wildest innovator of an age of revolutions."[19]

Without giving examples, Webster complained to his friend the distinguished scientist, physician, and politician Samuel Latham Mitchill that the English approved of aspects of his dictionary more than did the Americans. (Webster was annoyed that Mitchill himself, in fact, had failed to remark on it.) This only made him more irritated with his own nation, "perhaps . . . the only country on the globe where men are determined not to have their errors disturbed, where men fix their opinions upon a particular standard without knowing whether it is right or wrong and grow angry at the man who proves it inaccurate." In Great Britain there is "far more liberality," he added, in an apparently breathtaking turnaround in his views of a country he once called a "harlot," "and if I had not a family, I would quit a country where men who propose improvements on certain books are sure to be abused." This is not a "patriotic" sentiment, to be sure, but it is one that does highlight his resentment and frustration over the wave of disapproval that had greeted his first dictionary.[20]

4

Displacing Delilah

Money was indeed a problem. Webster had been receiving a little more income from his speller after a few of his rights to royalties had reverted back to him in 1804, but his family had grown, and with it, his expenses. His 1806 dictionary was yielding scarcely any income. "Even now my resources are inadequate to the work," he told Joel Barlow in November 1807; "my income barely supports my family, and I want five hundred dollars' worth of books from Europe which I cannot obtain here and which I cannot afford to purchase." One way to raise money was through subscriptions to the intended dictionary. Two or three hundred, he felt, would be all he needed. But people were frightened off by his extreme views and ways of expressing them, his drive to "overturn, overturn."[1] Barlow, incidentally, was feeling rather good about himself just then, publishing his poem *The Columbiad* that year, a visionary but turgid national epic of American history that for a time looked to become a foundational text for the United States, although in the end it did not.

Webster's editorial vantage point after 1808 became more complicated by his religious "awakening" to "the doctrines of the Christian faith," impelled partly by his desire to join the rest of his family in public Calvinist worship. If he had kept his conversion private, it would not have affected the reception of his work, but in July 1809 he felt compelled to publish in the *Panoplist* a lengthy explanation of how he had arrived at his current religious stance. Although many appreciated his "apologia" and wrote to tell him so, many others (especially Massachusetts Unitarians, notably at Harvard) were spooked that his judgment would now be complicated by religious zeal, further distorting his handling of the language—that "your own sentiments ["peculiar doctrine"] would get into the work, as the true and only definition," wrote his brother-in-law Dawes. Krapp's take on the influence of Webster's religious conversion on his lexicography signals the problem: "In short, it was really spiritual, not phonological truth in which Webster was primarily interested, and he seems to have thought . . . that the truth of a word, that is the primitive and original radical value of the word, was equivalent to the truth of the idea."[2]

Nor did Webster retreat from his anti-Johnson campaign. David Ramsay's warning to him about Boston in August 1807—that "prejudices against any American attempts to improve Dr. Johnson are very strong in that city"— only fanned the embers of his smoldering resentment. Webster ignored the admonition and responded by bombarding Ramsay with a vigorous twelve-page letter, following that up immediately with a thirty-two-page pamphlet, *A Letter to Dr. Ramsay, of Charleston (S.C.) Respecting the Errors in Johnson's Dictionary and Other Lexicons.* The pamphlet only deepened the existing bias against his lexicographical ambitions. Nothing Johnson did lexicographically was right, Webster wrote in his letter to Ramsay, and the "blind admiration" Americans had for him was stunting their intellectual growth, serving as "the insidious Delilah by which the Samsons of our country are shorn of their locks. . . . Johnson's Dictionary . . . furnishes no standard of correct English, but in its present form tends very much to corrupt and pervert the language. . . . Johnson has transgressed the rules of lexicography beyond any other compiler; for his work contains more of the lowest of all vulgar words than any other now extant. . . ." That was a risky claim, given that Webster certainly did not undertake an exhaustive search for vulgar words through a long line of eighteenth-century dictionaries. He went on, "Let the admirers of Johnson's Dictionary be a little more critical in comparing his vocabulary and mine and blush for their illiberal treatment of me!" John Jay, former president of the Continental Congress and the first chief justice of the Supreme Court, one of the few people who sent Webster subscription money, cheered him on but also sobered him by telling him his efforts to gain subscriptions were hampered by considerable apprehension that his dictionary would "impair" the sameness of the English language and its orthography in Britain and America, and that most people were biased against it because of that. As Webster makes quite clear in his *Dissertations on the English Language,* "As a nation, we have a very great interest in opposing the introduction of any plan of uniformity with the British language." He was not about to let John Jay or any nostalgic defenders of British English, nor the principle that the "sameness" of the language in the two countries should be preserved, persuade him to abandon that mission just so he could obtain subscriptions.[3]

Webster's views and methods, the size of the dictionary, the costs—they all worked against his obtaining subscriptions. "Many men are loth to advance money for a book to be finished 12 years hence," Dawes insisted, "when the author may be impaired or in his grave." His old Yale classmate Oliver Wolcott told him bluntly, "I cannot encourage you to expect success by means of a popular subscription, unless the public impressions are different in other places, from what they are in New York." They were not, at least not in cities and large towns. Webster's circular letter dated February 17, 1807, "To the Friends of Literature in the United States," soliciting "gentlemen of property" for subscriptions, brought none. He may have turned still more people against the project with his extravagant claims of having studied the Hebrew, Celtic, and "Teutonic" languages and thus obtained what he described as his unmatchable command of the history of the English language. It was the tone of his plea for subscriptions, as if he were the unappreciated resident prophet of American lexicography in the country, that tended to put people off. "The imperfections and inaccuracies of the best English dictionaries have been long known and regretted by men of letters in Great Britain," he wrote, and some philologists are trying to "supply the defect," but "by men incompetent to the task." With the "valuable materials" he has collected, he proposed to remedy this deplorable situation, once and for all, with his dictionary. In the middle of all this, he was brought down to earth by his father, Noah Webster Sr., who wrote to him in June 1807 asking for a loan of $10 to $20 to pay for "post and rails" needed for a new fence on the farm. Webster did send his father $10, which he could ill afford. Increasingly desperate, two years later he even petitioned James Madison, soon to become president of the United States, for some sort of appointment in Europe with a "considerable emolument" so he could gain access to books he had no hope of finding in America. Nothing came of that request either—just as well, perhaps, because it is improbable that Rebecca would have allowed him to uproot his young family by moving to another country.[4]

Letters from him followed one after another for years, public and private, complaining, protesting, imploring, explaining, justifying, and boasting. All he could do was "trudge on," the lonely warrior, resilient and undefeated: "The labor requisite to accomplish the work upon my plan is certainly double to that which Dr. *Johnson* bestowed upon his dictionary. My etymological inquiries alone . . . will probably incur as much labor as the whole execution of Johnson's works."[5]

2

In the meantime, his money was running out, and there was no alternative but to leave New Haven and settle somewhere less expensive so that he could "get bread for my children." He sold his New Haven house and in 1812 purchased a "humble cottage in the country"—in fact, a sizable house—in the sleepy farming town of Amherst, Massachusetts, where he could continue working "with comfort" and fewer distractions. Rebecca was supportive but distraught. Their daughters wept on leaving New Haven.[6]

Once settled in the large study of his new home, from which he looked out across the town "green" to what now is Amherst College, an institution he would help to establish (he delivered the address at the laying of the cornerstone of Amherst College in August 1820 and became president of its board of trustees), he immediately began work on his magnum opus. That study became his dictionary room. He placed in it what became a legendary round table he brought with him from New Haven. His daughter Eliza many years later remembered the table, the room, and her father working in it:

> In the second story of his new home, in a large room, with windows looking to the south and east, Webster set up anew the large circular table which he had used for some years at New Haven. This table was about two feet wide, built in the form of a hollow circle. Dictionaries and grammars of all obtainable languages were laid in successive order upon its surface. Webster would take the word under investigation, and standing at the right end of the lexicographer's table, look it up in the first dictionary which lay at that end. He made a note, examined a grammar, considered some kindred word, and then passed to the next dictionary of some other tongue. He took each word through the twenty or thirty dictionaries, making notes of his discoveries, and passing around his table many times in the course of a day's labor of minute and careful study.

The "hollow" part of this doughnut-shaped table was the space inside the circle into which Webster could walk through a small opening.[7]

3

He was ready for work but decided to devote himself first to sorting out once and for all the etymology of the language. It was a detour of monumental proportions, ten long years of fantastic conjectures that virtually froze his progress on the main body of the dictionary. He saw his decade of intensive research, however, as a substantial breakthrough in etymological understanding. By 1813, he was collating, as he put it, "the radical words [the form of a word without the affixes or morphemes that are used to make other words] in 20 languages, including the seven Asiatic languages or dialects of the Assyrian stocks." He had happened on a "field entirely new," he claimed, which was true in the sense that all preceding dictionaries were woefully inadequate in their etymologies.[8]

Webster embarked on the study of etymology without much more than a negligible familiarity with the scientifically based philological research in Europe that was breaking new and revolutionary ground in the history of languages. Johnson's young friend Sir William Jones (1746–94), at age twenty-six one of England's most promising orientalists, may be said to have inaugurated the study of modern philology with his pioneering discoveries regarding ancient Hindu Sanskrit and its relationship to the family of languages known as Indo-European. The German linguists Karl Wilhelm Friedrich Schlegel (1772–1829) and Franz Bopp (1791–1867) had begun doing major work in this field well before Webster plunged headlong into his version of etymology. Their work on the relationship of Sanskrit to the grammatical forms of Indo-European languages was fairly well known by English philologists by 1820.[9]

Unlike William Jones, who had done important work on the roles of vowels in the making of languages, Webster virtually ignored vowels in tracing the evolution of language: "little or no regard is to be had to them, in ascertaining the origin and affinity of languages." He was more comprehensively rebelling against language historians in general who, like Jones, angered Webster by remarking, "I beg leave, as a philologer, to enter my protest against conjectural etymology in historical researches, and principally against the licentiousness of etymologists in transposing and inserting letters, in substituting at pleasure any consonant for another of the same order, and in totally disregarding the vowels." If Webster had heeded that protest, he might have saved himself much of his work during those tedious ten years, though doubtless he benefited from the exercise as he propelled himself daily around his dictionary table from one bilingual dictionary of Semitic and European languages to another on the principle of radicals and roots: that "a radical identity between two words [exists] if they exhibit only a moderate degree of similarity in their consonantal structure." He also believed the biblical account of God's confounding languages at the Tower of Babel, and he was convinced all languages had their origins in the ancient languages—Shemitic or Semitic (Shem supposedly was the oldest son of the biblical Noah), Japhetic (Japheth supposedly was the third son of Noah), and Chaldean (the Aramaic vernacular of the Semitic people of Babylonia). He remained dogmatic, not likely to have listened to Jones or any of the German philologists, even if he had been more aware of their research and discoveries in this field. While his methodology was herculean but unscientific, he convinced himself it was thoroughly systematic. And having spent many years searching for the casual external similarities of words, he was not about give it all up in deference to European philologists who did not have, he felt, an inside track to the final answer. Years later, in 1839, he wrote this in his address to the Mercantile Library Association: "In this branch of etymology, even the German scholars, the most accurate philologists in Europe, appear to be wholly deficient. To this investigation I devoted ten years, and my reward is ample."[10]

If not from learned Americans, the learned English elite, or German philologists, where did Webster get much of his inspiration for his etymological journey? It was, surprisingly, from England in the late eighteenth century, but certainly not from English traditional views of language and education. His English linguistic and etymological hero, so to speak, was John Horne Tooke, a learned English political agitator and erratic member of Parliament who, incidentally, reviled the dictionary compiled by his contemporary, Dr. Johnson, and has been described as "one of the most systematically frantic etymologists who ever lived." In his *Dissertations on the English Language*, Webster confesses "an affection" for Horne Tooke, who was influential as a linguist because in his book *Diversions of Purley* (1786) he promoted the radical idea that the origins of language could philosophically be discovered by unscientific, almost mystical, speculation over the etymologies of words. He drew conclusions from the superficial resemblance of words. In this regard he played his part in retarding the development of English philology; he also made, as we shall see, an unfortunate and wasteful impression on

Noah Webster. Webster was particularly drawn to Horne Tooke because at the root of the latter's linguistic ideas was the conservative principle that the plain speech of the common man could be traced to Anglo-Saxon, not to Latin and Greek. As the scholar Marilyn Butler puts it, John Horne Tooke "set the comparative study of language on an eccentric course in England just when philology was taking off in Germany." An inspiration for Webster, and as we shall see, also for Webster's emerging rival, the influential English lexicographer Charles Richardson, Horne Tooke defiantly turned his back on the considerably exciting philological discoveries the Germans had already made.[11]

4

Attacks on Webster's work continued. A major one, already mentioned, came in 1816 in the form of an address by John Pickering, philologist, politician, and jurist, to the distinguished American Academy of Arts and Sciences in Cambridge, Massachusetts. Webster, however, read it later in Pickering's analysis of the "present state of the English language" when it appeared in print as the preface to Pickering's *Vocabulary*. Pickering listed certain "provincialisms" or "Americanisms"—these included new words, old words with new meanings, and local words by then obsolete in England—of which he thought the public should be more aware. A firm believer in British authority and the "purity" of the language inherited by America, he advocated that "Americanisms" unknown to intelligent and educated Americans (and British)—described by one contemporary British reviewer as "barbarous phraseology"—should never be given the legitimacy of inclusion in a dictionary. In effect, Pickering's book amounted to a rejection of much of what Webster stood for: "I expect to encounter the displeasure of our American reformers, who think we ought to throw off our native tongue as one of the badges of English servitude, and establish a new tongue for ourselves." The "best scholars in our country treat such a scheme with derision," Pickering insisted; to turn our backs on "a language which is common to ourselves and the illustrious writers and orators of our mother country," would be madness. It would not have pleased Webster to know that after Pickering's address to the academy, Thomas Dawes had rushed up to him in great excitement and said, "There! That is what I have been trying to bring my brother Webster to agree to; but he won't do it!"[12]

Webster took his revenge the following year in *A Letter to the Honorable John Pickering*—not a private letter to Pickering but a published pamphlet of no fewer than sixty-four pages. He challenges Pickering word-by-word, indignantly assailing the resistance that Pickering had thrown into his path toward becoming America's great language reformer. He coaxes his argument inevitably into the realm of morality: "I deprecate the effects of a blind acquiescence in the opinions of men and the passive reception of every thing that comes from a foreign press. My mind revolts at the reverence for foreign authors which stifles inquiry, restrains investigation, benumbs the vigor of the intellectual faculties, subdues and debases the mind. I regret to see the young Hercules of genius in America chained to his cradle." He had read Pickering's *Vocabulary* with quivering anger, especially when he came to an insulting allusion he was certain was to himself: "in this country, as in England, we have thirsty reformers and presumptuous sciolists, who would unsettle the whole of our admirable language for the purpose of making it conform to their whimsical notions of propriety." Webster now pretends not to care. "Whether you number me with the thirsty reformers and presumptuous sciolists [people who traffic in superficial knowledge]," he writes, "is a fact I shall take no pains to discover, nor if known, would the fact give me the smallest concern." But he is outraged that anyone should have the temerity to pick on him like that, the self-appointed savior of the American language. He lashes out with a passage against Pickering's "dictatorial authority" that, with a little pause and some reflection, might have occurred to him could apply to himself at least as much as to Pickering: "The man who undertakes to censure others for the use of certain words and to decide what is or is not correct in language seems to arrogate to himself a dictatorial authority, the legitimacy of which will always be denied."[13]

It also irks him that Pickering was straying into territory he had staked out as his own. He denies Pickering's charge that he is out to "unsettle" the language by recording and promoting differences between the languages of the two countries. He maintains that he is not the enemy of Britain: "I venerate the men and their writings," he announces. "I venerate the literature, the laws, the institutions, and the charities of the land of my fathers." But if called to battle, he will fight: "I wish to be on good terms with the English: it is in my interest and the interest of my fellow citizens to treat them as friends and brethren. But I will be neither frowned nor ridiculed into error. . . . I will examine subjects for myself. . . . If I must measure swords with their travellers and their reviewers . . . I shall not decline the combat." He concludes on a lugubrious note, complaining that Americans are already forgetting what he had done for the country, but he holds out some hope for himself, his books, and the nation: "I have contributed in a small degree to the instruction of at least four millions of the rising generation; and it is not unreasonable to expect that a few seeds of improvement planted by my hand may germinate and grow and ripen into valuable fruit when my remains shall be mingled with the dust."[14]

5

By November 1821, Webster had reached the letter *H* in his dictionary. He had also completed a "Synopsis of the Principal Words in Twenty Languages," in which he recorded his etymological conclusions for an appendix to the dictionary, a piece of scholarship that would never be published—it presently languishes in the archives of the New York Public Library. He hoped to finish in five years, but his isolation worried him, "retired from libraries and from men of erudition, whose aid I want and must have in revising the work." A move to either Boston or back to New Haven, where there were more books available, therefore became necessary, and he thought he might even have to visit Europe, especially England, where he could seek out the books he needed and perhaps even secure a publisher with the correct assortment of types for foreign languages that the book would require and were not available in America. John Jay sent him money in 1821, but he needed far more patronage from wealthy men than was forthcoming. By his reckoning he had already spent $25,000 of his own money on it, money of which his family had been deprived during its years of greatest need when the children were growing up.[15]

It helped his finances that the family ranks in Amherst had thinned. In 1813, Webster's daughter Emily married William Ellsworth, who would become governor of Connecticut and a Supreme Court justice, and moved to Hartford. And in 1816, his daughter Julia married Chauncey Allen Goodrich, an impressive young tutor at Yale studying for the ministry. The following year Goodrich became a professor of rhetoric at Yale, following in the footsteps of his grandfather Elizur Goodrich, and he and his wife settled in New Haven. Ellsworth and Goodrich, but especially the astute Goodrich, would both figure prominently in the dictionary wars in the ensuing years.

6

Rebecca favored New Haven, so in 1822 they returned there. Their daughter Eliza recalled the reasons the family left Amherst for New Haven in a letter to her sister Emily in 1885: "I do know one reason why Father left Amherst because he several times mentioned it before me. He intended going to Europe & wished to leave Mother & Louise [another sister, with some intellectual disabilities] under the protection of brother & sister [Julia] Goodrich. The comfort which sister Julia could give to Mother he appreciated, & then too he needed the aid of books from the Yale library." They first rented a small house and then, evidently intending this move to be permanent, Webster built a larger house on the corner of Temple and Grove Streets, a good location close to the hub of college life—next to where many of Webster's archives lie today at the Beinecke Rare Book and Manuscript Library. They were delighted to be back in New Haven. Rebecca was glad to be with her old friends again and living close to Julia. And Webster's proximity now to his resourceful son-in-law Chauncey Goodrich would become crucial to the fate of his dictionary in both useful and painful ways.[16]

Returning to the dictionary in New Haven without the tangled distractions of further etymological forays into other languages, he worked hard and made rapid progress, reaching the letter *R* by December 1823. He soon became convinced, however, of his need to travel to France and England to complete his work. "I rejoice that a man of your uncommon learning and facility of Investigation is not to give up his great Dictionary; but you must feel younger [at sixty-five] than *I* do," Dawes wrote to him in February 1824, "to carry the manuscript across the Atlantic." His friend William Cranch, a federal judge and the nephew of Abigail Adams, thought it was a fine idea to travel where his work surely would be better appreciated: "I have no doubt that your labours will be more justly estimated in England than they have been here. The greatest difficulty will be to make them believe it possible that any man but an Englishman can obtain a knowledge of the English language. This Country [America] has not given you credit for one half your merit as a literary character, because you have been so unbending to the prejudices of our literary men."[17]

He left for Paris on June 15, 1824, accompanied by his twenty-two-year-old son, William, who was to serve as his copyist. He did not much like France. At the royal library, which later became the Bibliothèque Nationale de France, he managed to examine "the latest works on the physical sciences," where he found "the new terms . . . I have been seeking for my dictionary," but he was out of place and uncomfortable. Someone he knew from home saw him in his Paris hotel one morning, an unmistakable, darkly-clothed New Englander, and later wrote: "I saw a tall, slender form, with a black coat, black small-clothes, black silk stockings, moving back and forth, with its hands behind it, and evidently in a state of meditation. It was a curious, quaint, Connecticut looking apparition, strangely in contrast to the prevailing forms and aspects in this gay metropolis. I said to myself—'If it were possible, I should say that was Noah Webster!' I went up to him, and found it was indeed he. At the age of sixty-six he had come to Europe to perfect his Dictionary."[18]

After little more than two not very productive months in Paris, Webster crossed the Channel to Brighton, England, headed for Cambridge University, where he intended to spend the winter consulting books in the library and completing the writing of his dictionary. He had written to Professor Samuel Lee at Trinity College, professor of Arabic and Hebrew languages, and himself a brilliant philologist and lexicographer—he became Regius Professor of Hebrew in 1831—stating he would be coming. William wrote to his mother that for their ride to Cambridge they preferred to hire "a private conveyance" of "a chariot and a couple of horses" rather than have to endure "a hasty ride in a crowded stage coach." It did not take Webster long to be disillusioned with Cambridge. William wrote to his mother, "My father is almost discouraged on account of the character Professor Lee gives of the inhabitants of Cambridge. According to his description of the people, and his account is confirmed by other respectable inhabitants, the morals of the greater part of the population are wretchedly depraved." They had not arranged to stay in one of the Cambridge colleges, so they had no choice but to obtain lodgings, consisting of "a parlor & two bedrooms," in the town for eight months. The appearance of the college buildings themselves did not seem to have pleased them either: "old stone buildings, which look very heavy, cold & gloomy to an American accustomed to the new public buildings in our country." As for books, which was the reason he came abroad, he seemed to be getting them from wherever he could, from a bookseller's library in town for a quarterly payment, the university library, and probably from Trinity College library.[19]

Professor Lee may not have fully understood why the Websters were in Cambridge in the first place. At any rate, Lee was ill for much of their time there, so the one potential contact for introducing them to the faculty was largely out of circulation until nearly the end of their stay. Webster had hoped to engage a few of the faculty in discussions about the language, but for most of his time in Cambridge he was almost totally neglected. He did make an effort to overcome his isolation, however. In a more accommodating mood than he usually demonstrated when railing against the British and their language, he retreated from his dogmatic position in the *Dissertations* that Americans must have no interest in encouraging a sameness between their language and that of Britain. He wrote to Professor Lee suggesting a meeting of Oxford and Cambridge scholars, in which he would play a part, to the end of bringing about "some agreement or coincidence of opinions in regard to unsettled points in pronunciation and grammatical construction" and "the evils of our irregular orthography": "The English language is the language of the United States; and it is desirable that as far as the people have the same things and the same ideas, the words to express them should remain the same." One can imagine the Cambridge response to this virtually unknown American on his first visit to England—unknown at least to the Cambridge dons—suggesting such a major overhaul of the language. In any case, for the most part he was ignored. Not until late January 1825 did several Fellows of Trinity College finally discover him and regret they had not met him earlier; and at about that time Lee's health improved enough to enable him to read Webster's "Synopsis" and declare himself "much interested in the ingenuity of [Webster's] remarks." So far as we know, that seems to have been the extent of his interest in Webster's work. Webster told Rebecca on December 6, "I have no reason to be discouraged nor to regret the voyage, as yet, but I have some months labor yet to perform." By nearly the end of their visit, though, Webster and his son were enjoying themselves. Cambridge was, after all, "a place endeared to us . . . by an acquaintance with some interesting families and some gentlemen of the University, whose uniform kindness to us will form a pleasurable source of recollections of this venerable seat of literature and science."[20]

In his relative academic solitude, Webster soldiered on, William proving to be extremely helpful by transcribing the entire manuscript into a fair copy. "He devotes most of his time to copying for me," Webster reassured Rebecca. The day after Christmas 1824, he wrote again, "William is gone to the Chapel for evening service. His eyes have been weaker these three weeks past, owing to straining them by writing at night. But they are gaining strength." He complained of pains in his own right hand, especially "the right thumb, the strength of which is almost exhausted. I am approaching the end of my work, & by care, I hope to have strength to proceed, without interruption."[21]

Much sooner apparently than he expected, on a memorable day in January 1825, he completed the last word for his dictionary: *zymome* or *zimome*, which (apparently not mustering enough energy to elaborate) he defined simply as "one of the constituents of gluten." It was a moment that almost overwhelmed him physically and emotionally: "I finished writing my Dictionary in January, 1825, at my lodgings in Cambridge, England. When I had come to the last word, I was seized with a trembling which made it somewhat difficult to hold my pen steady for writing. The cause seems to have been the thought that I might not then live to finish the work, or the thought that I was so near the end of my labor. But I summoned strength to finish the last word, & then walking about the room a few minutes I recovered." "Worn out" with writing and eager to leave Cambridge for London, where he intended to find a publisher, he thought the odds were against him, for "it is uncertain what difficulties I may have to encounter from the *prejudices* of the English & from the *interest* which the principal booksellers have in Johnson's dictionary by Todd." He was referring to Henry John Todd's revision of Johnson in 1818—there would be another Todd edition in 1827—and he was right. In London he met with indifference toward his work by scholars and booksellers alike. There was no use staying in England. If he was to secure a publisher, it would have to be in America. They sailed for home soon afterward, Webster clutching the manuscript he had struggled for twenty years to complete.[22]

Webster arrived home in the early summer of 1825, buoyed up at first by the jubilation of his family and friends over his having completed his colossal work. As the months passed, however, he grew increasingly desperate that he could not find anyone to publish his dictionary. He was sixty-seven and tired, and a huge amount of editing and proofreading lay ahead of him. The expense involved before the public could read a single word he had written was daunting and a formidable deterrent to potential publishers and printers. It gradually dawned on him he might himself have to pay for his book's publication, although this would mean severe financial hardship for his family from which they might never recover.

In late 1825 or early in 1826, his son-in-law Chauncey Allen Goodrich stepped in to help him find a publisher. He did not have far to look, offering the book to Sherman Converse, a native of Connecticut and enterprising young graduate of Yale in 1813 who had remained in New Haven and launched himself into the publishing business, first as editor of the *Connecticut Journal* and later by starting what soon became one of the largest publishing houses in New England. Webster might earlier have considered using Converse as his publisher and dismissed the idea because Converse had gained something of a dubious local reputation as a controversial and combative newspaper editor. Only four years earlier Converse had lost a major two-year court case in the Connecticut Supreme Court of Errors (with two appeals) over a libel suit against him for slander as editor of the *Connecticut Journal.* "This Mr. Converse has scattered firebrands, arrows, and death," declared the plaintiff's attorney, adding that "he has aimed a fatal dart at the bosom of my client." Converse's tenaciousness was borne out by his publishing the proceedings of the trials in 1822, in which he boldly accused the court and the judge of playing politics.[23]

Goodrich was not unduly bothered. He judged that with his Connecticut background Converse would be sympathetic to Webster's dictionary and eager to publish it. He was correct. For Converse this was a unique opportunity that had fallen into his lap, one that was sure to widen his publishing interests outside Connecticut and have his name linked with what looked to be an unusually important book. Webster felt relieved, although he was compelled to pay a sum out of his own pocket because Converse did not have the resources to bear all the costs. What Converse lacked in publishing experience and reputation, however, as well as money, he more than made up for with audacity and energy. He wrote to numerous highly placed politicians, educators, and authors in search of patronage. Aiming for the jackpot, he enclosed samples of Webster's lexicography together with his "Dictionary Prospectus" and boldly sent them off in February 1826 to Thomas Jefferson at Monticello, pleading for a recommendation he hoped would generate some badly needed financial support. It had become obligatory by this time to mention—with a stiff dose of hyperbole—Webster's untiring language service to the country across several decades: "Mr. W[ebster] has bestowed upon this work . . . almost 30 years of industrious labor" and "compiled a work which comprises more philological research than all the English Lexicon hitherto published, and which if published will do great credit to Mr. Webster and to our country."

Vastly more philological work on the English language had been done in England before Webster rose from his obscurity in Hartford, Connecticut, but never mind. If Jefferson would favor Converse with a generous response, "I may obtain sufficient patronage to lay it [the dictionary] before the public." Jefferson, however, as we have seen, had never been a fan of Webster's and had actually mocked him, so he was hardly likely to join in, even if he had been in better health—he died only five months after he received Converse's letter. He replied to Converse, "worn down with age, infirmity and pain, my mind is no longer in a tone for such services. I can only therefore express my regret that I cannot be useful to you in that way. . . ." Too many people, like Jefferson, by then distrusted Webster's self-promotion and prowess with the language, so money trickled in unimpressively.[24]

Publication, moreover, was delayed no fewer than a couple of years by the laborious task of revision and editing that had been given to the meticulous James Gates Percival, another Yale graduate and resident of New Haven. Percival was a man of "shrinking and morbid sensitiveness," a reclusive and temperamentally eccentric poet, accomplished linguist, geologist, and doctor. He lived penuriously in New Haven for most of his life, unconnected to Yale in any way since his graduation. He had matriculated at Yale at age sixteen and graduated in 1820 at the top of his class. After he acquired a degree in medicine there, he tried unsuccessfully to practice, attributing his failure to his poetry: "I got my name up for writing . . . verses and found myself ruined. When a person is really ill he will not send for a poet to cure him." One of his classmates remarked about Percival, "I never knew one who could acquire correct knowledge quicker than Percival." Another confirmed his reputation as an eccentric: "I think he had few acquaintances in college, though I never knew he had any enemies. The fact that his intercourse was so circumscribed was doubtless to be attributed to constitutional reserve, and not to the consciousness of his own superiority. Everybody looked upon him as a good-natured, sensitive, thoughtful, odd, gifted fellow." On the recommendation of another of Webster's sons-in-law, William Fowler, a classmate of Percival's at Yale, Converse gave him the massive job of reading most of the proofs several times.[25]

7

While he was involved in the tedious process of preparing his dictionary for the press, Webster became distraught again from what he regarded as the serious inadequacy of the American Copyright Act of 1790, which provided copyright protection for an initial period of only fourteen years and no protection whatever from the commercial competition of cheap pirated British books. The act also specified that if the author were to die during the term of copyright—a distinct possibility in the case of the seventy-year-old Webster—the copyright would lapse, and the author's heirs after that would be denied any royalties. What Webster advocated was the extension of the initial term of copyright protection and the assignment of copyright to the author's legal heirs, but his fondest hope was for Congress to legislate perpetual copyright to authors and their heirs.

In a letter to Daniel Webster (no relation), a member of the House of Representatives and soon to be a US senator, in 1826 he urged congressional action: "The right of a farmer and mechanic to the exclusive enjoyment and right of disposal of what they *make* or *produce* is never questioned," he asserted, so why should not an author's? It was not until December 1830 that at last a new copyright bill was successfully brought to a vote. It ensured an initial period of twenty-eight years of copyright, with the provision of inheritance of rights for heirs should the author die before those twenty-eight years elapsed. The heirs also had the option to renew copyright for another fourteen years after the first twenty-eight. This was not perpetual copyright for heirs, but it was a huge step forward. Authors all over the land rejoiced. Although many others had agitated for the legislation, Webster believed he was the chief reason for its passing, as he wrote to son-in-law Fowler on a visit to Washington, DC, in 1831, where he was lobbying politicians: "My presence here has, I believe, been very useful and perhaps necessary to the accomplishment of the object. . . . [I]t was necessary that something extra should occur to awaken" Congress's attention, and his visit was it. The result convinced him that "my fellow citizens consider me as their benefactor and the benefactor of my country." The lack of international copyright law, however, would not be redressed until long after Webster's death, when Congress passed the International Copyright Act of 1891.[26]

8

Percival was no average proofreader. He was a more competent scholar of etymology than Webster, said to have been able to read ten languages fluently. Independently, he had been studying the advanced etymological research of the German philologists and spotted numbers of Webster's errors concerning etymology that he could not bring himself to pass over silently. One anonymous observer of Percival's methods during this work described his habits: "He could only work in his own time and way. Nothing could be passed over until thoroughly finished; and the consequence was, that he would sometime spend days upon some single insignificant word, whose history, if attainable, was of no importance. In the meantime, printers, compositors, and proofreaders must be paid for standing idle. . . ."[27]

Months went by. While the printing of the book continued, Percival plagued Webster with corrections he felt had to be made—as he put it, "obliged to correct the blunders of ignorance . . . I feel like the living tied to the dead." Percival complained in July, "at the present rate of progression, it will be almost a life-interest with me." Even Webster's son-in-law Chauncey Goodrich appears to have been involved in assisting Percival by allowing him to consult his well-stocked library in his Yale rooms. One of Goodrich's colleagues one day walked in on Percival reading in Goodrich's rooms: "I occasionally saw him at Professor Goodrich's rooms. He pursued his investigations standing by the side of the book-shelves; generally holding two or three books in his hands, having a pile of others collected at his feet, wearing on his head his ragged leather cap, usually keeping his back turned toward any persons in the room, and never, while I was present, speaking or raising his eyes from the work."[28]

By December, Percival was threatening to pull out under the strain, tired of Webster telling him he was being obsessive and pedantic. He worked nonstop every day until seven in the evening, then took the sheets he had corrected to a cranky Webster in order to "make revisions on his authorities, and settle with him the corrections." "This has been my employment for most of six months," he complained in December, "and I am now done with it. I cannot, and will not go through twenty months at least of such incessant labor; for it will take fully that time to finish. The world may cry out what they choose; but when I find myself bound by Gordian knots, I will cut them. Some arrangement must be made to lighten my task, or I shall resign it entirely. . . . My situation is therefore one of disgust and toil. . . . I regret that I have ever engaged in the thing. It will be one of the miseries of my life to think of it." Converse raised his pay, gave him a few assistants, and the project inched its way to completion.[29]

Webster's frustration with Percival's scrupulousness turned inevitably to anger. Converse angered him, too, since he was the one who had hired Percival. His patience at an end, he fired Percival. "I can only say that I was compelled to take the steps I did," he wrote to Converse on May 23, 1828, just six months before publication, "for I am certain, had I not done it, I should ere this have been unfit for any superintendence of the dictionary. As it is, I am not certain that I shall not sink under the labor, before it is finished." In his dictionary, he acknowledged Percival's extensive help with a single vague reference. Fowler continued to help him with the proofreading, but his contribution was intermittent and not thorough. Webster's own revision was haphazard. Without the continuation of Percival's extremely detailed corrections and editing, many errors remained in the manuscript that came to haunt him in the months to come.[30]

In the meantime, Webster and Converse began an advertising campaign inflated by extravagant promotional claims and spelling out exactly in what ways this dictionary would outshine existing British rivals. There would be twenty thousand words that had never before appeared in any dictionary, five thousand of which were scientific terms; "precise and technical definitions"; between thirty thousand and fifty thousand new senses and connotations of words; etymologies; and pronunciations that Webster maintained would substantiate his contention that the orthoepy, or pronunciation, of the language in the Englishman John Walker's *A Critical Pronouncing Dictionary* (1791), then the chief authority on the subject in both Britain and America, was comprehensively incorrect. In his promotion of the publication, Webster cast Walker as his main antagonist, whom he characterized as no authority at all, even in Britain, and whose book he urged readers to avoid. This attack was the beginning of his war against other lexicographers besides Johnson. His own book, he announced, would stabilize both orthography and orthoepy in America for good by promoting sensible consistency, discouraging dialects, and declaring the independence of American pronunciation from English. Webster had long felt that one of the ways to achieve this consistency of pronunciation was to simplify and regularize spelling, since it was the present state of orthography that confused people as to how to pronounce words. Walker was making things worse with too much complexity, "too much niceness and exactness," and "hypercritical fastidiousness" in his representation of sounds (especially of vowels) on the pages of his dictionary. Moreover, one of Walker's greatest sins, Webster declared, was his alteration of spelling to bring it into line with the fashionable speech of English society. The Englishman Charles Richardson—more about him later—who was becoming Webster's hostile lexicographical rival in America, as well as in England, on this point praised Webster's new dictionary because its pages are "not disfigured by the appearance of such ill-looking vocables as are sometimes made to represent the sounds in other dictionaries." Although Webster was advocating "sameness of pronunciation" throughout America, he was not advocating total segregation of the American from the English tongue. In his book on dictionaries and lexicographers, *Chasing the Sun*, Jonathon Green notes that in a letter to Queen Victoria in 1841 accompanying his gift to her of the second edition of the dictionary, Webster expressed his hope that "genuine descendants of English ancestors born on the west of the Atlantic, have not forgotten either the land or the language of their fathers." Green comments on this: "It was all a far cry from the post-Revolutionary hothead of the 1780s."[31]

But his son-in-law Goodrich was nervous about this assault on Walker's authority in America. He wrote to Edward Everett to see what he thought. Everett's reply to Goodrich has not been preserved, but in a letter to Webster about Walker in 1829, although he equivocated somewhat, he came down strongly in favor of Walker: "There can be no doubt . . . that Walker had access to the best sources of information, as to the fashionable pronunciation of the language. He was selected by Edmund Burke, as his son's master in elocution. . . . Now where the actual usage of living societies is regarded as the standard, no book can be. The most that any book can aspire to do, is faithfully to record the usage, for the time being; and I must own that I am not acquainted with any other book, which appears to be so good a record of the pronunciation of our language as Walker's." As far as he knew, nobody by then had done a better job than Walker. In fact, on reading Webster's dictionary, Everett turned squarely against Webster: "[W]e think the cases must be very rare, and present a very well admitted ambiguity, to authorize us, as Mr. Webster proposes, to resort to principles of the English language, in defiance of the received English pronunciation. We also deny wholly the propriety of making a distinction between the American usage and the English usage, *as such*, and the setting up of a standard for each."[32]

9

Webster's large, unabridged dictionary, *An American Dictionary of the English Language*, was published at last in December 1828. Priced at $20 (in the region of $450 today), its massive two quarto volumes contained almost two thousand pages and about seventy thousand entry words, almost twice as many as in his *Compendious Dictionary* and Walker's latest edition. (As a reminder, a quarto is a large volume, suitable for unabridged dictionaries, formed by folding a printer's sheet twice to produce four leaves or eight pages.) Webster did without many of Johnson's illustrative quotations but ended up making his book even larger than Johnson's by inflating his list with five categories of entry words that he specifies in his preface: "words of common use," "participles of verbs," "terms of frequent occurrence in historical works" (especially proper names), "legal terms," and "terms in the arts and sciences." Given his antipathy toward Johnson's lexicography, by the way, it may seem surprising that on the title page Webster includes a quotation from the great moralist (without mentioning his name) taken from *Rambler*, no. 51: "He that wishes to be counted among the benefactors of posterity, must add, by his own toil, to the acquisitions of his ancestors." Presumably, he also took note of another passage in that *Rambler* essay: "The man whose genius qualifies him for great undertakings, must at least be content to learn from books the present state of human knowledge," so that "he may not ascribe to himself the invention of arts generally known." Webster never again quoted Johnson on the title page of any of his dictionary editions.[33]

The sprinkling of Americanisms—regardless of what Webster claims for them as contributing to his book's American character—are few in number, about one-fifth of the figure he had boasted were contained in his *Compendious Dictionary*: "I have not been able to find many words, in respectable use, which can be so denominated." His book's chief claim to being American, he states, was its inclusion of new American senses of old words, though there were not many of those either. Still, his new title strategically stresses that this dictionary is an *American* product, designed, as he writes in his preface, "to furnish a standard of *our* [my italics] vernacular tongue, which we shall not be ashamed to bequeath to three hundred millions of people, who are destined to occupy, and I hope, to adorn the vast territory within our jurisdiction." It was that word *American* in the title that angered many on both sides of the Atlantic, but which won him many more readers and supporters at home than otherwise he might have had. Paradoxically, the broad-mindedness or liberality of tastes and interests evident in Webster's

FIGURE 1. This portrait of Noah Webster first appeared as a frontispiece in his 1828 *American Dictionary of the English Language*. The image reappeared in later Webster editions for most of the nineteenth century. Courtesy of the Beinecke Rare Book and Manuscript Library, Yale University, G. and C. Merriam Company Papers.

entry words and definitions is frequently offset by the provincialisms of a New England environment, which are out of place in what is supposed to be an American, not New England, dictionary. Take, for example, these pieces of homely wisdom and local custom—*curfew*: "This word is not used in America; although the practice of ringing a bell at nine o'clock continues in many places, and is considered in New England as a signal for people to retire from company to their own abode; and, in general, the signal is obeyed"; *rail*: "In New England we never call this series a *rail*, but by the general term *railing*"; *sauce*: "In New England culinary vegetables and roots eaten with flesh. Sauce consisting of stewed apples is a great article in some parts of New England; but cranberries make the most delicious sauce"; *tackle*: "To seize; to lay hold of; as, a wrestler *tackles* his antagonist; a dog tackles the game. This is a common popular use of the word in New England, though not elegant. But it retains the primitive idea, to put on, to fall or throw on."[34]

In his preface and introduction, Webster regales his readers with how his dictionary surpasses all previous dictionaries, touching on his advances in every department of lexicography. The English lexicographer Charles Richardson had other ideas. Like Webster, a follower of John Horne Tooke's philological theories, Charles Richardson was one of the fiercest of Samuel Johnson's critics and author of his own *New Dictionary of the English Language* (editions in 1835–37). He published his *Illustrations to English Philology* in 1815 (2nd ed., 1826), which contained a two hundred–page section titled "A Critical Examination of the Dictionary of Dr. Johnson," a frontal attack on Johnson and defense of Horne Tooke's *Diversions*. Richardson later found himself in competition with Webster, and in his *New Dictionary* severely condemns Webster for turning his back on "the elders of English lexicography in his own dictionaries." He has particular fun at the expense of Webster's etymology: "There is a display of oriental reading in his preliminary essays, which, as introductory to a dictionary of the English language seems as appropriate and useful as a reference to the code of gentoo [the indigenous people of India] laws to decide a question of English inheritance." While he is on that scent, he sneaks in a dig at Webster's alleged indifference to, and even ignorance of, English literature and his lack of literary taste in general: "Dr. Webster was entirely unacquainted with our old authors." An exaggeration, to be sure, but it is largely correct, notwithstanding Webster's claims of familiarity. Much of that, of course, was motivated by rivalry. Not one for taking such abuse lightly, Webster returns the favor in his *Mistakes and Corrections* in 1837 by attacking Richardson for his ignorance of oriental languages: "Tooke's principle that a word has one meaning, and one only, and that from this all usages must spring, is substantially correct; but he has, in most cases, failed to find that meaning"; and shifting his attention to Richardson, adds, "and you have rarely or never advanced a step beyond him." All of that among these three men sounds disturbingly like a case of the blind leading the blind.[35]

Webster did not include in his quarto the bulk of his "Synopsis" on etymology, but he did nevertheless make a good show of it by including in his prefatory material a forty-five-page section titled "An Introductory Dissertation on the Origin, History, and Connection of the Languages of Western

PREFACE.

In the year 1783, just at the close of the revolution, I published an elementary book for facilitating the acquisition of our vernacular tongue, and for correcting a vicious pronunciation, which prevailed extensively among the common people of this country. Soon after the publication of that work, I believe in the following year, that learned and respectable scholar, the Rev. Dr. Goodrich of Durham, one of the trustees of Yale College, suggested to me, the propriety and expediency of my compiling a dictionary, which should complete a system for the instruction of the citizens of this country in the language. At that time, I could not indulge the thought, much less the hope, of undertaking such a work; as I was neither qualified by research, nor had I the means of support, during the execution of the work, had I been disposed to undertake it. For many years therefore, though I considered such a work as very desirable, yet it appeared to me impracticable; as I was under the necessity of devoting my time to other occupations for obtaining subsistence.

About twenty seven years ago, I began to think of attempting the compilation of a Dictionary. I was induced to this undertaking, not more by the suggestion of friends, than by my own experience of the want of such a work, while reading modern books of science. In this pursuit, I found almost insuperable difficulties, from the want of a dictionary, for explaining many new words, which recent discoveries in the physical sciences had introduced into use. To remedy this defect in part, I published my Compendious Dictionary in 1806; and soon after made preparations for undertaking a larger work.

My original design did not extend to an investigation of the origin and progress of our language; much less of other languages. I limited my views to the correcting of certain errors in the best English Dictionaries, and to the supplying of words in which they are deficient. But after writing through two letters of the alphabet, I determined to change my plan. I found myself embarrassed, at every step, for want of a knowledge of the origin of words, which Johnson, Bailey, Junius, Skinner and some other authors do not afford the means of obtaining. Then laying aside my manuscripts, and all books treating of language, except lexicons and dictionaries, I endeavored, by a diligent comparison of words, having the same or cognate radical letters, in about twenty languages, to obtain a more correct knowledge of the primary sense of original words, of the affinities between the English and many other languages, and thus to enable myself to trace words to their source.

I had not pursued this course more than three or four years, before I discovered that I had to unlearn a great deal that I had spent years in learning, and that it was necessary for me to go back to the first rudiments of a branch of erudition, which I had before cultivated, as I had supposed, with success.

I spent ten years in this comparison of radical words, and in forming a synopsis of the principal words in twenty languages, arranged in classes, under their primary elements or letters. The result has been to open what are to me new views of language, and to unfold what appear to be the genuine principles on which these languages are constructed.

After completing this synopsis, I proceeded to correct what I had written of the Dictionary, and to complete the remaining part of the work. But before I had finished it, I determined on a voyage to Europe, with the view of obtaining some books and some assistance which I wanted; of learning the real state of the pronunciation of our language in England, as well as the general state of philology in that country; and of attempting to bring about some agreement or coincidence of opinions, in regard to unsettled points in pronunciation and grammatical construction. In some of these objects I failed; in others, my designs were answered.

It is not only important, but, in a degree necessary, that the people of this country, should have an *American Dictionary* of the English Language; for, although the body of the language is the same as in England, and it is desirable to perpetuate that sameness, yet some differences must exist. Language is the expression of ideas; and if the people of one country cannot preserve an identity of ideas, they cannot retain an identity of language. Now an

FIGURE 2. In the preface to his 1828 *American Dictionary of the English Language*, Noah Webster writes, "Language is an expression of ideas; and if the people of one country cannot preserve an identity of ideas, they cannot retain an identity of language." Courtesy of Indiana State University Special Collections, Cordell Collection of Dictionaries.

Asia and of Europe"—a treatise he features by broadcasting it in bold letters on his title page. Here, greatly but not sufficiently abbreviated for all but the most erudite philologists, he rehearses indefatigably his intricate "discoveries" about the origin of languages. As with his *Dissertations on the English Language*, one is amazed at the parade of detail, the fruit of ten years' labor. His debts in it to both John Horne Tooke and Charles Richardson are abundant, though neither of them went into the subject quite to the extent he did. "Philology is yet in its infancy," he writes; "I am not at all surprised at the common prejudice existing against etymology." Not so much in its "infancy," one might add, to justify his shutting his mind to it except for fleeting allusions here and there. On the other hand, "Should my synopsis ever be published," he hopes "the learned enquirer might pursue the subject at his leisure."

Webster's spelling innovations were in some cases more influential and lasting, though still controversial in spite of his continuing efforts to moderate his reforms. Most of those (a small portion) that have become standard in American orthography, such as the removal of redundant letters like *e* from *furore*, *k* from *frolick* and *musick*, and *u* from *ardour*, *endeavour*, and *terrour*, were based on sensible and appealing principles of economy and regularity. Others, like changing the *re* to *er* at the end of words such as *metre*—hence *meter, scepter, specter, theater*—were the result of Webster's desire to anglicize them from the French and spell them as they are pronounced; and, on the same principle, the *ce* in words such as *expence, offence*, and *pretence* should be altered to *se*. He also pronounced that if a verb with two or more syllables ends with a consonant preceded by a vowel, that consonant should not be doubled, as it was (and still is) in England in its derivative forms (past and present participle tenses). So the spelling of *travelled* and *travelling*, and *worshipped* and *worshipping*, for example, must not continue in the United States. The same goes for nouns from such verbs (e.g., *worshipper*). He had urged these and other reforms before in his *Dissertations on the English Language*, in the preface to his *Compendious Dictionary*, and piecemeal in various essays and letters.[36]

From the moment Webster's *American Dictionary* appeared in American culture, the brilliance of his definitions was generally recognized. Sir James Murray, editor of the *Oxford English Dictionary* from the 1870s, described Webster as "a great man, a born definer of words." George Philip Krapp agreed that in his definitions Webster "reveals a clearness of mind, soundness of judgment and catholicity of interest that puts him intellectually in the same class with Franklin." Webster himself thought the quality of his definitions were the best part of his book, boasting that he had written up to forty thousand definitions of words that had never before appeared in an English dictionary (see examples below). In spite of his stated determination not to follow Johnson with his definitions, however, he drew many of them directly from the 1799 edition of Johnson's edition or else raided Johnson's phrasing for them.[37]

We can quantify this borrowing, thanks to Joseph Reed, a Johnson scholar who actually counted the number of definitions Webster lifted, one way or another, from Johnson's dictionary. He pointed out that some 7 percent of Webster's definitions are verbatim borrowings, 22 percent are altered only by a word or two, and many more are paraphrased. The astonishing total number of these borrowings, Reed calculated, amounted to one-third of all of Webster's definitions. (It is difficult, incidentally, to credit Webster's claim that forty thousand of his definitions had never before appeared in a dictionary when one-third of the total was taken from Johnson and many more from other British lexicographers. The claim is more plausible if he had in mind the entire text of his lengthy definitions, as well as definitions for each of his five different categories of entry words.) What this heavy debt to Johnson tells us, among other things, is that Webster, like many lexicographers over the preceding two hundred years, was not immune to leaning heavily on his predecessors while at the same time sharply criticizing them. The main difference here between him and his predecessors was that he vehemently denied any such debt. That was imperative for him to do, of course, because part of his mission was to convince the public he had cast aside Johnson (chiefly), along with other British lexicographers on his solitary journey toward producing an American dictionary.[38]

Webster also took hundreds of his citations from Johnson, not least those Johnson had taken from his vast and intimate knowledge of English literature, although Webster accused Johnson of featuring many citations for entry words that did not need any illustration because their meaning was obvious. Johnson's use of thousands of citations, drawn largely from Britain's great literary heritage, was, as he states in the preface to his *Dictionary*, a means of defining words by celebrating that tradition and its language: "to preserve the purity and ascertain the meaning of our English idiom." With his citations Webster also wanted to do far more than just illustrate how a word has been used and what it means. In his own preface, he cites Johnson's famous remark, "The chief glory of a nation arises from its authors," but he is thinking in larger patriotic, rather than literary, terms of his country's future greatness as an independent nation. Johnson was a literary man; Webster essentially was not. When Webster argues that the writing of American national leaders and politicians like Washington, John Adams, John Jay, and Jonathan Trumbull Jr. epitomize the literature of a country that "in purity, in elegance, and in technical precision is equalled only by that of the best British authors"—Shakespeare, Milton, John Dryden, and Joseph Addison, for example—his patriotism prevails over his critical sense. His purpose was not to celebrate America's writers as much as to encourage American literature and society to blossom by endowing American English with added legitimacy, in the process instilling greater confidence and pride in the American vernacular. That kind of nationalism is evident in one of his citations for *citizen*. One of his senses (or definitions) of the word is: "In *a general sense*, a native or permanent resident in a city or country; as the *citizens* of London or Philadelphia; the *citizens* of the United States." Another is: "In *the U. States*, a person, native or naturalized, who has the privilege of exercising the elective franchise. . . ." Then he moralizes somewhat with this from George Washington: "If the citizens of the United States should not be free and happy, the fault will be entirely their own."

Webster's citations also served another purpose. He took a high proportion of them from the Bible, again borrowing many of them from Johnson. For the letter *S* alone, 52 percent of the biblical quotations cited by Johnson were also used by Webster.[39] Both were pious men, Johnson a lifelong Anglican and Webster devoted to Calvinist teachings after his conversion in 1808. Webster's intent was to use biblical citations not only to help define entry words but also to present Christian contexts for the words. Take his citations for *abide*, for example. One of his senses of the word is "to remain, not cease or fall," which he illustrates with the verse in Psalms (125:1): "They that trust in the Lord shall be as Mount Zion, which cannot be removed, but *abideth* for ever." Another meaning is "to continue in the same state," for which he cites from Proverbs (19:23): "The fear of the Lord tendeth to life; and he that hath it shall *abide* satisfied." There are quotations for that single word from Genesis, Acts, Jeremiah, 2 Samuel, Joel, and Hosea; *lust* (verb and noun) is illustrated with excerpts from Exodus, Romans, 2 Peter, James,

Psalms, Deuteronomy, Proverbs, Matthew, James, and 1 Corinthians. One is left in no doubt as to how the Bible configures *lust*. Webster felt that with his definitions he had also made his edition, among other things, a guide to a moral and Christian life, a foundation for Christian leadership, and even a reference work for the King James version of the Bible—a kind of biblical commentary. In later revised editions after his death, the majority of these biblical citations disappeared.

A closer look at a few of Webster's definitions and their linguistic significance tells us more about how he presented his biographies of words. *Education* he defines with an explicit moral and social dimension:

> EDUCATION, n. [L. *educatio*.] The bringing up, as of a child; instruction; formation of manners. Education comprehends all that series of instruction and discipline which is intended to enlighten the understanding, correct the temper, and form the manners and habits of youth, and fit them for usefulness in their future stations. To give children a good *education* in manners, arts and science, is important; to give them a religious *education* is indispensable; and an immense responsibility rests on parents and guardians who neglect these duties.

Similarly, he focuses his definition of *marriage* on the moral and religious:

> [M]arriage was instituted by God himself for the purpose of preventing the promiscuous intercourse of the sexes, for promoting domestic felicity, and for securing the maintenance and education of children.

To *purpose* he gives a religious and biblical twist, terminating the first sense with an exclamation mark:

> PURPOSE, n. [Fr, *propos*; Sp. It. *proposito*; L. *propositum, propono*; *pro*, before, and *pono*, to set or place.] 1. That which a person sets before himself as an object to be reached or accomplished; the end or aim to which the view is directed in any plan, measure or exertion. We believe the Supreme Being created intelligent beings for some benevolent and glorious *purpose*, and if so, how glorious and benevolent must be his *purpose* in the plan of redemption!

All the definitions are much longer than the one-word phrases in the *Compendious*, but they vary considerably in length. *High*, for example, is defined

EDU | EFF | EFF

Those who know how volumes of the fathers are generally *edited*. *Christ. Observer.*

2. To publish.

Abelard wrote many philosophical treatises which have never been *edited*. *Enfield.*

ED'ITED, *pp.* Published ; corrected ; prepared and published.

ED'ITING, *ppr.* Publishing ; preparing for publication.

EDI''TION, *n.* [L. *editio*, from *edo*, to publish.]

1. The publication of any book or writing ; as the first *edition* of a new work.

2. Republication, sometimes with revision and correction ; as the second *edition* of a work.

3. Any publication of a book before published ; also, one impression or the whole number of copies published at once ; as the tenth *edition*.

ED'ITOR, *n.* [L. from *edo*, to publish.] A publisher ; particularly, a person who superintends an impression of a book ; the person who revises, corrects and prepares a book for publication ; as Erasmus, Scaliger, &c.

2. One who superintends the publication of a newspaper.

EDITO'RIAL, *a.* Pertaining to an editor, as *editorial* labors ; written by an editor, as *editorial* remarks.

ED'ITORSHIP, *n.* The business of an editor ; the care and superintendence of a publication. *Walsh.*

EDIT'UATE, *v. t.* [Low L. *ædituor*, from *ædes*, a temple or house.]

To defend or govern the house or temple. [*Not in use.*] *Gregory.*

ED'UCATE, *v. t.* [L. *educo, educare ; e* and *duco*, to lead ; It. *educare ;* Sp. *educar.*]

To bring up, as a child ; to instruct ; to inform and enlighten the understanding ; to instill into the mind principles of arts, science, morals, religion and behavior. To *educate* children well is one of the most important duties of parents and guardians.

ED'UCATED, *pp.* Brought up ; instructed ; furnished with knowledge or principles ; trained ; disciplined.

ED'UCATING, *ppr.* Instructing ; enlightening the understanding, and forming the manners.

EDUCA'TION, *n.* [L. *educatio.*] The bringing up, as of a child ; instruction ; formation of manners. Education comprehends all that series of instruction and discipline which is intended to enlighten the understanding, correct the temper, and form the manners and habits of youth, and fit them for usefulness in their future stations. To give children a good *education* in manners, arts and science, is important ; to give them a religious *education* is indispensable ; and an immense responsibility rests on parents and guardians who neglect these duties.

EDUCA'TIONAL, *a.* Pertaining to education ; derived from education ; as *educational* habits. *Smith.*

ED'UCATOR, *n.* One who educates. *Beddoes.*

EDU'CE, *v. t.* [L. *educo, eduxi ; e* and *duco*, to lead.]

To bring or draw out ; to extract ; to produce from a state of occultation.

Th' eternal art *educing* good from ill. *Pope.*

EDU'CED, *pp.* Drawn forth ; extracted ; prod

EDUL'CORATE, *v. t.* [Low L. *edulco*, from *dulcis*, sweet ; Fr. *edulcorer.*]

1. To purify ; to sweeten. In *chimistry*, to render substances more mild, by freeing them from acids and salts or other soluble impurities, by washing. *Encyc.*

2. To sweeten by adding sugar, sirup, &c. *Encyc.*

EDUL'CORATED, *pp.* Sweetened ; purified from acid or saline substances, and rendered more mild.

EDUL'CORATING, *ppr.* Sweetening ; rendering more mild.

EDULCORA'TION, *n.* The act of sweetening or rendering more mild, by freeing from acid or saline substances, or from any soluble impurities.

2. The act of sweetening by admixture of some saccharine substance.

EDUL'CORATIVE, *a.* Having the quality of sweetening.

EEK. [See *Eke.*]

EEL, *n.* [Sax. *æl ;* G. *aal ;* D. *aal ;* Dan. *id. ;* Sw. *ål ;* Gypsey, *alo ;* Turk. *ilan.* The word, in Saxon, is written precisely like *awl.*]

A species of Muræna, a genus of fishes belonging to the order of apodes. The head is smooth ; there are ten rays in the membrane of the gills ; the eyes are covered with a common skin ; the body is cylindrical and slimy. Eels, in some respects, resemble reptiles, particularly in their manner of moving by a serpentine winding of the body ; and they often creep upon land and wander about at night in search of snails or other food. In winter, they lie buried in mud, being very impatient of cold. They grow to the weight of 15 or 20 pounds ; and the conger eel is said to grow to a hundred pounds in weight, and to 10 feet in length. They are esteemed good food. *Encyc.*

EE'L-FISHING, *n.* The act or art of catching eels.

EE'LPOT, *n.* A kind of basket used for catching eels.

EE'LPOUT, *n.* A species of Gadus, somewhat resembling an eel, but shorter in proportion, seldom exceeding a foot in length. It is a delicate fish. *Encyc. Dict. Nat. Hist.*

EE'LSKIN, *n.* The skin of an eel.

EE'LSPEAR, *n.* A forked instrument used for stabbing eels.

E'EN, contracted from *even*, which see.

I have *e'en* done with you. *L'Estrange.*

EFF, *n.* A lizard.

EF'FABLE, *a.* [L. *effabilis*, from *effor ; ex* and *for*, to speak.]

Utterable ; that may be uttered or spoken.

to *efface* is to rub out or destroy, so as to render invisible.

EFFA'CED, *pp.* Rubbed or worn out ; destroyed, as a figure or impression.

EFFA'CING, *ppr.* Destroying a figure, character or impression, on any thing.

EFFECT', *n.* [L. *effectus*, from *efficio ; ex* and *facio*, to make ; It. *effetto ;* Fr. *effet.*]

1. That which is produced by an agent or cause ; as the *effect* of luxury ; the *effect* of intemperance.

Poverty, disease and disgrace are the natural *effects* of dissipation.

2. Consequence ; event.

To say that a composition is imperfect, is *in effect* to say the author is a man. *Anon.*

3. Purpose ; general intent.

They spoke to her to that *effect*. 2 Chron. xxxiv.

4. Consequence intended ; utility ; profit ; advantage.

Christ is become of no *effect* to you. Gal. v.

5. Force ; validity. The obligation is void and of no *effect*.

6. Completion ; perfection.

Not so worthily to be brought to heroical *effect* by fortune or necessity. *Sidney.*

7. Reality ; not mere appearance ; fact.

No other in *effect* than what it seems. *Denham.*

8. In the plural, *effects* are goods ; movables ; personal estate. The people escaped from the town with their *effects*.

EFFECT', *v. t.* [from the Noun.] To produce, as a cause or agent ; to cause to be. The revolution in France *effected* a great change of property.

2. To bring to pass ; to achieve ; to accomplish ; as, to *effect* an object or purpose.

EFFECT'ED, *pp.* Done ; performed ; accomplished.

EFFECT'IBLE, *a.* That may be done or achieved ; practicable ; feasible. *Brown.*

EFFECT'ING, *ppr.* Producing ; performing ; accomplishing.

EFFECT'IVE, *a.* Having the power to cause or produce ; efficacious.

They are not *effective* of any thing. *Bacon.*

2. Operative ; active ; having the quality of producing effects.

Time is not *effective*, nor are bodies destroyed by it. *Brown.*

3. Efficient ; causing to be ; as an *effective* cause. *Taylor.*

4. Having the power of active operation ; able ; as *effective* men in an army ; an *effective* force.

ED'ITOR, *n.* [L. from *edo*, to publish.] A publisher ; particularly, a person who superintends an impression of a book ; the person who revises, corrects and prepares a book for publication ; as Erasmus, Scaliger, &c.

2. One who superintends the publication of a newspaper.

FIGURE 3. Some definitions in Webster's 1828 *American Dictionary of the English Language*, such as *education*, include moral dimensions. Detail: Definition of *editor*. Courtesy of Indiana State University Special Collections, Cordell Collection of Dictionaries.

with no fewer than thirty-four senses, *hold* (verb) with twenty-five, and *honor* with fourteen. *War* (noun) has six, but the first is typically long and essaylike, touched, as many definitions are, with reference to Christianity:

> WAR, noun [G., to perplex, embroil, disturb. The primary sense of the root is to strive, struggle, urge, drive, or to turn, to twist.] . . . When war is commenced by attacking a nation in peace, it is called an offensive war and such attack is aggressive. When war is undertaken to repel invasion or the attacks of an enemy, it is called defensive, and a defensive war is considered as justifiable. Very few of the wars that have desolated nations and deluged the earth with blood, have been justifiable. Happy would it be for mankind, if the prevalence of Christian principles might ultimately extinguish the spirit of war and if the ambition to be great, might yield to the ambition of being good. Preparation for war is sometimes the best security for peace.

For *woman* we are given an admonitory, social, physical, and biblical emphasis:

> WOMAN, *noun plural* women. [a compound of womb and man.] 1. The female of the human race, grown to adult years. And the rib, which the Lord god had taken from the man, made he a woman. Genesis 2:22. Women are soft, mild, pitiful, and flexible. We see every day women perish with infamy, by having been too willing to set their beauty to show. I have observed among all nations that the women ornament themselves more than the men; that wherever found, they are the same kind, civil, obliging, humane, tender beings, inclined to be gay and cheerful, timorous and modest. 2. a female attendant or servant.
>
> WOMAN, *verb intransitive* To make pliant.

From this point on, through a succession of revisions, we shall see that Webster's definitions became shorter and shorter, more compact and with fewer illustrative citations and senses, as editors became increasingly definite about curtailing his discursive, rambling style.

Largely because of his definitions, thousands of which the public read as mini-encyclopedia entries, Webster was triumphant. In spite of all the skeptics and naysayers, working mostly alone except for some help from a handful of Yale faculty and what he grudgingly received from Percival, and after at least ten years of grueling and mostly misconceived etymological work that delayed his completion of the dictionary, the dictionary reminded the American public, including linguists, of what he had claimed by virtue of his spelling books and the 1806 edition: that he was a major authority on the English language in the United States. The distinguished American jurist and legal historian James Kent gushed that Webster had done more for America than "Alfred [the Great] did for England, or Cadmus for Greece." Not content with that, Kent added that, along with Washington and Jefferson, Webster made up "our trinity of fame." Schools, universities, state school systems, and legal institutions across the country all chimed in to celebrate Webster's patriotic achievement. Praise and recognition poured in also from England and France. After 3,000 copies of an edition of the *American Dictionary* were printed in England in periodical installments between 1830 and 1832—compared, incidentally, to only 2,500 copies in America—in its excitement, the *Times* of London called it "the most elaborate and successful undertaking of the kind which has ever appeared."[40]

That said, there was also harsh criticism in England. One of the most damaging attacks came from perhaps the most eminent English comparative philologist of the age, Richard Garnett, who in the *Quarterly Review* in 1835 could scarcely believe Webster's "crudities and errors" as he went about tracing the derivations of words: "There is everywhere a great parade of erudition, and a great lack of real knowledge; in short, we do not recollect ever to have witnessed . . . more pains taken to so little purpose." It was based on research a modern scholar has felicitously described as "a magical mystery tour through the history of language from God and Adam chatting in the Garden of Eden, by way of the earlier Noah and his linguistically significant sons" to England and early America.[41]

Webster was now seventy and assumed he could sit back and enjoy his hard-won fame in his New Haven sanctuary among friends and family. But that was not to be. Bad reviews, unexpected competition from within his own family in New Haven, and surprisingly formidable and erudite American competition from a quiet scholar in Cambridge, Massachusetts, soon dimmed the glow of success and reignited his combativeness.

5

The Lexicographer's
Fifth Column

In 1828, Webster was ailing. He tired easily and hoped he had seen the last of any heavy dictionary work, including major revisions of his quarto. One of many problems for him, and in the long term for his heirs, was that even before the unabridged quarto was published, he knew it would never make much money. It would be too expensive and bulky for most people, as has been the case with most unabridged printed dictionaries ever since, and would not pay its way.

It was also clear even to Webster, and especially to Percival, who knew the unabridged manuscript better than anyone except Webster himself, that it would meet with criticism because of its orthographical eccentricities (e.g. *bridegoom* for *bridegroom, ieland* for *island, turnep* for *turnip, wo* for *woe*) and the flawed etymology he inherited from Horne Tooke. This was a particular problem, since the object of education was to instruct pupils, not confuse them. The demand of the hour was for a revised, smaller, single-volume octavo abridgment of the 1828 quarto (an octavo size is formed by folding a printer's sheet three times, making eight leaves or sixteen pages), one less expensive and more accessible and practical for the average user that would tap into the larger market waiting to be exploited by an imaginative publisher and editor. Such an edition would need to answer the requirements and demands of an increasingly large and receptive literate mass market. He would be entering uncharted editorial and commercial waters; and his hesitancy proved to be well-founded, when through various miscalculations and failures, he was never able to capitalize on the market that existed.

A more immediate obstacle to a compact octavo edition, however, was Webster himself. Convinced that his work was the product of a sacred "duty" and mission that he continued to hold in trust in behalf of the American people, he felt a calling to protect it from less inspired and knowledgeable, even if well-meaning, editors who might wish to meddle with the bond he imagined existed between himself and the American reading public. He feared potential efforts by others to reconstitute his 1828 edition with revisions that in his "retirement" he would be less able to control. Anyone who attempted such revisions would therefore have him to reckon with. As for alleged poaching by competing lexicographers, they of course had to be fought off like predatory wolves.

2

It was no mere coincidence that the publication of Webster's 1828 unabridged edition, and the dictionary wars that broke out full force soon afterward, coincided with a print revolution between 1825 and 1850 that greatly advanced the age of mass communication. At the center of this development was the invention of the steam-powered printing press by the Germans Friedrich Koenig and Andreas Friedrich Bauer, in 1802, and then refined by Koenig in London around 1810. The invention used steam to power the rotary motion of cylinders that replaced the flatbed on which paper, or whatever was to be printed, had been placed. (Very labor intensive, flatbed printing had been the mechanized method for centuries, ever since Gutenberg invented his printing press in the fifteenth century.) The ink was applied to the type by these rollers. The invention enabled rapid printing, requiring far less manpower, on a scale never before possible.

The machine was first installed in the United States in 1826 by the American Tract Society, after which media in the country expanded in a rush of many different types of both entertaining and informative printed information: small town and city newspapers, magazines, annuals, the penny press, pamphlets, literary periodicals, book publishers, civic and reform groups that published books promoting their causes, and government reports of one kind or another on a widening array of subjects. At the same time, the proliferation of printed material encouraged literacy, since people had a greater quantity of inexpensively available printed material to read and therefore enjoyed a valuable incentive for learning both to read and write. "Where the press is free, and every man able to read, all is safe," wrote Thomas Jefferson in 1816.[1]

Among other factors driving literacy were an expanding middle-class readership; the increase of free public schooling and female teachers; a growing link between education and a strong republican government; population diversity; a decline in regionalism; a diversity of occupations and increased wealth; a larger urban population; the evangelical Protestant tradition, with its emphasis on Bible reading and publication of new editions; advances in printing techniques such as stereotyping (see appendix C), which made books less expensive; and the developing morality of individual aspiration. America by the end of the eighteenth century was not lagging behind England in literacy rates. Available evidence has it that the United States by the time Webster's dictionary was launched had even a higher rate of literacy than England.[2]

3

Even before the unabridged 1828 dictionary was published, Webster had in mind an octavo abridgment—not a school dictionary—for the general market, but one that would not involve much work, merely streamline the 1828 edition by getting rid of illustrative quotations and most of the etymological commentary, shorten definitions, and give the whole work a perkier look. His friends advised him that such an edition was needed if he ever hoped to make money from his work.

Webster mentioned his idea of a compact octavo edition to his publisher, Sherman Converse, and made it clear he did not want to do the work involved. It was at this point that Converse angered Webster. Webster had written impatiently and dismissively to Converse shortly before the quarto was published on May 23, 1828: "Your letter of the 20th contains remarks respecting my proposal to stereotype a small dictionary, which it was and is improper for you to make. You are not acquainted with the circumstances and views by which I am governed, nor are your rights in the least concerned in my plans. . . . My friends here all agree that the Dictionary must be abridged into the Octavo form, but I cannot do the work myself & who shall be procured to do the work, I do not know." But Converse maintained a couple of years later that when Webster mentioned an octavo abridgment to him, he was skeptical, feeling that it would be too much work to turn the 1828 quarto into a saleable commodity: "As to an abridgement of the Dictionary, I never had any intention, wish, or thought of making one, or causing one to be made. I don't think the idea ever crossed my mind that such a thing could be done. If it did, I have no recollection of it, and were I sufficiently destitute of principles I should be unwilling to compass myself so great a blockhead as to attempt it."[3]

Converse already was on very uncertain ground with Webster. After Webster returned to New Haven from England and was growing desperate because he could not find anyone in America willing to risk the investment of publishing the dictionary, Converse had saved the day. One might have thought Webster forever after would be grateful to Converse, but he was not. He thought instead that Converse was the one who ought to be grateful for the fame and chance offered to him to have a part in the publication of what he believed was a major work in American history. On top of that, Webster was accusing Converse of defrauding him and charging for extra expenses resulting from poor sales, a "penalty for being unfortunate," as he explained on December 8, 1829, to Hezekiah Howe, the book's printer, from whom Converse had borrowed money to publish the book. He complained that Converse "has charged me also with a large sum for proof-reading, which is contrary to all justice," as well as for engraving his picture, which he refused to pay. One way to save money there, of course, would have been to abandon Webster's idea of including his picture. After all, not even Johnson included his own picture in his first edition, nor did Webster's major competition later on. This was his reward, Webster groused, for the "liberality" and generosity he had manifested toward Converse: "During the execution of the work, I received letters from Mr. Converse filled with abusive language wholly unmerited, and which was not easy for me to overlook." He wanted nothing more to do with the man "after the vexation and embarrassment I have experienced from Mr. Converse for two or three years past." For his part, Converse did feel some guilt about the exasperated way he had written to Webster, but he could not recollect he had ever written anything "abusive": "I asked his forgiveness from I hope right motives. I hope he has forgiven me, and that I also have forgiven him in my heart."[4]

There was more to Webster's resentment than just Converse's dealings with him over the 1828 quarto. Since Webster was uncertain about whom to hire to edit the octavo, Converse took it upon himself to begin looking around for someone to take it on. His attention was caught by a new edition in 1828 of Alexander Chalmers's 1820 octavo abridgment of John Todd's edition of Johnson's *Dictionary*. It was edited by a retiring scholar and bachelor living in Cambridge, Massachusetts, a few hundred yards from Harvard College. His name was Joseph Emerson Worcester.

4

Born in 1784 in Bedford, New Hampshire, the very year Samuel Johnson died, Joseph Worcester was twenty-six years Webster's junior. He grew up on his father's farm in Hollis, New Hampshire, with his eight brothers and six sisters. The family was well schooled and had a reputation for erudition. The children's father, Jesse, spent a few years teaching, was an occasional contributor to public journals, and authored at least one book. Four of Worcester's brothers attended Harvard; and one, Yale. A younger brother, Samuel, wrote a sequel to Webster's speller in 1831, and in 1833 the *American Primary Spelling Book*.

Young Joseph, the second of the brothers, graduated with distinction from Phillips Academy in Andover in 1807—he and his elder brother, Jesse, who also graduated with distinction, were there together for four years. There is a sketch of Joseph in the *Phillips Bulletin*, written more than a century later but sounding accurate, which portrays him as having all the makings of a retiring, private scholar, not one by nature inclined to mingle in the lives and activities of the other boys or likely to make a big splash in the company of men and women:

> In his manner he was reserved, and he was hesitant in his speech, as if in quest of the right word. His natural shyness had been accentuated by his rather lonely existence, for he had few friends. His qualities were substantial, not showy. He was no romantic figure, full of dash and fire; it was his function,—and his pleasure—, to plod doggedly along, producing one reference book after another. The lure of philological research, the joy of building an exact definition, the satisfaction of hunting a word to its origins,—these were his delights. He had little originality. . . . It is men of this type who bear the burdens of the world.

As for his character, the sketch highlights qualities universally confirmed by all who knew him, and countless who did not: "[H]e was without a stain. He bore suffering with equanimity and aspersion without complaint." One of his nephews spoke of his "forbearance, gentleness, and kindness." Joseph and his brother Jesse both planned to go on to Dartmouth College, but Jesse took ill that summer and soon afterward died, whereupon Joseph decided to enter Yale instead as a sophomore in 1809 at the age of twenty-five, where he discovered his affinity for debate and was elected to Phi Beta Kappa in the top four of his class. He graduated in two years after establishing himself there as a promising scholar. At the age of twenty-eight he made his way to Salem, Massachusetts, where he taught at a private academy for several years. He may have chosen Salem as the place to open his school because his uncle Samuel Worcester lived there, a feisty orthodox minister at the Tabernacle Church who had turned down a professorship of theology at Dartmouth.[5]

In one of those literary coincidences over which one can only marvel, one of Worcester's thirty pupils at Salem was Nathaniel Hawthorne, who was born there in 1804. For the first eight months of his formal education, Hawthorne attended Worcester's school like any other pupil, but in November 1812 a ball hit his foot violently at school, which rendered him lame and sentenced him to more than a year of painful convalescence. In a conscientious and caring manner, Worcester then took it upon himself to teach Hawthorne at home during that period. He was a taskmaster with high standards, however, who appears at times to have made the boy grumble to his parents. Patiently and with his own wide reading to draw on, Worcester exposed his captive pupil to a wide range of authors, including John Bunyan, John Milton, Edmund Spenser, Jean-Jacques Rousseau, Sir Walter Scott's "Waverley" novels, the poet George Gordon, Lord Byron, and particularly Shakespeare. According to one of Hawthorne's biographers, he may even have acquainted Hawthorne with James Boswell's *Life of Johnson*, a significant addition in light of Worcester's lifelong devotion to Samuel Johnson. Hawthorne once reminisced that Worcester had taught him the value of words. Worcester in later years referred to him as "a very pleasant and interesting young pupil."[6]

Tired of the arduous life of a teacher, in 1816 Worcester moved to Andover, Massachusetts, where scholarship now became his life. It is not clear how he made a living, but he promptly began doing research on geography, his first love. For scholarly work on the scale he envisioned himself doing, however, he needed to be near large libraries, so in 1819 he moved to Cambridge, Massachusetts, where he lived within walking distance of Harvard's vast collections. He immediately thrived in that world, partaking of the cultural, social, and literary life of both Boston and Harvard. Between 1817 and 1828, he published several major works on geography and history that earned him highly favorable national attention as well as an excellent income—among them, *Elements of Geography: Ancient and Modern with an Atlas* (1819), *An Epitome of Modern Geography with Maps: For the Use of Common Schools* (1820), *Epitome of History* (1820), a two-volume *Sketch of the Earth and Its Inhabitants* (1823), and *Elements of History, Ancient and Modern* (1826). In 1825, he was elected a member of the American Academy of Arts and Sciences, founded by John Adams and others during the War of Independence and headquartered in Cambridge. Several of his books surpassed all previous works on their subjects and became standard texts for schools. It was after 1825 that he began to take a greater interest in history and then language.[7]

Quickly after his move to Cambridge, Worcester's character and temperament became well-known there. William Newell, governor of New Jersey and of the Washington Territory, wrote in a memoir for the American Historical Association in Boston in 1880 that Worcester "had nothing of the selfishness of the mere literary recluse and hard worker. His absorption in his studies never made him forgetful of the wants and claims of others." Another biographical sketch of Worcester recalling those early Cambridge years was provided some thirty years after Worcester's death by Thomas Wentworth Higginson. A native of Cambridge, Higginson remembered him there during the 1830s, when Worcester was about fifty and Higginson in his teens. Higginson in his own right became an interesting figure in American social thought. A liberal thinker and prolific author on a variety of subjects, he is remembered perhaps mostly for his long and fruitful friendship with Emily Dickinson, who called her her "Preceptor." His affectionate anecdote about Worcester captures a glimpse of the latter's quietly industrious and retiring character:

> Among the various academic guests who used to gather in my mother's hospitable parlor on Sunday evenings, no figure is more vivid in my memory than one whom [James Russell] Lowell in his *Fireside Travels* has omitted to sketch. This was Dr. Joseph E. Worcester, whose "Elements of History, Ancient and Modern," I had faithfully studied at school; and who was wont to sit silent, literally by the hour, a slumbering volcano of facts and statistics, while others talked. He was tall, stiff, gentle, and benignant, wearing blue spectacles [shielding his eyes], and

with his head as it were ingulfed in the high coat collar of other days. He rocked to and fro, placidly listening to what was said, and might perhaps have been suspected of a gentle slumber, when the casual mention of some city in the West, then dimly known, would rouse him to action. He would then cease rocking, would lean forward, and say in his peaceful voice: "Chillicothe? What is the present population of Chillicothe?" or, "Columbus? What is the population of Columbus?" and then, putting away the item in some appropriate pigeon-hold of his vast memory, would relapse into his rocking-chair once more.[8]

5

Worcester's reputation as an exacting scholar was the primary reason he was hired to undertake revision of the *Todd-Johnson* dictionary, which was published less than a year before the appearance of Webster's 1828 quarto. More importantly, it was Worcester's work on that particular book that recommended him to Converse. His role in the edition was summed up by a reviewer in the February 1832 issue of the *American Monthly Review*, who testified to his universally respected scholarship: "This was edited by Mr. J. E. Worcester, a gentleman then already well known for accuracy of learning, diligent research, and judicious application of his knowledge in regard to some other subjects." The reviewer concluded that the dictionary was "faithfully and judiciously compiled, [and] may justly be regarded as a great accession to English Lexicography; containing as it does so complete a vocabulary, and exhibiting in respect to words of doubtful pronunciation, the authorities of other orthoëpists, in those cases, in which they vary from Walker."[9]

Worcester's edition of *Todd-Johnson* had given him the opportunity to introduce into lexicography a major emphasis on pronunciation, an area that his exploration of lexicographical history, including recent American lexicography, told him had been neglected and clumsily misrepresented in dictionaries. He settled on the idea, for example, of citing the "most popular" English orthoepist authorities—such as William Kenrick, Thomas Sheridan, William Perry, Sir William Jones, and G. Fulton and G. Knight—for the pronunciation of words about which the Americans and British disagreed, going beyond even Walker. For an appendix on words of "doubtful pronunciation," Worcester happens to mention one of Webster's arch-enemies, John Pickering, his "learned and respected friend," whose work on American vocabulary has had "a salutary influence on our own literature, by calling the attention of scholars to the occasional deviations of American writers from pure English." That remark leaves little doubt regarding Worcester's views of American radical "innovations," generally known then to be identified with Webster's lexicography. At that point, however, Webster himself was only of remote interest to Worcester, although in his preface to the Todd-Johnson edition, he credited "Mr. Webster's Dictionary" in 1806—the *Compendious Dictionary*—"with regard to such of the [American] words as are found in that work, from which the definitions of them have also been partly taken."[10]

Converse had a look at Worcester's work on the *Todd-Johnson* and was promptly convinced by his scholarship that this was the man to prepare the octavo abridgment. Moreover, Worcester had not come to Todd's edition of Johnson cold. He had already decided that lexicography was his great calling and begun work on his own independent dictionary of English, a much smaller work than Webster's, suitable for schools but also for the general public and intellectual community, easy to use, inexpensive, and one that could compete in the market. He was deeply immersed in that dictionary when Converse wrote to him.

Converse realized in 1828 that Worcester could be trusted to moderate Webster's controversial pronunciation, spelling, and etymology, as well as drastically shorten definitions and etymologies, and produce an octavo that would have wide appeal. What better man for the job could there be? Whether Converse checked first with Webster before approaching Worcester, as he said he did, is unknown. What we do know is that Webster told Fowler a couple of years later that Converse had exceeded his authority by hiring Worcester:

> I had been informed that Hilliard, Gray & Co. [later the firm became Little, Brown, & Company in Boston, founded by two of William Hilliard's publishing partners] were stereotyping and publishing an abridgement of my Dictionary . . . but I could not believe what I suspected that this was the doing of Mr. Converse. In this he has manifested the worst trait in his character or spirit of vindictiveness. He wanted to have the publication of an abridgement promised to him before I had determined to make one. This I absolutely refused but said to him these words, "If I ever make an abridgement, you will probably have the offer of it." This

he would have had, if his subsequent conduct towards me had not destroyed my confidence in him. Now he alleges that I *promised* him the work, which is absolutely false. His efforts to wrong me will produce serious results.[11]

It was obvious to Converse that Webster was extremely reluctant to allow anyone apart from himself to tamper with vital elements of his dictionary, such as orthography, pronunciation, and definitions. Nonetheless, Converse felt that was a hurdle that could be, must be, negotiated, if anyone was ever going to make money from the dictionary, even if Webster protested every step of the way. Converse hoped he could convince Worcester to take on a revision that would involve much exhausting, detailed work. Years later, he recounted his own version of what happened: "When I applied to Mr. Worcester to abridge the quarto, he objected on the grounds that he had already projected a school dictionary and that such an undertaking would interfere both with his plans and his interests, that he could not abridge Mr. Webster's work without suspending his own. . . ." Other than having to suspend his work to edit Webster's, Worcester apparently saw no obvious conflict of interest in working on both dictionaries, because his school edition involved rewriting definitions and pronunciation guides as well as reducing the number and types of entry words. Worcester was familiar enough with Webster's writings on the English language, however, to realize that to attach his name to an octavo that, under Webster's pressure, might end up being only moderately different from Webster's 1828 quarto would place him in an awkward position in relation to his own work when it was published, and perhaps even damage his reputation. Converse wrote again, and again Worcester declined. Undeterred, Converse traveled to Cambridge to see if he could win over Worcester in person. He offered Worcester $2,000 (approximately $50,000 today) for what turned out to be about eight months' arduous work. The fee probably helped persuade Worcester to edit the octavo, but it is also feasible that, on thinking about it, he may have liked the idea of having a hand in improving the first large comprehensive dictionary to be published in America. He also had Converse's assurance that the plan played to his strengths: to correct Webster's egregious spelling innovations in the quarto and make the pronunciation more systematic and rational by citing a string of orthoepists. He would also have the freedom to add to the word list, and he generously agreed to contribute his own "Synopsis of Words Differently Pronounced by Different Orthoepists." The "Synopsis" would include words whose "correct" pronunciation was uncertain and inconsistent in both America and England and offer alternatives to Webster by several of the leading English orthoepists.[12]

Converse hoped the abridgment would also include the bonus of John Walker's celebrated 103-page *Key to the Classical Pronunciation of Greek, Latin, and Scripture Proper Names* (1798). Most but not all of the many editions of Walker's *Critical Pronouncing Dictionary* published in America in the early nineteenth century included his *Key*. It would bring added value to the octavo, as it was already popular in America: at least seventeen editions of it had been separately published there by 1829. Worcester, however, was reluctant to include it because he had included and made much of the *Key* in his own update of *Todd-Johnson*. In the absence of an international copyright agreement, of course, there was nothing to prohibit Converse from including the *Key* in the abridgment, regardless of Worcester's ethical qualms. That awkwardness could always be sorted out later. In the meantime, Converse would accept all the risks of stereotyping plates for the octavo and absorbing costs, but Webster would have to pay one-quarter, or $500, of Worcester's $2,000 fee, an ironic detail in light of what lay ahead in their relationship. It seemed like a large project, but Worcester was well primed for it, had the best private library of dictionaries in America on which to draw, and was confident he could complete the work in not much more than a year.

Converse's comment on his visit to Cambridge was, "I must say that my persuasive powers were very severely taxed in securing the desired result."[13] But it is more likely that Webster's shrewd son-in-law persuaded Worcester. Goodrich had chosen Converse to publish the quarto to begin with, and he went along with Converse on his first visit to Cambridge to meet Worcester. It is easy to imagine Converse mostly listening as the more erudite Worcester and Goodrich talked about language history, dictionaries, Webster, and Worcester's own lexicography. Goodrich's presence encouraged Worcester, who insisted that Goodrich must also play a central part in the editing. The meeting can be seen as a happy conjunction of Yale and Harvard, New Haven and Cambridge, the competitive spheres of influence. Since Converse and Webster were not on the best of terms, Goodrich was well placed to impress upon his father-in-law the urgency of getting on with an abridgment in order to earn some badly needed income from his twenty-five years of work. He had also made a study of Worcester and recognized not only his linguistic expertise but also his remarkable concentration and ability to get the job done. He could assure Webster that he would act as his representative and shepherd the edition along to ensure that Converse in New York and Worcester in Cambridge would make editorial decisions significantly improving the reputation of the dictionary and, above all, making sense commercially.

6

Goodrich was a complicated man. A respected linguist, rhetorician, and lecturer on theology and composition, first as professor of rhetoric and after 1817 as professor of theology and rhetoric at Yale, he had quickly made a name for himself as a scholar and personality, turning down the presidency of Williams College in 1820 to remain at Yale. He was also a resourceful tactician in getting his own way. Highly principled and essentially compassionate, he was tough-minded and could be ruthless if he detected dishonesty or deception. He was devoutly religious and a devoted husband and father. An ordained minister but without any trace of theological bitterness and narrowness in his pastoral work, he was awarded the honorary degree of doctor of divinity by Brown College (now Brown University) in 1837.

His friend and faculty colleague at Yale, Theodore D. Woolsey, who later became president of Yale and delivered Goodrich's memorial commemoration in Center Church on the Green in New Haven in 1860, spoke of his "Pauline temperament," his strong character, efficiency, and "practical power." Goodrich, he said, was devoted to "practical religion," spoke every week in the chapel to students and faculty as part of his course of lectures on eloquence and oratory, and met with students individually on a regular basis to help them become "vigorous and effective writers." Commenting on Goodrich's working life, Woolsey observed, "He was . . . qualified to throw off work fast" and yet capable of "unwearied painstaking" labor: "I have often wondered how such a man, so natively restless, and of so nervous a temperament, could endure the drudgery of drilling in speaking and composition, day after day, as he did while he was Professor of Rhetoric." It was not part of his career plans in 1828, when he became involved in his father-in-law's

FIGURE 4. Chauncey Allen Goodrich, a professor of rhetoric at Yale University and Noah Webster's son-in-law, became the primary editor and thorough reviser of Webster's dictionaries from 1829 to 1860, including early revisions for the 1864 edition. Courtesy of *Appleton's Cyclopaedia of American Biography*, ed. James Grant Wilson, 1888.

dictionary, but the project would occupy him in unforeseen ways for the remaining years of his life.[14]

7

Webster was furious when he learned from Converse of the proportions of the agreement reached by Converse, Goodrich, and Worcester—and that he had been deliberately left out of the planning stage. Nonetheless, he grudgingly went along with it, perhaps at first not fully realizing either who Worcester was or the implications of what Goodrich and Converse would encourage Worcester to do. He wrote to Worcester on July 27, 1828—this was still before the quarto was published—with not a very enthusiastic welcome: "Mr. Converse has engaged you to abridge my Dictionary, and has requested me to forward you the copy of the first volume. This was unexpected to me; but under the circumstances, I have consented to it, and shall send the copy." Goodrich also wrote to Worcester the next day on an entirely different note:

"This gives me and Mr. Webster's other friends [at Yale] the highest satisfaction; for there is no man in the United States, as you know from conversation with me, who would be equally acceptable."[15]

Goodrich quickly established a working relationship with both Converse and Worcester that for the most part ignored Webster and enabled them to navigate efficiently through the quarto and the rough waters that Webster's demands and complaints might otherwise have created for everyone concerned. Worcester would do the editing, but Goodrich would be at the center of the whole enterprise: "Cases of doubt, arising in the application of the [Webster's] principles," Goodrich would write of himself in the preface to the octavo, "and such changes and modifications of the original as seemed desirable, in a work of this kind, intended for general use, have been referred, for decision, to PROF. GOODRICH, of *Yale College*, who was requested by the author to act, on these subjects, as his representative."[16]

Goodrich could not have come to the study of language from a more different world and point of view than Webster's. For one thing, and this is crucially important, Goodrich was, unlike Webster, a literary man whose "well-known literary tastes" and "long and familiar acquaintance with English literature," said the *Methodist Quarterly Review* in January 1848, enabled him to judge the meanings of words from their use in Anglo-American literature. This was thought to be an indispensable background and ability because there was widespread agreement that written prose was "the foundation of a reliable English dictionary." Furthermore, Goodrich and his father-in-law could not have been more apart in their ideas about language. Where Webster was unorthodox and experimental, and relatively untrained in the history of rhetoric and oratory, classical and modern, Goodrich was "utterly orthodox" and superbly qualified to take up his professorship in 1817. He was a fine classical scholar, having published a Greek grammar in 1814 and *Greek and Latin Lessons* in 1832; and in 1852, he would publish *Select British Eloquence*, nearly one thousand pages of "the best speeches of the most distinguished English orators, accompanied by critical and biographical sketches, arguments, and notes." As Woolsey put it in his Goodrich memorial address, *Select British Eloquence* manifested Goodrich's "many years of familiarity with British models . . . and he took great delight in the subject. No one can help feeling that he was at home." The book reflected his desire "to put the reader in a position to understand what he reads, nearly as well as could be done when the speeches were delivered." Goodrich taught his students out of a deep and natural appreciation and understanding of the elegance of traditional classical and British oratory and grammar. He had found in Worcester a kindred spirit.[17]

Converse, for his part, was relieved to be working with Goodrich, happy to be staying clear of Webster in the lines of communication. He and Goodrich together again visited Worcester in Cambridge soon after their agreement, "when the matter of variations was settled" regarding how to proceed. Without doubt, Converse was an opportunist and might well have thought this collaborative link with Goodrich was an indirect way of encouraging his relationship with Webster to improve slowly, or at least keep it from worsening, for the sake of any future editions Webster might agree to let him publish.[18]

Once the octavo was given the go-ahead, Worcester shifted from his own work to Webster's dictionary. His understanding was that his principal contact would be Goodrich, not Webster, almost entirely by mail, although Webster occasionally did stir himself enough to send Worcester additions to the word list as well as the occasional random correction of the quarto. Goodrich also visited Worcester in Cambridge on his own several times as the work moved ahead, where they could freely discuss proposed revisions and adaptations of the quarto's pronunciation and spelling that he knew were sure to anger Webster. Goodrich then in his conversations with Webster could delicately discuss Worcester's proposals, filtering out what he knew would alarm Webster as most toxic to his reputation and work. Twenty-five years later, Goodrich glowingly described Worcester's role and ethical conduct throughout their collaboration:

> Mr. Worcester made no changes of a literary or any other kind, except under the direction of Dr. Webster and myself. He was exceedingly delicate on this point, sending on lists of some hundreds of words with queries whether their pronunciation or spelling should be changed. I answered these queries for Dr. Webster, and Mr. Worcester acted accordingly. His abridging was performed almost wholly by erasure; but now and then he condensed definitions, or threw in connecting words of his own. . . . I have always said, that Mr. Worcester's abridgement was *well made*. Every one knows that the changes of orthography and pronunciation made by my direction (as Dr. Webster's representative)

were highly advantageous. Some of his [Webster's] spelling & pronunciation were so obnoxious to the public that Dr. Webster's best friends feared greatly for their effect. There was danger that the large work, encumbered by these, would be considered as a book for the learned alone. It was the Octavo abridgement, thus *popularized* in orthography & pronunciation, which gave a decided favourable turn to the popular mind at this crisis.[19]

8

In his first surviving letter to Goodrich, on October 28, 1828—after most of the unabridged quarto had been printed but about one month before it was published—Worcester was concerned that his and Goodrich's revisions thus far were not reducing the quarto's text enough and that the octavo would swell to a self-defeating size. He was also frustrated that proofs of the quarto needing to be forwarded to him in the prepublication stage were not arriving quickly enough to enable him to get up to speed. He urged Goodrich to send him prompt responses to his suggestions once he had had a chance to talk to Webster about them: "I shall endeavor to forward the early pages as soon as opportunity offers that you and Mr. Webster may see them and judge whether much more can be properly erased."[20]

It was Webster's treatment of spelling and pronunciation that worried Worcester most, which were incompatible with all the leading authorities like Johnson, Todd, Walker, Chalmers, and a host of others whom Webster wished largely to ignore. Webster allowed the following as alternatives to the conventional preferred spellings, which most people did not think should be any part of a dictionary of English: *duce* for *deuce, nehbor* for *neighbor, nusance* for *nuisance, spred* for *spread,* and *turky* for *turkey.* As for pronunciation, Worcester reminded Goodrich: "You mentioned to me that you should go through an examination of the Dictionary and anticipate me in your remarks on the pronunciation of words which I hope you will be able to do." He wanted to get on with it. In the meantime, he was sending Goodrich lengthy lists of words that he had tentatively decided should be pronounced this or that way, either leaving them as they appeared in the quarto or returning them to conventional orthography. But without clearer directives, he was becoming doubtful about how to proceed. He pressed Goodrich again three days later to make decisions promptly after talking to Webster: "I would thank you to specify as definitely as you can, what words, which are found in the quarto in a new orthography, are to be restored in the definitions to their usual form." "Am I or am I not to introduce other pronunciation with authorities?" he questioned. In December 1828, Worcester thought it best "to send a list of all the words that will be inserted in his Synopsis, together with various others about which there may be a question of some sort." That way there would be less confusion, less chance of recrimination, although he admitted he seldom had the "leisure to make all the explanations and queries that might be useful."[21]

All in all, Worcester was finding it a perplexing process to edit the work of a man he had met only two or three times, to whom he knew his revisions would be anathema: "It is a matter of delicacy and difficulty to fix the pronunciation of various foreign words, and I fear that I will not always do it in a manner that Dr. Webster and yourself would approve." "I regret that some points relating to the abridgement were not more definitely fixed," he told Goodrich. As for recording inconsistencies in Webster's pronunciations in the quarto, he supposed "it is Mr. Webster's wish that I should not [do so] in any instance, nor am I desirous to do it, provided the work will not suffer and Mr. Converse will be satisfied." He was nervous that his own "Synopsis" might be muddied with "instances of words which are not proper to be inserted" in it and "of which the pronunciation given in [Webster's] dictionary is certainly questionable." He still remained uncertain how far he could go, whether the "orthography is to be restored or not" in many of Webster's words, such as *ax, cloke,* and *zink*. In the end, Goodrich decided to include a few of Webster's reformed spellings, but he degraded them: "old orthography takes the lead, and is immediately followed by the one proposed." Moreover, Worcester was troubled with doubts that this project was going to succeed or do him personally any good: "It is difficult to make such a work as this conformable to the views of another who is 150 miles distant. It is my wish to give satisfaction to those interested, but fear the work will have more blemishes than could be wished."[22]

As the days and months passed, however, Worcester became less tentative, confident that Goodrich was behind him all the way. Goodrich continued to visit him in Cambridge, and the two men were becoming good friends. Worcester was pleased to hear from his brother, then living in New Haven, that Goodrich had been "good enough to call" on him there. Still, the persistent hazard in their collaboration was that Goodrich had to be extremely careful not to anger his father-in-law who might at any moment attempt to put a stop to their work on the octavo. On December 30, Worcester returned to his main complaint, still feeling at sea in Websterian waters: "I cannot but regret that the principles on which the abridgement is to be formed were not better settled before it was commenced. The work must suffer somewhat on this account, though I hope not very much, and it must cost some more labor and trouble."

Goodrich for the most part agreed with Worcester's objections to Webster. Webster's spelling oddities should not be allowed to stand further on in the entry than their first mention, in the definitions, for instance, and in derivatives of words. An example of what both Goodrich and Worcester wished to avoid in the octavo is Webster's entry word, *bridegoom*. The reader who looks up *bridegroom* in the quarto is told to go to *bridegoom*, defined thus: "A compound of *bride* and *gum, guma*, a man, which, by our ancestors, was pronounced *goom*. This word, by a mispronouncing the last syllable, has been corrupted into *bridegroom*, which signifies a *bride's hostler; groom* being a Persian word, signifying a man who has the care of horses. Such a gross corruption or blunder ought not to remain a reproach to philology." And they agreed that entry words ought to be alphabetized according to conventional spelling. That way a substantial part of Webster's display of unorthodoxy, eccentricity, and occasional defiance could be eliminated or downgraded—a type of lexical housecleaning without knocking over all the furniture.[23]

Near the end of the collaboration, Worcester began to feel restless and uncomfortable about conflicts of interest. It worried him especially that Converse had decided to include Walker's *Key* in the octavo after he had assured Worcester he would not do so. Worcester made no secret of it to Goodrich that his own publishers were upset:

You may perhaps have understood that the publishers of [Todd-]Johnson and Walker's Dictionaries have had some unpleasant feelings about my having undertaken to abridge Dr. Webster's dictionary, but I have not felt that they have any right to oppose it. When I undertook the business, Mr. Converse said that he did not expect to add Walker's *Key*; and afterwards when the plan, in this particular, was changed, I told him that I could have nothing to do with that part of the book. My reason was that having edited the work for other publishers, they would complain if I should do it for him, nor should I feel satisfied with myself to do it.[24]

That was in early April 1829, by which time all the proofs for the octavo had been printed and reviewed by Worcester, just over nine hundred pages of them. The end was in sight, and he longed to return to the completion of his own dictionary. "I wish to be released from the confinement of the work, as soon as I can," he wrote to Goodrich. "Please to say how many pages of introductory matter you expect to furnish, and when it will be ready."

A final visit to Cambridge by Goodrich to tidy up details and enjoy Worcester's company concluded their collaboration. The work was done, bringing both relief and renewed doubts, but neither Goodrich nor Worcester—nor Converse for that matter—came anywhere near anticipating the damaging repercussions of their productive collaboration in the remainder of their lives and on the course of early American lexicography.

6

Tea and Copyright

Goodrich Takes Over

The one-volume octavo abridgment came out in late 1829. At 940 pages, it was about half the length of the 1828 quarto. Worcester and Goodrich had extracted large amounts of text, chiefly from Webster's definitions and etymologies, streamlining many of Webster's and making them less wordy and more quickly understandable to the average user. A quick look at the entry word *deface* in the quarto and octavo illustrates somewhat representatively the shortening of definition in the octavo:

1828 QUARTO: TO UNDO OR UNMAKE.

1. To destroy or mar the face or surface of a thing; to injure the superficies or beauty; to disfigure; as, to *deface* a monument; to *deface an edifice.*
2. To injure any thing; to destroy, spoil or mar; to erase or obliterate; as, to *deface* letters or writing; to *deface* a note, deed, or bond; to *deface* a record.
3. To injure the appearance; to disfigure.

1829 OCTAVO

1. To destroy or mar the face or surface of a thing; to injure the superficies or beauty; to disfigure.
2. To injure any thing; to destroy, spoil, or mar; to erase or obliterate.
3. To injure the appearance; to disfigure.

Worcester and Goodrich also added some thirty thousand to forty thousand new definitions and increased the number of entry words to 83,000, some

16,000 more than the quarto. One of their first decisions very likely was to banish Webster's long "Introductory Dissertation on the Origin, History, and Connection of the Languages of Western Asia and of Europe," which began by considering in what language Adam and Eve spoke to each other and going on from there to his theories about the origins of all languages. Instead of that, in a way adding insult to injury, they added Walker's *Key to the Classical Pronunciation of Greek, Latin, and Scripture Proper Names,* anathema to Webster. There was no denying that this was a superior dictionary to the 1828 quarto, and far more usable. Also it cost $6 (about $150 today), a price within the reach of thousands who could not afford the $20 quarto. Immediately, it sold well and continued to do so through the years in a series of printings, reaching a fifteenth in 1836, with a thoroughly revised edition under Goodrich's total control appearing in 1844.

To give some idea of Worcester and Goodrich's compression of Webster's definitions, we might look again at those cited earlier from the quarto (see chapter 4, section 9). It is good to keep in mind, as we consider them, Goodrich's major role at Yale as pastor and religious adviser. *Education* now is reduced to only the first two lines, or a quarter, of Webster's definition: "The bringing up, as of a child; instruction; formation of manners." *Marriage* is deprived entirely (the last six lines) of Webster's portrait of God's role in marriage. Two additional senses or meanings are added to *marriage,* "a feast made on the occasion of a marriage"; and the scriptural/theological sense, "the union between Christ and his church by the covenant of grace." For *purpose* all reference to a "Supreme Being" in the quarto is dropped; and while all five of Webster's senses remain, they are drastically reduced, with one being judged as "hardly to be distinguished from the former." Twenty-nine lines are cut down to nine. Forty-three long-winded lines of Webster's *war* are now compressed into eleven lines, though all six of his senses are retained. *Woman* is shortened from fourteen lines to three; Webster's two senses remain, but his religious and cautionary message is eliminated. No mention is made of a woman being "soft, mild, pitiful, and flexible." From these examples alone, it is obvious that the definitions are purged of Webster's personal views on these and thousands of other subjects.

In his preface to the edition, Goodrich takes, as he always would in future editing, a particular interest in the complexities of pronunciation, much more difficult in his eyes to sort out than Webster's orthographical eccentricities. "As a guide to *pronunciation,*" he writes, "the words have been carefully

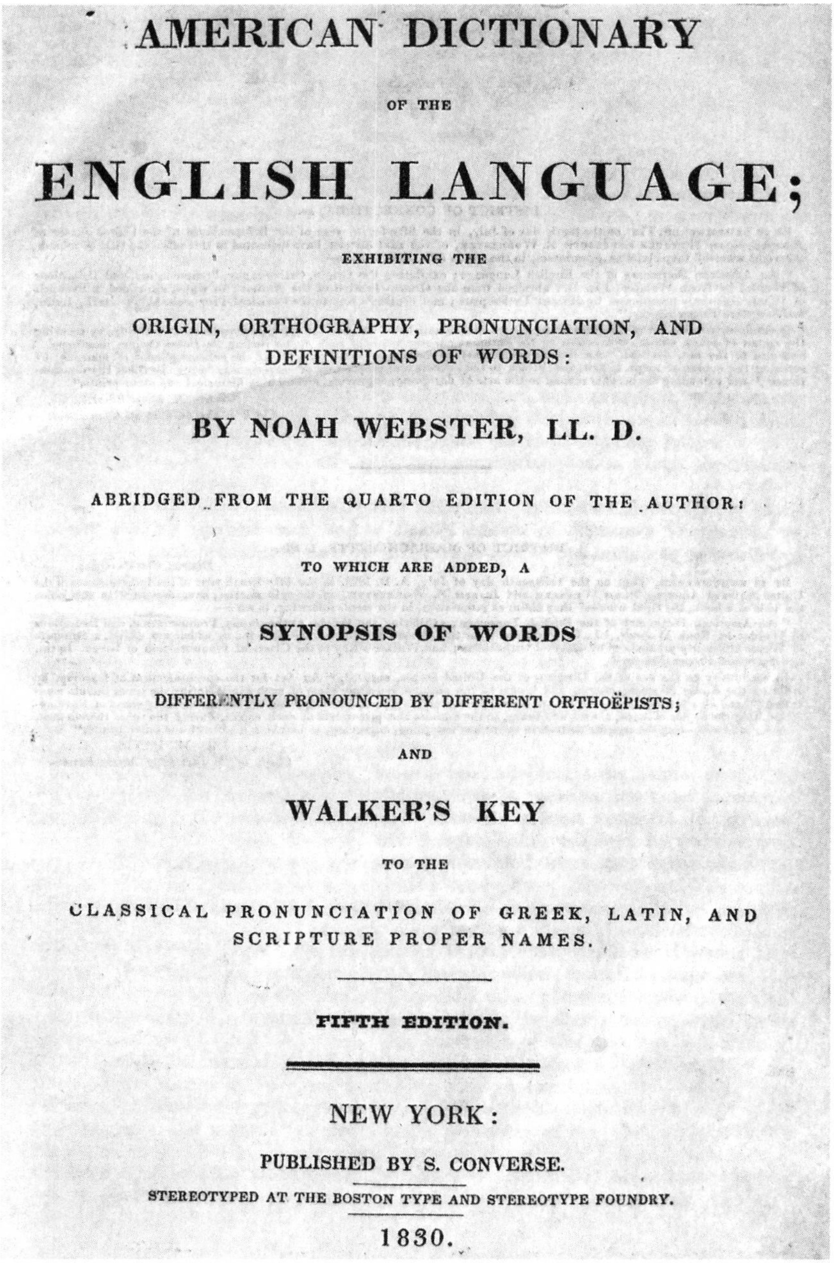

AMERICAN DICTIONARY

OF THE

ENGLISH LANGUAGE;

EXHIBITING THE

ORIGIN, ORTHOGRAPHY, PRONUNCIATION, AND
DEFINITIONS OF WORDS:

BY NOAH WEBSTER, LL. D.

ABRIDGED FROM THE QUARTO EDITION OF THE AUTHOR:

TO WHICH ARE ADDED, A

SYNOPSIS OF WORDS

DIFFERENTLY PRONOUNCED BY DIFFERENT ORTHOËPISTS;

AND

WALKER'S KEY

TO THE

CLASSICAL PRONUNCIATION OF GREEK, LATIN, AND
SCRIPTURE PROPER NAMES.

FIFTH EDITION.

NEW YORK:

PUBLISHED BY S. CONVERSE.

STEREOTYPED AT THE BOSTON TYPE AND STEREOTYPE FOUNDRY.

1830.

FIGURE 5. Title page from the 1830 octavo abridgment of Noah Webster's *American Dictionary of the English Language,* edited by Chauncey Goodrich and Joseph Worcester. Courtesy of Indiana State University Special Collections, Cordell Collection of Dictionaries.

divided into syllables. This, in the great majority of instances, decides at once the regular sound of the vowels in the respective syllables; and where the vowels depart from this regular sound, a *pointed* letter is used, denoting the sound which they receive in such cases." This renders unnecessary "the re-spelling of words, as a guide to pronunciation. . . ." As for disputed pronunciations, "different forms are frequently given," says Goodrich: "But the SYNOPSIS of Mr. Worcester exhibits these diversities much more fully, and gives, in one view, the decisions of the most approved Pronouncing Dictionaries respecting about eight hundred primitive words, which, of course, decide the pronunciation of a great number of derivatives." The result is that "nearly all the important points of difference in English orthoëpy" are accounted for, and readers are able to decide for themselves which they wish to adopt.

When Webster saw the completed work in print he was horrified. How could he have let this happen? The octavo made him look like someone who had written a first draft of a book with inconsistent and half-baked ideas, requiring experts to come in, clean up the mess, and make it fit for publication. It disordered his perception of himself as America's premier authority on the English language and made him appear just the latest in a long string of competing lexicographers. His sentiments began to turn against the mild and unsuspecting Worcester and his irritating Synopsis. "The object of the Synopsis," writes Worcester, "is to exhibit, at one view, the manner in which words of doubtful, disputed, or various pronunciation, are pronounced by the most eminent English orthoëpists." That alone was enough to anger Webster, who thought too much choice merely confused a user. He was upset with Goodrich, too, smelling foul play in what he saw as the breathtaking lengths to which his son-in-law had taken revisions of his dictionary's spelling and pronunciation—not to mention the definitions. The more he thought about it, the angrier he became.

2

"It is much to be regretted," Webster told Fowler as he looked back in April 1843, "that I suffered the American Dictionary to be abridged, not only as regards profits, but as regards its usefulness." The octavo "must not be considered as mine, though most of it is taken from mine." In any case, the Goodrich octavo was inferior to his quarto, he added, because it lacked a "History of the Language" as well as "the important principles which I have adopted to correct its anomalies"—not to mention that his definitions and etymology had been abridged and in his view were often defective.[1]

After what he felt was the fiasco of the Worcester-Goodrich octavo, Webster decided that one way at least to begin to recover his damaged credibility and momentum was to spring back promptly with his own small duodecimo (also called a square octavo, about five or seven inches square), *A Dictionary of the English Language, for the Use of Primary Schools and the Counting-House*, published in late 1829 by Hezekiah Howe, not by Converse. Webster's decision to use Howe, a local Connecticut publisher, instead of Converse in New York for the school edition was very likely a reaction against Converse for, as he believed, going over his head in securing Worcester as editor, with Goodrich's approval, for the octavo. This was the beginning of an irreparable estrangement between himself and Converse, which appears to have taken Converse completely by surprise. Outraged, Converse wrote to Webster: "[B]ut for me your Dictionary would have rested in Manuscript—There seems to be peculiar apprehension lest I should make something from my great labour and expense of time and money[,] and I suppose this is the reason why others are preferred." Webster's ego did not take kindly to being counseled in this manner by his publisher. But when Converse warned him of disaster if he tried to publish the book himself, Webster wrote "Menacing letter!" on the back of Converse's letter and turned his back on him forever.[2]

With forty-seven thousand entry words in 532 pages, Webster's school dictionary was supposed to earn Webster more, and it did: the number of pages is reduced by about 75 percent from that of the quarto, with tables added at the end; the definitions are almost all shortened to single lines of phrases (*above*: "higher, more"; *blistering*: "raising blisters"; *bloated*: "puffed, swelled, made turgid"; *dejection*: "depression of spirits, melancholy"); the notation is simplified to just eighteen symbols; the word count is halved; "uncommon" technical words are omitted, as are derivates and "primitive" (rarely used or obsolete) words; and participles of regular (but not irregular) verbs are almost entirely omitted. The edition was revised and published many times throughout the nineteenth century.

In the preface, which Webster wrote in December 1829 when he was sorely demoralized—this was the only word, he said, he had ever coined—by the

outlaw octavo, he defended himself. There were so many spelling and pronunciation discrepancies between his 1828 quarto and this corrected school
dictionary, he admitted, because he had spent most of his time on the quarto
working out the etymology and definitions and failed to devote enough time
to pronunciation and spelling. The reader need not worry. He had removed
inconsistencies, as he would have done in the octavo, he assured his readers,
had he been given a chance to "superintend" that edition. Therefore this
school dictionary, not the octavo, carries his authority since it was "all written and corrected by myself" and "is to be considered as containing the . . .
orthography and pronunciation which I most approve." It was a defensive
argument that carried the risk, of course, that readers would begin to doubt
his whole enterprise.[3]

"As far as it can be done," he told Fowler (now teaching at Middlebury College and fast becoming his confidant in preference to Goodrich) a few days
after Christmas 1829, his "spelling book and [school] duodecimo will be exactly alike, as soon as a few mistakes in the former can be corrected. . . ." With
this greater consistency, he hoped now to win more favor at institutions of
learning, especially the universities: "I understand from Mr. Converse, who
has lately been to Boston, that the President and Professors of Cambridge
[Harvard] have recommended my Dictionary to their students. I sincerely
hope that your Middlebury gentlemen will cooperate with Cambridge [Har-
vard] and Yale in this work of reform and uniformity. If our colleges go hand
in hand, the works will succeed." He then would be able to hold his head up
high when he visited literary institutions. He complained that the sounds
of Walkerisms (pronunciations sanctioned by Walker's dictionary), "operates
on me like a box on the ears."[4]

He then alarmed his family by telling them he might wipe the slate clean
and dissociate himself completely from what he considered the appalling
octavo by selling his rights to it. Goodrich feared that since Webster was
no businessman, he might indeed go ahead and sell the rights to the octavo
outside the family at far below its market value, just as he had done with
his speller. What appears to have happened next illustrates Goodrich's advantage in living just down the street from Webster. On July 10, 1829, over
a few cups of tea in Webster's home, he urged his father-in-law to sell the
copyright of the octavo to him. That way it would remain in the family. It
was logical for him to own the copyright, he felt, since after all he was its

chief editor. He reminded Webster he had received no payment whatever for his labors.[5]

Webster surrendered. For a while Goodrich kept members of the family, especially Fowler, in the dark that he now owned the copyright—at a knock-down price, incidentally. Fowler had asked Goodrich specifically to promise not to decide in his absence to whom the octavo would be sold, if it would be sold at all, and was beside himself when he learned what Goodrich had done. In justifying his purchase to his brother-in-law Ellsworth more than a decade later, Goodrich pointed out that purchasing the rights had not been without financial risks to himself and his own family. When the idea first came up, he maintained, "I remarked to Julia, 'if the work fails and there is danger of it owing to peculiar varieties in pronunciation and spelling, we shall have a millstone round our necks for life: and if it succeeds and becomes profitable to an extent correspondent with the risk, we shall be liable to the imputation of having a money-making spirit in respect to a parent.'" That was a fair reading.[6]

Converse continued as Goodrich's publisher of the book for four years, but the increased income from the octavo was still not enough to save him from bankruptcy in 1833, and Goodrich had to scramble to find another publisher. George and Charles Merriam, then small publishers in Springfield, Massachusetts, but later major dictionary publishers, turned him down. Goodrich had trouble finding someone to take Converse's place because prospective publishers were wary that Webster might suddenly decide to stereotype yet another abridgment of the 1828 quarto for schools and academies that would compete in the same market as the octavo. That could easily happen, because stereotyping enabled a printer to print quickly and relatively inexpensively, and a small school edition especially so. The publishers who were most interested in the octavo abridgment, Norman and Joseph White of New York, had reservations about taking it on precisely for that reason. The Whites urged Goodrich to ask for a formal, signed affidavit from Webster stating unequivocally that he would never publish a rival octavo for schools or of any other kind. So Goodrich trotted over to Webster's house for some more tea and appealed to his father-in-law's sense of fairness. Since he had paid his father-in-law for the copyright to the octavo, would it be decent of him someday to publish another octavo abridgment that would jeopardize his investment? Whether or not hours of persuasion were necessary is unknown, but Webster agreed to sign the needed legal document on May 7, 1833, witnessed by

Webster's wife, Rebecca. In it Webster promised "not [to] publish or permit to be published such an edition in octavo on stereotype plates, without some agreement with said Goodrich that I shall secure him and any persons who may be associated with him from any injury that may result from such publication, by reduction of the price of the larger work, & supplanting the octavo in the market." The Whites were still not satisfied, and, at their urging, a couple of months later Goodrich got Webster to be more exact: "I, Noah Webster in Connecticut, in consideration of the loss & sacrifices made by son-in-law Chauncey A. Goodrich in the purchase of the copyright and stereotype plates of the octavo form of my American Dictionary, do hereby grant and assign to the said Chauncey, and to his wife, my daughter Julia & to their children, all my right & interest in the premium for copyright of said book, for & during the remainder of . . . the term for which the copyright of said work is now secured to me by law."[7]

One thing was certain: Webster had signed away what could turn out to be a small fortune, and just to make sure nobody could accuse him of twisting Webster's arm, Goodrich had him add this blatantly untrue statement after his signature: "I hereby certify that I have made this grant spontaneously, and without the solicitation or previous knowledge of any person whatever." But even the second phrasing of the agreement, specifically the phrase "in the octavo form"—a book that could be interpreted as looking like an octavo but actually not be one—was slightly more ambivalent than Goodrich and his publishers wanted. So Goodrich pushed Webster again. This time Webster refused. Nonetheless, Goodrich and the Whites were content to draw up a contract on June 1, 1833, for the revision and republication of the octavo.[8]

3

Converse by this point had lost any sort of connection with Webster's dictionary, but more than that, he was persona non grata all around. Webster had rebuked him for charging too much for various services, failing to hand over copyright earnings when due, not supplying him with the contracted number of copies of the quarto, and not advertising the quarto sufficiently because of his stake in the octavo: "not one fifth part of the United States are supplied with the books." Such a comment, of course, ignored the inconvenient fact that the copies of the quarto that Converse did print did not sell well. When

Webster traveled to Washington in December 1830 to promote the passage of the copyright extension bill soon to come before Congress, he was incensed to learn that Goodrich had invited Converse to accompany him there as well. "I have not seen him & I hope I shall not," he wrote to Rebecca.[9]

Several letters between Converse and Goodrich between 1830 and 1833 reveal just how unpopular Converse had become with the Webster family and eventually with Goodrich, too. These letters also show how unbending Goodrich could be from his intellectual-moral high ground. He made his own observations and drew his own conclusions, but his opinion of Converse was bound to be influenced by "reports" from Webster. In November 1830, Converse tried desperately to set the record straight, writing to Goodrich that he felt "wronged and injured" and "deeply wounded" by Webster, and that he had "not so far forgotten Mr. Webster's rights as an author or my own character and obligations as a man, and a Christian, as to commit depredations on his works. . . . Slander in New Haven has been poured upon me without measure, and when I think of it, with the absolute wrongs I have suffered there, my soul turns away with loathing from the places I once loved." He assured Goodrich, however, that he had no "disposition to revenge" against Webster for not giving him the contract for the school dictionary. On the contrary, he had always demonstrated "good will in both act and motive" toward the lexicographer. The "stings of injury" from Webster, he admitted, had provoked him in the heat of misunderstandings to write two or three angry letters to him, but he had since in vain repeatedly asked for Webster's forgiveness. Webster was in no mood to forgive him.[10]

Converse failed. His attempt to recover Goodrich's good opinion of him managed only to destroy any chances he had of achieving that. His biggest mistake was to mortgage the stereotyped plates of the octavo to Messrs. Ames, papermakers in New York. They were not publishers but imagined they might make profitable use of the plates in the future. With the borrowed money, he then unwisely traveled to England in hopes of furthering his publishing interests there. While he was away, still financially stretched and distracted and depressed by his worsening financial situation, he defaulted on his mortgage payments to the Ameses. Unable to reach him, they took the initiative of writing to Goodrich to say that Converse was on the verge of forfeiting the plates. Since Goodrich for whatever reason chose not to help Converse, the Ames brothers assumed ownership of the forfeited plates.

When Converse returned to New York, he was crushed to find that the only way he could recover the plates was to buy them back from the Ames brothers. But he had no money to do that, a bitter impasse for him since it was he who had stereotyped the book in the first place, at great expense. He appealed to Goodrich for help, but Goodrich, shocked by what the Ames brothers had told him, reached an agreement himself with the Ameses to buy the plates: "It became apparent that my copyright would be worth but little unless the property could be got out of their hands." Without telling Converse, Goodrich offered the Ameses a price they could not resist, $11,000 (close to $275,000 today), and thus he became owner of both the copyright and the plates. On June 1, 1833, now rid of Converse, Goodrich contacted the newly formed publishers White, Gallagher, and White, who "agreed to take the publication and the plates, allowing me a certain interest in the latter, on condition that the premium in copyright should be merged in the right of publication, and no more kept as a distinct concern." No bookseller would have been interested on any other terms, Goodrich informed Ellsworth. For the remaining twenty-four years of the octavo copyright, the Whites would retain exclusive publishing rights. They would also employ Goodrich for that entire time to edit and revise the work. "When I sold out to Mr. White," Goodrich wrote in December 1844, "I bound myself to prepare a corrected copy with additional words, and all corrections, whenever he [White] should choose to stereotype the work anew."[11]

In vain, Converse continued to plead. Goodrich did not take Converse's protestations kindly and replied that he had given Converse plenty of time to try to recover the plates: "The abuse which you have heaped upon me in your last letter and the base and detestable motives to which you ascribe my purchase of the plates, would justify me, on the ordinary principles of intercourse among gentlemen in passing by your communication and the request which it contained with silent contempt. But you have written under the influence of inflamed passions, and I am willing to give you one opportunity more to consider what you are doing before you plunge yourself into deeper difficulties." He then explained that Converse was delusional in thinking he still had a right to the plates and had misconstrued everything that had happened: "You think that but for me you might have recovered that property. . . . When I commenced my arrangement for this purchase, I considered the property as much lost to you as though you were already in the grave. I believe so still." Converse was soon forgotten.[12]

7

Spelling Wars

The Rise of Lyman Cobb

As if Goodrich's swift and (as he thought) high-handed move to take control of the octavo abridgment were not enough, in the 1820s Webster was also caught off balance by an aggressive challenge at the root of the fame he claimed for himself as America's schoolmaster and linguistic champion. It concerned chiefly his spelling books, with major repercussions for his dictionary. The challenger was Lyman Cobb, an obscure and brash schoolteacher in upstate New York, forty-two years younger than he.

Lacking a formal education beyond what he received as a youth, very likely in a log schoolhouse in rural New York, Cobb began teaching in a similar school at the age of sixteen. Unhappy with the textbooks he had to use in the classroom, which included Webster's *American Spelling Book*—a new edition in 1804 had become a runaway bestseller—Cobb at the age of twenty-one published his own speller in 1821, *A Just Standard for Pronouncing the English Language Containing the Rudiments of the English Language . . . an Easy Scheme of Spelling and Pronunciation, Intermixed with Easy Reading Lessons . . . Calculated to Teach the Orthography of Walker*. After a revised second edition in 1825, it became widely known as "Cobb's Speller" and until midcentury sold as the chief rival to *Webster's Elementary Spelling Book*. No fewer than four million copies were sold up to then, most of them in New York State, Philadelphia, and Baltimore. Unfortunately, like Webster, for quick cash Cobb several times sold the rights to his speller-reader, thus depriving himself of considerable wealth and eventually sentencing himself to near poverty.[1]

Cobb's book was designed to teach spelling chiefly through a program of reading, as part of its title suggests. Its forward-looking strategy gave it a place in the reformist educational movement to displace old-fashioned school textbooks like Webster's. Indeed, the progressive journal *American Journal of Education*, founded in 1826 by its editor William Russell, was critical of Webster, although Cobb also proved to be a disappointment to Russell because he was judged to be still too dependent on memorization technique based on repetition. That Webster's speller remained popular throughout the nineteenth century in spite of this movement toward more advanced educational methods illustrates, among other things, his lasting grip on the American imagination.[2]

Webster had competitors other than Cobb in the spelling sweepstakes, notably Daniel Crandall's *The Columbian Spelling-Book* (1819), from which Cobb borrowed heavily, and *Marshall's Spelling Book of the English Language; or the American Tutor's Assistant* by Elihu F. Marshall (1821). Among other things, these editions largely ignored Webster's spelling reforms and championed Walker's system of pronunciation. It was this allegiance to Walker that posed a stark and audacious threat to Webster's wide-ranging language reforms and could be said to have launched the spelling battles that followed. In 1829, Webster returned to the spelling battleground with a new edition of his speller that affirmed his continued opposition to his Walker-inspired rivals. He knew that if he lost these wars over spelling, the bedrock of his reputation, he might well lose out to competitors like Worcester and live to see his whole American language enterprise collapse.

2

Cobb decided that the best way to shove Webster off his throne was to open up the market for his own speller with a sustained public exposure of Webster's allegedly glaring inconsistencies and absurdities. In 1827 and 1828, he took aim at Webster's speller in several articles in the *Albany Argus*, signed "The Examinator," which he later collected and circulated in a pamphlet titled *To the Teachers, School Committees or Inspectors, Clergymen, and to the Friends of Correct Elementary Instruction*. In it, his tone bordering on what Jennifer Monaghan has described as "apoplectic," he pounced on what he called Webster's errors and defects and argued that Webster, in the several editions of his speller and dictionaries, had failed to follow his own recommendations on spelling and pronunciation, failed to achieve the uniformity of spelling and pronunciation between his spelling books and dictionaries that was crucial in school instruction, and for decades had managed mainly to confuse Americans, especially teachers and children: Webster's "pretensions . . . indicate a greater share of pedantry and egotism than I am pleased to find in a countryman who has hitherto enjoyed so great a share of publick confidence and patronage." He asked educators to consider whether in light of these many imperfections they ought not to adopt Cobb's speller for the classroom instead of Webster's before any more damage was done. Cobb was making a move not only to take over the spelling book market but also to expose Webster's instability as a lexicographer.[3]

At first, Webster retaliated in a measured, eight-page letter to the editor of the *Argus* in December 1827. He simply explains he had revised a good deal in his speller and dictionaries since 1782, remarking "that there are some errors, defects, and inconsistencies in the work is not to be wondered at" after the passage of some forty-six years. He reminds readers that all English dictionaries had been similarly erroneous and inconsistent, including Walker's, which he describes with some hyperbole: "full of inconsistencies from beginning to end, and the attempt to make it a standard has done more to corrupt the language than any event which has taken place for five hundred years past." He could easily cite "*eight* to *ten thousand* instances of vowels marked in Walker's dictionary for an erroneous pronunciation." No fewer than three dictionaries, he adds, had since been published to correct Walker, though he does not say which. "But the evils of our philology lie deeper, and a mere dabbling in pronunciation will not reach them," he warns. The orthography is "unsettled: no two authors are agreed . . . and no dictionary is consistent with[in] itself." Definitions are chaotic, the vocabulary is "very incomplete," and the grammar is "in a condition equally bad." But he is coming to the rescue with his forthcoming quarto, which would "present the language purified from some of its corruptions" and, discouraging the formation of dialects, offer "something like regularity" and help to unify the United States.[4]

Cobb was getting good traction from his offensive. Webster's dictionary appeared a few months later in 1828, but the next year Cobb struck again, still anonymously, this time with an article in the more visible *New York Evening Post*, widening his net to include Webster's new *Primary School and Counting-House Dictionary* and *Elementary Spelling Book*, both published in 1829. Cobb claimed that Webster had recently hired assistants to help him revise his speller in light of the *Albany Argus* corrections, implying that

Webster had panicked and possibly plagiarized the work of others, and that his dictionary was irreparably flawed. On July 4, 1829, he boldly blitzed the battlefield with no fewer than seventeen articles under the name "Inquirer" for the *Morning Herald* in New York. He takes aim specifically at Webster's representation of himself as the one who would banish irregularities and establish consistency in the American language. Cobb claims he had assiduously combed through various editions of Webster's publications, identifying hundreds of words Webster spelled inconsistently and many more innovations of spelling based on mere whim and impulse, "as the notion strikes." He shows, for example, how Webster lopped off the final letters in words ending with *ff* as in *sheriff* and *b* as in *crumb*. As for the word *ache*, Cobb writes, Webster never could make up his mind whether to spell it that way or as *ake*. Any dictionary worth taking up space in a classroom or home, he argues, must have consistent orthography based on clearly stated rules and illustrated with comprehensible symbols and diacritical marks, without innovations unless identified with the label "anomaly." Neither should the same words be differently spelled from page to page. In none of these respects did Webster pass this test, Cobb concludes. Moreover, through his "mischievous influence of innovation" he had "done more to introduce irregularity in orthography than all of the other works published in this country within fifty years."[5]

In his thirteenth article, for good measure, Cobb also cites what he describes as a devastating remark by a friend of Webster's, Daniel H. Barnes. Beginning in 1827, before the *American Dictionary* was published, Barnes had been helping Webster revise his speller for the new edition in 1829, in light of Cobb's *Albany Argus* articles, when he was killed in an accident in late 1828. He had been going over Webster's dictionary at the same time, likely at the page proof stage, when it was too late to effect substantive changes, and he could not contain his surprise over the myriad tangled orthographic and other problems. Cobb quotes Barnes's amazement at the dictionary's legion of spelling contradictions and variations:

> These I have marked in that dictionary which Mr. Webster considers his best work, and such an appalling number I could not imagine or scarcely believe, had I not seen it and done it myself. . . . Mr. Webster has no idea of the multitudinous errors in his works. . . . I have not seen any of the mammoth bones; the owner is afraid if they are exposed

before the entire skeleton is set up, that they will crumble to pieces. He said to me "there must be no discussion of that kind while the work is in the press." By and by the mountain will bring forth, I hope not a moon-calf.—He cannot spell, what else he can [do], remains to be seen.—Reading his dictionary, as I have done, has taken away all hope that he will ever do more than to aggregate materials for a good work.[6]

Shortly afterward, Webster's publisher Sherman Converse, not yet fully estranged from the Webster orbit, sprang to Webster's defense—or, more accurately, the defense of his own investment—by firing back at Cobb in the *Morning Herald* of August 27, 1829. While by this time it was widely assumed that Cobb was the anonymous essayist hammering away at Webster, Converse removes all doubt, publicly exposing Cobb as stirring up a controversy purely out of self-interest. He deplores Cobb's insensitivity to the memory of Barnes, who, he maintains, genuinely approved of Webster's dictionary. He claims Barnes had told him that Cobb actually approved of Webster's orthographical principles in the dictionary, to which Cobb replies in the *Morning Herald* a week later that he had never had such a conversation with Barnes and that he could hardly have approved of Webster's lexicographical orthography at that time, as he had not yet seen his current manuscript. As for Cobb's revelations themselves, Converse reminds readers that Webster's books were written over many years during which the language had continued to change, and that in a dictionary of such length it was impossible to catch all the errors.[7]

After completing those seventeen articles on Webster's orthography for the *Herald*, Cobb grouped them together with his *Argus* articles and in 1831 published a fifty-six-page pamphlet titled *A Critical Review of the Orthography of Dr. Webster's Series of Books*. He appended to it a table of 720 words he chose from the several editions of Webster's spelling books and dictionaries over several decades to demonstrate the scope of his inconsistency between his 1782 speller, 1806 *Compendious*, 1828 quarto, 1831 octavo and duodecimo, and the revised 1829 *American Spelling Book*. He sent the pamphlet to members of Congress, university professors, and judges who he knew had endorsed Webster's books at one time or another, asking them to inspect Webster's books objectively in light of the evidence in his pamphlet. For years, Cobb continued to make Webster's life miserable by attacking his orthography. That his campaign against Webster was at least partially successful is borne out by sales of millions of his own books.[8]

3

As for Webster himself, his brief defense against Cobb's pamphlet in an open letter of November 1831, "To The Public," does not add much to what Converse had offered. Cobb's disparagement of his books, he writes, was not inspired and motivated by lofty principles but rather by a commercial need to "pave the way for introducing his own school books." He asks only to set the facts straight:

> The writer compares the orthography of my old books, published before my quarto Dictionary and some of them thirty or forty years ago, with that of my new series of books. This is glaring injustice. My last publications are *intended* to correct the former ones, and the differences between them are *not* errors but improvements. As my old books have been rejected by myself, and some of them are out of print, it is as improper to introduce them in this comparison as it would be to introduce Chaucer's *Canterbury Tales*. This sweeps away the foundation of a large part of all the writer's pamphlet.

It is a plausible defense, although one might quarrel a little with the distinction between improvements and errors if the former are made because of the latter. Webster admits that when he set out to write his *American Dictionary* he had not yet "settled any definite system of orthography in certain classes of words differently written," but the writings of "the best authors" teem with spelling variations: *civilize-civilise, gulf-gulph, inchant-enchant, inclose-enclose, inquire-enquire, insure-ensure, intrust-entrust, risk-risque, surprise-surprize.* "Some" of these "escaped me and the gentlemen who assisted me," he explains. His ambition was to have all the words in his books "uniformly written," but "my books, I believe, now contain the most uniform and most correct orthography of English words that has ever been presented to the public." That was a risky claim, considering Cobb's 720 examples, but he warns readers to beware of Cobb's "drudgery of *letter-hunting*."[9]

After these years of abuse from Cobb, Webster set about shedding layers of frustration and anger by writing a vindictive personal attack on him (never published) in at least two known personal letters in 1836 and 1837. They were virtually identical, which makes it likely he sent out several others similar to them. One on October 26, 1836, was a letter of thanks to Henry Henrick, the publisher of a Knoxville, Tennessee, newspaper, for publishing his piece, "Webster's Caution," warning readers to be alert to pirated editions of his speller, containing unauthorized revisions. There were many such fraudulent editions, even as far away as Dublin, Ireland. In his letter to Henrick, Webster indulged in some ad hominem Cobb-bashing:

> He is an extraordinary man. His history is shortly thus. He was a poor boy in Lenox, Mass. . . . He afterwards lived with a Mr. Bosworth of Albany, as a menial, but I am told he was addicted to lying for which he was flogged. He thus ran away and the first thing Bosworth heard from him was, he had made a Spelling Book. It seems he went westward and kept school, then in Walker's Dictionary adopted his plan of spelling and pronunciation. After he published his Sp[elling] book, he attacked MINE, marked everything in which I differ from Walker, published a long series of papers against me, first in an Albany newspaper, then in a pamphlet, which he sent by mail into all quarters. When my Dictionary appeared, he again wrote against me in a New York paper, finding fault with my discrepancies of orthography, [and] published a pamphlet which doubtless you have seen. In his [spelling] book there are . . . many plagiarisms from my dictionary. . . .[10]

He sent much the same letter in 1837 to Professor William Holmes McGuffey of Miami University in Oxford, Ohio, a leading figure in the American textbook world best known for his famous *McGuffey Readers*—a series of graded primers teaching reading and moral precepts for grade levels 1–6 that began appearing in the 1830s in Cincinnati, Ohio. McGuffey "might be amused to learn," Webster wrote, that Cobb was "the most indefatigable man on earth . . . of very low origin . . . a dull scholar in a common school. . . . Now it is no objection to him or his books that he was of low origin or destitute of any unusual advantages for education. But these facts show the reason of his extraordinary proceedings in regard to me, his vulgar abuse, & total want of common decorum, in circulating misrepresentations respecting my books."[11]

The barest outlines of this biographical vignette may resemble Cobb's background, but its most sensational feature is the venom that reveals the level of Webster's bitterness as he approached his eightieth birthday. After a long life of labor, "competition and plagiarists deprive me of a large portion of the reward," he complained to McGuffey. Still embittered by Cobb, four years later in 1841, two years before his death, Webster only slightly refined this indictment in an anonymous article, "The Age of Spelling Books," printed in the *New Hampshire Gazette* on November 30, 1841. Cobb was an "illiterate" schoolteacher, a mere "book-maker." "Cobb failed," he announces, "& laid one third of the towns in New York under bondage for many years." The article is signed "Teacher."

4

The public mostly took Webster's side. He felt its support, for example, on his trip to Washington to push for the new copyright bill in 1831. While he was there, President Andrew Jackson, whose populist politics Webster abhorred, honored him with an invitation to dinner at the White House on December 28, 1830, with thirty others, mostly members of the Senate and House of Representatives. Ever skeptical of great men and wary of public social events, Webster commented he "could not well avoid" attending the dinner. It was not just Jackson's politics that he deplored; he also was repelled by what he felt was Jackson's vulgarity. Jackson actually did him a great honor by seating him for dinner at his right hand, but for Webster the meal was simply pretentious. There was little that was American about it— in the official residence of the president of the United States, of all places. "As to *dining* at the President's table in the true sense of the word," he wrote grumpily to his daughter Harriet (Fowler's wife), "there is no such thing" because "foreign customs"—the food was not mainstream American—prevail "to the annoyance of American guests."[12]

The food and presidential ritual apart, Webster was gratified to discover that "members of both houses . . . were glad to see me" and praised him for the usefulness of his books. "It convinces me that my fellow citizens consider me as their benefactor and the benefactor of my country," he wrote to Fowler. To leave that point in less doubt, he also shrewdly composed an endorsement of his own dictionary that he persuaded many congressmen to sign and that later he used widely in advertising his books. One passage of it portrayed the dictionary as the uncompromising "standard": "It is very desirable that one standard dictionary should be used by the numerous millions of people who are to inhabit the vast extent of territory belonging to the United

States. . . . We rejoice that the *American Dictionary*, bids fair to become such a standard. . . ." But Cobb's challenge to Webster's supremacy would not go away, and Webster had to get used to Cobb's siphoning off sales of millions of copies of his speller.[13]

After Webster's spelling reforms ignited these spelling wars and much other bitter controversy relating to his efforts to Americanize the language, it was clearer than ever to the public that spelling differences between America and Britain had become an issue in both countries that would not soon disappear. It was and has remained intense, but this preoccupation with spelling also energized a uniquely American educational innovation, the spelling bee. Although the origin of the spelling bee can be traced back to the first decade of the nineteenth century, when it was called a "spelling match," once these competitions began to be staged publicly in communities across the country, they eventually became a feature of primary and secondary American education from the 1850s onward. The competition could become fierce, even in schools—perhaps not quite as chaotic and dangerous, though, as the one in a California mining town portrayed hilariously by the American author and humorist Bret Harte in his 1878 poem "The Spelling Bee at Angels," narrated by "Truthful James" (see appendix D for the entire poem). One cannot be certain what Webster would have thought of it, but the poem's rambunctious humor was the sort over which Mark Twain, for one, would have rejoiced. Both Webster and Worcester's dictionaries play their not greatly appreciated parts in the poem. Words like *phthisis* cause havoc, but when "*eider-duck*" comes up, there is general pandemonium and a near riot as various participants make for the exits. They are prevented from leaving by "Three-fingered Jack" who "locked the door and yelled":

> "No, not one mother's son goes out till that thar word is spelled!"
> But while the words were on his lips, he groaned and sank in pain,
> And sank with Webster on his chest and Worcester on his brain.[14]

Quite a weight, one must admit.

8

The "Common Thief"

A more formidable challenge than Cobb to Webster's kingdom came in the shape of new dictionary competition from Worcester, who posed a more serious and permanent threat to both the success of Webster's books and his place in American history. Far more than Cobb, whom Webster found it relatively easier to dismiss, Worcester would unintentionally haunt and anger Webster for the rest of his life. It was well known across the country that Worcester was a solid and reliable scholar with powerful Harvard and Boston friends, who had dared to venture onto Webster's turf and offer an exceedingly strong lexicographical alternative to the American public.

Bruised from Cobb's campaign against him and increasingly paranoid over criticism and competition, Webster deeply resented Worcester's intrusion into his lexicographical domain through his editing of the Goodrich octavo. From that time onward, he nursed a private grievance against him that threatened to go public. Worcester had inadvertently made an enemy and would soon rue the day he had given in to Converse and Goodrich. He was made to feel that the $2,000 he had earned from revising the octavo were sin's wages. As far as he was concerned, and as we shall see, the money became pitifully small compensation for the adversity it would cause him.

Even more disturbing to Webster than the Goodrich octavo was the Boston publication in 1830 of Worcester's first full-fledged bid for America's lexicographical attention, *A Comprehensive Pronouncing and Explanatory Dictionary of the English Language*. It was a small dictionary intended to be purchased by schools for their students. A second edition followed promptly in 1831, and another in 1835. Soon after its publication in 1830, Robert Dunglison, the first professor of medicine at the University of Virginia and personal physician to Thomas Jefferson, went on record in the *American Monthly*

Review regarding the dictionary's utilitarian value, especially its medical terms: "I can, without hesitation, award to this Dictionary the merit of being best adapted to the end in view of any I have examined. It is, in other words, the best portable pronouncing and explanatory dictionary that I have seen, and as such is deserving of very extensive circulation." A few years later, the *Common School Journal* (founded and edited by Horace Mann, the brother-in-law of Nathaniel Hawthorne and progressive champion of the common school movement—public schools with a wider curriculum and more nurturing environment than traditional schools of the time) praised the 1835 edition, as the dictionary historian Eva Mae Burkett explains, for "the number of words, on the inclusion of the imperfect and past participle forms of the verbs, on its lists of words of doubtful orthography, and on its pronouncing vocabularies of proper names." Apart from Webster's quarto, Worcester's was up to then the most reliable modern dictionary of English in existence, by an American lexicographer or anyone else. When Webster saw it, he recognized

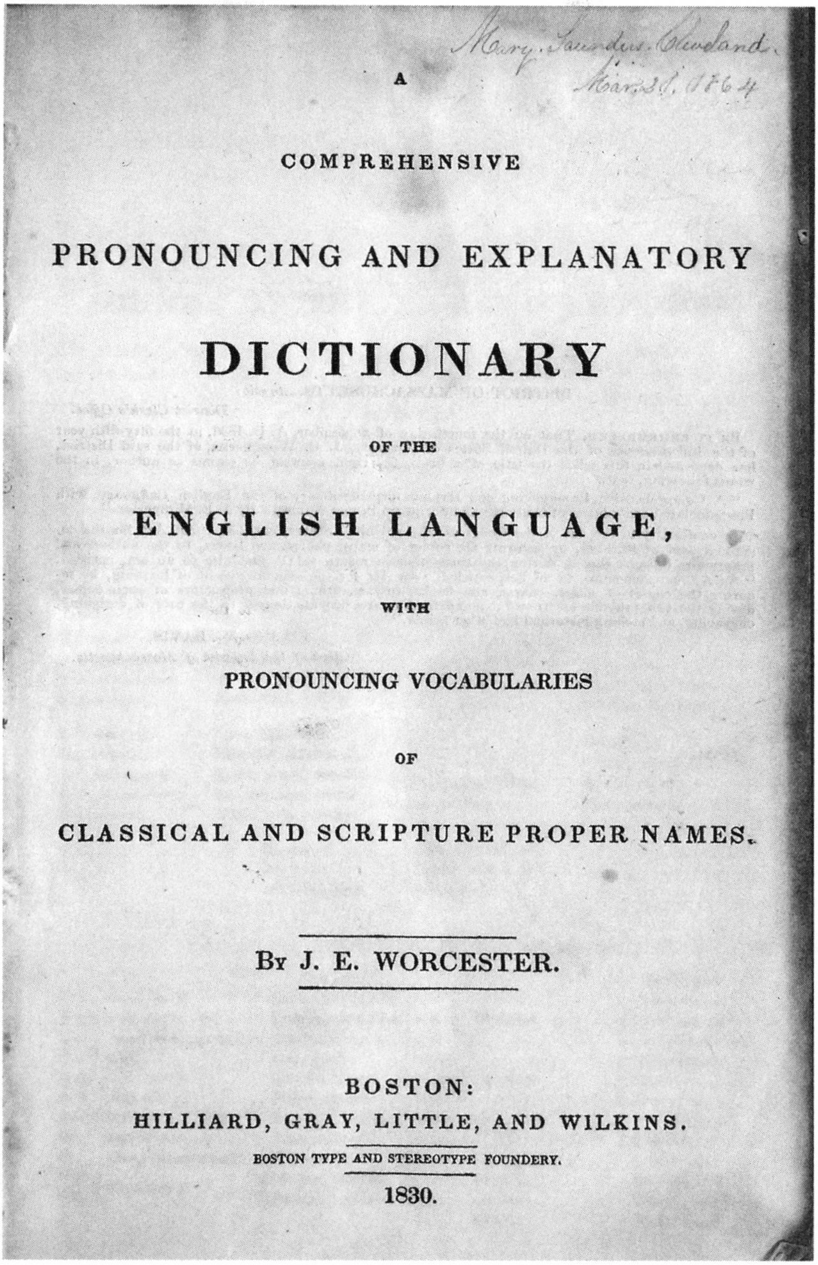

Mary Saunders Cleveland.
Mar. 28, 1864

A

COMPREHENSIVE

PRONOUNCING AND EXPLANATORY

DICTIONARY

OF THE

ENGLISH LANGUAGE,

WITH

PRONOUNCING VOCABULARIES

OF

CLASSICAL AND SCRIPTURE PROPER NAMES.

By J. E. WORCESTER.

BOSTON:
HILLIARD, GRAY, LITTLE, AND WILKINS.

BOSTON TYPE AND STEREOTYPE FOUNDERY.

1830.

FIGURE 7. Title page of Joseph Emerson Worcester's *Comprehensive Pronouncing and Explanatory Dictionary of the English Language*, 1830. Courtesy of Indiana State University Special Collections, Cordell Collection of Dictionaries.

it as a formidable competitor that risked throwing his world into disarray. "His book will probably injure the sales of mine," he wrote. A school edition competing with Webster's unabridged quarto would be like David facing Goliath, but Webster had a newfound fear of Worcester, and the threat from the latter at this early stage of the dictionary wars seemed to him very real.[1]

2

The first thing to notice about Worcester's dictionary is the author's generous acknowledgment in his preface of Webster's pioneering work a couple of years earlier: "a work of vast learning and research, containing far the most complete vocabulary of the language that has yet appeared, and comprising numerous and great improvements upon all works of the kind which preceded it, with respect to the etymology and definition of words." He might have bitten his tongue when mentioning Webster's etymology, and it is notable he does not mention Webster's system of orthography or orthoepy; instead, he provides his own tables of comparative pronunciation, as well as "A Vocabulary of Words of Doubtful or Various Orthography." With forty-three thousand entry words—six thousand more, he makes a point of stating, than Walker's *Critical Pronouncing Dictionary*, editions of which had recently been published in the United States—Worcester's dictionary claims to have added many new entry words never before included in a dictionary, quite a few of them drawn from a wide range of professions and sciences. It excludes, however, according to Worcester, many obsolete words and words of passing novelty that he thought might corrupt youth and mislead his general readership into thinking they were acceptable and had a future.

Webster complained to his son-in-law Fowler as early as November 1830 that although his dictionary contained about the same number of entry words as Worcester's, Worcester had inflated his list by including, in fact, far too many obsolete words like *abalienate, abative, abature, abearance,* and *abregation*—all inappropriate for a book that would find its way into classrooms. He repeated that charge in another letter to Fowler on April 20, 1831: "These are copied from dictionaries but are not in use and ought not to be inserted even in a larger work unless for antiquaries." Still, Worcester's book was lean and therefore inexpensive, another annoyance for Webster, who recognized, of course, that a lower price meant higher sales. Worcester's definitions were also dramatically concise, and they lacked etymology, but Worcester insisted they were as "comprehensive and exact as could be reasonably expected from the size of the volume." And cogent, even abrupt, they certainly are. The five definitions, for example, cited earlier (chapter 4, section 9; chapter 6, section 1) from Webster's 1828 quarto and Worcester and Goodrich's octavo revision, respectively, are even shorter in Worcester: *education*: "bringing up, nurture"; *marriage*: "The act of uniting a man and woman for life; wedlock; matrimony; *purpose*: "intention; design; effect"; *war*: "public contest; open hostility"; *woman*: "an adult female of the human race." Not weighed down by etymology, illustrative quotations, mystifying diacritics, and synonyms, their simplicity is just what young students needed.[2]

What Webster found especially galling about Worcester's book was its emphasis on pronunciation and its purported "comprehensive" range with so many citations from eighteenth-century orthoepists, implying that Webster's (among others) might be less so. Worcester did, and always would, particularly emphasize and document pronunciation, and in so doing demonstrated his undiminishing dependence on past English lexicographers. Whereas Webster went out of his way to distance himself from English lexicographers, maintaining that consulting them brought only chaos, not clarity, Worcester let them have major voices in his treatment of pronunciation, even providing tables comparing all of their pronunciations of words. Webster believed he had made a major contribution to the American language by lending his voice to the need for a national consensus about how words should be pronounced—to avoid the kind of widespread confusion that was rampant in Britain and found intolerable even in America. It was on that point that Webster, in the minds of readers, had the better idea: he was in favor of simplicity in the system of showing pronunciation, avoiding as much as possible these "ill-looking vocables," as the lexicographer Charles Richardson had put it, and a multitude of diacritical marks. Worcester, on the other hand, favored consulting numerous English orthoepists and providing a more complicated (at least for the reader) system of notations. And yet here was Worcester, Webster grumbled, writing that he had made pronunciation "his leading object" and given it "special attention": making a virtue of diversity, carefully recording variant pronunciations, and citing some twenty-six dictionaries and other sources for pronunciation in a discriminating and nuanced manner. Webster thought his rival's treatment of pronunciation was retrogressive. Worcester's system of notation, Webster protested, "goes to frustrate my plan

*Ĕc-clḗ-ṣĭ-ăṣ'tĭ-cụs, n. a book of the Apocrypha.
Ĕch-e-lŏn', (ĕsh-ē-lŏng') n. [Fr.] in military tactics, a movement of an army in the form of steps.
Ĕçh-ĭ-nāte', Ĕçh-ĭ-nā'tẹd, a. bristled; pointed.
E-chī'nụs, (ē-kī'nụs) n. a kind of sea-urchin; shell-fish.
Ĕçh'ọ, n. the reverberation of a sound.
Ĕçh'ọ, v. n. to resound; to be sounded back.
Ĕçh'ọ, (ŭk'kọ) v. a. to send back a voice.
Ĕ-chŏm'ē-tẹr, n. in music, a kind of scale, serving to measure the duration of sounds.
E-clair'cisse-ment, (ē-klȧr'sĭz-mĕnt) [ĕk-klȧr'sĭz-mĕnt, W. Ja.; ĕk-klĕr'sĭz-mĕnt, S.; ĕk-klȧr'sĭs-mŏn, P.; ĕk-klȧr'sĭz-mŏng, J.; ē-klȧr'sĭz-mäng, F.] n. [Fr.] explanation; the act of clearing up an affair.
Ĕ-clȧt', (ē-klä') [ē-klä', P. J. Ja. Wb.; ē-klȧw', S. W. E. F.] n. splendor; show; lustre.
Ec-lĕc'tĭc, a. selecting; choosing.
Ĕ-clipse', (ē-klĭps') n. obscuration; darkness.
Ĕ-clipse', v. a. to darken a luminary; to obscure.
Ĕ-clĭp'tĭc, n. a great circle of the sphere. [scure.
Ĕ-clĭp'tĭc, a. described by the ecliptic line.
Ĕc'lŏgue, (ĕk'lŏg) n. a pastoral poem.
*Ĕc-o-nŏm'ĭc, a. same as economical.
*Ĕc-o-nŏm'ĭ-cạl, [ĕk-o-nŏm'ē-kạl, W. J. F. Ja.; ē-ko-nŏm'ē-kạl, S. E.] a. frugal; thrifty.
*Ĕc-o-nŏm'ĭcs, n. household management.
Ĕ-cŏn'o-mĭst, n. one who is thrifty or frugal.
Ĕ-cŏn'o-mīze, v. a. to employ with economy.
Ĕ-cŏn'o-my, n. thrifty management; frugality; disposition of things; system of matter.
Ĕc-phō-nē'ṣĭs, n. in rhetoric, an exclamation.
Ĕc'stạ-ṣy, n. excessive joy; rapture; enthusiasm; a trance.
Ĕc-stăt'ĭc, Ĕc-stăt'ĭ-cạl, a. ravished; rapturous.
Ĕc-ụ-mĕn'ĭ-cạl, a. general; universal.
Ĕc'ụ-riẹ, (ĕk'kụ-rẹ) n. a stable for horses.
Ĕ-dā'cious, (ē-dā'shụs) a. eating; voracious.
Ĕ-dăç'ĭ-ty, n. voracity; ravenousness.
Ĕd'dẹr, n. wood on the top of fences.
Ĕd'dĭsh, n. a second crop of grass; aftermath.
Ĕd'dy, n. a contrary current; a whirlpool.
Ĕd'dy, a. whirling; moving circularly.
Ĕd'dy, v. n. to keep together in a whirl.
Ĕ-dēm-ạ-tōse', or Ĕ-dēm'ạ-toŭs, a. swelling.
Ē'dẹn, n. a garden; paradise.
Ĕ-dĕn-tā'tĭon, n. a pulling out of teeth.
Ĕdge, (ĕj) n. the sharp part of a blade; brink.
Ĕdge, (ĕj) v. a. to sharpen; to give an edge. [er.
Ĕdge, (ĕj) v. n. to move forward against any power.
Ĕdgẹd, (ĕjd, or ĕj'ẹd) p. a. sharp; not blunt.
Ĕdge'tōōl, n. a tool with a sharp edge.
Ĕdge'wīṣe, ad. in the direction of the edge.
Ĕdg'ing, n. a border; a fringe.
Ĕd'ĭ-ble, a. fit to be eaten; eatable.
Ē'dĭct, [ē'dĭkt, S. W. J. F. Ja. Wb.; ĕd'ĭkt, or ē'dĭkt, P.] n. a proclamation; order.
Ĕd-ĭ-fĭ-cā'tĭon, n. instruction; improvement.
Ĕd'ĭ-fĭce, (ĕd'ē-fĭs) n. a fabric; a building.
Ĕd-ĭ-fĭ''cĭạl, (ĕd-ē-fĭsh'ạl) a. relating to edifices.
Ĕd'ĭ-fĭ''ẹr, n. one who edifies.
Ĕd'ĭ-fy, (ĕd'ē-fī) v. a. to instruct; to improve.
Ē'dĭle, n. the title of a Roman magistrate.
Ĕd'ĭt, v. a. to superintend a publication.
Ĕ-dī''tĭon, (ē-dĭsh'ụn) n. publication of a book; the whole impression of a book; republication.
Ĕd-ĭ-tọr, n. one who superintends a publication.
Ĕd-ĭ-tō'rĭ-ạl, a. belonging to an editor.
Ĕd'ĭ-tọr-shĭp, n. the office and duty of an editor.
Ĕd'ụ-cāte, (ĕd'ū-kāt) [ĕd'ū-kāt, S. J. E. F.

Ja.; ĕd'jụ-kāt, W.] v. a. to bring up, as a child; to instruct.
Ĕd-ụ-cā'tĭon, n. a bringing up; nurture. [ern.

Ĕd'ĭ-tọr, n. one who superintends a publication.

Ĕ-dúc'tĭon, n. the act of bringing into view.
Ĕ-dŭl'cọ-rāte, v. a. to sweeten; to purify.
Ĕ-dŭl-cọ-rā'tĭon, n. the act of sweetening.
Ēek, (ēk) v. a. to supply. See Eke.
Ēel, (ēl) n. a serpentine, slimy fish.
Ē'ẹn, (ēn) ad. contracted from even. See Even.
Ĕf'fa-ble, a. expressible; utterable. [stroy.
Ĕf-fāce', v. a. to blot out; to strike out; to de-
Ĕf-fĕct', n. event produced; meaning; completion; reality.—pl. goods; movables.
Ĕf-fĕct', v. a. to bring to pass; to produce.
Ĕf-fĕct'ĭ-ble, a. performable; practicable.
Ĕf-fĕc'tĭon, n. a construction; a problem.
Ĕf-fĕc'tĭve, a. efficacious; efficient; useful.
Ĕf-fĕc'tĭve-ly, ad. powerfully; with effect.
Ĕf-fĕct'ụ-ạl, a. producing effect; efficacious.
Ĕf-fĕct'ụ-ạl-ly, ad. in an effectual manner.
Ĕf-fĕct'ụ-ạl-nĕss, n. quality of being effectual.
Ĕf-fĕct'ụ-āte, v. a. to bring to pass; to fulfill.
Ĕf-fĕm'ĭ-nạ-cy, n. softness; unmanly delicacy.
Ĕf-fĕm'ĭ-nạte, a. womanish; soft; voluptuous.
Ĕf-fĕm'ĭ-nāte, v. a. to make womanish.
Ĕf-fĕm'ĭ-nate-ly, ad. in an effeminate manner.
Ĕf-fĕm'ĭ-nate-nĕss, n. unmanly softness.
Ef-fĕn'dĭ, (ĕf-fĕn'dẹ) n. a Turkish officer.
Ĕf-fẹr-vĕsce', (ĕf-fẹr-vĕs') v. n. to generate heat by intestine motion; to bubble; to work.
Ĕf-fẹr-vĕs'çence, (ĕf-fẹr-vĕs'sẹns) n. a violent motion of a fluid, attended with heat.
Ĕf-fẹr-vĕs'çent, (ĕf-fẹr-vĕs') a. gently boiling or bubbling.
Ĕf-fēte', a. barren; worn out with age.
Ĕf-fĭ-cā'cious, (ĕf-fē-kā'shụs) a. effectual.
Ĕf-fĭ-cā'cious-ly, ad. effectually. [cious.
Ĕf-fĭ-cā'cious-nĕss, n. quality of being efficacious.
Ĕf'fĭ-cạ-cy, n. ability or power to produce effects.
Ĕf-fĭ''cĭence, (ĕf-fĭsh'yẹns) } n. act or power
Ĕf-fĭ''cĭen-cy, (ĕf-fĭsh'yẹn-sẹ) } of producing effects. [cause.
Ĕf-fĭ''cĭent, (ĕf-fĭsh'yẹnt) n. an agent; active
Ĕf-fĭ''cĭent, (ĕf-fĭsh'yẹnt) a. causing effects.
Ĕf-fĭ''cĭent-ly, (ĕf-fĭsh'yẹnt-lẹ) ad. effectively.
Ĕf'fĭ-ġy, n. image; likeness; representation.
Ĕf-flāte', v. a. to fill with the breath; to puff up.
Ĕf-flo-rĕsce', (ĕf-flọ-rĕs') v. n. to form dust or powder on the surface.
Ĕf-flo-rĕs'çence, } n. production of flowers; an
Ĕf-flo-rĕs'çen-cy, } eruption.
Ĕf-flo-rĕs'çent, a. shooting out in flowers, &c.
Ĕf'flụ-ençe, n. a flowing out.
Ĕf'flụ-ent, a. flowing out; issuing out of.
Ef-flū'vĭ-ạ, n. [L. pl. of Effluvium] small particles which are continually flying off from bodies.
Ef-flū'vĭ-ụm, n. [L.] vapor; a small particle.
Ĕf'flŭx, n. the act of flowing out; effusion.
Ĕf-flŭx'ĭon, (ĕf-flŭk'shụn) n. act of flowing out.
Ĕf'fŏrt, n. a struggle; strain; endeavor.
Ĕf-fŏs'sĭon, (ĕf-fŏsh'ụn) n. act of digging up.
Ĕf-frŏn'tẹr-y, n. boldness; impudence.
Ĕf-fŭlge', v. n. to send forth lustre.
Ĕf-fŭl'ġence, n. lustre; brightness.
Ĕf-fŭl'ġent, a. shining; bright; luminous.
Ĕf-fū-mạ-bĭl'ĭ-ty, n. evaporation.
Ĕf-fūṣe', v. a. to pour out; to spill; to shed.
Ĕf-fū'sĭon, (ĕf-fū'zhụn) n. a pouring out; waste.
Ĕf-fū'sĭve, a. pouring out; dispersing.

mīen, sȋr; mȯve, nör, sŏn; bŭll, bür, rûle.—Ç, Ġ, ç, ġ, soft; Ⅽ, Ḡ, ç, ġ, hard. ṣ as z; x as gz;—this.

FIGURE 8. A sample page from Worcester's 1830 dictionary, which favored a more complicated system of notations than Webster's dictionaries provided. Detail: The definition of *editor* is significantly shorter than in Webster's 1828 dictionary. Courtesy of Indiana State University Special Collections, Cordell Collection of Dictionaries.

of uniformity": one of his own "chief objects had been to banish complicated schemes of notation. . . ." Worcester's galaxy of past orthoepists, on the other hand, amounted to a survey of past British lexicography: Sheridan, Walker, Perry, Jones, Bailey, Johnson, Kenrick, Entick, Nares, and many others, "besides our own countryman Dr. Webster." The battle lines between the two men were being drawn, and Webster was drawing them.[3]

3

For several years after Worcester's dictionary appeared, Webster was distracted by the copyright bill passing through Congress and the completion of his new, revised edition of the Bible (based on the King James Version), *The Holy Bible, Containing the Old and New Testaments, in the Common Version with Amendments of the Language* (1833). He set out chiefly to banish words and phrases he thought were offensive, especially to youth and in polite company: "phrases very offensive to delicacy, and even to decency." "Language which cannot be uttered in company without a violation of decorum or the rules of good breeding," he writes, "exposes the scriptures to the scoffs of unbelievers, impairs their authority, and multiplies or confirms the enemies of our holy religion." *Fornication* becomes *lewdness*, for example; *putrefy* becomes *offensive; stink* is replaced by *odious* (which is now an adjective), *sucked* by *nursed*; and *whore* by *lewd woman*. In certain places, he seems to have had something against the word *womb*, for "took me out of the womb" (Psalms 22) becomes "brought me forth into life"; and "grow in the womb" becomes simply "conception" (Ecclesiastes 11); elsewhere, he left the word alone. Along the same lines, "the young one that cometh out from between her feet" is simplified to, "her own offspring." Such changes, known as the bowdlerization of a text, were all the rage in early-nineteenth-century America, especially after the appearance of *The Family Shakespeare*, an expurgated edition edited by Henrietta Maria Bowdler and long attributed to her brother, Thomas Bowdler, in 1807. Webster's own distaste for Shakespeare's "vulgar" language and his care to exclude it from his dictionaries was in step with his edition of the Bible and, more generally, this kind of policing of the language.

With this sort of attention to the Bible, Webster was also in step with the early-nineteenth-century Protestant evangelical "Second Great Awakening" and the religious landscape of the country. The insightful French observer of American manners and thought, Alexis de Tocqueville, was especially struck by this in his travels in America. He writes in *Democracy in America* (1835; chap. 17), "In the United States the sovereign authority is religious. . . . [T]here is no country in the world where the Christian religion retains a greater influence over the souls of men than in America." Whether or not it was true, as he claims, that "Americans pursue a peculiar form of worship, from habit more than from conviction," the centrality of religion to American culture was abundantly clear to both the foreign visitor and to Americans.

But for Webster his biblical detour was more than purely a religious experience. While he felt it was the culmination of his religious conversion twenty-five years earlier, he also envisioned a clear link between this new work on the Bible and his lifelong efforts in behalf of the American language: both sought to educate and inform and were written for a public seeking authority. The dictionary for Webster was in effect a "Bible," meant for an American public that read dictionaries for all sorts of wisdom and knowledge in a nation given to "lexicographicolatry" (meaning the reverence for dictionary authority that verges on idolatry).[4] Indeed, to some degree the dictionary today still is often thought of as a secular counterpart to the Bible, as one dictionary historian, Lynda Mugglestone, recently frames it: "[P]opular opinion tends to invest the word of the lexicographer with some of the same power as the Word of God—so much so that the dictionary and the Bible are often perceived as twin and (equally incontestable) sources of authority, one secular and the other divine. . . ." "The interplay between the pen and the pulpit," in another critic's words, that was an instinctual and deep-rooted characteristic of Webster's intellect, was of course far more common in his day than it is now: "In a world where men of letters were often also men of the cloth . . . it can be no surprise that the wordbooks acquired (and still retain for many today) a quality of Holy Writ . . . especially when the Bible was one of the main reasons for learning to read."[5]

Webster at first did not want to respond to Worcester's new dictionary. He lacked health, concentration, will, and (he believed) time to bother about it except to write disgruntled letters to family and friends. "If the public most approve of my plan which is altogether more simple than his," he wrote to Fowler, "then his notations will operate against his book." Rather loftily, Webster asked, "When will *truths*, the sole object of learning, triumph over custom and prejudice?" He was convinced that Worcester "has borrowed much from my dictionary," which was conduct "not less dishonourable nor immoral because it is common." It is odd that with such a comment he could overlook his own heavy borrowing from Johnson.[6]

A few months later, after the passage of the copyright bill and his return to New Haven from Washington, Webster was warming himself into a more proactive and militant frame of mind. The following April in a letter to Fowler he detailed several areas where he maintained Worcester had erred egregiously—a sign that he might have been preparing himself to make his "democratic" case to the general public:

—Introduction of words "not in use and some never used in our language": Some of these that Worcester lists were and remain archaic; others were not and exist today in our lexicon, such as *abactor, abalienate, abature, abregate.*

—Insertion of Latin and Greek words that were in Webster's view "improper," not belonging in a dictionary about common usage: "[T]he insertion of Greek and Latin names in a small book for non-English schools appears to me useless—a great part of them are never seen by English readers. But of this every man will judge for himself." Also, many of Worcester's technical words such as *acidulae, acroteria, agger, albugo, Alguazil, anamorphosis,* and *apogacum* do not belong in school, or in any but technical, dictionaries: "If the work is intended to contain all technical words, it is deficient in many thousands—if not, there is no more reason for inserting these and hundreds of others, than there would be to take all the technical words in *all* the sciences."

—"Omission of most of the participles of common English words," which every reader wants, in order to accommodate words that only "merely English" readers want, such as *adapting, adding, assessing, congregating, purifying,* and *travelling,* among many hundreds, all of which are included in Webster's 1828 quarto and none of which are in Worcester's *Comprehensive* (1830). Worcester states in his preface that the exception to his rule was participles of irregular verbs.

—"Mistakes in definition."

—Inclusion of words that "dandies use, and which are condemned": "Thus both *suit* and *suite* are inserted—the same word in fact, but differently pronounced."

—Worcester's "difficult" and largely "useless" system of notation is extremely confusing to young people: "The mode of notation is very bad. It is difficult and a great part of it entirely useless. . . . Who wants a mark *under a* [in] the first letter [of] *abandon* or *over a* in the second syllable? . . . One of my chief objects is to banish the complicated schemes of notation of the British [orthoepists]. And in the British notices of my dictionary . . . my scheme is applauded."

He adds that he regrets consenting, doubtless under pressure, to the insertion of "different modes of pronouncing many words" "in my octavo," "which is used by adults," but "Worcester's method must be perplexing both to teachers and pupils, and it tends to keep the pronunciation forever unsettled"; it also strikes a blow against his mission of a uniform language for a unified nation. Webster does present pronunciation differently in his own school dictionary, more simply and less cluttered with diacritical marks.[7]

This would not be the last time Worcester was attacked for parading the English orthoepists throughout his dictionaries. It was an argument that was bound to resonate with the average reader and in the classroom, especially in "common," or public, schools.

4

Once he had completed his edition of the Bible in 1833, and more than four years after Worcester had debuted his own dictionary, Webster's simmering hostility erupted. At that time, his anger at Worcester, Goodrich, Converse, Cobb, Walker, Johnson, and sometimes seemingly all the world might have cooled had it not been for his continuing financial distress and fear he was being wangled out of the dictionary market. An article appeared in the November 26, 1834, issue of the *Worcester Palladium* newspaper (named for the Massachusetts city of publication and having nothing to do with Joseph Worcester), under the heading "Webster's Dictionary," ostensibly written by the newspaper's editor but most likely written by Webster himself, accusing Worcester of "gross plagiarism" in his dictionary. The misprints in the piece suggest it might have been rushed into print. The article resembles advertising propaganda, but it is more venal than that. It is a nasty, personal attack maligning Worcester as a "common thief." In it, Webster is cast in the role of the famed and deserving but financially unrewarded redeemer of the language.

Webster's *Palladium* article marks the first time the quarrels between the two men had broken out into a public forum, the opening shot in the very public and confrontational dictionary and language wars between the two of them that lasted well beyond Webster's death. It alerts the public to Worcester's alleged methods and thefts, the first part of which needs to be quoted for a full appreciation of its acrid content:

> A gross plagiarism has been committed by Mr. J. E. Worcester on the literary property of Noah Webster Esq. It is well known that Mr. Webster has spent a life, which is now somewhat advanced, in writing a dictionary of the English language, which he published in 1828, in two quarto volumes. Three abridgments have since been made; one in an octavo form—and two still smaller, for families and primary schools. To aid in the drudgery of producing these abridgments, Mr. Webster employed Mr. Worcester who, after becoming acquainted with Mr. Webster's plan, immediately set about appropriating to his own benefit the valuable labors, acquisitions, and productions of Mr. Webster. He has since published a dictionary, which is a very close imitation of Webster's; and which, we regret to learn, has been introduced into many of the primary schools of the country. We regret this, because the public, inadvertently, do an act of great injustice to a man who has rendered the country an invaluable service, and ought to recieve [receive] the full benefit of his labors.

The article continues by returning to the theme of copyright: "If we had a statute which could fix its grasp on those who pilfer the products of the mind, as readily as our laws embrace the common thief, Mr. Worcester would hardly escape with a light mulct. At all events, before people buy his wares, they would do well to inquire how he came by them." The personal emotion in this passage, its detail and tone of self-pity and arrogance over Worcester's alleged effrontery, and its insulting phrasing were so poorly disguised that readers familiar with Webster's writings or the man himself might easily have identified him as its author, not some editor prevailed upon to publish it as written by himself.[8]

After that opening salvo, the article parades the virtues of Webster's quarto, the chief theme of which (as in many of Webster's letters during these years) was that since Webster had done so much work and spent so much of his money on the dictionary, he had a unique and indisputable claim on "the patronage of Americans": "His works have been produced only by immense labor, expense, and personal sacrifice; indefatigable application to all the means which Europe, as well as America, could furnish for a perfect Dictionary of our language. . . . [A]nd should literary pilferers rob him of his pecuniary rights, they cannot rob him of his well-earned fame." In both this attack and those that soon followed in the ensuing exchanges in the *Palladium*, Webster claims not merely a proprietary stake in the dictionary market but also that he was, as so often in the past, the hapless victim of conspiracy, exploitation, and misrepresentation. Plagiarism, at any rate, was at best a tenuous and difficult-to-prove accusation when talking about dictionaries.[9]

One wonders if at times like this he might have recalled his own remark a year earlier about the impression that something Samuel Johnson had written in the *Rambler* had made upon him in his youth: "Dr. Johnson well observes that to fear [Johnson wrote "dread"] no eye, to suspect no tongue is the great prerogative of innocence, an exemption granted only to invariable virtue. This remark of Dr. Johnson I committed to memory fifty-five years ago; it has had no inconsiderable influence in regulating my moral conduct."[10]

The article was immediately countered, not by Worcester, who had not yet seen it, but by his friend Sidney Willard, the Hancock Professor of Hebrew and Other Oriental Languages at Harvard. Willard was the first to tell Worcester about it. Willard had struck at Webster before with an article in the *North American Review* in 1817, retaliating against Webster's ill-natured "Letter" to John Pickering on the subject of Americanisms. More than a decade after Webster's defamatory article appeared, Worcester told how Willard's intervention came about: "At this time the *Christian Register*, published in Boston, was edited by Professor Sidney Willard, who happened to be as well acquainted with my lexicographical labors, and the circumstances relating to them, as almost any gentleman in the community; and he answered this (as he styled it) 'ferocious attack' in such a manner as he thought proper, before I had any knowledge that such an assault had been made." Among his several arguments and refutations, Willard highlighted what he called Worcester's practical, sane approach to lexicography: he never violated linguistic custom or prevalent usage, which determine "the laws of a language," in the interest of innovation, speculation, persona, political and religious ideology, or whatever other distorting personal agenda might steal across a lexicographer's radar. What was at stake here was Worcester's credibility, which Willard chose to defend not only by elaborating Worcester's personal and professional credibility and his solidity as a scholar but also by casting an oblique light on Webster's excesses.[11]

Worcester was not temperamentally suited to public controversies in the press. This letter, however, infuriated him. He could not remain silent. His response appeared in the *Palladium* on December 10. He begins by giving the editor the benefit of the doubt: "As you, Mr. Editor, are unknown to me, I am bound to believe that you were not aware that you were publishing a statement that is grossly false, but that you were informed that it was true. . . ." He quickly puts the record straight: "I, however, know it and declare it to be utterly false, and I have ample means of proving it to be so, before any impartial tribunal." With a sharp look in the direction of Webster, he adds, "I know not on whose evidence you have relied, but I do know that whoever has made you believe the truth of the statement has grossly imposed on you." He then tells the public with what authority and background he had come to write his own dictionary. He assures readers that he has no need or incentive to plagiarize Webster: "So far from appropriating the labors of Dr. Webster to my own use, I challenge any one to enumerate a dozen words in my Dictionary for which I cannot readily give other authorities than Dr. Webster, or to show that with respect to . . . orthography, or pronunciation of a dozen words, I have been governed solely or chiefly by his authority." On the contrary, "I have the most extensive collection of works on English Lexicography that I know of in the possession of any individual, or in any single library; and I have been for a good while attentive to this sort of literature. This I say, not from ostentation, but to show that in preparing such a work as I have published, I have little occasion to be indebted to Dr. Webster." In any case, his dictionary is "far from being 'a close imitation' of Dr. Webster's. It differs widely in . . . the selection of words, and in the orthography of a considerable number of words; the notation is entirely different; and the pronunciation is treated in a very different manner." He insists he never had laid eyes on the two "smaller" school dictionaries of Webster's before his book was published, one of which, moreover, was published just before his dictionary and one in 1833, no fewer than three years afterward. If called upon, he has "ample means of showing that I came as lawfully by my materials as Dr. Webster did by his." Worcester does not in this instance actually call Webster a liar or attack his dictionary, or use the occasion to advertise his own. He leaves it to Webster to decide if he was going to wade more deeply into such perilous waters.[12]

He did not have long to wait for an answer. One week later, on December 17, Webster replied in the *Palladium* with a short note to the editor stating that back in March 1831 he had asked Worcester outright whether he had borrowed "many" definitions and words from his dictionary, to which Worcester had replied on March 25, "not many." That was the opening Webster had been looking for. He interpreted it as an admission of guilt, snidely adding that Worcester's dictionary would have been "less defective and more correct" if he had borrowed more. Oddly, perhaps showing his age somewhat, or his lack of ready access to dictionaries in order to check the accuracy of his claims, Webster maintained there was no question Worcester had borrowed some words and definitions from him because these were not to be found in other dictionaries. In fact, virtually all of them could be found in several other dictionaries. Perhaps Worcester thought the charge was not worth dignifying with an answer, but those who were familiar with Webster's disposition could have told him that more of this same sort of splenetic attack was bound to follow.[13]

Worcester's Christmas cheer—what was left of it after this flare-up—surely was spoiled on December 24 by another editorial attack in the *Palladium*. It opens with a glancing reference to Sidney Willard and others from "the charmed circle of Harvard College" who predictably might rise to Worcester's defense. The editorial then recklessly asserts that because Worcester had published his dictionary shortly after completing Goodrich's octavo revision, he "undoubtedly" had pilfered some twenty-one words that it alleges were not to be found in any other dictionaries. Since this list was compiled from only "a cursory review" of Worcester's dictionary, the editorial maintains, there had to be many more besides. It also accuses Worcester of incompleteness because of the many words in Webster's tome that are not in his dictionary. The editorial concludes by proclaiming that Webster's dictionary is now a "standard work," widely used by members of Congress ("not always the best judges," it concedes), and that "the current of public opinion is in its favor." It assures readers it has "not a particle of personal interest" in whose dictionary is better or which will ultimately be accepted as the nation's "standard." What does concern the author of the editorial is "that the products of the mind, which have been garnered up with unwearied and long-continued toil, should be pillaged and appropriated to their own use by 'eleventh-hour' laborers."[14]

5

Webster came out into the open with a signed letter in the *Palladium* on January 25, 1835, addressed directly to Worcester. In it, he expands the list of 21 words in the Christmas editorial to 121, "which *prima facie* would seem to have been taken from my dictionary." This is only a random collection, he emphasizes, drawn from less than one-tenth of Worcester's book—at that rate there would be well over one thousand borrowings in the entire work. His list includes *muskrat, obsidian, outlay, prayerful, prayerless, repealable, rock-crystal, safety-valve, savings-bank, semiannual, slump, souvenier, sparse, spinning-jenny, spry, squirm, succotash, tirade, tomato, volcanist, waffle*, and *wilt*. Then comes the challenge: "to state in what other dictionary except mine, you found the foregoing words, and how many or which you borrowed from mine." That challenge was just what Worcester wanted to hear. It gave him an opening to confront Webster directly and refute these accusations once and for all. His reply begins with the observation that as a lawyer Webster ought to know the burden of proof rests with the accuser, not the accused. Nonetheless, he will respond to Webster's "unreasonable" demand "cheerfully" and "uprightly and faithfully" even in the face of his slander. Hinting that Webster has been lurking in the shadows of the *Palladium*'s editorials, he is "gratified" that he has finally broken cover: "[T]hough I have no love of contention, yet if I must be dragged into a newspaper controversy in defence of myself in this matter, I should prefer that, of all men in the world, it should be with yourself, writing under your own name."[15]

Webster would prove to be an easy target because he was less familiar with other dictionaries than the author of a dictionary ought to have been. Worcester devotes his entire letter to explaining the sources of his word list, and although he does it politely, he also implies Webster's incompetence and lapse in concentration:

> You evidently supposed, Sir, that none of the words in your list were to be found in any Dictionary that was published before the appearance of your own work; but I confess I am somewhat surprised at this fact, inasmuch as, from your reputation as a lexicographer, it might naturally be supposed that you were extensively acquainted with works of this sort, and especially with the works which are so well known to all

persons who have any just pretensions to much knowledge of this kind of literature, as are the several publications which I shall name.

"I shall not go out of my own library," he adds, "or mention any work that I was not in the habit of consulting in preparing my Dictionary."

He informs Webster (and the public) that of the allegedly purloined entry words he found twenty-one in Nathan Bailey's *Dictionarium Britannicum* (1730), thirty-five in John Ash's *New and Complete Dictionary of the English Language* (1775), thirty-seven in his own edition of *Todd-Johnson* ("published before the appearance of yours"), twenty-one in Pickering's *Vocabulary* (1816), and about sixty in the *Encyclopedia Americana* and Sir David Brewster's *New Edinburgh Encyclopaedia* (1807–30) combined. This is not counting the entry words he found in no fewer than fifty other English dictionaries and glossaries in his library. He goes on: "Of your one hundred and twenty-one words, six or seven are not to be found, so far as I can discover, in your Quarto Dictionary, and one of them is one of those three thousand words which are contained in Todd's Johnson's Dictionary, but are not to be found in your great work, and which were inserted by me in the octavo abridgment of your Dictionary."

It is as logical to conclude from all this, Worcester tells Webster, "that you have not seen, or at least have not carefully examined, many British Dictionaries, as it would [be] to infer, with respect to a list of words, that because you do not know of their existence in British Dictionaries, they must, therefore, have been taken from yours; for it appears sufficiently evident that there may be words in British Dictionaries that you are not aware of." Moreover, since Webster seems to have overlooked other sources as well, "it would not appear very wonderful, if I were able to find the few remaining words without any assistance from your labors." On top of that, in his dictionary Webster has cited authorities for only 39 of his 121 words, while "I can, without going out of my own library, furnish authorities, in all cases different from yours, for upwards of a hundred of them"—and that included American terms and expressions, and words describing American life, such as *chowder, clapboard, Congregationalist, grandjury, griddle, land-office, moccason* (i.e., *moccasin*), *pappoose* (i.e., *papoose*), *spring-jenny*, and *winter-kill*.

No entry word is Webster's exclusive property, Worcester continues, simply because it appears only in his dictionary; it belongs "to all who write and speak the language, to be used by them on all proper occasions." He gives as an example in Webster's list, *semi-annual,* not found in any other dictionary, "yet you cannot doubt that I was familiar with this word before your Dictionary was published; and as I have had occasion to use it repeatedly in my other publications, I thought myself authorized to insert it also in my Dictionary." Only the words that Webster has himself coined or re-spelled, like *canail, ieland,* and *nightmar,* is he entitled to call his own, but that is no problem, Worcester cannot resist saying with—one imagines—a wry smile at Webster's spelling reforms, for "it has been my intention scrupulously to avoid them, as being your own property . . . being willing you should for ever have the entire and exclusive use of them." As for words in his dictionary but not Webster's, Webster is welcome to slip them into his dictionary any time he wishes, since they all have "the sanction of respectable usage." Worcester then ends by asking a loaded question, which he puts in italics: Would Webster "*be so good as to inform me whether the charges against me in the Worcester Palladium were occasioned by any statements made by you, or whether you had ever made, or are now prepared to make, any such statements.*" In the middle of all this, Worcester noticed his eyesight had begun to fail him, which was aggravated by the tense and pressured effort to defend himself. It was out of character for him to challenge an author like this in the public press, and he could only hope that his letter ended the matter.

Webster was never a man to back off from a fight. The feisty seventy-six-year-old struck back quickly just a week later. The entry words seemed to have led to an embarrassing dead end, so he returns to Worcester's other alleged thefts, his definitions, and to his notations, which he maintained were bound to "unsettle the pronunciation, which in this country [unlike in Britain], has long been undisputed"—an astonishing contention. All of this "shows how improper it was for you to meddle with my books"—that is, in editing the octavo. Five years of pent-up resentment over that octavo now surface very publicly as he makes a pitch to win the public's emotional sympathy with his stock recitation of how hard he had worked: "My quarto Dictionary cost me about *twenty years labor and twenty thousand* dollars. For this labor and such an expense I could never receive remuneration, had the market been left open.—How unkind then was it for you, who had been intrusted with the task of making an abridgment, and been well rewarded for it, to sit down and introduce some of my improvements into a book of your own compilation. . . . Now, Sir, rather than treat you in this manner, I would beg my bread." He defends his pronunciation and spelling reforms, calling himself, not Worcester, the true American lexicographer with a "duty" to perform: "I have thought and I still think it the duty of the lexicographer [to] correct such palpable mistakes, and not to follow implicitly the English books. Whether the corrections shall be received or not I shall be satisfied that I have done my duty." "If, in regard to the use you have made of my books, in your compilation," he finishes sarcastically, "your mind is quite at ease, long may you enjoy it."[16]

Webster had conjured up new charges in this last letter that Worcester could not ignore. In March, four long months after this controversy first rocked his scholarly and tranquil life, Worcester took the fight again to his antagonist. He begins by reminding readers that when he first joined this quarrel he stated openly he had nothing to fear from being "thoroughly investigated" and that since then he has "not met with an individual who has intimated an opinion that any thing wrong has been proved against me." In a way, he notes, that is troubling, because it suggests "there must be something far from right elsewhere." It bears thinking about because "it is better to suffer wrong than to do wrong," and he feels that something in the Webster camp—or perhaps in Webster's mind—must be amiss. He dares not speculate.

Still, he is not going to suffer in silence. Webster, he explains, had leveled three new charges against him: (1) he had used Webster's definitions for words found in other dictionaries; (2) he had borrowed Webster's rules of orthography; and (3) on every page of his book he had cited Webster's authority on pronunciation. As for the first two, they are charges made "without proof," and he warns Webster that any further efforts to substantiate them "will be found as ineffectual as have been similar attempts which have been made." Any cursory look at his dictionary will reveal that he had made ample use of Johnson and Walker but had "little occasion to be indebted to you for rules or orthography which I adopted." There is abundant evidence that, for better or for worse, "I decided independently of your authority." He had not referred to Webster on every page but had indeed done so "in a great part of the pages" along with a long line of the most eminent English orthoepists—Sheridan, Walker, Entick, Sir William Jones, and William Perry, to name but a few: "I thought it was treating you with respect to do so, and never dreamed it would displease you. If I had known that you would rather be entirely omitted, I should have been inclined to act accordingly."[17]

Worcester could be forgiven for thinking again that Webster was damning him both for at times following his rules of pronunciation and for ignoring them and thus "unsettling" the language by citing English authorities. For Webster to complain that Worcester had cited him mainly because he might in subsequent editions change his mind about the orthography and orthoepy is curiously inept. Webster had already been witheringly criticized for his unreliable orthography, notwithstanding his valued contribution to the spelling reform of certain classes of words. The obstacle Worcester could never surmount, however, nor perhaps ever fully understand, was that Webster was not inclined to allow his status in America to be eclipsed even partially by sharing the spotlight with the leading lexicographers and linguists in the history of the English language. That most of them were English did not help matters. That obsessiveness perhaps was the elusive key to Webster's complex persona that Worcester sensed was "far from right."

Before dropping the subject for what he hoped was the last time, Worcester returns to his blunt, unanswered question in his previous letter: Had Webster "occasioned" the editorial remarks in the *Palladium* that actually started this dictionary war? Webster had chosen "to dodge the question," and at the same time was appealing "to the public sympathy under the pretense of having been injured."

Needing desperately to have the last word, Webster sent one more tired short letter, more like a note, to the *Palladium*, but not to answer that question. Instead, he repeats his charge about the definitions, using the word *clapboard* as an example. Webster maintains he was the first to include that entry word, that it does not appear in any previous dictionary, either in America or England. Worcester could easily have replied, but did not, that he got the word from Pickering's *Vocabulary*, who took it from Webster's *Compendious Dictionary*. He would have had more trouble refuting Webster's assertion that he (Worcester) copied the word's definition verbatim from Webster. Webster's comparison of his definition, "a thin narrow board for covering houses," with Worcester's, "a thin narrow-board for covering houses," does suggest that Worcester took the definition verbatim from Webster. But it could be equally argued that since a clapboard is indeed a narrow piece of wood used to cover houses, those are the words, in that order, anyone might reasonably have used in a definition. Johnson had written in *Rambler* no. 143, "all definitions of the same thing must be nearly the same." *Clapboard*, in fact, does illustrate the difficulty in tracing borrowings from dictionary to dictionary, and that it is futile and senseless to accuse fellow lexicographers of excessive types of borrowing when any single dictionary historically is a blend of several other dictionaries.[18]

Like most newspaper controversies, the *Palladium* skirmish concluded without either man emerging as a clear winner. And like many sensationalist newspaper controversies stirred up by journalists to increase their circulation, it did little more than damage the reputations of both Worcester and Webster. It commanded a good deal of attention among the literati, university professors, the cultured classes, and anyone interested in the progress of the language and role of dictionaries in the young nation, but it was not particularly edifying. For Worcester it was a huge distraction; for Webster, another convenient way to strike out at those who presumed to compete with him, have the temerity to question his destiny as America's language savior, or disagree with his reforms and his view of the history of the English language.

One major beneficial effect of the controversy, however, was that the journalistic publicity of this skirmish inevitably raised the American consciousness of the role lexicographers were beginning to play in American society. While the *Palladium* quarrel itself did not reveal much about the authority of dictionaries per se in America in 1834–35—how they related to usage, for example, or what it meant, or could mean, for a dictionary to be the "standard" for a country in the lexicographical areas of spelling, pronunciation, etymology, and meaning, or in definitions of what it meant to be an American—it alerted the American public to the complicated identity and role of the individual lexicographers. That happened in these pages of the *Palladium* for the first time in a forceful, personal, psychologically revealing manner. These lexicographers were fighting, not about commercial gain but over how they saw themselves, and wished the public to see them, as serving the public. And the intensity of the controversy enabled the public to recognize the importance to the lexicographers, and to itself, of what was involved and why the issues raised mattered so much to everyone. Dictionaries belonged to everyone, and what they contained was important to society. Perhaps the key phrase in the heated exchange was Worcester's, when he said that no entry word belongs to any one lexicographer, or (by implication) to one part of society more than another, or to one religion, or to one educational background: the language *"belongs to all who write and speak the language."* Worcester is reminding the public that the work of a lexicographer, private, lonely, and personal as it is, is the property of everyone. From these points of view, the subtext of the *Palladium* exchange is ultimately about democracy. Something the English philosopher Edmund Burke remarked to Lord Berkeley in the late eighteenth century as he introduced "Elocution [John] Walker" to him, strikes this same universal note: "Mr. Walker, whom not to know . . . would argue want of knowledge of the harmonies, cadences, and proprieties of our language." The *Palladium* controversy did not just open the first significant chapter of the dictionary wars between two men; it revealed to the public there were issues to be considered in the future that had not occurred to them so clearly before.[19]

6

Throughout the 1830s in Cambridge, Worcester quietly got on with his dictionaries and other reference works. The *Palladium* controversy had disturbed him and thrown him somewhat off balance, but it had not deterred him. He was in the race to stay. Just a few months after the *Palladium* clash, he came out with his *Elementary Dictionary for the Common Schools with Pronouncing Vocabularies of Classical, Scripture, and Modern Geographical Names* (1835; 2nd ed., 1843). It was a bold move by Worcester in a school market that Webster had sought to dominate. The *Elementary Dictionary* was a small (duodecimo), condensed version of his *Comprehensive Dictionary* in 350 pages and with forty-four thousand entry words, published by the Boston firm Jenks and Palmer. Jenks later would play his part in the fierce dictionary war that flared up between publishers. In his preface, Worcester explains how he had achieved such a compact book:

> This work is substantially a reduced form of the "Comprehensive Dictionary," and it has been brought to its present size by abridging a part of the definitions, by not retaining the notices of synonyms, and the various modes of pronunciation of words differently pronounced with their authorities annexed, and by the omission of most of such words as are obsolete or very rarely used, of many technical terms, and of some words from foreign languages. But notwithstanding these omissions,

it contains a very full vocabulary of the common and well-authorized words of the language.[20]

The book was inexpensive; sold well, as had most of his previous scholarship; and was reprinted in several editions until the 1850s. He also continued his editorship of the *American Almanac and Repository of Useful Knowledge*, a popular annual founded in 1830 by his friend and president of Harvard, Jared Sparks.

Worcester remained a wealthy and quiet bachelor during these years, eventually moving in the late 1830s to large rented rooms in the three-story Craigie "mansion" (built in 1759 and now the Longfellow House) on Brattle Street in Cambridge. Brattle Street was the handsome and expensive street known as "Tory Row" because most of the houses on the street before the Revolutionary War had been owned by British Loyalists forced to leave the country. The Craigie house had already become famous because George Washington adopted it as his headquarters during the Siege of Boston in 1775. The owner of the house, Andrew Craigie, the first apothecary general of the American army, had died in 1819, leaving his wife in debt and compelled to take in boarders.

When Worcester moved into the house, another tenant was the poet Henry Wadsworth Longfellow, then a recent widower who had taken up the position at Harvard of Smith Professor of Modern Languages and Belles Lettres. In a journal recording his experiences at Craigie House, Longfellow remembered when Worcester arrived: "The next tenant of the vacant rooms was Mr. Worcester the geographer and lexicographer, who [later] purchased an undivided quarter of the estate—a tall, lean, crooked man, very slow of speech. He never gave a direct answer to any question put to him. He was then a forlorn bachelor, but has since been married and built himself a house near the island. At Mrs. Craigie's death in 1841 he became the chief tenant of the house and lands. He was fond of gardening and took pride in pears and wring-necked squashes." Longfellow also mentioned that when some poplar trees along Brattle Street showed some signs of dying, Worcester had them pruned so severely that they all died. Other boarders from time to time included three presidents of Harvard—Jared Sparks, Edward Everett, and Josiah Quincy—so in Craigie House Worcester found himself living more closely within the world of the higher reaches of Harvard.[21]

FIGURE 9. Longfellow House, Brattle Street, Cambridge, Massachusetts. Joseph Emerson Worcester and Henry Wadsworth Longfellow were fellow boarders in the house until the 1840s, when Longfellow purchased the house and Worcester built his own grand house next door. Worcester sometimes complained mildly about his neighbor's noisy children. Courtesy of National Park Service, Longfellow House–Washington's Headquarters, National Historic Site.

In 1841, his life changed: at the age of fifty-seven, the "forlorn bachelor," as Longfellow called him, married Amy Elizabeth McKean, thirty-nine-year-old daughter of the late Boylston Professor of Rhetoric, Oratory, and Elocution at Harvard, Joseph McKean, the founder of Harvard's exclusive Porcellian Club. Amy Elizabeth and her father had been living in Fay House, which he owned, down the road from Craigie House, which later became part of Radcliffe College. When McKean died in Havana in 1818, where he had fled for his health, Amy Elizabeth had continued to live in Fay House for several years, teaching and administering a school in the building. Worcester had courted her for six years, getting to know her perhaps at popular social evenings at Fay House attended by several members of the Harvard faculty like Edward Everett and Longfellow and others, including Oliver Wendell Holmes and James Russell Lowell.

"My friend and fellow lodger Mr. Worcester is about making a rush into the Elysian Fields of matrimony," Longfellow wrote, "thereby illustrating the great doctrine of the Perseverance of the Saints. He has been for six years looking over that fence with longing eyes; and has at last cleared the ditch at a leap, and to all appearances is revelling in clover."[22] With a new wife, Worcester needed to leave Craigie House, so when the Craigie land came up for sale, he bought thirty-two acres of it, including a large adjacent plot on the west side of the house containing a long, picturesque pond, which because of his presence there came to be known by its local name, Dictionary Lake. He immediately began to build his "mansion," a grand, sprawling house—too big, in fact, for just him and his wife—in a modified Greek Revival style. He and Amy Elizabeth continued to rent their quarters in Craigie House until their house was completed. Longfellow's new father-in-law, Nathan Appleton, meanwhile purchased and gave Craigie House to Longfellow. His wife, Fanny Appleton, wrote in May 1844, the "Worcester family left us in complete possession, with rooms nicely cleaned, and uncarpeted stairs and entries." Worcester and his bride lived in their new home for the rest of their lives.[23]

Life, therefore, was looking better than ever to Worcester. Married life and his new house clearly suited him. Amy Elizabeth was ready and willing to help him with his work in any way she could. He felt settled as never before and was about to enter a highly productive stage in his professional life as an author and editor. In less than two years after he and Amy Elizabeth moved into their "mansion," he would publish the most important dictionary of English in either America or England since Webster's first 1828 edition.

9

Webster's Decline

Webster had trouble moving on. Throughout the 1830s, he continued to fume about how the competition and his detractors had dimmed his star as a lexicographer and reduced the income from his decades of hard work. His large quarto dictionary never sold much, but his speller sold phenomenally well, and the Goodrich/Worcester octavo continued modestly to outsell Worcester's *Comprehensive Pronouncing and Explanatory Dictionary* in the United States—except in regional markets such as metropolitan Boston. He realized no income from the octavo, however, because Goodrich got it all. He was unable to rid himself of the feeling he was essentially an outsider who had to scrap for every advantage and recognition. What he felt he needed more than anything else, apart from money, was to get back in the game, to prepare a new edition of the quarto that would contain all the revisions and corrections he knew he had to make. Publishers were hard to find, however, and the money for it was scarce.

He was approaching eighty and, if we are to believe his letters, his health was worsening. He does not sound sprightly in this description of himself he provided his daughter Harriet in November 1835: "I have an irregular action of the heart which I have experienced more or less ever since I was twenty; but which is more troublesome now than formerly. Sometimes it gives me inconvenience to walk any distance; but when I am quiet, I am at ease. It is probably connected with the state of my stomack which is weak and my stomack is sensibly affected by my heart, so that, you see, I must quiet [moderate] study—at least in a good degree." It would help, he added, if her husband, Fowler, could "take a few lessons in penmanship, or send us a Key for deciphering his letters," or have her write out fair copies of his letters for him. On the other hand, his granddaughter described him in and about New Haven at the age of eighty as elegant in bearing and conduct: "tall, erect, and slender, but not thin in figure or face. As a young man he had brown eyes, sometimes called gray, and abundant hair, well cared for, of an auburn tint, and the fair ruddy skin that accompanies the reddish hair." His ruddy face and thick head of auburn hair "seemed to give him the fire and enthusiasm of the sanguine temperaments with the stability and perseverance of the bilious races." A family friend at this time described him "walking across that beautiful lawn in front of good old Yale," a "tall, slender, remarkably erect figure with light elastic step." Asked to reveal his secret in maintaining a robust appearance, he replied it was due to retiring at an early hour, rising with the lark, combining mental labor with bodily exercise every single day, and studiously maintaining "a conscience void of offense toward God and man." As Joshua Kendall, Webster's most recent biographer, puts it, Webster was a readily recognized figure striding around New Haven with his "flaming red hair and remarkably erect bearing [that] made him a striking figure. He wore long-tailed coats and frilled shirts long after they went out of style."[1]

2

In good health or not, only five months after his last *Palladium* letter Webster was doing what he could to promote his book and keep it alive. He feared his grip on the dictionary market was slipping away and that the public was turning away from his other books as well, especially in schools. He was gratified in 1835 that "the faculty of Yale College have lately determined that candidates for admission shall be examined in [according to] my *Grammar*—another proof of the convalescent state of English learning," but he feared the future belonged to younger men like Worcester with energy and resources to carry the fight forward. All he could do was pin his hopes on a new edition of his 1828 quarto, stick to the drudgery of correcting the "mistakes" in his books, and keep writing letters advertising himself. In November of that year, he wrote out a full advertisement for a new edition, "Reasons for Adopting One Dictionary as a Standard of English Orthography"—by which he meant his own dictionary. He wanted Fowler, who was now acting as his constant confidant and sort of unofficial agent, to place the advertisement in the newspapers. All his works, it claims, were "constructed on the plan of uniform orthography," including "his dictionaries, elementary spelling books . . .

grammar and other books for schools." Mindful of the savage clobbering he had endured from Cobb and others regarding his inconsistencies of spelling and pronunciation—which he chalked up to "oversight or forgetfulness"—he promises to put them all right in future editions.[2]

Picking up again on his resonant anti-British theme that almost always worked for him with the general public, his advertisement is a frontal attack on "the most egregious errors in the British books." He directs his abuse at the British use of the language in the second half of the eighteenth century: the authoritative and pompous use of polite and ornate English practiced by the aristocracy and intellectuals as distinct from the speech of the common man; the affected "clamor of pedantry" of grammars that encouraged the study of dead languages (Greek and Latin); and the dominance of literary over popular speech, embodied by Dr. Johnson's Latinate syntax and Edward Gibbon's tediously ornamental rhetoric in *The Decline and Fall of the Roman Empire*. Webster had always been contemptuous of Johnson's elevated style, his circumlocutions, fondness for "hard" and polysyllabic words, rotundity of phrasing, and formulaic elaboration of ideas in complex sentences built from balanced or parallel words, phrases, and sentences. For him, this amounted to "corrupt" practice, a decline from what he regarded as sensibly elegant and clear English. However, he objected to Shakespeare and seventeenth-century drama in general, we recall, because of Shakespeare's use of vulgar words. As he told Thomas Dawes in 1809, "It was most injudicious in Johnson to select Shakespeare as one of his principal authorities. Play-writers in describing low scenes and vulgar characters use low language, language unfit for decent company; and their ribaldry has corrupted our speech as well as the public morals. I have made it a main point to reject words belonging to writings of this character, and shall proceed as far as propriety requires in cleansing the Augean stable."[3]

He parades in this latest advertisement all his old themes, which by the 1830s were sounding tired and worn. He decries the authoritative standards of pronunciation and spelling, formulated and codified as they had been by "polite" English society. He also promises to undo "the immense mischief" done by English orthoepists, especially Walker. He repeats his old claim, which still was incorrect: "We now learn that the pronunciation of Walker *is* not and never *has* been that of the higher classes of society in the nation in general; but [of] local peculiarities or more properly dandyism. . . . So that after having our children instructed thirty or forty years in dandyisms, we are now brought back, and by British authorities too, to our old pronunciation. So much for American obsequiousness; but the evil which Walker has done will not be corrected in half a century." American teachers were helpless; they did not know any better: "They are mistaken and ought to be appraised of the imposition." He announces he would continue the fight in behalf of America.[4]

3

Worcester had come along at both an opportune and awkward moment for Webster. Webster could cast him in the role of usurper of his self-proclaimed kingdom: the leading champion of British imposition, the American spoiler, a kind of American Trojan horse intent on reversing the linguistic progress and destiny of the new nation that Webster had tirelessly carved out.

Regarding the extent to which Webster was trying to normalize the language with his reforms, he had argued back in August 1807—in the pages of the religious monthly the *Panoplist*, defending himself against a review by a "learned" "English gentlemen" of his *Compendious Dictionary* that had recently appeared in the journal *Eclectic Review*—that "the lexicographer's business is to search for truth, to proscribe error, and repress anomaly." What he had in mind by the "truth," as regards orthography, was "common usage." Had not both the British and Americans, though, rejected campaigns for the creation of national language academies for the very reason that it is impossible to manipulate language trends with theories and programs, or by force of personality, especially orthography and pronunciation? You can legislate language as much as you want, but you can never win against "language's own life": "The American accent that Webster hoped to define, and eventually to institute, through an elaborate set of linguistic rules was far more prescriptive than the English accent taught at Harvard and enshrined in Worcester's dictionary," the scholar Elisa Tamarkin writes, adding that "Webster might have listened to how Americans spoke but only in order to codify what he heard as a set of abstract linguistic laws for all Americans to follow." While Worcester, on the other hand, was neither deaf nor indifferent to common American use, Tamarkin explains, his "determination to look to England is not just more conservative because it gives priority to precedent over an abstract idea of linguistic nationality but because it proceeds from the assumption that language should exist only as the world has made it." Yet here was Webster again, almost half a century since he began his campaign, still refusing to back off from his mission to shape the American language, still pressing for reforms, still rejecting the realities of language history in the interests of linguistic nationalism. As we shall see, though, he was not alone. Many who were offended by his authoritarian manner and at times seemingly arbitrary scale of reforms and innovations did nonetheless agree that the American language must be allowed to make its own way independent of the mother country, and that there must be less carping about it. A few years earlier, in 1818, Edward Everett remarked disapprovingly from Harvard: "American innovations on the English language are ipso facto corruptions, the British, improvements; and in this . . . I have found a resolute spirit of decrying every thing American to be pretty universal."[5]

4

One way Webster hoped to promote sales of his own dictionary and schoolbooks was to gain and retain the inside track with his booksellers and publishers. He could persuade them into pushing his books to the exclusion of others. He was not even beyond having members of his own family devote their lives to the cause. When Fowler told him in July 1836 that he was playing with the idea of leaving teaching at Middlebury College to open a business in bookselling, Webster rejoiced because he saw it as serving his own self-interest: "If you remove and enter into the business of bookselling, this course will render you serviceable to *my interest*, and this is *the interest of all my family.*" Fowler was thinking mainly of starting a business in Philadelphia or New York, while Webster had in mind his going to Cincinnati, the pivotal city in Webster's crucial western market—by the 1820s it was commonly known as the "Queen of the West" because of its spectacular growth—where he could join Webster's son, William, in the bookselling business. Something must be done immediately, Webster insisted, to come to the rescue of both the dictionary and schoolbooks: "The crisis now is important, as the question whether my elementary books are to be used generally as permanent school books is to be decided within a year or two. That such may be the case to a great extent is certain, if proper means are used. Conn[ecticut] and Vermont are undoubtedly in my interest. . . . The patronage of the West is to be retained at all hazards. I have it now, and it *must not be lost.*"[6]

William, out in Cincinnati, was supposed to be in harness to the great enterprise, but he felt differently and soon took a job as a teller in an Indiana bank. He had already damaged his eyes proofreading for his father at Cambridge University and apparently thought his dad was demanding too much. "I had always hoped," Webster wrote on December 8, 1837, "to have my son a bookseller, and a grandson also who might take an active part in sustaining my efforts, but I am disappointed. William, we hear, is appointed teller in the banks. . . ." One month later he was still fixated on the help he hoped for, but concluded he would not get, from his family in the bookselling business: "I wish, by some means, I could form a bookselling establishment that might have an interest in publishing my books," he confided to Fowler on January 9, 1838: "An edition of the quarto is wanted, and no house will undertake it, as the outlay would be large. . . . I wish, by some means, I could form a booksell-ing establishment that might have an interest in publishing my books. . . . All my books serve to support each other. But I must rely on the spelling books and dictionaries. . . . It would have been a great point gained for my family if a good bookselling house had been, some years ago, established, by my friends, either in New York or Philadelphia . . . [as the] success of books now depends very much or chiefly on booksellers. . . ." He still had his eye on poor Fowler on March 10: "I think my sons in law should think more of this plan. You are not a bookseller but if your family should go to [Philadelphia], I should go too, or be there for the most part and try to make an establishment for my books." Fowler was ready to help by spending his summers promoting his father-in-law but wisely decided after all not to give up teaching.[7]

Webster had concluded that if his dictionary was going to be rescued from eventual oblivion, it was a new edition of the original 1828 quarto that would have to do it. On September 19, 1836, in the New Haven *Daily Herald* he notified the public that the 1828 edition was sold out and that anyone who wanted a copy would have no choice but to buy the English edition that was still in print. Without copies to sell, there was only the Goodrich/ Worcester octavo and the small school editions left in America to carry his message to future generations, but Goodrich had total control of the former. Increasingly desperate, he asked Goodrich to speak to Norman White, the publisher of the octavo, to see if he was interested in publishing a revised quarto, but White wanted no part of it: "We think the demand would by no means justify the publication of an edition at present." White was mildly

receptive to what he called "the Websterian system" of orthography, as modified by Goodrich of course, and he was ready to continue publishing it by
staying with the octavo, certainly not by taking control of both the octavo
and a bank-breaking quarto.[8]

5

By early 1836, Webster had made up his mind in favor of a somewhat smaller,
two-volume (octavo) version of his 1828 quarto. This new edition would be
less bulky than the quarto, more widely usable and (presumably) salable, and
more interesting to a publisher. Such an edition would be slightly larger than
the Goodrich/Worcester octavo; nor under his supervision would it at all
resemble what he viewed as a notorious abridgment that had insulted him by
violating so many of his ideas about the English language. That was important, because he could then tell himself that according to the letter of the law
such an edition would not break his and Goodrich's signed agreement that
he would never publish a rival octavo. His family expressed concern over the
expenses of any new edition. Even his wife, Rebecca, loyal and self-sacrificing
as she was, protested when he announced to Fowler he was "willing" to mortgage or sell their house for a smaller one in order to pay for the new edition. He looked everywhere for money, confiding to Fowler on February 27,
1839, "I think sometimes of asking you and Harriet to lend me money for the
purpose. . . ." Ellsworth was not forthcoming with financial help, nor could
Webster count on Goodrich. Webster, it seemed, would have to assume the
economic risk himself: "I should now rather have a house of about half the
rooms which my present house has, and spend the short remainder of my
life in it. . . . I should not think it an *embarrassment* to have the value of the
house in the Dictionary."[9]

By July, the horizon had brightened. Webster felt the market for his new
edition had improved, and with sales of his *Elementary Spelling Book* sky-
rocketing, his hopes soared. As in the past, and in spite of Cobb's attacks, it
was his spelling book that would bankroll this new book. He had managed to
secure a printer for the new edition, and it was "pretty well determined that I
shall begin the printing of an edition of my large Dictionary in September or
October." He turned to faithful Fowler to provide new words in mineralogy
and geology and any others "deemed proper for insertion," along with their
definitions: "I wish you to make a paper book, alphabetical, in which words

FIGURE 10. Rebecca Greenleaf Webster. Oil on canvas, by Jared Bradley Flagg (1820–99). Courtesy of the Beinecke Rare Book and Manuscript Library, Yale University, Paul Leicester Ford papers.

deemed proper for insertion may be entered, accented and briefly explained. If you think I shall be likely to mistake your letters, you can write first on a scrap of paper, and let Emily [Webster's daughter] copy the words into the book. . . . If you can assist me in that way or any other, I shall make . . . compensation for the labor." He peremptorily commanded William and his wife to return to Connecticut from Indiana in order to help him with the edition, swallowing up in the process several hundred dollars of his son and daughter-in-law's savings.[10]

Far more important than either Fowler's or William's help with the new edition, however, was Goodrich's. Apparently reassured by Webster that the new edition would not encroach on his octavo abridgment, Goodrich consented to pitch in and (for the sake of the family) help his aged father-in-law, but only in the way that interested him, by returning to the dictionary to identify eccentric spellings, isolate errors that had to be put right, and search for new words. Anxious to get the book out, Webster agreed. It was a decision that would largely determine the course and tenor of the next twenty years of Goodrich's professional life. Eighteen months later they had finished the work, "I trust in a way to occasion me no embarrassment," Webster remarked. "The sales will probably be slow, but sure. It is a work for which there is at present no substitute, and it is not an easy thing to make one like it.[11]

Leaning persistently on Fowler and William, in the middle of all this Webster found time to indulge his vanity by ordering a bronze bust of himself done from a plaster cast by Chauncey Bradley Ives, a prolific and popular sculptor, then living and sculpting in New Haven, who went on to international fame. "The likeness is said to be very exact," Webster told Fowler on July 9; "Emily and her family are delighted with it. William has sent one for you." The bust was not just for family, however: "If the faculty of Amherst College will permit a copy of it to be set in the library, or other apartment, I will present one to the college for that purpose. Considering what interest I took in founding the institution, it seems to be, if not proper, at least not improper to place my bust in one of the public rooms." A copy of the bust was duly placed in the college library.[12]

The two-volume *An American Dictionary of the English Language*—called a royal octavo, measuring about 6.5 by 10 inches, slightly larger than a regular octavo (6 by 9 inches)—was published in 1841 in New York by the publishers White and Sheffield, thirteen years after the 1828 edition and twelve after the Goodrich/Worcester octavo abridgment. It contained 1,079 pages and was priced at $15. The title page announced it contained "the whole vocabulary of the [1828] quarto, with corrections, improvements and several [15,000] thousand additional [entry] words." Three thousand copies of the edition were printed. For some perspective on that print run, 2,500 copies of the 1828 quarto were published for the American market and 3,000 for the British, so not much had changed in the intervening years regarding low expectations of sales.

Oddly, given Webster's continuing censure of John Walker ever since his *Dissertations*, and also his animosity toward Worcester, Walker's *Key to the Classical Pronunciation of Greek, Latin, and Scripture Proper Names* finds its place in the edition and is even featured on the title page—a sign of Walker's continuing popularity in America and Goodrich's influence. Also unexpected

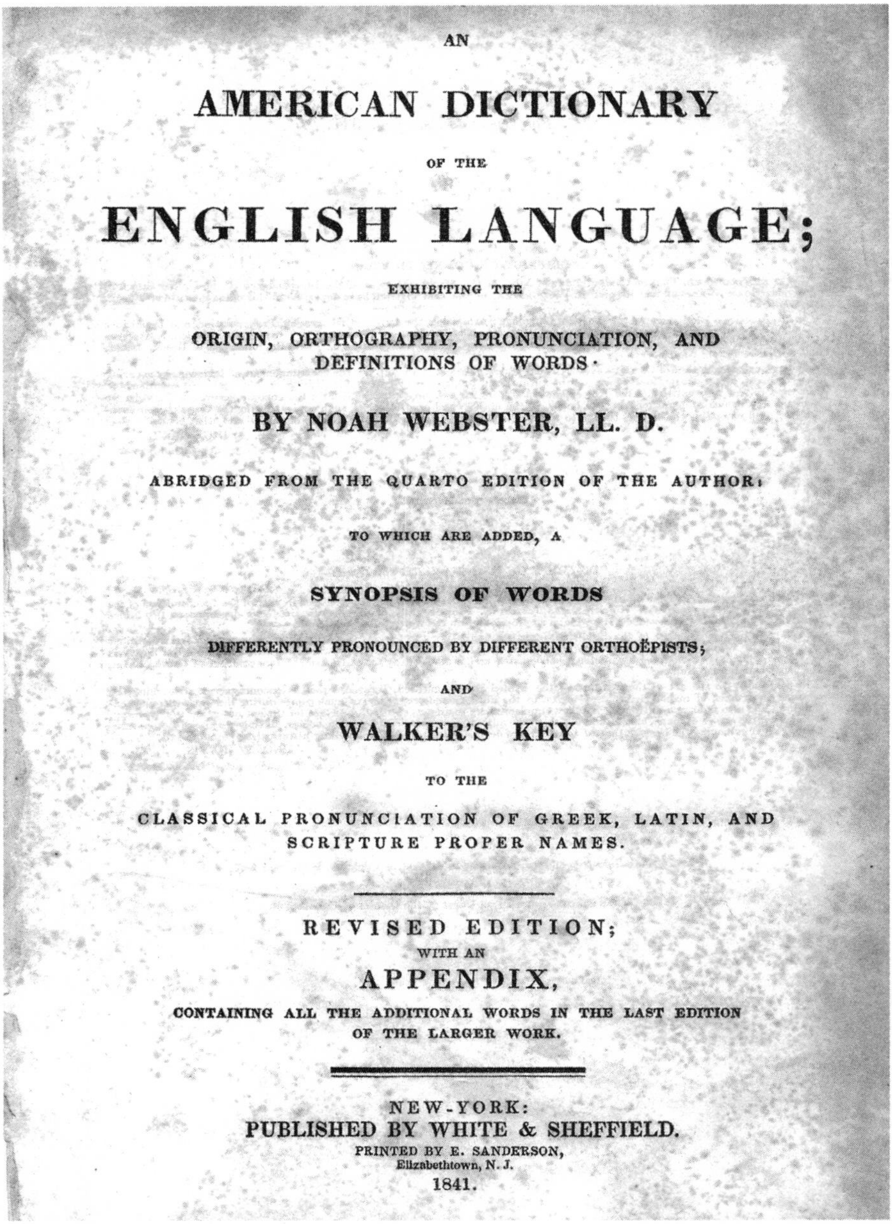

AN

AMERICAN DICTIONARY

OF THE

ENGLISH LANGUAGE;

EXHIBITING THE

ORIGIN, ORTHOGRAPHY, PRONUNCIATION, AND
DEFINITIONS OF WORDS·

BY NOAH WEBSTER, LL. D.

ABRIDGED FROM THE QUARTO EDITION OF THE AUTHOR;

TO WHICH ARE ADDED, A

SYNOPSIS OF WORDS

DIFFERENTLY PRONOUNCED BY DIFFERENT ORTHOËPISTS;

AND

WALKER'S KEY

TO THE

CLASSICAL PRONUNCIATION OF GREEK, LATIN, AND
SCRIPTURE PROPER NAMES.

REVISED EDITION;
WITH AN
APPENDIX,
CONTAINING ALL THE ADDITIONAL WORDS IN THE LAST EDITION
OF THE LARGER WORK.

NEW-YORK:
PUBLISHED BY WHITE & SHEFFIELD.
PRINTED BY E. SANDERSON,
Elizabethtown, N. J.
1841.

FIGURE 11. Title page of the 1841 revised and expanded, abridged, two-volume edition of *An American Dictionary of the English Language*, edited by Chauncey Allen Goodrich with Noah Webster's assistance. Courtesy of Indiana State University Special Collections, Cordell Collection of Dictionaries.

is the inclusion of Worcester's fourteen-page "Synopsis" of about 850 words of "disputed pronunciation" by six orthoepists, all English except for Webster, whose pronunciations are added for this edition, possibly by Goodrich, to those of the original six. That "Synopsis" is introduced and placed without any mention that Worcester had prepared it thirteen years earlier, creating the impression (on the part of those, at least, who did not know it in the Goodrich/Worcester octavo) that Webster was its author. That very likely was Goodrich's decision. So was, undoubtedly, the inclusion of Goodrich's preface to his and Worcester's octavo revision that Webster despised, which mentions Worcester's prominent role in that revision.

Notwithstanding the additional words, and even with Goodrich and Fowler's help, the edition was essentially the same book as the original 1828 quarto, a "hasty piece of work" in eighteen months, far from the comprehensive revision that Goodrich, and Converse before him, knew the quarto badly needed. The approximately fifteen thousand additional words, mostly foreign and a string of scientific terms gleaned mainly from a professor of medicine at Yale, not from Fowler, were stuck into an appendix in the second volume because of Webster's lingering reservations about the inclusion of too many scientific and technical terms in the lexicon. Goodrich made a somewhat perfunctory stab, as these things go in lexicography, at altering spelling and pronunciation in favor of more conventional usage. He, or Webster, or both, decided to scrap many more of Webster's early orthographical eccentricities: for example, *maiz* was returned to its former self, *maize*, as was *sovereign* from *suveran*. Nonetheless, Webster refused to be nudged from such as *aker* (for *acre*), *grotesk* (grotesque), *porpess* (*porpoise*), and *tung* (*tongue*).[13] The pronunciation of some "disputed words" in the "Synopsis," we are told, was altered "in conformity with . . . more recent usage" and entered in the body of the work. Definitions were expanded somewhat, with new senses slipped in, and definitions of scientific words were also corrected.

While this edition was making its way through the press, Webster was still writing notes for "Addenda" comprising additional words and their definitions, which appear mostly in an 1844 edition published by Harper & Brothers, made up of unsold sheets of the 1841 edition. A few of these also found their way, however, into an appendix in the 1841 edition.[14]

In July 1841, Webster at first was sanguine about sales, reporting that the new edition had "found a good market in our large towns," although "the a state in which the mind is arrested and fixed, or, as we say, lost ; a state in which the functions of the senses are suspended by the contemplation of some extraordinary or supernatural object. 2. Excessive joy ; rapture ; a degree of delight that ar[...] asm ; excessive eleva[...] treme delight. 4. Exc[...] *Shak.* 5. Madness ; dis[...] *medicine,* a species of [...] bers, after the paroxysm [...] the fit.

EC'STA-SY, *v. t.* To fill with rapture or enthusiasm.

EC-STAT'IC,   } *a.* 1. Arresting the mind ; suspending
EC-STAT'I-CAL, }   the senses ; entrancing. 2. Rapturous ; transporting ; ravishing ; delightful beyond measure 3. Tending to external objects ; [*not used.*]

EC'TY-PAL, *a.* Taken from the original. *Ellis.*

† EC'TYPE, *n.* [Gr. εκτυπος.] A copy. *Locke.*

EC-U-MEN'IC,   } *a.* [Gr. οικουμενικος.] General ; uni-
EC-U-MEN'I-CAL, } versal.

EC'U-RIE, *n.* [Fr.] A stable ; a covered place for horses.

E-DA'CIOUS, *a.* [L. *edax.*] Eating ; given to eating ; greedy ; voracious.

E-DAC'I-TY, *n.* [L. *edacitas.*] Greediness ; voracity ; ravenousness ; rapacity.

ED'DER, *n.* [qu. Sax. *eder.*] In *husbandry,* such wood as is worked into the top of hedge-stakes to bind them together.

ED'DER, *n.* [Sax. *ætter.*] A viper.

ED'DER, *v. t.* To bind or make tight by edder ; to fasten the tops of hedge-stakes, by interweaving edder. *Eng.*

ED'DISH, or EAD'ISH, *n.* The latter pasture or grass that comes after mowing or reaping ; called also *eagrass, earsh, etch.* [*Not used, I believe, in America.*]

ED'DOES, or ED'DERS, *n.* A name given to a variety of the *arum esculentum,* an esculent root.

ED'DY, *n.* [Sax. *ed* and *ea.*] 1. A current of water running back, or in a direction contrary to the main stream. 2. A whirlpool ; a current of water or air in a circular direction.

ED'DY, *v. i.* To move circularly, or as an eddy.

ED'DY, *a.* Whirling ; moving circularly. *Dryden.*

ED'DY-WA'TER, *n.* Among *seamen,* the water which falls back on the rudder of a ship under sail, called *deadwater*

ED'DY-WIND, *n.* The wind returned or beat back from a sail, a mountain or any thing that hinders its passage.

E'DEL-ITE, *n.* A siliceous stone of a light gray color.

E-DEM'A-TOUS, *a.* [Gr. οιδημα.] Swelling with a serous humor ; dropsical.

E-DEN, *n.* [Heb.] The country and garden in which Adam and Eve were placed by God himself.

E'DEN-IZED, *a.* Admitted into Paradise. *Davies.*

E-DEN'TA-TED, *a.* [L. *edentatus.*] Destitute or deprived of teeth. *Dict.*

† E-DEN-TA'TION, *n.* A pulling out of teeth. *Cockeram.*

EDGE, *n.* [Sax. *ecg* ; Dan. *eg.*] 1. In a *general sense,* the extreme border or point of any thing. It is particularly applied to the border, the thin cutting extremity of an instrument.—2. *Figuratively,* that which cuts or penetrates ; that which wounds or injures. 3. A narrow part rising from a broader. 4. Sharpness of mind or appetite ; keenness ; intenseness of desire ; fitness for action or operation. 5. Keenness ; sharpness ; acrimony.—*To set the teeth on edge,* to cause a tingling or grating sensation in the teeth. *Bacon.*

EDGE, *v. t.* [W. *hogi* ; Sax. *eggian.*] 1. To sharpen. 2. To furnish with an edge. 3. To border ; to fringe. 4. To border ; to furnish with an ornamental border. 5. To sharpen ; to exasperate ; to embitter. 6. To incite ; to provoke ; to urge on ; to instigate ; that is, to push on as with a sharp point ; to goad. 7. To move sideways ; to move by little and little.

EDGE, *v. i.* 1. To move sideways ; to move gradually. 2. To sail close to the wind.—*To edge away,* in *sailing,* is to decline gradually from the shore or from the line of the course.—*To edge in with,* to draw near to, as a ship in chasing.

EDG'ED, *pp.* 1. Furnished with an edge or border. 2. Incited ; instigated. 3. *a.* Sharp ; keen.

EDGE'LESS, *a.* Not sharp ; blunt ; obtuse ; unfit to cut or penetrate. *Shak.*

EDGE'TOOL, *n.* An instrument having a sharp edge.

EDGE'WISE, *adv.* 1. With the edge turned forward, or towards a particular point ; in the direction of the edge. 2. Sideways ; with the side foremost.

EDG'ING, *ppr.* 1. Giving an edge ; furnishing with an edge. 2. Inciting ; urging on ; goading ; stimulating ; instigating. 3. Moving gradually or sideways. 4. Furnishing with a borde[...].

EDG'ING, *n.* 1. That which is added on the border, or which forms the edge ; as lace, fringe, trimming, added to a garment for ornament. 2. A narrow lace.—3. In

gardening, a row of small plants set along the border of a flower-bed.

ED'I-BLE, *a.* [L. *edo.*] Eatable ; fit to be eaten as food ; esculent.

ED'I-TOR, *n.* [L.] 1. A publisher ; *particularly,* a person who superintends an impression of a book ; the person who revises, corrects and prepares a book for publication. 2. One who superintends the publication of a newspaper

in a moral and religious sense ; instruction ; improvement and progress of the mind, in knowledge, in morals, or in faith and holiness. 2. Instruction ; improvement of the mind in any species of useful knowledge.

ED-I-FI-CA-TO-RY, or E-DIF'I-CA-TO-RY, *a.* Tending to edification. *Hall.*

ED'I-FICE, *n.* [L. *ædificium.*] A building ; a structure ; a fabric ; but *appropriately,* a large or splendid building.

ED-I-FI'CIAL, *a.* Pertaining to edifices or to structure.

ED'I-FIED, *pp.* Instructed ; improved in literary, moral or religious knowledge.

ED'I-FI-ER, *n.* One that improves another by instructing him.

ED'I-FY, *v. t.* [L. *ædifico.*] 1. To build, in a *literal sense ;* [*not now used.*] 2. To instruct and improve the mind in knowledge generally, and particularly in moral and religious knowledge, in faith and holiness. 3. To teach or persuade ; [*not used.*]

ED'I-FY-ING, *ppr.* Building up in Christian knowledge ; instructing ; improving the mind.

ED'I-FY-ING-LY, *adv.* In an edifying manner.

E'DILE, *n.* [L. *ædilis.*] A Roman magistrate whose chief business was to superintend buildings of all kinds, more especially public edifices, temples, bridges, aqueducts, &c.

E'DILE-SHIP, *n.* The office of edile in ancient Rome.

ED'IT, *v. t.* [L. *edo.*] 1. *Properly,* to publish ; *more usually,* to superintend a publication ; to prepare a book or paper for the public eye, by writing, correcting or selecting the matter. 2. To publish.

ED'IT-ED, *pp.* Published ; corrected ; prepared and published.

ED'IT-ING, *ppr.* Publishing ; preparing for publication.

E-DI'TION, *n.* [L. *editio.*] 1. The publication of any book or writing. 2. Republication ; sometimes with revision and correction. 3. Any publication of a book before published ; also, one impression or the whole number of copies published at once.

† E-DI'TION-ER, *n.* The old word for *editor. Gregory.*

ED'I-TOR, *n.* [L.] 1. A publisher ; *particularly,* a person who superintends an impression of a book ; the person who revises, corrects and prepares a book for publication. 2. One who superintends the publication of a newspaper

ED-I-TO'RI-AL, *a.* Pertaining to an editor ; written by an editor

ED'I-TOR-SHIP, *n.* The business of an editor.

† E-DIT'U-ATE, *v. t.* [Low L. *ædituor.*] To defend or govern the house or temple.

ED'U-CATE, *v. t.* [L. *educo.*] To bring up, as a child ; to instruct ; to inform and enlighten the understanding ; to instill into the mind principles of arts, science, morals, religion and behavior.

ED'U-CA-TED, *pp.* Brought up ; instructed ; furnished with knowledge or principles ; trained ; disciplined.

ED'U-CA-TING, *ppr.* Instructing ; enlightening the understanding, and forming the manners.

ED-U-CA'TION, *n.* [L. *educatio.*] The bringing up, as of a child ; instruction ; formation of manners.

ED-U-CA'TION-AL, *a.* Pertaining to education ; derived from education. *Smith.*

ED-U-CA-TOR, *n.* One who educates. *Beddoes.*

E-DUCE', *v. t.* [L. *educo.*] To bring or draw out ; to extract ; to produce from a state of occultation.

E-DU'CED, (e-dūst') *pp.* Drawn forth ; extracted ; produced.

E-DU'CING, *ppr.* Drawing forth ; producing.

E'DUCT, *n.* [L. *eductum.*] Extracted matter ; that which is educed.

E-DUC'TION, *n.* The act of drawing out or bringing into view.

E-DUC'TOR, *n.* That which brings forth, elicits or extracts

E-DUL'CO-RATE, *v. t.* [Low L. *edulco.*] 1. To purify , to sweeten.—In *chemistry,* to render substances more mild, by freeing them from acids and salts or other soluble impurities, by washing. 2. To sweeten, by adding sugar, sirup, &c.

E-DUL'CO-RA-TED, *pp.* Sweetened ; purified from acid or saline substances, and rendered more mild.

E-DUL'CO-RA-TING, *ppr.* Sweetening ; rendering more mild.

E-DUL-CO-RA'TION, *n.* 1. The act of sweetening or rendering more mild, by freeing from acid or saline substances, or from any soluble impurities. 2. The act of sweetening by admixture of some saccharine substance.

FIGURE 12. The 1841 edition of *An American Dictionary* removed some of Webster's orthographical eccentricities. Detail: The definition of *editor* has been revised slightly from the 1828 edition. Courtesy of Indiana State University Special Collections, Cordell Collection of Dictionaries.

price is too high for many clergymen and teachers"—at $15 it was priced $3 higher than Webster had hoped it would be, and a far cry from the $6 price tag of the Goodrich/Worcester in 1829. The price was far too high for the general public. Webster spent the rest of his life in a futile effort to increase its sales one way or another: "I have to struggle alone and this I shall not long be able and disposed to do." He would end his days knowing that his dictionaries had never enjoyed financial success. He told Fowler in the parlor of his living room—their last conversation—that Goodrich "shall never again have the power to alter my dictionary." It was not one of his more accurate prophecies. Goodrich's "power" over revisions to his dictionaries would increase, not decrease, after Webster's death.[15]

6

In 1843, the shades were closing in on Webster. He did not suffer from any lingering illness or physically debilitating handicap in the last months of his life. He had his aches and pains but looked young for his age. He was active with his family, still helping his son William financially, interested in gardening, and a regular visitor to his daughters and old Yale friends, including professors Benjamin Silliman and James Luce Kingsley, and former college president Ezra Stiles. Just the year before, he had rounded up his own essays, written over a period of some fifty years, for a substantial volume with notes, *A Collection of Papers on Political, Literary and Moral Subjects* (1843), which was published only a few days before he died. In early May, he even completed some corrections for a new edition of his speller. On May 22, with a lame foot he had injured while sitting in his rocking chair, he twice walked three-quarters of a mile to the local post office on a clear but cold day. He struggled home the second time with a chill that quickly worsened into pleurisy, an inflammation of the lung. Finding it difficult to breathe, he took to his bed in his study.

We have a detailed account of his last days from his daughter Eliza, who, along with many other members of the family, stayed with him in his dying hours and recorded some of the last conversations they had together. He told her, "I have struggled with many difficulties. Some I have been able to overcome, and by some I have been overcome. I have made many mistakes, but I love my country, and I have labored for the youth of my country. . . ." His "literary labors were all ended," he told Eliza. According to her, he did not specifically mention his lexicographical labors—perhaps an indication he did not think they would stand the test of time. He presented one of his grandsons with a treasured early edition of his speller. He spoke of his constant patriotism and closeness to God. "I'm ready to go," he whispered, "my work is all done; I know in whom I have believed." Asked by one of his daughters if he suffered much, he replied significantly, "Not acute suffering dear, but with an indescribable uneasiness." He died a few hours later, on May 28, 1843, clutching a copy of his speller, the book that far more than his dictionary had made him famous.[16]

All of New Haven, where he had lived with his family for more than forty years, seemed in mourning. Several memorial services were held in Center Church on New Haven Green and at Amherst College. His long funeral procession included all his family, the entire Yale faculty and student body, and schoolchildren from New Haven and surrounding communities. He was buried near his home, in Grove Street Cemetery, the burial place of many Yale presidents, joined by his wife, Rebecca, four years later. Soon after his death, Benjamin Silliman wrote in his diary about his old friend Webster: "He died in the fulness of reputation, of health, of mental power, and of Christian faith. He has left a brilliant fame. Millions have been instructed by his writings, and millions more will study them in years to come. He encountered no small opposition, which was due quite as much to his personal peculiarities as to the boldness and novelty of some of his speculations. His elementary works for schools have received a universal sanction and many other works remain to instruct mankind. . . ."[17]

PART TWO

THE MERRIAMS AT WAR

10

Taking Webster out of Webster

From Family Feuds to the Merriam Brothers

Webster's death exposed suppressed strife in his family that took years to sort out. Ill feeling and misunderstanding within the family, as we have seen, had existed for some time between the sons-in-law and between Webster himself and Goodrich. The daughters additionally resented the amount of money their father for years had spent propping up his only son, William, in his various unsuccessful business ventures. Harriet, Fowler's wife, did not mince her words on February 13, 1837: "I feel ashamed of my brother, who is *willing* that continual sums should be advanced for him by his father who has already advanced so much. He ought to go and find employment." Just before Webster died, he alarmed everyone by granting William copyright ownership of the spellers, the real money-makers, a decision that outraged William's siblings and brothers-in-law even more since it jeopardized their income portions of the estate. Much of the resentment was reserved for Goodrich, however, Webster's son-in-law, whom they regarded as an opportunist who had taken unfair advantage of an old man by coaxing from him exclusive rights to the copyright (and profits) of the Goodrich/Worcester octavo edition. To make matters worse, that edition posed obstacles for the progress of any new Webster editions until its copyright ran out in 1857. When Webster's will was read out, it excluded his daughter Julia from her annual portion of the estate income up to the amount the Goodrich/Worcester octavo had earned. Resentment flared up again. Webster felt that Julia, Goodrich's wife, had earned more than her share of her inheritance from the series of Goodrich/Worcester editions that by rights ought to have been the property of the entire family.[1]

Goodrich was shocked. Grudgingly, he eventually agreed to give up the profits "at a pecuniary loss," provided that Julia was restored to equal legacy rights with her sisters and brother, but he went further. He stoutly defended himself in October 1843, facing down his brother-in-law Ellsworth, the chief executor of Webster's estate, by summarizing for him the publishing history of the offending abridgment. Goodrich had never earned as much money from it as they all thought, he told Ellsworth: in nine years, two editions per year on average had been published, each of only one thousand copies, earning him a total of $6,468: "It has succeeded to such an extent as to give me a handsome recompense for my risk and trouble," but "anyone acquainted with the business will say it is a very moderate profit for the risk and care. I presume some of my friends [i.e., family] have thought the profit more. . . ." Anyone in the book business can tell you, he added, that "it is the bookseller and not the holder of the copyright who makes most of the profits on a work of extensive sale. My purchase from the Ameses was an extremely fortunate one, and the activity of the Whites when they became the publishers has made it moreso. My chief profit then has been on this purchase and not . . . in the purchase which I made from father Webster." In preparing the octavo abridgment, he argued, he had spent $5,000 on trips to Boston, on working with Worcester, and on adding new material from Webster, not to mention the countless hours of his spare time he had stolen from his professorial Yale duties in editing the entire volume and seeing it through the press. He argued that his motives had always been selfless: "If I know my own heart, I have never been actuated by selfish motives in any of my dealings with Dr. Webster or his children. I took the copy-right at his urgent request. . . . I took it under the full conviction of his physicians and friends that the relief this afforded [him] was essential to his enjoying the requisite health for the completion [revision] of the larger work." The correspondence at the time of his acquiring the copyright from Webster clearly reveals this was not achieved at Webster's "urgent request" as he claimed, but because it had happened some ten years earlier, the family now would have to take Goodrich's word for how it came to pass.[2]

The interest and importance of these exchanges are not so much in the details of who was responsible for what, but in Goodrich's astuteness and efficiency when so much was at stake. His letters show an inexhaustible capacity to dominate his opposition with elaborate and morally plausible arguments.

The single-mindedness, intellectual keenness, and insight he demonstrated, from the inception of his work with Worcester to his continuing revisions of Webster's work, earn him a place in the Websterian saga of the nineteenth century in some ways almost as important as Webster's. He had become the central, controlling player for all concerned with Webster's dictionary, even while Webster himself was still alive. And after Webster's death, no future publisher of the Webster dictionaries could afford to be without his services.

2

There were five executors named in the will: Webster's wife, Rebecca; his son, William; his son-in-law William Ellsworth; Goodrich's publisher, Henry White; and Roger S. Baldwin (later governor of Connecticut and US senator). Goodrich conspicuously was not mentioned. Baldwin never played a part in the executorship of Webster's estate or in the subsequent quarrels of the heirs. Of these, William Ellsworth would emerge as dominant. As chief executor, he found he had been given a huge and unenviable job. For one thing, there were still 1,200 copies in unbound sheets of the last 1841 royal octavo languishing in some warehouse that had to be placed with a publisher, but who would buy them with imminent editions of the Goodrich/Worcester abridgment on the horizon? And then, because of Webster's half-hearted efforts and tired plans, there was the persistent problem of lack of uniformity of spelling and pronunciation among his various works—spellers, school dictionaries, the 1828 quarto, and the most recent rushed royal octavo. Without this uniformity, he maintained, he would never see the day when "all the people of this country should follow one dictionary [his, of course] & Spelling book, that all may speak & write alike. This is a matter of national importance." Webster's orthography as yet had been far from comprehensively revised. All that would be hugely expensive, provided of course the executors of Webster's estate could find a willing publisher with adequate resources for the job. The obvious first step was to encourage Goodrich to take on, or rather continue, the task of removing much of Webster from Webster.[3]

Ellsworth therefore found himself in a commanding position. As a lawyer and former governor of Connecticut, he had the authority and skill to take on the formidable chore of unifying the family concerning editions, editors and publishers, copyrights, legacies, profits, and Webster's reputation. The manner in which he dealt with the family and the decisions he had to

FIGURE 13. William Webster, Noah Webster's son. Courtesy of New Haven Museum and Historical Society.

make in these critical months and years would determine the future of Webster's dictionary and how posterity would regard him. It could all so easily go wrong. He churned out letter after letter well into the 1850s to get it right. Since he was no lexicographer and had little interest in the subject, he had to rely on the advice and judgment of others. The only three family members in a position to influence him in that area were William Webster, Goodrich, and Fowler. Totally devoted to promoting his father's books, whatever inconvenience that meant for himself and his family, William nevertheless marginalized his own role as executor by moving again, this time to New York shortly before his father died, in hopes of running a bookstore of his own from which he could serve as his father's agent most effectively. The family now resented that William had been given total control of the speller by his father, who worried constantly about his only son's money woes and general lack of focus and, for reasons having as much to do with his father's whims and directions as his own business limitations, failure to succeed in his jobs in Cincinnati and Indiana. As the speller was the money-maker, something had to be done right away about wresting control of it from William. Ellsworth wrote to him impatiently on July 6, 1843, pointing out it would be madness to leave the speller in his hands. It "*must* be *managed* by some *active bookseller*," he stated firmly, implying that William had not yet proved to be successfully "active" in the bookselling business. William was now engaged mostly in "other business," Ellsworth insisted, and could not give the speller the attention required. He would soon "run the book down." The family would not allow that to happen. Besides, he added, "your father never contemplated your managing the spelling book." In just a couple of months, the other executors managed to regain possession of the speller by buying out a publisher to whom William already, for some quick cash, had granted partial rights over the book.[4]

3

Full of complaints about how the Goodrich/Worcester abridgment "well nigh ruins the large dictionary," Ellsworth was delighted to find a purchaser for the unsold sheets after being turned down by fourteen other publishers. The firm J. S. & C. Adams of Amherst agreed in late 1843 to purchase the sheets for $2,800. The brothers who owned the firm had been Webster's friends from the days when he lived in Amherst, "three of the *very* best names" in the town, Ellsworth assured his family. Ellsworth's main idea then, as he told William in December 1844, had been to sell out the interest in these sheets so that "after that I should have no connexion with it." That sounded blunt enough. He fantasized that publication of these sheets could somehow fill the country with Websters "to the exclusion of Worcester's new *large* Dictionary, now advertised." According to the terms of the sale, the Adams brothers had three years to do something with the sheets, after which the executors re-served the right to find a publisher of their own for an entirely new edition.[5]

The Adams's purchase was a long shot that failed. Within a year they were relieved to be able to sell the remaining unbound sheets to the determined brothers Charles and George Merriam for $1,000 more than they themselves had paid for them. Since 1797, the Merriam brothers' father, Daniel, and his brother Ebenezer had run a small printing and bookselling establishment, with a printing press once owned by Benjamin Franklin, in West Brook-field, central Massachusetts. It was a shoestring operation, but just successful enough to enable Daniel to send his sons to Boston to be apprenticed in the printing business. Eventually, he and Ebenezer gave up the profession, but his sons, who had received no formal education after the age of twelve, opened their own printing and bookselling shop in Springfield, Massachu-setts in 1831. They had been trained in printing and binding books, especially in the relatively new process of stereotyping, but it was at least as important that they turned out to be superb and canny businessmen with an eye for promising commercial opportunities.

By the early 1840s, the ambitious Merriam brothers had generated a suc-cessful business in the production and sale of legal books, schoolbooks, Bibles, and sundry other volumes. They had passed up a lucrative oppor-tunity to gain the rights to Goodrich's abridgment of Webster's dictionary in the early 1830s simply because they lacked the money to take it on. But in 1843, they spotted a way to capitalize on Webster's unsold sheets when it came to their attention that the Adams brothers were trying to sell them. They knew Goodrich's abridgment of Webster's dictionary had sold well and recognized that "Webster" was a name they could exploit. New editions of his dictionary, properly handled, might just make them some money. They judged it was worth taking a risk and purchased the sheets.

In possession of the sheets, the Merriams moved quickly. They immedi-ately wrote to Ellsworth saying they wanted a contract to publish right away a new edition of the 1841 (royal octavo) *American Dictionary*. Although Ells-worth was ready to back them, he had his doubts. He replied on March 4, 1844, that it was not that simple. He well understood the fractious nature of the Webster family: "you cannot secure to yourself what you now wish, without a binding contract with *all* these persons *now* in life. . . . My belief is that it will be in vain to attempt getting a safe and binding contract from the heirs and widow." Nonetheless, he volunteered to "advance your interests" personally with "the widow and children of Dr. Webster." Ellsworth did as he said, keenly putting the case to the family by emphasizing the likely financial benefits, and he eventually was able to convince all of them that this was a great opportunity not to be passed up.[6]

The Merriams had recognized the opportunity but had not then seen the troubled road ahead, congested as it was with Webster family rivalries and unexpected contractual complications. Writing with hindsight to Ellsworth three years later in 1847, they reminded him how much they had done during the intervening years for the Webster family by taking on the huge task of a new edition when all the signs suggested the project could become an albatross around their necks. One of the Merriams was heard to remark that the sheets of the 1841 royal octavo had been "lying stranded like Robinson Crusoe's boat, a vessel too big for the builder to launch." They had paid for the right to publish the dictionary "at a time when it had lain a year and a half after the decease of Dr. Webster, without a purchaser, or, so far as we know, without an offer," because of Worcester and Goodrich's abridgment. After "three of the best business years of our lives" devoted to the new edition in hand, continually plagued by "a source of anxiety" and involving an investment of more than $25,000 (more than half a million dollars today), they grumbled that "hardly any business inducements whatever would tempt us again to pass through" that trial.[7]

When they began talking vaguely of revisions that had to be made for their intended edition, Ellsworth—who described both the brothers-in-law Goodrich and Fowler as "able scholars and judicious critics"—recommended Goodrich as editor. He need not have done so. The Merriams had already determined for themselves that no other scholar was as familiar with the dictionary. And Goodrich seemed available. In a letter to Fowler years later, Goodrich wrote of his surprise at being asked: "I had never had the slightest communication with the Merriams on any subjects, and in fact did not know either of them by sight." He naturally believed it was his connection with Yale that made them think of him, though in light of his work with Worcester on the octavo, it hardly seems surprising they should ask him. At that point, neither they, nor Ellsworth, nor Goodrich saw any insurmountable conflict of interest between Goodrich's octavo abridgment and the new large edition the Merriams had in mind, nor any with Goodrich as editor of future editions of both. Goodrich's revisions toward a new Merriam edition could have benefits all around if they were coordinated with revisions of the other Webster dictionaries as well, thus establishing consistency in spelling, pronunciation, and definitions among them that had never existed and that Webster had given up hope of ever seeing in his lifetime.[8]

Goodrich was uncertain about taking on the monumental task, one that might well determine the course of the rest of his life. He had three main reservations: the massive amount of work required to make Webster's dictionary respectable; how the octavo and its publishers the Whites would fit into the scheme; and the likelihood that certain members of the Webster family, out of loyalty to the lexicographer, would push against the revision Goodrich had in mind every step of the way. He wanted a watertight assurance that all the family and trustees would support his revisions as he made his way through the dictionary. He would not tolerate second guessing, distracting conflicts of interest, and the delays that any disputes would cause. He wrote to Ellsworth in January 1844 that this project could not proceed unless the family agreed to his terms. He used strong language: many of Webster's linguistic and lexicographical principles were so egregious and embarrassing that they had met with hostility at both Harvard and Princeton—he does not mention Yale, an environment always more sympathetic to Webster—and were frequently cited "as specimens of perverted English." Ellsworth was on his side, but the rest of the family—their feelings undoubtedly hurt by Goodrich's critique of Webster's work—was suspicious and hesitant. Could Goodrich be trusted? Ellsworth went to work on them and managed to put their minds at ease. Everyone eventually decided to back Goodrich completely, except for Webster's confidant, Fowler, who insisted Goodrich must interrupt his work regularly to keep the family informed in detail about the revisions.[9]

Although at first Goodrich's publishers, the Whites, were nervous that he was getting into bed with a competitor, they came around to accepting the Merriams' entrance into this complicated mix of editions after Goodrich reassured them that all the work he would do for the Merriam edition he would also use, with the agreement of the Merriams, to keep his octavo abridgment up to date. And it would work the other way, too. The revisions of the two editions would be kept in step with each other regarding spelling, pronunciation, definitions, and etymology. Goodrich told the Merriams they need not worry about the Whites, whose recent sales of the octavo had dropped and who would be glad to be pulled along by the fresh horsepower of the larger dictionary: "If you can arrange with Mr White, there is nothing to prevent my superintending this work, and contributing the results of some years' study to the design." Nobody else, he told them, could make the two editions "correspondent to each other." The Merriams then acted with the speed that became their trademark, writing briskly to Norman White, receiving his reply, and replying to Goodrich all within the space of six days. White had no objections to any of the arrangements because he understood that without uniformity of spelling and pronunciation among the several dictionaries, the complex of Webster dictionaries in print would remain forever fatally flawed, very likely turning the public away from Webster. The Merriams took both a short view and a long view of revisions of Webster, especially his orthoepy: "We should not think it practicable, nor all things considered, desirable to change, or essentially to modify at this period [for an octavo abridgment], the system he adopted. It occurs to us however, that in preparing the larger [unabridged] work for the press, *this* might be done."[10]

4

The Merriams were making themselves the engine and bankroller of new Webster editions and new initiatives against Worcester. Their goal was to make something marketable out of the unabridged quarto, the heart and soul of Webster's career. They would leave nothing to chance, acting immediately on issues that came up and seeking the best advice and editorial expertise they could find. "Do it now!" was their motto. Other publishers could have taken up the challenges and rich opportunities offered by the unabridged edition. It had been an open door, but only the Merriams had the courage to walk through it.

Goodrich needed to know exactly how much was expected of him—what kind of edition the Merriams had in mind. On December 19, 1844, he wrote to them, "It would be impossible for me to say what compensation ought to be paid for preparing Dr. Webster's dictionary for the press, without an exact specification of the things to be done." What did they mean when they spoke of "adding" pronunciation? They needed to "fully understand" Webster's system of pronunciation, he wrote, in order to appreciate the magnitude of how much work it would take to revise it. Neither was he clear whether they intended to increase the number of entry words and revise definitions. "You would be surprised if I were to mention words and meanings which did not occur to Dr. Webster, and which you would instantly say ought to be found in the dictionary. For instance, the meaning of a *check*, as for the ticket given you in a rail-road car, is not there. The word *Chief Justice* is omitted in the vocabulary, while *Chief Justiceship* is inserted." Sheets with many similar examples could easily be filled, he cautioned the Merriams, and it would be a "very considerable task" to go through the entire dictionary to identify and supply these omissions. Not to mention the orthography. That was a sobering report, not something the Merriams were happy to hear, because they had not been thinking of anything near that scale of revision. Was Goodrich trying to discourage them? They might well have wondered whose side he was on.[11]

Goodrich even struck at Webster's definitions, which had always been deemed a strength but in which he saw worrying weaknesses. "Inaccuracies in definition" abound, he lamented, that are "palpably erroneous," about one hundred in the last hundred pages alone, owing to the unfortunate fact that Webster unwisely had relied on "old authorities": *Chuckle*, for example, "which we all know means to laugh in a suppressed manner, or inwardly" but that Webster had defined as "convulsive laughter." From there he moved on to a major concern, the dictionary's treatment of orthography. They had to get rid of Webster's particularly unorthodox spellings, such as *beleev* for *believe* and *cloke* for *cloak, determin-determine, giv-give, greef-grief, groop-group, iland-island, korus-chorus, neer-near, nightmar-nightmare, soop-soup, steddy-steady, stile-style, thum-thumb, tung-tongue, turnep-turnip, wimmen-women*—the list seemed endless. Goodrich did not have in mind a clean sweep of all of Webster's so-called spelling reforms, however. Certain classes of them—such as the elimination of *k* in *ck* and *u* in some words—already had a foothold in America. And the substitution of *er* for *re* for some word endings was, as we have seen, already common practice in America as well.

For these and many other types of overhaul, Goodrich insisted that the dictionary the Merriams had taken on must catch up with his abridgment, which fifteen years before had begun the process of bringing Webster closer in line with conventional American (and British) spelling. Concerned that the Merriams were beginning to worry about how competent a lexicographer Webster really was, he softened the blow, adding, "I can only say, that a dictionary must necessarily be imperfect—that no man can always have his thoughts about him." Webster's work undoubtedly is a monument of industry, he wrote, "but all his friends knew that important improvements might be made by a careful revision. Many inadvertences might be removed—many errors corrected." It was up to the Merriams to decide how far they wanted to go down that path, but Goodrich's literary friends were telling him it was now or never. If the work were printed now without thorough revision and "locked up" until 1856 when the copyright ran out, it might by then have ceased to be competitive. Worcester by that time could have become the new American lexicographic hero by consolidating his emerging status as America's most trustworthy and scholarly lexicographer—and stolen much of their market.[12]

Goodrich also impressed on the Merriams that if he did throw himself into this monumental process, he did not want either them or the Whites to grumble about whose edition was becoming superior in the course of the revisions. There must be no shortcuts either, he told them. Indeed, at first that is precisely what they had in mind—to bring out a quick edition out before Worcester could finish the one everyone knew he had in progress. Let there be no doubt, Goodrich warned them: if that happened, the critics would pounce on them. The resulting inferior product would open the way even more widely for Worcester to prevail with his careful, thorough, and superior scholarship.

Several versions of the contract between Goodrich and the Merriams were exchanged before Goodrich was satisfied they fully understood each other. They finally signed a contract on January 30, 1845, for what turned out to be three years' work. Goodrich would be paid $2,000 to $3,000. By contrast, Converse and Webster had paid Worcester $2,000 in 1828 for just eight months of work on the octavo abridgment.[13]

5

Fowler supported the plans for a new edition, but only just. His jealousy of Goodrich ran so deep that Goodrich for some time had been reluctant even to invite his children to stay with him and his wife in New Haven, lest Fowler should think he was trying to curry favor with them to their father's disadvantage. Webster had always trusted Fowler implicitly. He had written to his son William in Cincinnati back in July 1836: "As to your prejudice against Mr. Fowler, I care not a cent for it. You & the family have no better friend than Mr. Fowler, & he is deeply impressed with the importance of sustaining my publications—& no man can do more to effect in this business." In 1837 and

1838, he had repeatedly tried to convince Fowler to become joint editor with him in the preparation of the 1841 royal octavo edition. Fowler—who would emerge from relative obscurity to become one of the nation's authorities in linguistics with the appearance of his *English Language in Its Elements and Forms* (1850)—seriously considered the proposal. At Webster's urging, he even spoke about it independently to the New York firm Harper & Brothers, who liked the idea of publishing the proposed new edition, provided they could do so "unencumbered by the check which Mr. Goodrich [because of the octavo abridgment] held upon it." They promised a "pretty fortune" to Webster if this could be arranged. Goodrich stood in the way, however: with no way around that, Harpers' had no choice but to drop the idea. After Webster's death, Fowler came to resent what he considered Goodrich's foxlike intrigue in securing the copyright for the octavo abridgment, the root of a long antipathy between them that agitated Fowler far more than Goodrich.[14]

Acting on his father-in-law's trust and confidence in him as the preserver of the "sacred" dictionary, Fowler had independently secured a publisher for his own duodecimo edition (about the same size as Webster's 1829 *School and Counting-House* edition), what he called the *University* edition, an abridgment published by the New York firm F. J. Huntington and Savage in 1845 (with a revised edition in 1850).[15] For that edition, he decided, above all, not to make any revisions that would dishonor and violate Webster's system of spelling and pronunciation, and (in case anyone was listening) he insisted that the spelling in the projected Merriam edition should be guided by his own *University* edition exactly, not the Goodrich/Worcester abridgment. He feared the wholesale evisceration of Webster's lexicography. His entire rationale, therefore, was to defend Webster and protect his lexicographical legacy at all costs. Had he succeeded, he would have played perfectly into Worcester's hands.

Fowler issued in 1845 a privately circulated pamphlet, *Printed, but Not Published*, in which he rehearsed his grievances against his brother-in-law, offering a detailed account of how Goodrich allegedly had aborted Webster's plans and how Fowler himself, Webster's most trusted literary executor, had been sidelined. Goodrich's "shrewdness and skill," he wrote, had enabled him to achieve his "sharp bargain" with Webster. In vain Fowler had implored Goodrich to let him in on the act, share a portion of his royalties with Webster, and release Webster from his legally binding agreement not to publish a rival abridgment of similar size. Goodrich's main defense was that he was using the royalties for "holy purposes" at Yale, and that he had given the university $5,000 as an endowment toward a new divinity professorship there—a chair to which he was appointed, incidentally. Fowler's reasonable reply was that the family would have preferred to find their own ways of spending royalties rightfully belonging to Webster and his family.[16]

Fowler's pamphlet was so disturbing that Goodrich was moved to compose a prayer about it in his diary. It testified to his deeply religious nature and how Fowler had tested it: "I cannot doubt that I needed exactly this trial to humble and purify my soul. It is impossible to penetrate the depth of self-complacency. . . . Here was the tenderest place in which to touch me. I hope before God I can say . . . 1) That I have never prayed more fervently for any one than for the author of this attack. My heart warm[ed] toward him in prayer. . . . 2) I feel much more dead to worldly things, especially to public estimation. This is what I needed."[17]

Ellsworth told Fowler again that he was fussing too much, and that he should start working constructively with Goodrich. Curiously, Fowler interpreted this to mean that the trustees were putting him in total control of revisions for all editions—"I thus had the whole subject of alterations committed to me without reserve"—and began to act as if Goodrich were obliged to do as he said. Insisting on regular meetings and correspondence between them, he was adamant that all revisions be run by him before copy could be sent to the Merriams. He stood ready to fight back at every turn against Goodrich's anticipated corrections, deletions, and additions.[18]

He soon discovered he was no match for Goodrich. He described in a later account how Goodrich got the better of him: "I received a letter from Mr. Goodrich, stating that he was about to edit the large work for the Merriams, and *requesting me to authorize him, without consulting any one, to make alterations!* . . . I regarded this as a very cool piece of arrogance towards me, who was acting as an editor of the University edition, with full power to make alterations." In a huff, Fowler rushed down to New Haven from Middlebury to settle this matter with Goodrich in person. They talked for hours, well into the night. Several years later, Goodrich reminded Fowler of what he had told him sometime around midnight: "[Y]ou came to New Haven and proposed to unite yourself with me, as joint editor of this revision. I declined, stating that the compensation would be wholly inadequate, since you would be compelled to reside here, but putting my objection chiefly on the ground mentioned above, that the supervision of a *single* responsible editor was indispensable to the success of such an undertaking." The prospect of Fowler giving up his job to come to New Haven to pester him with interminable disagreement struck Goodrich as slow torture. They had reached an impasse, so the next day the two of them made their separate ways to Ellsworth in Hartford, who managed to get them to agree to work together for several months at least to make the orthography in the *University* edition and the Merriam edition the same. Even that arrangement was insufferable to Goodrich. It slowed the process to a crawl, precisely what Goodrich feared might happen.[19]

"You will, I know," Ellsworth wrote to Goodrich, "be able to urge good reasons for the alterations you design, and such reasons will influence me." But Fowler would not surrender. "I stated to you when last in Hartford," an exasperated Goodrich wrote to Ellsworth in February, that in declining to act as joint editor with Mr. Fowler, which he said he would have done "in respect to any other man," he had no desire to be secretive about what he was doing as editor. "I would cheerfully submit to Mr. Fowler the alterations which I made . . . in respect to spelling and pronunciation. . . ." Now, of all things, Fowler had just appeared on his doorstep in New Haven, thrust a paper at him for him to sign, demanding that Goodrich submit any revisions to him on a regular basis, and that he had the power of overruling any he did not like. Goodrich refused to sign. Poor Ellsworth felt helpless to patch it up between two scrapping brothers-in-law, but he privately reassured Goodrich he would have his way most of the time. The best thing to do was ignore Fowler and carry on with revisions, submit them to the trustees and family, and then send copy to the printers.[20]

There was never much doubt that Goodrich would prevail in that internecine rivalry, but Fowler's meddling was taking its toll both on the edition and Goodrich's mental and physical health. Other family members gave him mixed messages of support. He was about to wash his hands of the entire lot, carry on just with the Whites, and concentrate on his teaching and pastoral work at Yale. "The alterations in spelling which I have been able to obtain have cost me considerable pain of feeling from the resistance in that quarter, and much more must yet be experienced on other subjects," he wrote; "my health has suffered from this cause, and I expect it will suffer much more."

Fowler was "hostile to any considerable change, and your work," he cautioned the Merriams. Their edition "must . . . come forth at a great disadvantage as compared with Worcester . . . on the principle which he espouses." For the time being, he would continue and hope for the best: "I mean, as God gives me strength, to urge all changes which I think ought to be made for the benefit of the work and the promotion of your interests."[21]

Goodrich and the Merriams' agreement that drastic revisions of Webster must be made at all costs was vindicated in September 1845, Goodrich recalled, when "violent attacks were made upon Webster's orthography in various parts of the country, with an evident reference to the Merriams' well-publicized forthcoming edition. A report was also circulated and reported in Rochester, condemning Dr. Webster's system in the strongest terms." There were also "pointed remarks against us" in the New York Evangelist, supported even by the editor who previously "had been our friend." Particularly damaging, the editor of the New York Observer put together a report bitterly treating Webster's spelling "with the utmost contempt." The Merriams were convinced that an orchestrated effort from somewhere was under way to sink plans for their new edition. Panicking, they began sending Goodrich other such reports in the press, insisting frantically that he stick resolutely to the task of overhauling Webster's orthography—as if he needed persuading.[22]

The seemingly insurmountable problem by this time, caused partly by all these delays, concerned the goal of uniformity throughout all Webster editions. "I told the Merriams that it appeared to me too late," Goodrich wrote to Fowler: "[T]he stereotyping of the University was already completed, and every change would of course destroy the uniformity at which we aimed, unless correspondent changes were made in the plates of that work"—an expensive proposition. Goodrich refused to spend any more of his time with revisions unless Fowler's publisher, Huntington, agreed either to let the Merriam edition go ahead and let the University edition make its own way with an imperfect text, or pay for revising his plates.[23]

Another emergency meeting in New Haven on October 28 was called apparently by the Merriams and the unreliable William, who now found himself agreeing with Goodrich and the Merriams. The Merriams, William, Goodrich, Huntington, and Ellsworth were all there. Fowler seems not to have heard of the meeting—or perhaps he was deliberately excluded—and in his absence Huntington agreed to alter his stereotyped plates for the University edition, adopting the extensive revisions Goodrich already had under way. When Fowler learned that the meeting had occurred without him, he was furious: "[I]n violation of faith, in violation of honor, he [Goodrich] broke his agreement with me. . . . [H]e foisted into a book, edited by me . . . his alterations of Dr. Webster's system, and called them my alterations. . . . Thus was he guilty of a literary forgery. . . ." Goodrich would have none of this nonsense: "The Messrs. Merriams and Mr. [William] Webster will testify that the meeting originated with them and not with me." For good measure, he added, "If any man ever aimed to guard the rights of others, I aimed in that case to guard the rights of yourself and Mr. Huntington." The crowning insult, as Fowler saw it, was that when Huntington published the *University* edition in 1850, its title page did not even include Fowler's name.[24]

To put the record straight, nine years later, in his angry January 1854 letter to Fowler, Goodrich recounted that when by February 1846 Goodrich had already completed three hundred pages of revisions ready to be approved by the family, Fowler had asked him again to agree to give him access to that copy before sending it to the family for approval. Fowler had also demanded that the proof sheets be sent directly to him from the printer in Boston so he could keep track of the work in progress. To this Goodrich had coolly replied he could see the copy in Hartford when other members of the family saw it. Still, he conceded, if the Merriams and Ellsworth agreed, he was not averse to sending him the proofs, provided it was understood that Goodrich was not to be delayed by waiting for his suggestions. All he wanted was "harmony and peace." A couple of days later, Fowler accused him of deviously going forward with the final printing without consulting him: "I need not say that I felt deeply injured. . . . Earnestly and formally do I hereby enter a protest against your course in this affair as a violation of my rights and a breach of faith." That was too much for Goodrich: "By your letter . . . you [have] created the present separation between us. You carried things to the last extremity. You used language which one gentleman never applies to another except with the deliberate intention to render all further intercourse *impossible*. . . . I never cherished unkind or resentful feelings towards you; and I have never ceased, as in earlier days, to wish and pray for the happiness and prosperity of yourself and your children."[25]

Fowler continued to live in a fool's paradise regarding his influence on the Merriam edition. Eventually, even Ellsworth had had enough. "After some 6 letters between Mr. Fowler & myself," he wrote to William in February 1847, "I utterly despair of all cordial intercourse or friendly cooperation on his part, for the future. . . . He is the most extraordinary man I ever met with. . . . [H]e will not assent to *anything*; tis his very principle of action. His late letters to me have been little better than an insult." Fowler's story was over. He had been banished from editorial roles, and with the death of his wife, Harriet, in 1844 he was no longer even an heir and therefore no longer legally eligible to receive income from Webster's books—although the family relented, including him anyway following a good deal of soul-searching on their part.[26]

Goodrich's pursuit of total editorial control over Webster's dictionaries, however many there might be, had succeeded. He had struck a hard bargain. He could proceed without anyone constantly looking over his shoulder. This is not what the Merriams had in mind at the start: they had envisaged instead a publication that would somehow spring fully armed from the Goodrich/Worcester abridgment but not take much time to get out to the public. But Goodrich's plan made possible the thorough housecleaning required throughout Webster's lexicography before any new edition from the Merriams could be offered to the public.

11

Waiting for Worcester

From the very beginning of their interest in Webster's dictionaries, the Merriams' greatest fear was Worcester. Every historical, geographical, and lexicographical work to which Worcester had ever turned his hand had met with general approval, high commendation, and commercial success. He was acknowledged by Goodrich, among others, to be a superior lexicographer to Webster. Worcester was without doubt at the height of his powers and on the move, but he had not reckoned with the commercial hostility and extraordinarily intense entrepreneurship of George and Charles Merriam.[1]

The imminent publication of Worcester's 1846 edition worried them. There were things they could do right away to sully Worcester's reputation and discredit him by restaging the old allegations against him, reviving the charges that Webster had egregiously paraded before the public in 1834–35. "Worcester, as you know," Charles Merriam wrote to Ellsworth on March 2, 1846, "was employed by Dr. Webster to abridge his work . . . [and] in this way possessed himself fully of Dr. Webster's plan and the whole art of dictionary making." Worcester had done the unthinkable: while Webster was still alive, Merriam continued, Worcester had deviously never let it be known he planned to write his own dictionary, which the "community would have esteemed disingenuous, if not dishonorable, and morally wrong." Now, Merriam added, with Webster dead, Worcester was free to steal from Webster's work: "No one supposes he could sit down and compile such a work as he will bring out, seriously affecting, as it doubtless will, the sale of Webster . . . if Dr. Webster had not written his large work." Worcester had every right to write a dictionary of English, of course—never mind what Webster was doing. In any case, Worcester surely felt that his work on Todd's edition of Johnson's dictionary was a far better tutorial toward his own edition than was

Webster's work, given that Johnson's notions of English matched his own far more than Webster's did thus far.[2]

The Merriams even contemplated legal action against Worcester but decided against it because of costs. Their best option, they concluded, was to return the favor and pillage from Worcester's dictionary: "Professor Goodrich's view has been, therefore, that we look at Worcester, when [his book is] out, and avail ourselves, as we legally and righteously may, of his labors, so that his work shall not combine the results of Webster's labors and his own, while ours has Webster's only."[3] Legally, yes, but perhaps not righteously. The knotty problem was that Webster's claims of Worcester's alleged thefts had never been substantiated. On the contrary, Worcester had defiantly refuted these allegations, when they first were leveled at him, and had publicly shown Webster to be seriously misguided and oddly unfamiliar with British lexicography, or any lexicography anywhere else for that matter.

Charles maintained that Goodrich had long been convinced Worcester would "avail himself largely of Dr. Webster's labors." The reverse, in fact, was true. The Merriams preferred to overlook Goodrich's unequivocal remark to them just a few months earlier that, if anything, the borrowing was the other way around. "Now the fact is," Goodrich told them, "Dr. Webster did borrow directly from the 8vo [octavo] abridgment, a good deal of matter which Mr. Worcester and I put there." He did some counting and cited an unspecified "three thousand words which we had inserted from other dictionaries" and numerous words and their definitions new to dictionaries.[4]

Everyone knew Worcester was about to publish a new dictionary that was expected to reconfigure the American dictionary landscape. But the Merriams did not know when it was likely to be published, nor did they know enough about it—details they needed in order to devise their strategies effectively. They scouted through their Boston network to see if they could discover some insider information and came up with a look at a few of Worcester's printed sheets and an idea of just how much further he had to go before he completed his present edition: "His work has not yet appeared," Charles Merriam wrote to Ellsworth in March 1846, "having been delayed by the great care and pains-taking with which he has elaborated it. . . . The Stereotyper is upon the letter *w* and it will yet be three months before it appears, perhaps a little longer." They were under no illusions. Worcester was going to produce a fine dictionary: "We have seen some of the paper, and so has Professor Goodrich. His [Worcester's] draughts upon Webster are apparent, and his own additional labors are also important." Without giving examples, Merriam mentioned that "on a single page Worcester has 19 words not in Webster; on another, 30, and so on." It was crucial for them to know when Worcester's dictionary was likely to be published so they could plan their own publishing and advertising strategy. "Shall we await the appearance of Worcester?" Merriam wondered. As long as they obeyed the terms of their contract to come out with the new edition, Ellsworth did not much care whether they waited or not. Ask Goodrich, he replied a couple of days later. In the end, they decided to wait just in case Worcester's edition exhibited the degree of borrowing from Webster they hoped for and which they could publicize as part of their negative advertising campaign.[5]

2

They did not have long to wait. Worcester at last published his *Universal and Critical Dictionary of the English Language* in 1846 with the Boston publisher Wilkins, Carter and Company. It was a larger octavo (947 pages, of which 76 pages were prefatory material) than his *Comprehensive Dictionary* and was based on *Todd-Johnson*, integrating Walker's *Critical Pronouncing Dictionary*, and containing no fewer than about twenty-seven thousand additional entry words for a total of about eighty-three thousand, more than any dictionary then bearing Webster's name—without resorting to the practice in other dictionaries of including many thousands of entry words in their participial forms ending in *ing* and *ed*. The edition gave Goodrich and the Merriams more to think about than they had bargained for. (It is noteworthy, incidentally, that unlike Webster, whose self-advertising was ceaseless, Worcester did not in this dictionary, or any of his dictionaries printed in America, ever adorn his edition with a frontispiece displaying an engraving of himself. It was always Webster's way to do so; it was not Worcester's.)

Worcester explained in his preface that as he began preparing his *Comprehensive Dictionary* back in 1828, he had "adopted the practice of recording all the English words which he met with, used by respectable authors, and not found in Todd's edition of Johnson's Dictionary." His plan for his new dictionary at first was simply to enlarge his *Comprehensive*, but having "found the words which were not registered in any dictionary more numerous" than anticipated, he decided a new dictionary was in order, containing "as complete a vocabulary of the language as he should be able to make." There may well

Ē-DĔL-FŎR'SĪTE,* n. (Min.) A species of red zeolite. Dana.
Ē-DĔM-A-TŌSE', a. [oἴδημα.] Full of humors; edematous.
Ē-DĔM'A-TOŬS,* a. Relating to œdema; full of humors; swelling; œdematous. H...
Ē'DEN, n. [Heb.] Paradise...
Ē'DEN-ĪZED, (ē'den-īzd) a...
Ē-DĔN'TAL,* n. (Zool.) O...
mammals including those...
paratus is more or less in...
Ē-DĔN'TA-LOŬS,* a. Tooth...
Ē-DĔN'TĀ-TĘD, a. [edentat... ley. [R.]

ĒDGE'-RĀIL,* n. An iron bar or rail upon which the wheels of a railroad car revolve, a flange being formed upon the inner edge of the rail, projecting about an inch, in order to prevent the wheels from sliding off. Tanner.

Ē-DĔN-TĀ'TION, n. A pulling out of teeth. Cockeram. [R.]
EDGE, (ĕj) n. The sharp or cutting part or side of a blade or cutting instrument; a narrow part rising from a broader; brink; margin; border; rim; verge; extremity; sharpness; intenseness of desire; keenness; acrimony of temper.— To set teeth on edge, to cause an uneasy tingling in the teeth.
EDGE, (ĕj) v. a. [i. EDGED; pp. EDGING, EDGED.] To sharpen; to furnish with an edge; to border with any thing; to fringe; to exasperate; to embitter; to put forward beyond a line.
EDGE, v. n. To move forward sideways, or by little and little.
EDGE,* a. Having an edge; sharp; edged:—applied to a railroad in which the carriages run upon rails or edges of rails, as in common railroads,—in distinction to such roads as are made of flat blocks. Francis.
EDGED, (ĕjd or ĕd'jĕd) p. a. Sharp; not blunt.
EDGE'LESS, a. Having no edge; blunt. Shak.
EDGE'-RAIL,* n. An iron bar or rail upon which the wheels of a railroad car revolve, a flange being formed upon the inner edge of the rail, projecting about an inch, in order to prevent the wheels from sliding off. Tanner.
EDGE'-TOOL, n. A sharp tool to cut with; an axe or knife.
EDGE'-WISE, ad. In the direction of the edge.
EDG'ING, n. A border; a fringe; a narrow lace.
ED'I-BLE, a. [edo, L.] Eatable; fit to be eaten.
ED'I-BLE-NESS,* n. The quality of being edible. Scott.
E'DICT, (ē'dĭkt, S. W. J. F. Ja. K. Sm. Wb.; ĕd'ĭkt or ē'dĭkt, P.] n. [edictum, L.] A public ordinance or decree issued by a sovereign or high power; an order; a proclamation.
ED'I-FI-CĂNT, [ĕd'ę-fę-kănt, K. Sm. Wb.; ę-dĭf'ę-kănt, Ja. Todd.] a. Building; constructing. Dugard. [R.]
ED-I-FI-CĀ'TION, n. Act of edifying; state of being edified; instruction in religion and morals; improvement in disposition and character; improvement.
ED'I-FĪ-CA-TO-RY, a. Tending to edification. Bp. Hall. [R.]
ED'I-FICE, (ĕd'ę-fĭs) n. A fabric; a building; a structure.
ED-I-FI''CIAL, (ĕd-ę-fĭsh'al) a. Relating to edifices.
ED'I-FĪ-ER, n. One who edifies.
ED'I-FŸ, v. a. [ædifico, L.] [i. EDIFIED; pp. EDIFYING, EDIFIED.] To instruct so as to improve in religious character; to instruct; to improve; to teach. [† To build. Spenser.]
ED'I-FŸ-ING, n. Instruction; teaching.
ED'I-FŸ-ING,* p. a. Tending to edify; instructive.
ED'I-FŸ-ING-LY, ad. In an instructive manner. Killingbeck.
E'DILE, n. [ædilis, L.] A magistrate in ancient Rome, who had the charge of the temples, public buildings, streets, &c.
E'DILE-SHIP,* n. The office of edile. Gray.
ED'ING-TON-ITE,* n. (Min.) A mineral found in Scotland, in small, grayish-white, translucent prisms; a crystallized felspar. Brande.
ED'IT, v. a. [éditer, Fr.] [i. EDITED; pp. EDITING, EDITED.] To superintend, revise, or prepare for publication, as a book, newspaper, &c.; to conduct; to manage, as a literary publication. Brit. Crit.
E-DI''TION, (ę-dĭsh'ųn) n. [editio, L.] The publication of a book; the whole impression of a book; republication.
†Ę-DI''TION-ER, n. A publisher; an editor. Gregory.
Ę-DI''TI-ō PRIN'CEPS,* (ę-dĭsh'ę-ō) [L.] The first or earliest edition of a book. Hamilton.
ED'I-TOR, n. One who edits; one who superintends, revises, or prepares a work for publication; the conductor of a newspaper, journal, &c.
ED-I-TŌ'RI-AL, a. Belonging to or written by an editor.
ED'I-TOR-SHIP,* n. The office and duty of an editor.
ED'I-TRESS,* n. A female editor. Ec. Rev.
†Ē-DIT'U-ĀTE, v. a. [æedituo, low L.] To govern a house. Gregory.
ED-RI-OPH-THĂL'MA,* n. [ἐδραῖος and ὀφθαλμός.] (Zool.) A class of crustaceous animals, with sessile eyes situated on the sides of the head. P. Cyc.
ED-U-CA-BIL'I-TY,* n. Capacity of being educated. Chalmers. [R.]
ED'U-CA-BLE,* a. That may be educated; teachable. Chambers. [R.]
ED'U-CĀTE, (ĕd'yu-kāt) [ĕd'ü-kāt, S. J. E. F. Ja.; ĕd'jū-kāt, W.] v. a. [educo, L.] [i. EDUCATED; pp. EDUCATING, EDUCATED.] To bring forth and form the natural faculties; to bring up; to instruct youth; to nurture; to teach.

ED'U-CĀT-ED,* p. a. Having received education; instructed.
ED-U-CĀ'TION, n. Act of educating; the act of developing and cultivating the various physical, intellectual, and...
E-DŪCE', v. a. [educo, L.] [i. EDUCED; pp. EDUCING, EDUCED.] To draw out; to bring out; to extract.
Ę-DŪ'CI-BLE,* a. That may be educed. Martineau.
Ę-DŪCT',* n. That which is educed or elicited. Brande.
Ę-DŪC'TION, n. Act of bringing out.
Ę-DŪC'TIVE,* a. Drawing out; extractive. Boyle.
Ę-DŪC'TOR,* n. He or that which elicits. Smart.
Ę-DŪL'CO-RĀTE, v. a. [dulcoro, L.] [i. EDULCORATED; pp. EDULCORATING, EDULCORATED.] To sweeten; to purify; to wash; to free from acids, salts, &c.
Ę-DŪL-CO-RĀ'TION, n. The act of edulcorating.— (Chem.) Purification from salts, &c.
Ę-DŪL'CO-RA-TIVE, a. Having the quality of sweetening. Browne.
†Ę-DŪL'IOUS, (ę-dūl'yus) a. [edulium, L.] Eatable. Sir T. Browne.
ĒEK, v. a. To supply. See EKE.
ĒEK'ING, n. Augmentation; increase. Spenser.
ĒEL, (ēl) n. A serpentine, slimy fish that lurks in mud.
ĒEL'POŪT, n. A small kind of eel; a burbot.
ĒEL'-SHAPED,* (ēl'shāpt) a. Shaped like an eel. Pennant.
ĒEL'-SKIN,* n. The skin of an eel. Shak.
Ē'EN, (ēn) ad. A contraction of even.
ĒFF, (ĕf) n. A small lizard. See EFT.
†ĒF'FA-BLE, a. [effabilis, L.] Utterable. Wallis.
ĘF-FĀCE', v. a. [i. EFFACED; pp. EFFACING, EFFACED.] To blot out; to expunge; to erase; to obliterate; to cancel; to destroy any thing painted or carved; to rub off; to blow out; to strike out; to destroy; to wear away.
ĘF-FĀCE'A-BLE,* a. Capable of being effaced.
ĘF-FĀCE'MENT,* n. Obliteration; act of effacing. Perry.
†ĘF-FĀS'CI-NĀTE, v. a. To bewitch; to fascinate. Cockeram.
†ĘF-FĀS-CI-NĀ'TION, n. Fascination. Shelford.
ĘF-FĔCT', n. [effectus, L.] That which is produced by an operating cause; result; issue; consequence; event; purpose; meaning; general intent; success; completion; successful performance; reality; operation of a law.— pl. Goods; movables; property.
ĘF-FĔCT', v. a. [i. EFFECTED; pp. EFFECTING, EFFECTED.] To accomplish; to fulfil; to achieve; to complete; to execute; to bring to pass; to produce as a cause.
ĘF-FĔCT'ER, n. See EFFECTOR.
ĘF-FĔCT'I-BLE, a. Practicable; feasible. Browne. [R.]
ĘF-FĔC'TION, n. (Geom.) An effect of a general proposition; the geometrical construction of a proposition.
ĘF-FĔC'TIVE, a. Having the power to produce effects; producing effect; efficacious; effectual; operative; active; efficient; useful.
ĘF-FĔC'TIVE-LY, ad. In an effective manner.
ĘF-FĔC'TIVE-NESS,* n. The quality of being effective. Ash.
ĘF-FĔCT'LESS, a. Without effect; impotent; useless.
ĘF-FĔC'TOR, n. He or that which effects; a maker.
ĘF-FĔCTS',* n. pl. Movables; goods; furniture. Johnson.
ĘF-FĔCT'U-AL, (ef-fĕkt'yu-al) a. Producing decisive effect; productive of effects; powerful; efficacious; adequate.
ĘF-FĔCT'U-AL-LY, ad. In an effectual manner.
ĘF-FĔCT'U-AL-NESS, n. The quality of being effectual. Scott.
ĘF-FĔCT'U-ĀTE, v. a. [i. EFFECTUATED; pp. EFFECTUATING, EFFECTUATED.] To bring to pass; to effect. Barrow.
ĘF-FĔCT-U-Ā'TION,* n. Act of effectuating. Coleridge. [R.]
†ĘF-FĔCT'U-ŌSE, a. Effectual. Joye.
†ĘF-FĔCT'U-OŬS, a. Effectual. Barret.
†ĘF-FĔCT'U-OŬS-LY, ad. Effectually. Stapleton.
ĘF-FĔM'I-NA-CY, n. Quality of being effeminate; softness; unbecoming a man; womanish delicacy; lasciviousness.
ĘF-FĔM'I-NĀTE, a. [effeminatus, L.] Having the qualities of a woman; womanish; soft to an unmanly degree; feminine; voluptuous; tender; delicate.
ĘF-FĔM'I-NĀTE, v. a. [i. EFFEMINATED; pp. EFFEMINATING, EFFEMINATED.] To make womanish; to emasculate; to unman.
ĘF-FĔM'I-NĀTE, v. n. To grow womanish; to soften. Pope.
ĘF-FĔM'I-NĀTE,* n. An effeminate person. Cowper.
ĘF-FĔM'I-NĀTE-LY, ad. In an effeminate manner.
ĘF-FĔM'I-NĀTE-NESS, n. Unmanly softness; effeminacy.
†ĘF-FĔM-I-NĀ'TION, n. Effeminacy. Browne.
ĘF-FĔN'DI,* n. A Turkish word which signifies lord, master, or superior, and is joined as a title of respect to ecclesiastical, legal, and other civil functionaries, in contradistinction to aga, the title by which high military personages are designated; as, Reis Effendi, the title of the principal secretary of state and prime minister of the Ottoman empire. P. Cyc.

FIGURE 14. Worcester's *A Universal and Critical Dictionary of the English Language* was published in 1846. Detail: Definition of *edge-rail*, a technical term. Courtesy of Indiana State University Special Collections, Cordell Collection of Dictionaries.

have been other, more personal, factors behind that decision, such as the understandable human emotion to push back at the Merriams, whose behavior
since they appeared on the Webster stage did not strike him as "righteous." In
any case, this was not good news for the fate of Webster. He had taken many
words from eighteenth- and early-nineteenth-century English dictionaries,
especially those by John Ash, Charles Richardson, and B. H. Smart, as well
as from several scientific volumes. Another important source was William
Allen, former president of Bowdoin College and Dartmouth College, assistant librarian of Harvard, and author in 1809 of *An American Biographical
and Historical Dictionary*. He had collected some ten thousand words not to
be found in any standard dictionaries, many of them technical. At first, Allen
agreed to supply the Merriams with the words, at the rate of $10 per one hun-
dred words, but ultimately they did not publish many, because a large number were compound words and therefore "of little worth." Allen then passed
the manuscript on to Worcester, from which Worcester obtained upwards of
1,500 additional words he had missed.[6]

Allen's collection is an example of the American amateur preoccupation
and fascination with words at the time, for the most part independent of the
work of lexicographers: collecting, counting, evaluating, sharing, populariz-
ing, philosophizing, politicizing, and writing about them. This was the era
of the rise of democratic urges about the English language, expressed in the
precipitous growth of literacy and access to literature of all kinds rolling off
the mechanized presses, fresh interest in the language of the Bible, establishment of "common schools" and public libraries, accelerated coinage of new
words, and the development of technology, science, and medicine. Words
had become democratized, social equalizers, no longer the concern chiefly of
the learned and social elite. The general public claimed ownership. Ten thousand words sounds like a large number, and it was for the amateur enthusiast,
but for the lexicographers this era of surging interest in words was a field day.
Words were springing up everywhere. It was the job of dictionaries to keep
up with and sort them. If a lexicographer could boast he had more words in
his dictionary than existed in any other, he might be able to sell more copies.
Worcester was more fortunate than Webster, it must be said, that he lived,
collected, and wrote further into this new lexical universe, although he had
no interest in chucking out the old to let in the new. On the other hand, Webster had a head start in linking up with new patriotic, democratic linguistic

trends in America, launching himself as the voice of the people. And his legacy was perpetuated by his editors in the coming decades.[7]

In a lengthy introduction to the *Universal and Critical Dictionary*, Worcester's impressive scholarship is on display. It includes strongly worded sections on pronunciation; orthography; grammar; the history of the language; Americanisms and provincialisms (and archaisms); a lucid history of British and American lexicography; and two catalogs, one of "English Dictionaries of Words" going back to the fifteenth century, and the other of "American Dictionaries of English"—both drawn mostly from his world-class private collection of lexicons. What is striking about the dictionary is Worcester's scholarly and practical consistency, his quiet but authoritative tone, born of sound research and alert lexicography. People felt they could trust Worcester. His friend and Harvard academic Sidney Willard summed up Worcester's achievement in 1846: "He does not belong to the corps of militant etymologists, who war against custom, which establishes the laws of language. On the contrary, he pays due fealty to these laws, and gives no countenance to a revolutionary spirit. We have discovered no instance in which he has changed the orthography of a word to make it conform to an assumed theory. In these respects, he has, wherever we have traced him, shown that fidelity to our language as we found it, which makes him worthy of entire confidence."[8]

Although he risked the ire of outspoken patriotic readers and devoted Websterians, Worcester is not shy in stating in his preface that the authorities for most of his entry words are "mostly English"—mainly Johnson and Walker, in fact—or that he has cited English rather than American authors "of equal or even higher respectability" because "it is satisfactory to many readers to know, in relation to a new, uncommon, or doubtful word, that it is not peculiar to American writers, but that a respectable English authority may be adduced in support of its use." To which Webster might well have replied, "Why do we need English support for the uses of our words in the first place?" But Worcester approached all aspects of the dictionary with, as one critic has called it, "judicious moderation." Having been wounded more than once by Webster and not wishing to take chances that someday his ghost, in the voice of a new, antagonistic publisher, might resurrect the old attacks on him, in his preface he reviews how, when, and why he had begun writing dictionaries. Webster's work did not enter into his calculations, he says: "With respect to Webster's Dictionary, which the Compiler several years since abridged, he is not aware of having taken a single word, or the definition of a word, from that work. . . ." He had vigorously made this point, we must recall, in defending himself in the 1831 *Worcester Palladium* controversy against Webster's allegations that he had plagiarized from him. Whether his claim is plausible is virtually impossible to document given the nature of lexicography and the manner in which lexicographers had "borrowed" from each other for centuries. Nevertheless, Worcester argues that he went out of his way to avoid taking words or definitions from Webster. But regarding words of "disputed" pronunciation, he has given Webster's "authority" its due, along with that of several eminent English orthoepists.[9]

Worcester raises one more pointed objection to Webster on the matter of pronunciation: "The standard of pronunciation is not the authority of any dictionary, or of any orthoepist; . . . it is the present usage of literary and well-bred society." This contention, of course, appears to contradict Webster's popular (or populist) belief that the standard of pronunciation in America must, for the sake at least of national unity, be that of "common" people. But what Webster was tuned into was not the speech and orthography of the people as much as his own language theories—partly political and nationalistic, partly philosophically derived from the dubious Horne Tooke (although he had drifted away from this mentor in his later work) and Charles Richardson, and partly etymological. What Worcester really opposed was Webster's perceived manipulation of language according to "rational" or schematized linguistic conceptions. Worcester was not, and never had been, adumbrating social, political, philosophical, or schematized linguistic principles. He can be seen as a "conservative" linguist not because he was a defender of the language as used in England, or a champion of Samuel Johnson and John Walker, but because he abhorred indulgence. Worcester did, in fact, keep his eyes on American usage, although he never branded his books "American" dictionaries. Where Webster pushed for "radical" linguistic schemes based on analogy and essentially incorrect etymology to determine spelling and pronunciation, Worcester's lexicographical purpose was to write dictionaries that record the language as it existed in America. He never opposed American words. The corollary of that was not that therefore he would need to have rejected elegance and correctness as a model for literature and speech—and that if he did not, he would not qualify as a lexicographer of the people. A dictionary must contain, he writes, "all the words of the language," which recalls his remark in the *Palladium* controversy that no lexicographer owned entry words. The fact was that both sides of these dictionary wars—in the newspapers, universities, schools, writings of literary figures, politics, and speech of men and women of "the highest literary culture"—agreed, as Kenneth Cmiel puts it, "that Anglo-American literature, broadly meaning prose published in books, was the foundation of a solid English dictionary." There was such a thing as "authentic elegance." In the middle of all the fighting over the language that was going on, Worcester nevertheless still honors Webster in his preface to the 1846 edition, generously calling him "the greatest and most important" English lexicographer since Johnson and describing his quarto as "of great learning and research," with "many and great improvements with respect both to the etymology and definitions of the words." Having written that, however, Worcester slips in a caveat, "the taste and judgment of the author [meaning Webster] are not generally esteemed equal to his industry and erudition."[10]

Worcester's "judicious moderation" is apparent in a number of ways. To begin with, he decided he would include etymology sparingly, where useful, not dealing with it as an independent study in parallel with definitions. His principle is that since Anglo-Saxon is the "mother tongue" of English and that most of the words frequently used derive from it "with more or less change of their orthography," he omits most of the etymology of such words. He certainly was not going to launch himself into the kind of etymological journey that consumed so much of Webster's time, not because he was not competent to do so, but rather because he did not believe a dictionary was the appropriate forum for testing such theories. As regards vocabulary, most of his additional entry words, he explains, were drawn from years of reading, and from Johnson and Walker—he places asterisks on the thousands of words he did not take from them—but all of them were "revised with much labor and care, in relation to their orthography, pronunciation, etymology, and definitions." There is also a large increase—over any other dictionary ever published—in the lexicon of words relating to the arts and sciences. Again, he took many from Johnson, but hundreds of them he drew from encyclopedias and various specialized dictionaries of fine arts, war, medicine, technology, manufacturing, mining, gardening and agriculture, commerce, building, architecture, archaeology, chemistry, mineralogy, midwifery, anatomy, veterinary science, the military, and marine life. Virtually all of those words "have been defined entirely new."[11]

Worcester chooses to include a good selection of foreign words and, more controversially, archaic and "many words which are obsolete, and many which are low or unworthy of being countenanced," but he maintains that since readers come across them all the time in their reading, they will be grateful to be able to look them up in an English dictionary. He anticipates that many critics will feel he has been too "liberal" in throwing his net out too far and wide to draw in words. This is not a newfound concern on his part. Indeed, Webster had chastised him precisely for including so many obsolete, archaic, foreign, and scientific words in his 1830 *Comprehensive Dictionary*; but as he writes, "a dictionary which is designed to be a complete glossary to all English books that are now read, must contain" many such words.[12]

All things considered, it was his definitions in which readers were most interested. They vary considerably in length, at least half of them only one line long, others (rarely) as much as twenty or more lines. A characteristic succession of several related words following each other in quick succession in a definition often illustrates his impatience with imprecision, as he patiently chooses one word after another to introduce senses that unfold the biography of the entry word as fully as possible. A sample of a few of his definitions:

Function: "Performance; employment; office; occupation; office of a member of the body; place; charge, faculty; power;—a mathematical expression considered with reference to its form."

Mother: "She that has borne offspring: a female parent; correlative to *son* or *daughter*; that which has produced any thing:—that which has preceded in time; as, a mother church to chapels:—a familiar term of address to a matron or old woman.— . . . A thick, slimy substance formed in liquors, especially in vinegar."

Patriot: "One who loves and faithfully serves his country. It is sometimes used ironically [as Johnson did when he defined 'patriotism' as 'a factious disturber of the government']."

Pauser: "One who pauses or deliberates."

Thin: "Not thick; rare; not dense; not close; separate by large spaces; not closely compacted or accumulated;—exile; small;—not coarse; not gross in substance; as, a *thin* veil:—not abounding; not fat; not bulky; lean; slim; slender; meagre; slight; unsubstantial.

An especially long definition of almost thirty lines invariably includes some etymology, as in *sirloin*, in which he cites part of Johnson's definition and relates the word's etymology to its orthography: "It is not found in any English dictionary previous to that of Johnson, with the orthography of *sirloin*. [Nathan] Bailey's Dictionary has *surloin of beef*, corresponding to the French *surlonge de beouf*, the obvious or probable etymology. *Surloin* is also given by [Robert] Ainsworth; and the word occurs repeatedly in [Randle] Cotgrave's Dictionary, the first published in 1611, with the orthography of *surloine* and *surloyne*."

For those who still held his and Goodrich's octavo abridgment against him, Worcester insists it had not been his idea: he "was induced to undertake the labor of making the octavo abridgment of Dr. Webster's 'American Dictionary of the English Language.'" He "had no responsibility" in his editing beyond the "rules" that were part of his understanding with Goodrich. Having got that off his chest, he apparently felt himself well above and beyond the fray and safe from further sniping by Webster's militia of defenders. It would not be long before he discovered he was not as safe as he thought.[13]

3

Soon after Worcester's *Universal and Critical Dictionary of the English Language* was published in 1846, the Merriams began a deliberate and sustained hunt for evidence of Worcester's alleged thefts, hoping to tilt the competition in their favor even before they published their edition. William Webster was in New York, removed from the hotbed of these clashing interests in Massachusetts, but they wrote to him for assistance anyway. Search through Worcester's *Universal* dictionary, they instructed him, for evidence that Worcester had taken "the exact language" from Webster. William read over Worcester's new dictionary and failed to find any. He was surprised more by the "meagerness of his definitions" and concluded that Worcester did not steal from Webster, and the Merriams had little to worry about from him. That was not exactly what the Merriams wanted to hear. It was the sinning, not the virtuous, Worcester they wished to portray.[14]

They also called on Noah Porter, a graduate of Yale and a professor of moral philosophy and metaphysics there since 1846, to spearhead an attack on Worcester. Porter, who would become president of the university in 1871, had a worldwide reputation as a philosopher and theologian, having written on a wide variety of subjects. His best-known work, *The Human Intellect*, would be published in 1868. Apart from the Yale connection and the fact that this conflict was shaping up partly as a Yale versus Harvard contest, he had no apparent reason to turn against Worcester at this particular moment if the Merriams had not commissioned him to do so. If Goodrich advised him against any attack on the integrity of his friend, Porter ignored him, for he was quite blunt in an unattributed review article he published in the May 1847 issue of the *American Review*, a magazine particularly favorable to Webster. Whether he received a fee for writing this, or did it as part of the general Yale faculty support of Webster, is unknown.

Porter's discourse describes what he thinks all modern dictionaries of English should aspire to be like by midcentury. He starts off neutrally enough: "What is wanted in such a dictionary is the good usage of educated and sensible people in England and America—not the ultra and impracticable affectations of the salon, not the stiff and studied overdoing of the actor, or the professed doctor of pronunciation, not the refined nor the coarse cockneyisms of the city, nor again the negligent and vulgar provincialisms of Old or New England; but the actual use of the intelligent and refined who speak the English language." He agrees with Worcester that greater notice should be taken of English usage than of American, but without importing the language habits of the "affected Englishman" into the American language: "[W]e had rather err from provincial ignorance than from mistakes of affected imitators."

Porter divides the rest of his review into four sections: pronunciation, orthography, new words, and definitions, mostly dedicated to finding shortcomings in Worcester. He praises Worcester for his expansion of the lexicon to reflect the progress of the arts and physical sciences but insists he is too liberal when he includes, among his twenty-seven thousand new entry words not included in the latest edition of Johnson's *Dictionary* any word that has been used even just once by a writer, English or American, be it ever so contrived, absurd, or coined for a merely immediate effect. His examples of such offensive words that he says Worcester put in, all of which are part of our lexicon today, include *cantankerous, cutter, dandyize, dyssillabification, facsimile, scruff, shopocracy,* and *squirearchy*. (Except for one of these, Porter is correct: none is mentioned in either Worcester's 1830 *Comprehensive* or Webster's 1841 edition, but *cutter* appears in both.) He surmises that Worcester has done this simply to make his book sell well by inflating the entry word count. For every word Webster had introduced, he argues, with absurd exaggeration, Worcester has flooded the language with a hundred.

As for definitions, Webster's strong suit, Porter continues, Worcester is "unequal," usually correct but resorting too often to synonyms in definitions rather than to descriptions, "with little attention to the development of meaning" that is crucial to a more complete understanding of a word. Worcester is not even close to Webster's artistry in defining words, Porter contends. He then comments, accurately, on twenty-five examples of the incompleteness or erroneousness of Worcester's definitions, such as *neology*: "A term applied to a new system of interpretation of the Scriptures in Germany." "How much information does this convey?" Porter asks. "Why not tell what system of interpretation?" Porter also questions Worcester's definition of *saddle-cloth* as "A cover for saddle," which is not "the more common signification" of a blanket between the saddle and the horse; and of *kraal*, which Worcester defines as "a rude hut or cabin of Hottentots, with conical or round tops."[15] Not correct, says Porter: "[I]t is a village of such huts, never a single one." (Worcester accepted such corrections and expanded or corrected all of these in his 1860 edition.)[16]

The last page of Porter's "review" is less an analysis of Worcester's dictionary than a defense of Webster and an advertisement for the Goodrich-Merriam edition about to be released. With this review Porter strengthened his credentials in the eyes of the Merriams as an able Yale-based defender of any future Merriam-Webster editions, should he ever be needed.

4

The new, one-volume Goodrich-Merriam quarto edition of the *American Dictionary*, with a lexicon of 1,281 pages, was published late in 1847 with the title *The American Dictionary of the English Language by Noah Webster . . . Revised and Enlarged by Chauncey A. Goodrich*. The purpose in publishing it as a quarto was to have it create a greater impression as a more substantial work than Worcester's 1846 octavo. In order to achieve that in one volume, the Merriams were obliged to use smaller type. It was put on the market at the low price of $6 (more than $150 today)—substantially less expensive than the $20 price of Webster's 1828 two-volume quarto and the same price as Worcester's 1846 edition. Goodrich remarks in the preface that it is "the fruit of nearly three years of care and attention." Because work on the edition had survived the concerns of the Webster family about how extensively the new Merriam edition would revise Webster's lexicography, and also because Fowler had complicated Goodrich's work by wanting to have a major part in it, Goodrich makes a point of stating that he "has not acted . . . upon his own personal responsibility," but has, from time to time, laid open the sheets to the inspection of the other members of the family. . . ."[17]

Unlike both Webster and Worcester, in his preface to this edition Goodrich does not indulge in the numbers game of boasting how many new words he has added. He says only "some thousands." More to the point, he warns against the damaging effect of "a hasty introduction" of new terms and innovations into the lexicon: "There is at the present day, especially in England, a boldness of innovations on this subject which amounts to absolute licentiousness. . . . Our vocabulary is already encumbered with a multitude of words which have never formed a permanent part of English literature." It is a "serious evil" to insert any more, he adds—a pertinent statement in light of how rapidly new words were then popping up in the American language. Worcester thought the same thing. Obsolete and archaic words, however, that are found in the works of Bacon, Spenser, Shakespeare, and others are not the problem, and they ought to be included if the writings of England's great authors are to continue to be understood. So-called Americanisms are not a concern, since there are very few of them in any way worthy of being in a dictionary, Goodrich asserts, most of which have come over from Britain.[18]

According to Goodrich's preface, the new dictionary is "designed to present, on a reduced scale, a clear, accurate, and full exhibition of the *American Dictionary* in all its parts." The book is meant for a wide market, for use in academies and other institutions of higher learning, counting houses (business accounting and bookkeeping offices), and the family, and as a tool to aid in writing and pronunciation. The definitions are easily understandable and economically worded in "short descriptive sentences and clauses" for a wide range of users. Gone forever are the 1828 quarto's at times seemingly endless essaylike, discursive, personal definitions. Goodrich stresses that the

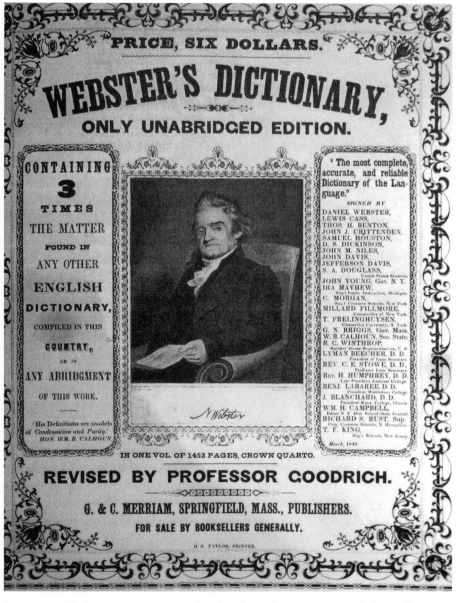

FIGURE 15. The first Merriam edition of Webster's dictionary, published in 1847–48, advertised Goodrich as editor. Courtesy of the Beinecke Rare Book and Manuscript Library, Yale University, G. and C. Merriam Company Papers.

dictionary has now been made into a "Synonymous Dictionary": "Every one engaged in literary composition has felt, at times, the want of such a work . . . to discriminate nicely between the shades of meaning in similar terms . . . to present, under each of the important words, an extended list of others having the same general import, out of which a selection may be made. . . . This arrangement, it is hoped, will be found of frequent use even to those who are practiced in composition; while it will afford important aid to young writers in attaining grace, variety, and copiousness of diction." Examples are *abiding*: "dwelling, remaining, continuing, enduring, awaiting"; and *peaceable*: "peaceful, pacific, tranquil, quiet, undisturbed, serene, mild, still." In Worcester's footsteps, discriminating synonyms thereafter became a staple of Merriam-Webster dictionaries.[19]

Goodrich also stresses in the preface the vital role of the edition in clarifying and stabilizing pronunciation. He had opted to continue to use Worcester's "Synopsis" (mentioned on the title page though not identified there as Worcester's) as a major authority citing different pronunciations by many distinguished orthoepists in both America and England in cases of disputed pronunciation. But that has now been "completely remodeled," he adds. The principal authorities are B. H. Smart and Worcester himself, "whose long-continued labors on this subject entitle his decisions to high consideration." For good measure, the introduction includes a section called "Principles of Pronunciation and Remarks on the Key." Walker's *Key*, though, has been "enlarged and improved," with more than three thousand words added by English academics in London and Oxford. Not only in the treatment of pronunciation but throughout the entire edition, we can trace an influence straight back to the popularity in America of Worcester's *Critical Pronouncing Dictionary*, his preoccupation with pronunciation in his role as chief editor of the original 1829 abridgment, and his prominent use in that octavo of Walker's *Key*, which he included in an appendix. The presence of Walker's *Key* in this new Goodrich-Merriam edition was tantamount to a major rejection of Webster's well-advertised early abhorrence of Walker and, as he thought, his negative influence on American speech and spelling.[20]

As for the orthography, Goodrich included Webster's both disputed and commonly accepted spellings, explaining that (in the 1841 edition) he had rejected many of Webster's innovations after twelve years of reflection on the subject following the publication of the 1828 quarto. In 1849, he wrote to the

Morning Courier and New York Enquirer, less tactfully than in the preface, openly informing the general public of the stunning news that the orthography in the first Merriam edition of 1847 was "not Webster's orthography at all" and that in his most recent edition "the most offensive peculiarities of his former system are laid aside; and there is really nothing left which can with any propriety be called *his*." While this claim has to be taken with a grain of salt, given the great numbers of contested spellings at play and Goodrich's stake in convincing the Merriams he was making a clean sweep of them, he was essentially correct. The Webster family may have flinched a little on reading this, but Goodrich was under no illusions about the consequences if he failed in this great purge. The only reason certain American spellings attributed to Webster, such as the *s* in words like *offense* and *pretense*, have survived is that Goodrich allowed them into his 1847 Merriam-Webster edition. As for the *ck* spellings in such words as *frolick, magick, mimick, physick*, and *traffick*, which were regarded as eccentric even in Johnson's day and were listed as secondary spellings in dictionaries by John Ash and Benjamin Martin, Goodrich had allowed Webster to keep such reforms in the 1841 royal octavo but decided to remove them entirely in the 1847 dictionary.[21]

The 1847 Goodrich-Merriam edition represented a significant turning point in the history of Webster dictionaries. It sold well, and after the copyright was renewed, Merriam was able to pay the Webster family considerable royalties. One critic half a century later looked back and judged that the edition "embraced, or ultimately affected, all the editions and sizes of Webster's Dictionary. . . ."[22] The edition not only removed Webster's "innovations" and excessive claims that had always dragged down his dictionary but also signaled that the proper function of an American dictionary was, without being overly authoritarian, to help people from all walks of life understand how to speak and write the language. That function had never been more important. Between 1790 and 1820, about one million immigrants had arrived in the United States, but that figure had risen to one million more in the 1840s alone. Between 1840 and 1890, about fifteen million flowed in, mostly Germans, Irish, British, and Scandinavians. Goodrich claimed in his preface that the new edition "was the most populist dictionary yet published in either America or England," by which he chiefly meant that he had made it a practical compendium, without confusing spelling innovations, with a good selection of the most recent vocabulary current in the country, and with a guide to pronunciation that was more prescriptive than Worcester's, whose citations from multiple orthoepists left too much up to the user. The edition's feature most appreciated by the public, especially those millions of immigrants pouring into the country, was the guidance and authority it provided for them.

Goodrich and the Merriams recognized they had to firm up Webster's reputation in the wake of such a wholesale revision of his lexicography. Goodrich, undoubtedly with some help from the Merriams and the family, therefore added after the preface what has to be one of the more remarkable memoirs of an author's life to appear in an edition of his work; it was printed in every Merriam edition, along with his portrait, for almost half a century. (Worcester's editions had neither of himself until much later.) When the Merriams took over the dictionary, Webster's name had cachet, but his self-proclaimed iconic status needed polishing up because of the lexicographical controversies he had stirred up in the last fifteen years of his life, of which journalistic coverage had made the public aware. And the Merriams knew there would be fiercer fights ahead in the papers and magazines, since they themselves intended to raise the temperature of the dictionary wars. The public needed to be reminded what a great man Webster was. Most of the details of the memoir were written by Webster himself in 1833 for *The National Portrait Gallery of Distinguished Americans* (1834). Goodrich added to this and virtually canonized Webster as an early American saint. The memoir is a step toward the perpetuation, the branding, of the Websterian myth that to this day has powered editions of dictionaries bearing his name, and that presented a formidable headwind against whatever private hopes Worcester may have entertained of surpassing Webster as America's lexicographical leader. Month by month and year by year, we follow Webster's life in the eight-page, double-column memoir, much of which is not very edifying but apparently was thought to be necessary in order to humanize the moral and spiritual account of how he overcame his highly advertised obstacles. For a taste of the eulogy, this will do: "[T]he name of NOAH WEBSTER . . . is known familiarly to a greater number of the inhabitants of the United States, than the name, probably, of any other individual except the 'FATHER OF HIS COUNTRY.' Whatever influence he thus acquired was used at all times to promote the best interests of his fellow-men."[23]

Refreshingly, and less seriously, Mark Twain had some fun over the size and weight of this quarto. (It is the quarto's size that makes it likely he is writing about this edition.) In his travelogue *Roughing It* (1872), he writes tongue-in-cheek of the problems the dictionary's bulk had posed for him in 1861 when he packed his belongings for a journey from Missouri to Nevada and points west with his brother. His brother had the bright idea of taking along Webster's massive volume, which weighed six pounds and posed serious baggage problems, because passengers were limited to twenty-five pounds each on the stagecoach: "And we had another nuisance, which was an Unabridged [Webster] Dictionary. It weighed about a thousand pounds, and was a ruinous expense, because the stagecoach Company charged for extra baggage by the ounce. We could have kept a family for a time on what that dictionary cost in the way of extra freight—and it wasn't a good dictionary anyway—didn't have any modern words in it—only had obsolete ones that they used to use when Noah Webster was a child." Not only that, but en route "every time we avalanched from one end of the stage[coach] to the other, the Unabridged Dictionary would come too; and every time it came it damaged somebody"—once it launched itself into Twain's stomach. Of course, by the time he wrote *Roughing It*, he might have said the same about Worcester's quarto.[24]

5

Worcester had struggled with his eyesight for years and finally lost it almost entirely. Goodrich felt for him, and admonished the Merriams on December 1, 1847, that Worcester was to be pitied, not attacked: "Mr. Worcester has ruined his eyes by his labors on the fine print of a dictionary. He has to live in a dark room, and has undergone a number of operations." Worcester remained virtually blind from 1847 to 1849, and after three operations on the right eye, which failed, and two on the left, he recovered his sight only partially in the left eye. In these years he could do little research and writing, and was, among other things, neither able to read Porter's article for himself when it came out nor keep track of the resurgence of dictionary controversies in the press generated by the Merriams and the publisher and critic William Draper Swan (more about him later). As Worcester explained a few years later, "There has been, as I have understood, considerable controversy relating to the Dictionaries in the newspapers and literary journals, particularly in the city of New York; but it took place when I had little use of my eyesight, and I have seen little of it. While my Dictionary was passing through press, one of my eyes became blind by a cataract, and not a great while after, the sight of the other eye was lost in the same way. . . ."[25]

It was only when Worcester partially recovered his eyesight in early 1849 that he was able to read Porter's attack on him. He was staggered by its polemical tone and content, surprised that a professor at Yale could be suborned by the Merriams as a "public advocate" of their edition and detractor of his, not primarily in order to further the understanding and progress of American lexicography but apparently for commercial advertising reasons. He wrote later that he had reason "to be entirely satisfied" with numerous reviews of his dictionary except for Porter's article on it in the *American Review*, "which is in remarkable contrast to any other review of the work" and most of which the Merriams "have seen fit to insert . . . in their Advertising Pamphlet." Worcester singles out facetiously one "specimen of candor and truthfulness" in Porter's review that he felt warranted special comment. He quotes Porter, who had targeted one of his main innovations in illustrating pronunciation in a dictionary: "He [Worcester] has . . . collected and attached to every important word, every method of pronouncing it that has ever been recommended by a writer, whether great or small, conceited or well-informed, judicious or affected." Not true, Worcester protests, and furthermore Porter surely knew he was twisting the truth if he had read what Worcester had stated in the preface to his dictionary—that his sources were not indiscriminately chosen writers but eleven of the best-known English pronouncing dictionaries, and at least twelve lexicographers, aside from "the distinguished American lexicographer, Dr. Webster."[26]

Charles Merriam countered that Worcester, through no fault of his own, was ignorant of the facts concerning who started the new phase of the "wars" now rising up again. It was not Porter at their bidding, he claimed, but Worcester's new publishers Jenks, Hickling, and Swan who fired the first shot. The Merriams took the condescending line that Worcester was a good but naive scholar who, especially in his blindness, had no idea what his publishers were up to. They were right that while he was blind he was able to keep track of very little in the newspapers and in the larger literary world, but to link that to an alleged general naïveté sounded underhanded: "If Mr. Worcester knew the facts in the case and designs to represent Professor Porter as a mercenary, a hired 'public advocate of our work,' he does what 'no honorable or honest man would do.' We feel sure, [however] that he did *not* know, as in other particulars he has not known, the 'facts in the case.'"[27]

12

The Bohn Affair

In August 1853, Worcester by chance spotted in an English journal an advertisement for a dictionary published in London in 1851, "in the title of which my name was connected with that of Dr. Noah Webster, in a way that I did not understand, and could not account for." The next thing he knew, in the August 5 issue of the *Boston Daily Advertiser*, he came across a disturbing announcement by the Merriams accusing him of plagiarism all over again. "Now mark this fact," they announced: "An edition of Worcester's Dictionary has recently been published in London, and sought to be pushed there . . . which is advertised as 'Webster's Critical and pronouncing Dictionary &c., enlarged and revised by Worcester.' On the title-page Webster is placed first, in large type, and Worcester follows in another line in smaller type; and the book is lettered on the back, 'Webster's and Worcester's Dictionary'!" The edition in question was, in fact, Worcester's 1846 edition. All of that "was new and surprising to me," Worcester wrote, "for I did not know that my Dictionary had been published in London."[1]

Baffled and angry, he promptly made for the Boston offices of his publishers. Wilkins and Carter were not there, but he learned that Wilkins did indeed own a copy of this London edition. Why, then, had Wilkins never told him about it? A couple of days later, Wilkins sent him his copy without comment. When Worcester saw the title page and read the preface, the blood doubtless drained from his face. A disreputable London publisher named Henry G. Bohn had deliberately and significantly altered his title page, changing the title itself and stating that the book was compiled from the "materials" of Noah Webster. Even more disturbing to Worcester, Bohn or someone he hired treacherously had "garbled and much altered" his preface, omitting much of it. The most damaging omission from the preface, in light of the Merriams' offensive that was already taking shape, was his vigorous assertion that he "was not aware of having taken a single word or the definition of a word" from Webster. The apparent reason for the conspicuous deletion was that Bohn, believing that Webster was better known in England than Worcester, preferred the public to believe that this was essentially Worcester's edition of Webster's dictionary.[2] It was what Washington Irving once called "a bookseller's trick." If Bohn had left Worcester's refutation in the preface, it would have undermined that strategy and exposed his fraud. As Worcester told Wilkins, "the person who remodelled the Title and Preface . . . must have known that he was contradicting the statement which I made in my Preface."[3]

All Carter could offer by way of an explanation was that Bohn had approached him and his partner for the "privilege" of publishing Worcester six years earlier, in late 1846, and that they had struck a deal with him soon afterward, sending him the stereotyped plates in October. When they heard nothing back from him and then pressed him to publish, they received a puzzlingly vague reply that he was sorry they had gone to the trouble of sending the plates—which he never returned. In the meantime, Bohn added insult to injury by bringing out a handsome London edition of the 1847 Webster edition. When it failed to sell well, he decided he would try his luck again, eventually publishing Worcester's book dressed as Webster's in 1852. Bohn's reasoning apparently was that although the Webster edition had not sold well, Webster's name was far better known in England than Worcester's, and therefore, since he already had the Worcester plates, it was worth another try to sell the latter's dictionary under that name.

Carter admitted he had foolishly assumed Bohn was "an honorable man." It was a reckless and costly assumption. With a little research into Bohn's dealings in London, he would have discovered that Bohn was a secondhand bookseller, book auctioneer, and shrewd publisher of cheap reprints, not regarded in London as a reputable publisher. It turned out that Bohn had a Websterian track record: he had been the London publisher of Webster's dictionary in 1840, as well as the Merriams' 1847 edition, and he was the Merriams' licensee in London—a poor choice if ever there was one. Wilkins confessed to Worcester, with no little embarrassment, "You may well think it strange that I did not at the time call your attention to the subject of this literary imposition; but as I did not see any means of remedying the evil, and knowing that the condition of your eyes was such that you could make but little if any use of them, I did not feel in haste to trouble you with a knowledge of it." The way Bohn did business, Wilkins added, was "as commercially dishonorable, as this literary enterprise is fraudulent and disgraceful."[4]

The Bohn fraud illustrates just how much of a publishing free-for-all still existed both in England and America in the mid-nineteenth century. Bohn felt he was merely reciprocating the shoddy practices of American publishers who, without adequate international copyright restrictions to hinder them, commonly published English books in America at knockdown prices. A revealing passage from the *Illustrated London News* in 1853 describes the climate of fierce rough-and-tumble competition between American and English publishers for cheap publications of one another's books. It locates most of the blame this time with the English:

> At present . . . the whole race of English booksellers, with few exceptions worth mentioning, are greater literary pirates than the Americans. No sooner does a tolerably good book appear in America, that [*sic*] the whole tribe of English publishers pounce upon it, and rival each other who shall first stock the market with it. There is nothing to pay the author. The book trade goes on swimmingly; and the English public have cheap "Uncle Toms" [Harriet Beecher Stowe's 1852 best seller, *Uncle Tom's Cabin*]. In the meantime the English writer is at a greater discount than ever in his own country, and sinks a step lower in the social scale.[5]

Bohn never publicly defended his conduct until more than ten years later, oddly enough in his 1864 revision of *The Bibliographer's Manual of English Literature* by W. T. Lowndes, in which he brazenly and cavalierly alludes to Worcester's pamphlet and dictionary: "Mr. Worcester has protested against my associating his [Webster's] name in the . . . dictionary, which he declares to be exclusively his own. I can only say that when I engaged to purchase the book in 1846, on a sample of the sheets, I understood it to be an enlarged and anglicized edition of the [Goodrich/Webster] abridgment that had previously been compiled by him under the name of Webster. After having extensively announced it as a joint production, I could not alter my advertisements without great inconvenience." A legitimate response to this could have been, "Why not?" Although he was the Merriams' licensee in London, Bohn afterward thought better of Worcester's work than Webster's. Webster's spelling, he writes in his *Manual*, was "fanciful" and "very little examination will convince any scholar of [Worcester's] superiority." In any case, in 1864 he shortsightedly sold his Webster stock to the publishers Bell and Daldy, later George Bell & Sons, who for decades made a small fortune as the Merriams' British distributor of Webster dictionaries.[6]

The Bohn-Merriam controversy highlights British-American publishing problems in the absence of an international copyright law that could protect both American and British authors and publishers from sales of their books at a discount. The market for American books in England was strong, particularly at those lower prices. More copies of Webster's 1828 quarto, for example, had been sent to England for sale than were sold in America. (There was an English appetite for it because it was the strongest comprehensive dictionary of the language since Johnson's.) American spelling always presented a problem in England, however, and English publishers were careful to change American spelling to English. This was a complication regarding dictionaries, of course, that involved the larger debate over the existence or legitimacy of "American English." David Micklethwait provides an interesting perspective on that debate, suggesting the possibility that after Harpers in New York audaciously published Thomas Babington Macaulay's *History of England* (1848) using American spellings authorized in Goodrich's 1847 Merriam edition, antagonism in England deterred Bohn for years from publishing a reprint of Worcester's dictionary. Micklethwait quotes a correspondent in England who wrote to the Merriams anxiously, in effect warning them: "I find there is a great prejudice against all American dictionaries here now, & it has been increased very much by the notices of the alterations of Macaulay in the U.S. in the American periodicals—you have no idea how strong the English feeling is on this subject since it has been awakend."[7]

2

At least equally iniquitous, Worcester thought, was that now the Merriams were perpetuating the fraud by "endeavoring to make use of this dishonest proceeding of the London publisher to my injury." In their pamphlet dated May 1853, titled *The English Dictionaries of Webster and Worcester*, they sneer at Worcester's 1846 edition, which they claim had been "palmed off in England as Webster's, to give it currency"—an allusion perhaps to a recent reprinting in 1850 of the Merriam 1847 edition. What they really meant was cashing in on Webster's name in England. "What is to be done in this matter?" Worcester asked Wilkins. "You will not suppose that I ought to feel satisfied to have it remain uncontradicted. . . . I am entitled to be protected from being injured." Normally, he added, "I am very averse to appear before the public in any controversy relating to a publication of my own. . . . [M]y habit has been to leave my books to the management of the publishers, without defending them from any attack, or doing anything to injure any works that may come in competition with them; nor do I wish ever to deviate from this course." Although the last thing he wanted to do was spur his publishers to stir up a dictionary controversy, the Merriams posed a unique challenge. Since the recovery of his eyesight, Worcester had witnessed their aggressiveness and readiness to organize and publicize, whether true or false, whatever they needed to say in order to defeat him. So it was crucial to be careful: "I do not wish anything ever to be said or done," he writes in his public response, "in order to promote the circulation of my literary publications, that is not in strict accordance with truth and propriety, or that can give reasonable offence to anyone." After all, he adds, there is plenty of room in America for more than one so-called national dictionary, as Webster frequently was fond of describing his own: "The world is wide enough, and the demand for useful books sufficient, to give employment to all literary laborers, who make use of proper means for preparing books which will promote the improvement of society; and I see no good reason for hostile contention between those who make such books, or between those who sell them."[8]

Unfortunately for Worcester, the Merriams did not think the world was wide enough for two dictionaries, both vying for supremacy in the American and British literary marketplace. "Hostile contention" was their modus operandi. Worcester knew Bohn's deception was potentially disastrous for him. He knew it was bound to make the public suspicious of him and that he would be swept into endless attacks and counterattacks in a tawdry face-off between his publishers and the Merriams. While Wilkins and Carter apparently had little taste for prolonging the conflict, he felt he had no choice but to fire back; in any case, it was their incompetence that had opened the way for the likes of Bohn. Instead of the fair competition between dictionaries that Worcester had hoped for after Webster's death, the conflict between the promoters of the Websterian legacy and Worcester (and his publishers) now descended to the most vituperative and public level ever. Wilkins and Carter by this time, however, had tired of having to carry the burden as Worcester's publisher and of the controversy for which they were partly responsible—their firm was experiencing financial hardship as well—so in 1851 they sold all their rights to the dictionary to the Boston publishers Jenks, Hickling, and Swan. With these new, more resourceful, and provocative publishers, Worcester drew himself up and in October 1853 retaliated in a pamphlet, *A Gross Literary Fraud Exposed, Relating to the Publication of Worcester's Dictionary in London.*[9]

3

In *A Gross Literary Fraud Exposed*, Worcester registers his revulsion before the American public over the way the Merriams did business: "[T]he publishers of Webster's dictionary seem to insinuate very strongly . . . as they have also done on other occasions," that he had stolen words and definitions from Webster and that his denial of this accusation was "not correct." How many more times would he have to say this? He repeats, in italics: "*Having had some knowledge of Dr. Webster's readiness to complain of improper use being made of his work, I resolved that, in preparing my dictionary, I would forego all the benefit which might be derived from the use of the materials found in his work, so that I might not give the least occasion for an accusation of the kind, and might be enabled to make the statement which I did make, and which I challenge any one to disprove.*" For good measure, he tacks on an appendix to the first printing of the pamphlet containing a blow-by-blow account of the exchanges between himself and Webster in the pages of the *Palladium* in 1834–35. He then takes up other "false statements" made by the Merriams in their pamphlets, their advertising, and the Boston *Daily Advertiser*, which, "because they have not been publicly contradicted have undoubtedly done me injury in the minds of many." The Merriams persist, he writes, in reviving the old charge that he had been employed by Webster or his family (rather than by Converse) to take on the major editorial work for the Webster abridgment, embellishing the facts with "other injurious reflections" on his alleged duplicity and treachery.[10]

This turned out to be a vital issue. In a sense, though, Worcester was playing into the sullying hands of the scheming Merriams, who wanted nothing more than to lure him into another period of having to defend his honor. If he had not taken the bait, they would have been less able to resurrect Webster's accusations of plagiarism, thicken the plot against him, remind the public and professional literary world all about it, and relentlessly push Worcester into an unflattering, unwinnable, defensive posture. If the Merriams could establish that in editing the abridgment he was under an ethical obligation to Webster for hiring him, they could further darken their accusation that he violated the trust and investment Webster had placed in him. Of course, Webster had placed no such "trust" in Worcester. He did more or less trust Goodrich. As far as we know, Webster and Worcester had virtually no communication with each other over the abridgment. The Merriams, however, could, and did, argue that in entering into Webster's orbit, Worcester obtained privileged access, enabling him to steal from Webster at will for the benefit of the dictionary he himself was about to publish.

On October 25, 1853, Worcester sent the Merriams a copy of his pamphlet, assuming they would wish to know the facts, even if they were inconvenient. Within two weeks of receiving the pamphlet from him and having been told the inescapable facts about the fraud, they published their own pamphlet, *Worcester's Dictionary Published in England under the Guise of Webster's Dictionary*. In it, they pretend to agree there is plenty of room in America for two or more major dictionaries of English but take the fight to Worcester anyway, ignoring or at least dismissing Worcester's factual account and claiming brazenly he had conspired to ride on Webster's coattails in London: "Worcester is of so little repute, and Webster so highly esteemed [in England], that Worcester's dictionary could only succeed by being published under the guise of Webster." If Worcester thinks otherwise, he is "either ignorant or misinformed as to the facts." Depicting Worcester as out of touch, the Merriams counsel him to wake up, "pay attention to the facts," and reign in his publishers who "vilify" and "defame" Webster by calling him a "plodding Yankee" and other names. It was actually, however, not so much the defamation of Webster that disturbed the Merriams about the Bohn controversy as their belief that this publishing swindle was enabling Worcester to make money in London from the Webster name. Worcester, of course, was making no money from the fraud; instead, he had been defrauded from making some. Apart from launching the Merriams' personal offensive against him, the publication of the Bohn edition in London was in his view particularly contemptible because it used his labor and what he and much of the informed public considered his superior scholarship to benefit the Webster name.[11]

The Merriams' outrageous claims are "void of truth," Worcester insists in his own pamphlet—and he has proof in Sherman Converse himself, the publisher who hired him, whom he makes plain he had not seen more than once in the past fifteen years. To resurrect Converse from retirement and get him to lend weight to his defense, he tracked him down in New Jersey, where he was living in semi-poverty, and sent him a copy of his pamphlet along with samples of the Merriam offensive, asking him whether he knew of "anything wrong or dishonorable" on his part in regard to the abridgment. In an appendix to another edition of his pamphlet, he reproduces both his letter to Converse and Converse's immediate and firm response in its entirety.[12]

Worcester never had a more vigorous and authoritative public defender than Converse. It was he himself, not Webster, Converse states emphatically, who hired Worcester and paid him the bulk of his fee for his work. Webster had not even wanted what turned out to be the far more lucrative abridgment and was only later persuaded by Goodrich to allow it to proceed. Converse writes that it was difficult to persuade Worcester to join in; he succeeded only by going to visit him at his home in Cambridge, at least once with Goodrich, to speak to him in person. "The result of our interview was an agreement on your part," he tells Worcester, "to abridge the Dictionary for *me*, and to allow me to use your Synopsis, with the express reservation of the right to use it as your own, for your own Dictionary. . . . And I am free to say you performed it to my entire satisfaction, and I believe to that of Professor Goodrich also, for I never heard any intimation to the contrary."[13]

The other corroborative witness Worcester could call on was Goodrich himself. He did not doubt that Goodrich would spring to his defense. Goodrich, of course, knew the history of the abridgment as well as Converse and Worcester, so Worcester sent him a copy of his pamphlet as well, with an accompanying letter that he later quoted in a second appendix to his pamphlet printed in January 1854: "You have never intimated to me that you thought I had done anything wrong or improper, in relation to that work," he wrote, "at the time of performing the labor of abridging it, or since. I cannot doubt that you suppose I have been unjustly censured, and that I have little reason to fear the strictest scrutiny on the subject. I am not aware that my character has suffered in the estimation of those who know best the facts in the case; though doubtless many have been made to believe the false charges that have been made against me." He also raised the matter of the Bohn fraud and the distress the Merriams, specifically, were causing him over it.[14]

Worcester then, presumably with Goodrich's permission, added to his pamphlet the following "courteous" reply from his friend on November 2, 1853. Goodrich's endorsement bears no trace of ambiguity. It is, in fact, a strong rebuke of the Merriams and, Worcester thought, ought to have silenced them and ended the quarrel for good:

> I never for a moment supposed, nor do I think any of your friends supposed, that you had the least knowledge of Mr. Bohn's change of the title page of your Dictionary, or any concern whatever with that transaction. It is perfectly true, as you say, that I was entirely satisfied with respect to your management, in abridging the American Dictionary. I have always spoken in high terms of the exactness and delicacy with which you conducted that difficult concern.
>
> I have always felt & said, that I knew of no ground whatever for any imputation upon you, as though you had made any undue use of Dr. Webster's Dictionary in the production of your own. On the contrary, I have uniformly stated that you had acted, in my view, with great delicacy on this subject, & that if any coincidences should be discovered between the two works, I had no belief they were intentional, or conscious ones on your part.

So far, so good—but then Goodrich defended Charles Merriam. Goodrich had dropped in on Charles briefly in Springfield, where they spoke of "the London title page and Preface." Goodrich assured Worcester that Merriam had spoken "in a way which shewed that he had not the least suspicion of your being concerned in that transaction. . . . [T]he whole tenor of his conversation showed me, that he had no intention whatever to cast any personal reflections on you." Worcester was unimpressed. It mattered little to him what the Merriams thought of him and said privately. What they circulated about him in the press was another matter. He felt let down when his old friend remarked that the Merriams felt more sinned against than sinning by Worcester's pamphlet. Goodrich also urged Worcester to rein in his publishers, the only troublemakers in this public clash: "I ought also to say in justice to the Messrs. Merriams, that they have uniformly deprecated, in their conversations with me, any collision with your publishers. They are high-minded men, of true piety"; "if they have erred, I am for myself satisfied that they have done it through inadvertence, not by design." Worcester was doing just that, imploring his publishers to back off, but he did not believe there was anything inadvertent about the Merriams' campaign of misinformation. The exchange illustrates just how fine a line Goodrich was treading in this controversy between his friend Worcester, his employers the Merriams, and the facts.[15]

For obvious reasons, Worcester did not include in his pamphlet that section of Goodrich's letter praising the Merriams. He alluded to it instead, with undisguised irritation, in his reply to Goodrich on November 21—a reply he does add to his second appendix for the reading public to see: "I would take the liberty to ask you, if persons wholly unknown to you, should publish far and wide, things relating to yourself, equally false and injurious, whether you would not be likely to regard them as unscrupulous men of the world, and not as men who felt it incumbent on them 'to do unto others as they would that others should do unto them'?—and whether you would be likely to place them in the latter class, till they were ready to give as extensive a publicity to the reparation, as they had given to the wrong?" As for his publishers, he adds, "perhaps you may feel, that when they [the Merriams] made the complaints which you spoke of, you might with propriety, have referred them to Matthew vii: 5, for their consideration and benefit ['Thou hypocrite, first cast out the beam out of thine own eye; and then shalt thou see clearly to cast out the mote out of thy brother's eye']."[16] The anger toward Goodrich that surfaces in such passages reveals how important the issue of morality in scholarship was to Worcester, not to mention the principles and value of lexicography he felt were important to the nation and at stake in the frantic commercial free-for-all that the publishers were generating.

Far from making the "reparation" Worcester felt was due, the Merriams renewed their assault on him and his publishers in December by printing another pamphlet in response to Worcester's. Turning to Worcester directly, they declare bluntly, "Our statement, we submit to you and the public, in its fair intent and spirit, is *not* void of truth, and you were employed by Dr. Webster or his family, through Mr. C [Converse], as their agent, to abridge his Dictionary." The Merriams' audacity took Worcester's breath away. "Instead of making any reparation, they have added to the 'falsehood and wrong' in attempting to defend what they have published; though I think I may safely

say they have not disproved, and that they cannot disprove, a single statement that I have made . . . I have therefore no occasion to modify any thing
that I have said."[17]

He wrote again to Converse on December 13, 1853, "Is it, or is it not so?
You were the only person that I had any thing to do with in undertaking to
perform that labor, and I supposed you acted on your own responsibility, as
in an affair of your own." Converse replied on December 19 without a flicker
of hesitation: "I acted as *agent of no man*. . . . I determined to stereotype
the work; and as the whole responsibility of the undertaking rested on *me
alone*, I could think of but *one man* to whom I felt willing to confide the
important trust of making an abridgment, which involved a risk so great.
Your attainments and pursuits had eminently qualified you for the task, and
I decided at once to engage your services if possible." Except for Goodrich,
who strongly supported Converse's choice of Worcester, "the family of Mr.
Webster had no share in either." Since Webster was left out of the choice,
except to go along with it later grudgingly, how could he be thought to have
"employed" Worcester?[18]

The Merriams understood better than most that the best way to attack an
adversary was to throw doubt on what is generally considered his strength. In
Worcester's case, they eyed his dictionary's orthography and pronunciation,
which the Merriams declare were "inconsistent" with what he had presented
in his revision of *Todd-Johnson*. Worcester was not guided by "any system or
principles of his own," they charge, but sought "to fall in with the constantly
changing practice of the hour. . . ."[19]

Nonsense, Worcester replies: "As the orthography of this Dictionary was
that of Johnson, so the orthography of the Abridgment of Webster's Dictionary made by me, was that of Webster, with some variations which were
decided upon by 'his representative' [Goodrich], and over which I had no
control. The only orthography for which I am responsible is that found in my
own Dictionaries." As for Webster's own "peculiarities," which the Merriams
charged him with mechanically importing into his own dictionary while he
was acting as Webster's "pupil" and "assistant," he replies sharply, "I am not
aware of having adopted any of Dr. Webster's 'peculiarities', relating either to
orthography or pronunciation; and if any such can be found in my dictionary,
I should certainly not regard them as adding to the value of the work." He
had spoken to Webster no more than "three or four times during his life," so

how could he have been his pupil and assistant? He threatens that, like Converse, he could himself tell tales and quote letters of Webster's he had in his possession, the publication of which "would probably not be desired by the friends of Dr. Webster." (These letters, incidentally, have not come to light.) He adds that at the moment he does not wish to reveal this information to the public. He does allow himself to wonder, though, whether in the last 1847 Webster edition "an abstinence from the use of mine was observed equal to that which I practiced in relation to Webster's. . . . I do not shrink from the strictest scrutiny in this matter." He asks the reader to decide "whether there was ever known a grave charge to be made more completely destitute of support by evidence, or less creditable to those who made it?"[20]

4

Worcester now was in the middle of the kind of pamphlet warfare he had always eschewed. The Merriams kept fueling the plagiarism controversy and pressing Goodrich for incriminating evidence against him, but in spite of some prevarication on Goodrich's part that Worcester saw creeping into Goodrich's remarks, Worcester still held out some hope that he could count on Goodrich's support. On January 31, 1854, he impatiently sought further affirmation by sending Goodrich his second appendix, which he was certain would appeal to Goodrich's sense of fairness. Whether Goodrich thought it proper to continue to defend the Merriams, Worcester wrote to him, "you will of course judge for yourself; but you must allow me to believe that, were you in my position, you would think no better of their conduct, nor bear it more patiently, than I do." Regarding the Merriams' charge that he had stolen from Webster's 1828 quarto in preparing his own 1830 edition, Worcester felt he was crying in the wilderness: "I do not believe that you can find, in literary history, a case of the kind, in which so scrupulous an abstinence from the use of the materials of a previous work (affording so valuable materials for the preparation of a new one), was observed, as was observed by me in relation to Dr. Webster's dictionary." He has a right to expect from Goodrich "entire exemption from all blame, from first to last, in relation to this matter."[21]

Goodrich did not want to play the Merriams' game. "I cannot see how all this has the slightest connection with any matters now at issue. I have always said that Mr. Worcester's abridgment was well made. . . . It has no relevancy in the world to Worcester's book, as published in England. The whole, so far as I can see, is a mere attempt to divert public attention in another direction. . . . Mr. Worcester will not claim any literary merit but that of an abridger. All other changes were made by Mr. Webster through me." What he then told the Merriams was decidedly a nuisance for their propaganda and campaign offensive: "[W]hen a man of Christian character publicly declares that 'he is not aware of having taken a single word, or the definition of a word, from that work,' I feel bound to believe him even though I should see some instances of apparent resemblance."[22]

Worcester appears not to have appreciated that Goodrich had much more at stake than just Worcester's friendship; or perhaps he believed that the mutual friendship and respect between himself and Goodrich over a period of almost thirty years would certainly trump whatever entanglements Goodrich had with the Merriams and Webster family. But the work Goodrich was doing for the Merriams in behalf of Webster and the Webster family, and also as a representative of Yale College's long-term loyalty to Webster and his dictionaries, gave him little choice ultimately but to side with the Merriams. Loyalty to the family and commercial interests prevailed over a personal friendship. It was Worcester's own hard-hitting pamphlet that, ironically, appears to have pushed Goodrich to give way to the Merriams' relentless entreaties. It shocked Goodrich, actually, how effectively the pamphlet exposed the Merriams and posed a threat to Webster's reputation and their own. The increasingly belligerent Worcester had become for Goodrich and the Merriams a greater adversary than his publishers.

The Merriams were not going to ease up on their assault on Worcester, whatever Goodrich implored them to do. In March 1854, they published a third pamphlet called *A Gross Literary Fraud Exposed; Relating to the Publication of Worcester's Dictionary in London, as Webster's Dictionary*—not to be confused with the similarly titled pamphlet by Worcester. In it, they heap criticism on Converse, attack the alleged lies of Worcester's publishers, and throw a good deal of doubt on Worcester's integrity. Before publishing it, they sent Goodrich, as before, a draft for his comments. In his reply he tried to play the role of the conciliator, offering them some tactical advice he was sure would cool Worcester's anger. He recommended, for example, that the Merriams refer to their adversary respectfully as "Dr. Worcester" because he had an honorary degree from Harvard and he and his circle of Harvard friends might well take the omission to be "a designed contempt." (Worcester had also been awarded an honorary LL.D. degree from Brown in 1847 and would receive another one from Dartmouth College in 1856.) Goodrich also urged the Merriams to state they had never believed Worcester knew all the facts about the contract for the Goodrich/Worcester abridgment because Converse kept it from him. This would win Worcester's gratitude, he said, while at the same time further blackening Converse's character, although he admonished them to deal less severely with Converse than they had in their draft because the public might otherwise read this as "kicking a fallen man"—as indeed it was. They could ill afford "to multiply such enmities."[23]

Even as Worcester realized that Goodrich still showed signs of turning against him, Goodrich found the controversy more unbearable and repugnant than ever. In letters to Charles Merriam in the spring of 1854, undoubtedly written under the moral pressure Worcester had exerted on him, Goodrich expressed even more displeasure and disillusionment with the brothers' conduct. His health was failing, and he wanted no further part in the fight. "There is no reason why I should be personally drawn into this matter," he told Charles Merriam yet again. He had gone further in betraying Worcester than he had ever imagined he would, but he had reached the end of his tether with the Merriams: "Any attempt to go farther would, I am persuaded, be injurious to you. . . . Dr. Worcester has been my personal friend throughout life," he told them plainly. "Surely few other men would have been this abstinent; and *he* would not have been so except [that] he was employed on the octavo abridgement." While he was at it, Goodrich reminded the Merriams that both he and Webster had borrowed a good deal from Worcester for the 1841 royal octavo, as he had done on his own for the 1847 edition, so why should Worcester not return the favor and borrow from Webster? He repeated, "I cannot consent to be brought into any personal collision with Dr. Worcester."[24]

Neither should the Merriams underestimate the gentlemanly and modest Worcester either as a lexicographer or combatant if his back were to the wall, Goodrich warned them: "Dr. Worcester can do more harm to the Webster Series than most men in the country. He will now feel exempt from all obligations of delicacy as to availing himself of Dr. Webster's labors. . . . He is now preparing a quarto dictionary; and with his tact and industry he might transfer all Dr. Webster's improvements in *definitions* to his own work. . . . If a contest goes on, he can pick flaws in our dictionary; for any work of this kind has many imperfections; and no man in the country is so able as he is to detect errors of this kind." If this man feels "aggrieved by me and Dr. Webster's family," he wrote, "he might do us a great and irreparable injury in respect to the octavo abridgement. . . . [A] break with him and his family might bring the most disastrous consequences upon us all, involving the quarto in its remote result." Let us not, he concluded, further "inflame his mind."[25]

5

The pressure to join the attack on Worcester eventually, however, proved too great for Goodrich to resist any longer, and he ultimately buckled under the Merriam juggernaut. On March 31, 1854, he gave them ammunition for further offensives:

> There is an opportunity . . . to make a much stronger case against Mr. Worcester, and in so doing to attack him respecting that on which he vaunts himself most, viz. his giving different authorities as to the pronunciation of leading words. . . . There can hardly be a greater perversion of our language. Who ever read such pronunciation as this? *Ingkubus* (*incubus*), *sangtify* (*sanctify*), *fung-shun* (*function*) . . . and some hundreds of others of the same class. . . . Mr. Worcester, however, contradicts himself continually on this very point. He gives us *singk* (*sink*), *sungk* (*sunk*), but not *dringk* (*drink*), *drungk* (*drunk*). . . . The fact is, Walker never pronounced according to this re-spelling, nor any man in England or this country.

In fact, these are reasonably good transcriptions of modern pronunciations, but that criticism attacked one of Worcester's principal strengths as a lexicographer: "This plan on which he so much vaunts himself, that of giving different authorities as to pronunciations, is the worst feature of Mr. Worcester's book. It serves only to confuse. . . . What can be more pernicious, especially in a schoolbook?" Goodrich wrote. *Pernicious* surely is too strong a word, but he had a point: how useful were all these orthoepic authorities to the public? Did they merely confuse the reader?[26]

To illustrate the differences between Worcester's pronunciations in 1846 and Webster's in 1847, Goodrich recorded in his "Synopsis" the differing pronunciation of a long list of words by several orthoepists. The dominant impression one obtains from his lengthy table is of Webster's simplicity and the greater (but not dramatically greater) complexity of Worcester. For almost their entire careers as lexicographers, Webster urged usage as his principal guide, whereas Worcester depended on (and cited) the pronunciation by numerous British orthoepists. (Where orthography was concerned, the reverse was generally the case: Worcester consulted American usage, whereas Webster was guided by the analogy between words.)

Goodrich also raised the specter of something apparently more sinister against Worcester, from whom he had not recently heard. "I hope my last letter will at least induce him to remain silent," Goodrich confided ominously to Charles Merriam on May 3. It seems he had threatened Worcester with some kind of public exposure, but there is no record of what that might have been. "He has sent me no answer, and I presume he feels it keenly. I do not believe he will be willing to do anything which will make it necessary for me to tell the public what I have told him in that letter." Goodrich was right. Worcester declined to publish yet another rebuttal. He rests his case in September 1854 and appeals to the public in *A Gross Literary Fraud Exposed*: "I will, at present, merely request every person who may take an interest, in this controversy, to read all that has been published on both sides, and ask himself, what offense, on my part, has been proved;—or what statement that I have made has been disproved;—how I could have pursued my literary labors in a more inoffensive manner than I have done;—and whether, in what I have written in this disagreeable affair (for a personal controversy is to me exceedingly disagreeable) my object has been, not to injure others, but merely to defend myself from *misrepresentation* and *falsehood*."[27]

Worcester was wounded by this shift in Goodrich's maneuvers and had more or less given up any hope of support from him. Matters between them had reached their lowest ebb, and their friendship (so far as we know) never recovered. After reading the Merriams' renewed attack on him in their third pamphlet, in which they accuse him of collusion with Bohn, whom they there identify as his publisher, a highly agitated Worcester wrote bluntly to Goodrich on April 14, 1854. He rejected outright any suggestion of such chicanery on his part and was appalled by Goodrich's duplicity: "I was surprised at your undertaking to defend them from a charge which I never made, and which I did not then know that any person had understood me as having made. The supposition that I could have taken any part in that 'literary fraud' seems too absurd to be believed by any intelligent person;

and how you or anyone should suppose that I accused the Messrs. Merriam of charging it upon me, I know not." What he had rebuked them for, with "harsh language," was their charge that he had stolen from Webster, "but of this you took no notice."[28]

No further correspondence survives between Worcester and Goodrich. Little more remained to be said about the controversy; each had hurt the other and said things that could not be unsaid. However much or little Americans before this had paid heed to the dictionary wars, this forgery hullabaloo—with its sensational personal animus, insults hurled all around, and private dramas unfolding before their eyes—was just the sort of plot that the newspapers and magazines were eager to dramatize and that captivated the American public. Dictionaries and the state of the language were now as close to center stage as they ever would be. Uncharacteristically, however, Worcester could not resist adding at the close of his defense a veiled threat calculated to worry Goodrich and the Merriams and get them to put an end to their attacks over the Bohn affair: "I again drop this controversy for the present,—I hope for ever. I have kept back matters which, perhaps, I may have occasion hereafter to bring forward; but I hope it will not be necessary."[29]

Worcester was doing his best not to allow his whole attention be consumed by the Bohn affair. He was working to turn out new editions of his dictionary. He had recently published his *Comprehensive Pronouncing and Explanatory Dictionary of the English Language, with Vocabularies of Classical, Scripture, and Modern Geographical Names* (1853), and he was now moving ahead boldly with a large, unabridged, quarto dictionary. It would be his magnum opus and, he hoped, his final and triumphant contribution to lexicography. He left Goodrich to his own devices and resigned himself to letting the publishers fight it out. Converse, on the other hand, was not willing to give up the fight—not quite yet, anyway—and his smaller though important role in this era of American language history obliges us to visit him once more in his lonely corner of obscurity in New Jersey.[30]

13

Converse's Complaint

Once Converse was drawn into the public scrap that sprang from the Bohn affair, bitter memories of his rejection by Webster and Goodrich a quarter of a century earlier returned to haunt him. He lived alone in Morristown, New Jersey. His second wife had died in 1845, and his only son, age twenty-five, was preoccupied with his teaching career in Boston. Eking out a meager existence, suffering badly from rheumatism and scarcely able to walk, uncertain where his next meal was coming from, without friends except for a nurse who looked in on him occasionally, Converse had been suffering for years. "My poor legs don't get well yet and I suppose they gain strength and improve a little every day although scarcely perceptible," he wrote to his son from New York City on March 3, 1851.[1]

He was not entirely forgotten, however, as he discovered, to his amazement, when he received Worcester's letter asking for support in his fight against the Merriams. For a few months Worcester's letters brought Converse, an old man living in his memories and rehearsing in his mind dreadful disappointments, to life again. They also revived his taste and capacity for tart, sardonic prose. Usually he was devoutly religious and ready to give people the benefit of the doubt, but his bitterness turned to anger when he discovered what the Merriams were up to.

Converse wrote that he "cherished no unkind feelings towards those gentlemen"; nontheless, it astonished him that all these years later they had picked a fight with him, "a *rude* and *unprovoked* attack." In their second pamphlet, they refer to his "sufficiently egotistical letter," presumably because, long forgotten as a protagonist in the Webster saga, he dared show himself again and recount the facts about how he had organized the abridgment and rescued Webster's quarto from impending oblivion. The Merriams' booklet alerts the public that they had received from "the Webster family" a copy of the 1828 contract between Converse and Worcester, showing in black and white that Webster, not Converse, was Worcester's employer. "Thus much for Mr. Converse," the Merriams scoff: "we do not think we need waste time" on him to comment any further. They had recommended that Converse and Worcester's publishers might themselves profit from consulting the Gospel of Matthew, which "would lead them to be more charitable. Yet we presume Dr. Worcester never saw this contract . . . . We bring no charge of want of veracity in the matter against him."

Converse reentered the fray with a letter to Worcester printed in *A Gross Literary Fraud Exposed* under the title "Mr. Converse's Answer." The Merriams, Worcester announces, "have published a garbled form of Mr. Converse's second letter to me," with remarks on Converse "not of the most kindly character; and they have attempted to prove, and claim to have proved, some of his statements to be false." "Mr. Converse has felt himself so much injured," Worcester writes, "that he has deemed it necessary, in order to vindicate the truth of his statements, to be at the expense of publishing the following 'Answer.'" Converse had written out his "Answer" in a passion and sent it to Worcester with the request, as Worcester notes, that it be inserted in his third appendix to his pamphlet "or printed in a proper manner to be circulated separately."[2]

"Sorry to be under the necessity of pursuing this matter further," Worcester gives Converse an opportunity in this third appendix to defend himself from the Merriams. He regrets the misery Converse is being put through, for "[w]hen I wrote to him, I had no expectation that he would be injured in this manner. . . . That a gentleman—so prostrated, as he is, by misfortune and long-continued chronic illness, yet compelled, by painful efforts, to obtain his daily bread—should be subjected to such vexation and expense for doing what he did (to use his own words) 'simply from a sense of duty,' is to me a matter of much regret; and one would think it would cause 'compunctious visitings' in other persons concerned," Worcester writes. With no evidence that the Merriams entertained "compunctious visitings" or natural feelings of pity of any kind, Worcester says he had reluctantly decided "it was high time" for him to tell the entire history again of Webster's irresponsible charges of plagiarism. After that, he adds, more with hope than conviction, "I again drop this controversy for the present,—I hope for ever."

He repeats his threat, averring he had "kept back matters which, perhaps, I may have occasion hereafter to bring forward; but I hope it will not be necessary."[3]

2

Converse's "Answer," in the form of a letter addressed to Worcester, amounts to a resounding demonization of the Merriams: "Fortunate, indeed, that the Merriam thunder is without lightning, and 'I still live.'" He complains that the Merriams' pamphlet had suppressed his first letter to Worcester and omitted what was essential in the second. He threatens, like Worcester, that if pressed he also might well make further revelations about his dealings with Webster that the public has never known, "to show you why he had failed to procure the publication of the original work, either in this country, England, or France. . . ." It seems he had preserved his correspondence relating to those half-forgotten negotiations and was prepared, if sufficiently provoked, to publish it. It was the Merriams, though, not Webster, with whom he and Worcester were now at war, and as the Merriams were not part of those events a quarter of a century before, perhaps there was not enough to be gained from making the correspondence public. For the moment, he says, he would speak only in the barest outlines of how he came to publish Webster and the unsaleable state of his dictionary when he took it on.[4]

Converse recounts that soon after Webster returned from England "greatly disheartened, if not in despair" over the prospect of ever getting his dictionary into print, Goodrich asked Converse if he would publish it. "My answer was Yes," he reports, provided that he would maintain the right to publish an abridgment with vital revisions. Webster agreed, but it was an agreement, which if it were true, Webster did not honor. Converse then tells how difficult it was for him as publisher of the abridgment to overcome public prejudice against Webster's language reforms and lexicography, explaining how for much of his career Webster's orthography had provoked the public's "utter misapprehension" and a "deep-rooted prejudice" against him as a lexicographer.[5] Converse relates that he was forced to "confer personally with a great number of the principal literary and influential men throughout the Union" so as to "*disabuse* their minds" before he could secure enough subscribers to enable him to proceed with the printing of the book. He lists fourteen of these people by name as well as the distinguished members of the Wistar Club of

Philadelphia (open only to members of the American Philosophical Society) and several members of Congress from all parts of the country. From these he had formed "a tolerably correct estimate of what would be popular or unpopular in a new dictionary," so he decided to start on the octavo abridgment right away, "*if* Dr. Webster would consent to sundry alterations."[6]

Webster did not consent. "This brings me to a passage in my intercourse with Dr. Webster, from the history of which I shall not lift the veil," Converse continues. "He has gone to his rest, and no man was witness to our interviews." From their clash over alterations they fell out: "Dr. Webster did not mean to treat me *unkindly* or *unjustly*, but I had placed him in a painful dilemma, and I do not believe he would ever have made the concessions he did but for a desire to do me a favor, superadded to the kind offices of Professor Goodrich exerted in my behalf." "The result of the whole matter was," Converse goes on, "that he gave me permission to employ a suitable person, if I could find one, to make the abridgment. He also gave me permission to introduce such modifications from the original . . . within such limits as he could prescribe." Converse also quotes from a letter from Webster to Worcester on July 27, 1828, that he felt should put the issue of who "employed" whom permanently to rest: "Mr. Converse has engaged you to abridge my Dictionary." In case that were not clear enough, Converse quotes from Webster's letter to him, "I shall submit the modifications to the discretion of Professor Goodrich and yourself, and [so] that I may not be responsibile for them as *author*, I shall give the copyright to *another*"—Goodrich, of course.

The clash had instigated Converse to use strong and impatient language to get Webster to act sensibly. He had acted in the role of a "businessman," he maintains, pushing for alterations of the dictionary that would "either increase the popularity of the work or protect it against injurious criticism." He knew in general what needed to be done and had the support of Goodrich who "denied me nothing." But Goodrich was keenly sensitive "not to transgress." He is sure, he says, that Worcester would remember how when Converse and Goodrich visited him at his rented rooms in Cambridge, "settling instructions for your guide, he [Goodrich] denied me a certain modification, till he had made a special journey to New Haven to consult Dr. Webster."[7]

The Merriams had claimed it was "preposterous" to believe, as Converse implies, that Webster would have given Converse "unqualified license." Converse had little patience with that assertion: "The mere schoolboy understands plain English better than to say that my letter *implies no control* over the abridgment. . . . Nor could the thick skull of a Hottentot so obscure the perception as to not comprehend the *necessity* of an author's consent and authority either to abridge or publish his work." He remembers he had already been working on the book for fifteen days without Webster's knowledge before the lexicographer finally gave him "authority to carry out what I had already undertaken." Now, twenty-five years later, warming to the fight against the Merriams and drifting toward mockery, Converse continues, "Far be it from *me* to believe the gentlemen would wilfully or knowingly utter a falsehood; though I could wish that, in their extracts from my letter, they had been *less careful* to suppress the truth." After almost a decade as publishers of a dictionary, of all books, one would have thought the Merriams knew "that to *authorize* a party to do an act is *one thing*, and to employ a party as *agent* to do the same act is *quite another*." As for their conduct, he encourages them to study the meaning of the words *courtesy* and *candor*.

This argument went on for months, and Converse becomes bitingly personal: "They have raked from the dust and repose of bygone years, a private contract with which they had no concern; have violated the confidence of its seal, for which they can offer no justification; and by misconstruction of its simple language, have assayed to sustain a bad cause by a worse argument. They have invaded the sanctuary of private feeling, and have dragged forth confidential transactions and personal misfortunes, having no relevancy whatever to the matter in debate, and committed them to the wings of the wind in pamphlets and newspapers." And they had done all this, he claims, because he had presumed to set the record straight regarding matters between himself and Worcester in 1828 about which the Merriams, as new boys on the block, knew nothing firsthand. Converse sees himself as the Merriams' convenient scapegoat, enabling them to construct with second- or thirdhand information a fictitious account promoting themselves as defenders of Webster and their Websterian editions. They have kicked him when he is down.[8]

"Time has been when an attack so wanton" as the Merriams', Converse continues in a more philosophical vein, "would have drawn from my pen a rebuke more scathing than they could have desired me to administer. . . . Such an enemy in one's own bosom must be like the Arch Fiend in Paradise, administering sweets to the taste to create bitterness in the *soul*." He

acknowledges that the Merriams have been successful, but "no man's mountain stands so firmly that it may not be shaken. . . . They are in possession
of wealth which, but for misfortune, would have been mine." "Rather than
misrepresent and abuse me," he observes, the Merriams ought "to send me
a copy of the Dictionary, handsomely bound, accompanied by a check for a
liberal amount on their bankers, with a kind note requesting my acceptance
of both, in acknowledgment of riches derived from the large dictionary, for
which, *primarily*, they have been so greatly indebted to my *efforts* and *misfortunes*." They can afford to be kind, he adds, and they should also try to
be "just." The Merriams responded neither kindly nor justly. They disagreed
that any relevant sense of justice obliged them to do as Converse facetiously
requested, although one wishes they might have been able to acknowledge
Converse for the crucial role he had played almost thirty years earlier in first
bringing Webster's dictionary before the public.[9]

3

In their third pamphlet in this series of attacks and counterattacks, the Merriams do not back down. They turn up the heat, accusing Converse of derid-
ing Webster and his dictionary and publishers—which he had indeed done—
and of "dark insinuations" against Webster's behavior. Converse does not pull
his punches in his reply on August 30, 1854, which also appears in the third
appendix to Worcester's *A Gross Literary Fraud Exposed*: "The Messrs. Merriams, I am told, are professors of the Christian Faith," he begins. "I confess
myself now more than astonished. In looking at that portion of their [recent]
pamphlet professedly devoted to me, the question was irresistibly forced
upon me, 'Can these gentlemen be really of sane mind?'" It is incredible, he
adds, that now, in 1854, the Merriams are presuming "to instruct me and the
public" about events that occurred so long ago and in which he was such a
vital player. As for "insinuations," he again raises the specter of further revelations, "grave reasons" that have so far kept him from "lifting the veil from
the whole history."[10]

Why do the Merriams continue to "garble" and refuse to circulate freely
what he has written to Worcester? He asks Worcester, "Was it consistent with
justice or truth, [for them] to undertake to make me a party to their controversy with *you*, when I had no connection with it, or interest in it, whatever?"
And what about their audacity in accusing him "of causing *them* injury!" he

says. "Is it not marvellous, that testifying to your integrity and honor, in matters between us in 1828, should work such terrible injury to Messrs. Merriam in 1854!"[11]

4

Converse's angry reappearance after many years of obscurity forced Goodrich to revisit his motives and feelings. Had he been fair to Converse in the early 1830s when he unceremoniously squeezed him out of the Webster enterprise? Had he acted in a Christian manner? Was he now betraying Worcester as well as Converse? Had he listened too much to Webster's declamations against the publisher? Momentarily remorseful, he offered to intercede with the Merriams in Converse's behalf at the same time he defended them. Unimpressed, Converse wrote Goodrich a letter on April 3, 1854, brimming with the pathos of a life of promise unfulfilled, opportunity lost, and achievements almost completely forgotten. He was in no mood for reconciliation: "I am sincerely obliged by your kind offer to mediate between me and the Messrs. Merriam," he began, "but after sending me two letters, arguing in their favor, you could hardly expect me to ask you to mediate, with your mind made up against me." The Merriams' audacity and refusal to back off from a single one of their claims against him had made Goodrich's offer to mediate laughable: "The case is very clear, that the Messrs. Merriam . . . would make no acknowledgement or apology except on the ground of a confession from me that I had been wrong and they *right*, the fact being exactly the reverse. . . . You say they are honorable men, and I don't mean to doubt it, but their garbling my letter does not speak *well* for their honor." All Goodrich needed do, according to Converse, was be honest and less circumspect: "When I wrote to you and requested you to say whether I had or had not stated the truth in my two letters, I committed the matter to you with perfect confidence that you would frankly and decidedly" tell the truth; "that would have ended the matter between me and the Messrs. Merriam."

It puzzled Converse that Goodrich had allowed himself to be seduced by the Merriams: "that *your* clear head should have so misconceived the true state of the case, *surprised* me." He suggested Goodrich had "misunderstood the Merriams, as well as myself," and if "a reply from me is ever published" he would make that even clearer to the public. That was another threat to worry Goodrich and the Merriams: "I have been misapprehended, misrepresented, and slandered in earlier life, when circumstances prevented my making a defense." Now he had nothing to lose—no stake in the Webster dictionary, and no Webster reputation to protect—so he could speak freely. "I do not think it my duty now, to submit to the attack of the Messrs. Merriam without making a reply," he wrote. "And when my defense shall have been made, I shall be perfectly willing to leave the matter to public decision."

Sick and bitter, but also hopeful, as he put it, of his rewards in heaven, he clouded his letter with reflections on how the years have defrauded him of his rightful share of material rewards from the dictionary: "I feel with *you* that with my crippled and feeble health, the shades of evening are fast closing around me, and I wish to retire to my rest, for the long and dark night, in peace, and there to remain, in hope and *expectation* of the glorious morning." "Time was," he continued, "my dear Sir, when you were with me, while I drank *deep* of 'the wormwood and the gall,' and to recall those scenes involuntarily opens the fountains of the soul." He should have spoken out when he could, he mourned, but now time has sealed his doom: "In later days, your mind was greatly abused [by Webster] both concerning my acts and motives. And for a long time I intended to show you how and why it was so. But the months and years rolled on, keeping us asunder, till it seemed as if the matter might as well rest, and forgiving it all, I let it pass." Now he felt there was no point in trying to set the record straight, since Goodrich's attitudes had hardened and his editorial and commercial interests had led him to align with the Merriams. It is far better to think of the first year of their relationship, when their excitement together at seeing Webster's dictionary into print, traveling together to Cambridge to convince Worcester to take on the abridgment, and working with Worcester as an effective trio in preparing the abridgment, brought him some measure of fulfillment: "Painful as such recollections are, early associations invest you with peculiar interest [admiration], whenever busy memory brings you to my mind, and that interest I hope never to lose, either in this world or the next."

His personal life was a shambles: "I am dependant now on my daily efforts for my daily bread, crippled and ill as I am. I have no home, and [nowhere] to lay my head, except I can earn enough in the day to give me food and lodging for the night. . . . Others are reaping fortunes from my great efforts in former years, but no man remembers 'this same poor man.'" He ended his letter with the resolve to fight on, "to defend my own veracity, while I live."[12]

If Converse expected to rouse Goodrich's compassion in his adversity, he was deluded. True, Goodrich was the only living person besides Worcester and Converse himself who could expose the mysterious publishing history of the first Webster quarto and its abridgment fully and frankly. But unlike Converse, Goodrich risked endangering much of his life's work if he did so. There was little he could do for Converse except send him money, which he did not do. He also failed to persuade the Merriams—if he tried at all—to stop publicly maligning both him and Worcester. On May 3, 1854, he informed the Merriams, "I hear nothing more from Mr. Converse. My last letter related to certain points of his early life to which he had referred in his letter. . . . I replied in a manner calculated to awaken strong [positive] emotion, and I hope to conciliate. . . . My hope is that he also will remain silent. I have felt a very strong desire that no reply may be made by either of them, and that you may then come off fully acquitted before the public without further contest."[13]

The Merriams had to have the last word. Instead of heeding Goodrich's advice, they risked turning the public against them by announcing that if Converse publicly confessed his mistakes and errors of judgment, they would present him with "a handsome copy of WEBSTER UNABRIDGED" and honor his draft for $100. Converse ignored the insulting bribe and told Worcester on August 30, 1854, that he believed "they would give twice that amount, to feel an honest conviction that they had done me no wrong, and were not wholly in the wrong themselves."[14]

That is the last we hear from Converse about the Merriams. Not a vindictive man, he was more likely to pray for his adversaries than attempt to sink them, but at the time he was heartbroken, physically ailing, and bitter. Goodrich expressed relief when it looked as though Converse had given up the fight. Converse silently faded away.

In 1863, Converse moved to Boston to live with his son. Although he scarcely ever left his room for the last ten years of his life, in his last days he moved back to New Haven, where he once had known happier days. He was buried there beside his first wife, not far from Goodrich's house.

14

Children, Money, and "Trash"

In the heat of the Bohn affair, it was crucial for Worcester that his publishers, Jenks, Hickling, and Swan, were prepared to lead the charge against the Merriams. Only one member of the firm, however—William Draper Swan— fought valiantly for Worcester and plunged deeply into the complicated battle that he knew lay ahead. Swan was a mason-turned-schoolteacher, turned politician, turned publisher who had already made a small fortune writing school textbooks. With a good understanding of the dictionary wars and linguistics in general, he was eager to take the fight to the Merriams. From the start, he was outgunned by the scholar-warriors Goodrich and Porter, along with the Webster patriot legacy. But Swan proved to be a slippery and effective adversary for the Merriams. He was fighting a commercial war and, more personally, because his own spellers and readers were in direct competition with Webster's, he had everything to gain by discrediting or at least dulling Webster's reputation.

By early 1854, Swan was fed up with the Merriams' relentless attacks on Worcester in the wake of the Bohn fraud. He rolled up his sleeves and published that year a comprehensive rebuttal of the Merriams in his forty-five page blockbuster pamphlet, *A Reply to Messrs. G. and C. Merriam's Attack on the Character of Dr. Worcester and His Dictionaries.* This is the first time anyone with that kind of publishing power had ever defended Worcester. Swan argues that Webster was not, after all, a very good lexicographer. While his definitions "displayed much industry," the literary world regarded his spelling and pronunciation "a decided failure." Swan notes correctly that very few people in 1854 were even familiar with Webster's original dictionary work, because so much of it had been removed in later editions: the dictionaries "actually made [solely] by him have now become very rare."[1]

By way of diminishing Webster's reputation as a lexicographer, Swan cleverly implies that little remains of Webster's work after his death to compete with Worcester's current lexicography, but as Goodrich knew and kept telling the Merriams, there was plenty more for them to do to, as it were, take Webster out of Webster. Some of Webster's spelling innovations still remained, but because Goodrich had banished many of them before Webster died, and since then had removed almost all of them as headwords, they had become less conspicuous. And much remained to be done about Webster's chaotic etymology, strongly discredited by then. For several years now, even Webster's definitions, as we have seen, had been on Goodrich's target list for their prolixity and religious and moral agenda, although they still were generally accepted as Webster's strongest feature. And with the progress of science and technology, and the considerable influx of words into the language, Webster's dictionary would inevitably have faded away without Goodrich there to keep it up with the times.

Spelling was a subject that Swan felt strongly about, having written spellers and readers himself. He understood their value in the schoolroom, and also which spelling strategies worked and which did not. Swan opposed, for example, Goodrich's inclusion of conventional spellings side-by-side with Webster's orthographic innovations, a practice the Merriams' last edition had deployed. This was supposed to make readers aware of the choices and take their pick, but Swan thought this was madness, thoroughly confusing to children in particular. Bringing schoolchildren into the debate, in fact, became his and other Worcester defenders' way of trying to raise the tone of the controversy, lifting it from what many thought had become a degradingly shabby commercial war.

2

In an era that saw the publication of Horace Bushnell's widely read *Views of Christian Nurture* (1847), with its intense concern for the welfare and rearing of children, Swan would effectively raise an alarm over what harm could be done to the nation's children by the wrong kind of guidance. If this was the age of the speller, it was also the age of child education. Children became the focus of a huge amount of attention in the country's rapidly changing culture. The complex of factors that sharpened that attention and focus included the trends and materials that developed to support those cultural shifts: theories of education, guides to the effective teaching of children, manuals on how to raise children in families, books on family life in general, discourses on reading such as William McGuffey's *Treatise on Methods of Reading* (1833), the accelerating publication rate of school textbooks, the establishment of teachers' colleges, the increased importance of religion in bringing up children, and the role churches and ministers played in the moral education of children—all bore witness to a higher valuation of children's place in society. At the core of this concentration was the philosophical-religious notion that a moral self was present in all children, an innate moral faculty and "natural piety" that had to be strongly cherished and nourished.[2]

Webster had touched on morality in his spelling and reading schoolbooks, but that was in the early days, before America had begun to produce books on child development that he shaped as distinctly American. Webster's interest in child education, moreover, was linked to the new nationalism, his overarching theme of American patriotism and cultural independence from Britain. With the development of American dictionaries, educators paid greater attention to how language contributed, culturally and morally, to the education of children. This was all part of a movement, a new field of study and practice, that by the mid-nineteenth century represented a great advance from the homespun moral content of Webster's spellers.

One of the staunchest supporters of moral education, or education as a moral enterprise, in early-nineteenth-century America was John Witherspoon, a Scot whose emigration to America and eventual presidency of the College of New Jersey (now Princeton University) significantly influenced American educational thought. Religion, he wrote, was the "great polisher of the common people," and a religious home life was the precious ingredient in a child's enlightened education and future happiness. His *Letters on Education*, published in 1765, was reprinted five times in America by 1822 and resonated powerfully with its citizens.

With his background in education, Swan was well placed as a publisher to counter the Merriams' debunking of Worcester as a serious educator. In the dictionary wars he acted not simply as a linguist or combatant with commercial interests; he also had classroom experience and could speak about the ways children could use a dictionary in a schoolroom. In his *Reply to Messrs. G. and C. Merriam's Attack*, he questions the usefulness in the classroom of a weighty, virtually immovable dictionary like the Merriam-Webster quarto:

"[G]ood order cannot be maintained in a large school where children are constantly leaving their seats to consult a Dictionary." Swan cites a report in 1851 by the Boston committee for schools suggesting that this large book sitting on the teacher's desk in a schoolroom "might as well have been in Texas." (Swan here conveniently ignores that Webster had produced an abridged edition specifically for schoolchildren, and that his 1841 edition was not so large that it had to sit on the teacher's desk.)[3]

The Merriams contended that Webster's dictionary had indeed moved on: many of the lexicographer's confounding spelling aberrations had been expunged, in the spellers as well as the dictionary, and that therefore children would never be exposed to them. The issue at hand, the Merriams maintained, was which current dictionary was the best for children. They claimed that Webster was overwhelmingly the preferred choice of common schools, government institutions, universities, private citizens, scholars, and much of the literary world—indeed, by just about everyone.

The Merriams had testimonials and other sales figures to back up their claims, although the sales data they presented were *their* figures, and the book dealers they surveyed did not have a count for Worcester separately; they included his fewer sales in the much smaller category, "all dictionaries except Webster's." Nonetheless, the money pouring into the Merriams' coffers also confirmed they were winning the commercial war hands down. The Webster name, and the patriotic overtones attached to the dictionary even before the first edition was published in 1828, still guaranteed a huge tailwind for them that seemed unstoppable.[4]

3

Still, the Merriams were worried. They saw clouds gathering in the West and realized they needed to reconfigure their advertising strategy. In a letter Charles Merriam wrote to Goodrich on September 5, 1853, he seemed panicked over how, in his view, the press war had shifted in Worcester's favor in both New York and Boston, but his main concern was that Worcester's publishers appeared poised to make a move in the West, where Worcester up to then was little known—not "wholly unknown" as the Merriams maintained—and the Merriams had long dominated the dictionary market.[5] They needed to put even more resources and energy into the fight for that market. Adopting martial language, Merriam declared they had to act: "[I]f we have a fair field [in the West], we can meet their mine with our counter-mine and commence systematic and thorough operations before the ground is too much pre-occupied." They also needed to collect more endorsements and step up their attacks on Worcester and his dictionary.[6]

Charles Merriam was determined to "go forward in the prosecution of our plans with an energy commensurate with the magnitude and importance of the interests involved." But he needed insider information, some more spying on the competition, so they could construct their advertising and publication strategies with more cunning and precision. It was not that uncommon in the antebellum period for publishers to bribe printers, journalists, other publishers, and anyone well placed to provide inside information about rival manuscripts being printed—and he was getting it: "A friend of ours (not known to the other party as our friend)," he wrote to Goodrich, "in conversing with one of the Worcester agents lately at the West, learned from him that they had high hopes and were directing their efforts to that end, of securing the West for Worcester, specifying particular States—Iowa, Wisconsin, &c." He also needed to know how far Worcester had progressed with his work and when his large, unabridged magnum opus was likely to be published.[7]

While Charles Merriam publicly scoffed at Swan's loud warnings that Webster's orthography was potentially damaging to children's education, privately he worried about it. He knew it remained Webster's Achilles' heel: "I must confess that I have had a good deal of misgiving whether some of the remaining peculiarities of Webster's orthography could be made finally to prevail. . . . Our recent Boston controversy, with the *Daily Advertiser*, &c., is giving prominence to these peculiarities." The Merriams knew Webster's dictionary was on much more solid ground than when they became its publisher in 1843, but there were traces of Webster's "peculiarities" lingering in it, and they could not tolerate that. After three years of revisions, Goodrich still had not dealt with all of them in the 1847 edition. What alarmed Charles Merriam most was that the influential world of publishers and newspapers was still rejecting Webster's orthography in their publications: "[T]he periodical press and book publishers still generally, I think, or in a great many cases, follow the old [English] mode." The young *New York Times*, which was founded in September 1851, preferred Worcester's "old mode." This was surely a sign, he feared, that unless there was a thorough housecleaning and Webster's spelling reforms were more completely eradicated from the Merriam dictionaries, and that the public recognized the purge had been accomplished, he and his brother would eventually lose out to Worcester.[8]

Charles Merriam knew the war would be won or lost in the classroom: "[T]he battleground . . . is to be mainly with the School Dictionary series, since the bitterest enemies of Webster concede that the large work has other redeeming qualities which make it valuable to the mature scholar." "The effort now demanded in New Hampshire, in Ohio, in Wisconsin, &c.," he continued, had to be focused on the schools. By throwing everything they had at winning the schools market in New York, Massachusetts, Ohio, Iowa, Pennsylvania, Illinois, and Wisconsin, among other states, the Merriams hoped to stop Worcester whenever and wherever he appeared to be gaining traction.[9]

As for regional dynamics, common schools in the South generally preferred Worcester, scared off by what they saw as Webster's radicalism, although that did not particularly help Worcester, since the school system there was as yet relatively undeveloped, and state legislatures purchased few dictionaries, regardless of who wrote them. As late as the 1850s, dictionaries were little used anywhere in the South, either in schools or by the general public. In Connecticut, especially at Yale, and to the west, it was a different story, as the Merriams' endorsements and testimonials bear out—although it was going too far for them to assert that in the West Worcester was virtually a blank.[10]

4

Swan was optimistic he could gain the upper hand in schools and took hope in the common knowledge that leading American authors overwhelmingly preferred Worcester. The Merriams' statement that they preferred Webster was nonsense: nobody "having the slightest claim to eminence in scholarship has in his published works adopted Webster's orthography as a standard." "The purest writers of English refuse to admit," he writes in *A Reply to Messrs. G. and C. Merriam's Attack*, "that Webster, even in its de-Websterized state, should be the national and state of New York standard." Washington Irving found himself swept into the dictionary wars when in a new advertising campaign the Merriams used a remark he had made about Webster's dictionary. They had sent him a copy of the 1847 edition in early 1851, to which promptly he replied with thanks and praise for its usefulness as a book of reference, but added he did not make it his standard for spelling, and that Americans like Webster who try to deviate from London as "the standard usage" risked being considered provincial. Having said that, he wanted to make it absolutely clear, "I do not pretend to take any part in the controversy which is going on in the periodical press on the subject."[11]

Always on the lookout for an advantage or opportunity, the Merriams put Irving's praise to good use, featuring it in their advertising campaigns but (unsurprisingly) omitting his reservations. This "bookseller's trick," as Irving later called it, irritated him, but he let it pass until he received an inquiry in June 1851 from Hon. James W. Beekman, a member of the New York State Senate and chairman of the Committee on Literature for the state as well as one of the earliest members of the New York Historical Society. The Merriams had run an advertisement in 1851 in which they claimed that when the New York state legislature was considering recommending and supplying dictionaries to "common" schools throughout the state, Webster's was adopted and "Worcester was not once proposed or thought of." They included Irving's praise of the 1847 edition. Beekman knew the Merriams' account of the proceedings was misleading. He had been at the meeting. And Irving's praise did not ring true. He wanted to know exactly what Irving had actually written to the Merriams, so he asked him.

Irving had once approved of Worcester's dictionary as what he called the "Pugnacious Dictionary" and thought it would become particularly valuable in supplying "the wants of common schools," but he had never before crossed the threshold and said his piece in this dictionary war. He wanted to clarify where he stood. "Dear Sir," he wrote to Beekman on June 25, 1851, "Several months since, I received from Messrs. G. & C. Merriam a copy of their quarto edition of Webster's dictionary. In acknowledging the receipt of it, I expressly informed them that I did not make it my standard of orthography, and gave them my reasons for not doing so, and for considering it an unsafe standard for American writers to adopt. At the same time I observed the work had so much merit in many respects *that I made it quite a vade mecum* [a handbook, guide, or manual kept for ready reference]." They had taken his words and had "the disingenuousness to extract merely the part of my opinion which I have underlined, and to insert it among their puffs and advertisements, as if I had given a general and unqualified approbation of the work." Webster's dictionary should play no part in the schoolroom, he said, because it "is not a work advisable to be introduced 'by authority' into our schools as a standard of orthography."[12]

Beekman sent that letter to the editors of the Boston *Daily Advertiser*, which published it in an editorial on July 29, 1853. He caught the Merriams with seemingly little room to maneuver, but they made the best of a bad situation in an advertisement dressed up as an objective article for the next issue of the *Daily Advertiser* on August 5, 1853. The only reason they were silent concerning Irving's rejection of Webster's orthography, they announced spuriously, was to spare him from being sucked into the controversy. Worcester's followers, on the other hand, "notoriously interested parties," had no such restraint and "wormed from him [Irving] the letter." Irving suddenly discovered to his horror he was at the center of a populist controversy that was anathema to him.[13]

The Merriams also tried out a few populist themes: the conflict between the educated and "half-educated," the elite and common man, and how the language was reflecting that split. The line they took was that Worcester's rarefied Harvard connections linked him with the elite, while Webster's dictionary belonged to a vastly wider community or culture—overlooking, incidentally, Webster's own rarefied connections at Yale, the faculty of which unanimously supported his dictionary and contributed their expertise increasingly to succeeding editions. Referring clumsily to Harvard as "Cambridge University," they smugly cast the dictionary wars as a class conflict: "While . . . cherishing a high regard for the memory of Dr. Webster or his family, the purity of his character, and the intelligence and industry displayed in his works, we must yet confess that he committed one unpardonable sin—*he did not graduate at Cambridge University.* . . . [W]e should hope this might not be deemed a perpetual *casus belli* upon him, in his memory and his literary progeny." We do not know Worcester's response to this remark but can easily imagine it.[14]

Back in New York, in July 1851 Beekman made his own use of Irving's letter, including it in a long report to the New York Legislature disputing the legislature's legal right to authorize that state money be spent for all districts in the state to be supplied by a specified dictionary to the exclusion of all others. He described the threat of Webster starkly, reviving the theme of a cultured language under siege by barbarity and vulgarity: if Webster were allowed to continue to "unsettle" the language with his "innovations," confusion would reign in the country's classrooms, and Americans would soon see the shelves of their district libraries filled "with trash as vile as any which the ignorance of rural book buyers, as alleged by the friends of Webster, could select." To drive this point home, he related the story of a boy who resisted his teacher's correction of his spelling of the word *build* as *bild*, on the grounds that Webster had spelled it that way. "Upon being permitted by his teacher to go to the library" to check the spelling, the boy "returned, bearing Webster open at the place, in triumph, to prove himself right."[15]

5

Most of the leading authors and distinguished men of letters mentioned by Swan—Irving, Sidney Willard, Daniel Webster, Longfellow, Hawthorne, Oliver Wendell Holmes, and William Cullen Bryant, to name but a few— who spoke up for Worcester were from the Northeast and South. Literary journals and the more respected newspapers also heavily favored Worcester. Never mind the mountain of recommendations piled up by the Merriams from several of the country's famous statesmen, some 104 members of Congress, several professors, and even a few minor literary figures. Swan informs his readers that most of these were "courteous acknowledgement[s] for an elegantly-bound literary present," namely, copies of the 1847 edition. He cannot resist adding, "[I]t is not unreasonable to say that, while presidents of the United States and members of Congress are excellent judges of politics, clergymen equally good critics in matters ecclesiastical, and newspaper writers competent admirers of convenient encyclopedias, neither of these classes are authority on a matter of literature."[16]

Two of America's beloved writers at that time were Oliver Wendell Holmes and William Cullen Bryant, both of whom grew up in Massachusetts. Boston was Holmes's literary and cultural center of gravity. He instinctively believed that "Boston has enough of England about it to make a good English dictionary. . . ."[17] He associated the metropolis with "the correct habit of spelling the English language," as he puts it in his *Autocrat of the Breakfast-Table*. Bryant, too, had important links with Boston through the Boston-based *North American Review*, which published many of his poems through the years.[18]

Holmes had long been fascinated with dictionaries. For him, they were the high priests of language, disseminating civilized culture. Back in November 1831, at the age of twenty-two, while living in a boardinghouse during his study at a Boston medical college, he published an article in the *New England Magazine* introducing his "autocrat of the breakfast-table," which matured much later into the "Breakfast-Table" series of books, beginning in 1858. In a second article in February 1832, he writes: "When I feel inclined to read poetry I take down my Dictionary. The poetry of words is quite as beautiful as that of sentences. The author may arrange the gems efficiently, but their shape and lustre have been given by the attrition of ages." Now, in a letter of July 1852, he sent Worcester several words missing from the latest edition of his dictionary to be included in his next. "I have always felt I should add my mite," he added, in return for so large a contribution to the common literary stock. . . . If you will allow me, I shall continue my surveillance of the English language, of which I consider you the High Constable for this country, and . . . [report] all irregularities in the old citizens and all appearances of suspicious strangers within my limited sphere of observation."[19]

Holmes took up the subject again, while the dictionary wars were at their height, in his seriocomic *The Professor at the Breakfast-Table* (1860), in which he chastises those who were scrapping over the language and making war on the "nobility" of the English language. He alludes to the rivalry between Yale and Harvard over which dictionary was better and mocks the orthographical chaos Webster created in the American language. One morning at the breakfast table, a young "provincial" gentleman—that is, not a Bostonian— "innocently" asks for "Webster's Unabridged" to settle the meaning of a word. Scandalized by this intrusion of "Webster" into civil Bostonian conversation, a "little gentleman" shocks "the propriety of the breakfast-table by a loud utterance of three words, of which the two last were, 'Webster's Unabridged,' and the first was an emphatic monosyllable." "Beg pardon," he apologizes, "but let us have an English dictionary, if we are to have any. I don't believe in clipping the coin of the realm, Sir! . . . Mr. Webster could n't spell, Sir, or would n't spell, Sir,—at any rate, he did n't spell; and the end of it was a fight between the owners of some copyrights and the dignity of this noble language which we have inherited from our English fathers. . . . We know what language means too well here in Boston to play tricks with it. . . . I can't stand this meddling any better than you, Sir!" "But we have a great deal to be proud of in the lifelong labors of that old lexicographer," he concedes, "and we must n't be ungrateful. Besides, don't let us deceive ourselves,—the war of the dictionaries is only a disguised rivalry of cities, colleges, and especially of publishers." Even over breakfast, conversation about dictionaries could raise a room's temperature.[20]

Twelve years later, Holmes returns to the subject of English dictionaries in his third "breakfast-table" book, *The Poet at the Breakfast-Table* (1872). Here he alludes to the "advertising fiction" of the Merriams in championing the Connecticut Webster against the Bostonian Worcester. In the course of another breakfast conversation, someone observes that a particular monosyllabic word of insult—which he does not identify—was "considered vulgar by the nobility and gentry of the Mother Country, and it is not to be found in Mr. Worcester's Dictionary, on which, as is well known, the literary men of this metropolis are by special statute allowed to be sworn in place of the Bible. I know one, certainly, who never takes his oath on any other dictionary, any advertising fiction to the contrary, notwithstanding."[21]

The dictionary wars, then, mattered greatly to Holmes. He feared this feud was wearing out the images of both lexicographers, who were becoming fodder for gossip and humor, as in his own half-comical line in an 1866 poem praising the industrialist, banker, and benefactor George Peabody, who founded the George Peabody Library in Baltimore (transferred to Johns Hopkins University in 1982). Words literally fail him, Holmes writes, to praise Peabody properly, and not even the dictionaries of Worcester and Webster, whose publishers were trying mightily to destroy each other, could help him now:

> BANKRUPT—our pockets inside out!
> Empty of words to speak his praises!
> Worcester and Webster up the spout!
> Dead broke of laudatory phrases![22]

15

High Stakes

"Have We a National Standard of Language?"

No writing of any kind about dictionaries of English during the preceding three hundred years, either in Britain or America, had erupted as part of the public domain as strongly and persistently as it did in America at this time. The dramatic increase in the number of newspapers being published in the United States by the mid-nineteenth century made this possible, as did the widening of their readership to include not only the elite and well-educated but also readers from all social, economic, and ethnic groups. By 1800, about two hundred newspapers were published throughout the country—Philadelphia had six dailies; New York City, five; and Baltimore, three, for example. By 1850, this number had risen to more than two thousand, with unprecedented circulation. Between 1828 and 1840, the total circulation of newspapers had more than doubled, from 68 million to 148 million. "The number of periodicals and semi-periodicals in the United States surpasses all belief," wrote Alexis de Tocqueville in the 1830s; "there is hardly any small town without its newspaper."[1] This precipitous expansion was due partly to the same factors responsible for the rise in the literacy rate, and advances in printing technology were also crucial: the Fourdrinier machine that produced continuous rolls of paper (invented earlier but introduced into the United States in 1827); the steam-powered cylinder press in 1832 (a considerable advancement over the hand press); and the steam-powered rotary drum printer (patented in 1847). The growth of the newspaper industry manifested, among other things, the diffusion of civil culture and the increased pluralism of American society.

Not everyone was happy about how the public press was using the English language in its coverage of the dictionary wars. Where had gentlemanly discourse gone? Both Webster's and Worcester's advocates cited the newspaper industry as the arch-villain fomenting controversy, anger, and incivility. "We see no reason why the language of a newspaper should be very different from the language of decent society,—from the language used by gentlemen in their daily intercourse," wrote the *New York Times* in an 1868 editorial titled "Good Manners in Journalism." Edward Gould, who worked for the *New York Evening Post* and, as we shall see, wrote vigorously in behalf of Worcester, had this to say about the public press: "Among writers, those who do the most mischief are the original fabricators of error, to wit: the men generally who write for the newspapers." Gould lamented that newspapers, instead of books, had become the principal source of authoritative information, all too often distorting the facts. Adopting imagery of violence, Henry Ward Beecher noted, "Rome had her gladiators; Spain her bull-fights; England her bear-baits; and American has—her newspapers!" It was into such an arena of populism that the wars now moved.[2]

2

In his *Reply to Messrs. G. and C. Merriam's Attack*, Swan singles out William Cullen Bryant especially for a piece he published on June 20, 1854, in the *New York Evening Post*, of which Bryant had been editor from 1829 to 1840. Bryant was a so-called purist conservative regarding the use and misuse of the English language, and he used his editorship to promote his views. In this instance, he did so forcefully: "[S]o far is Webster's Dictionary from meeting with the general acceptance of scholars and the community, that of those who, in different parts of our country and of the world, employ our common language, that noble vehicle of thought which we call *English*, with a moderate degree of attention to its purity, there are not ten in a hundred who 'accept' Webster's Dictionary as a standard of language; nay, the majority of them have in fact no acquaintance with it."[3]

By *standard*, in this context, Bryant means a "national" standard, a dictionary almost universally accepted as America's ultimate authority on the language. The Merriams had been making the theme of a "national" dictionary one of their battle cries, moving the dictionary wars into the political realm because for Webster the American language had always been a matter of national pride. Many writers, including Irving, Holmes, and Bryant, deplored the nationalism inherent in that theme. They favored the view that the English language was an apolitical heritage, one that could and should be adapted to the realities of American life but not vulnerable either to the vagaries of nationalism or personal theories and ideologies.

It was Bryant's raising of the theme of a "standard of language" that impelled the Merriams in 1854 to publish another pamphlet, *Have We a National Standard of English Lexicography? Or, Some Comparison of the Claims of Webster's Dictionaries, and Worcester's Dictionaries.* Worcester's dictionary is scarcely in the running as a candidate for the national standard, the pamphlet states: Worcester adopted the principle of following "current usage" in spelling, but not American usage; sequestered in his Cambridge enclave, neither had he been listening to the way Americans actually spoke. This was a treacherous road to walk down. The pamphlet ignores Worcester's explanation of the complex interrelatedness of American and British English in his introduction to the 1846 edition: "The Americans have formed some new words; to some old ones they have affixed new significations; they have retained some which have become obsolete in England; some English provincialisms they have brought into common use; and there are many neologisms, consisting in part of new words, and in part of old words with new significations, in use both in England and in the United States with regard to which it is difficult to determine in which country they originated."[4]

In his 1846 edition, Worcester included at least as many Americanisms as Webster had, but the pamphlet does not take note of this. It was not American words, say the Merriams, that increased Worcester's number of entry words (some one hundred thousand), but "great multitudes of compound words" like *short-fingered* and *short-legged*, and once you get onto that path it is "easy to enlarge the list indefinitely by prefixing the word *short* to half the words of the language." (Most such words were allowed into later editions of Merriam-Webster.) The pamphlet includes a list of entry words chosen from hundreds of others in Worcester that no "intelligent man" or "teacher of youth" would ever approve of incorporating into the language, from *squeezable, strengthfulness,* and *suitability* to odd-sounding ones like *jiggumbob, pish-pash,* and *somberize.* As for definitions—rarely longer than two lines, the pamphlet incorrectly says—Worcester's user-friendly succinctness denied readers the nuanced precision people need for "accuracy of thought." To illustrate, they cite *acceptable*: "Sure to be accepted or well received; welcome;

grateful; pleasing"; *lampate*: "A substance formed of lampic acid with a base"; *landlocked*: "Enclosed with land"; and *landmark*: "A mark to designate the boundary; a guide on land for ships at sea." How can a dictionary, the Merriams ask, take the reader far enough into shades of meaning with such abrupt definitions?

The Merriams also skip over Worcester's technique of giving different forms of a word and his handling of idiomatic verb phrases containing that word. For instance, under the heading of the entry word *come* Worcester lists and gives definitions for the following: *come about, come at, come by, come into, come of, come off, come on, come over, come out, come out with, come round, come short, come to, come to one's self, come to pass, come up, come up to, come up with, come upon, to come* (in the future), *come your ways.* Such recording of the versatility and fine distinctions of a word in multiple idioms, working in concert with discriminated synonyms, cover much lexical territory and was much appreciated by people learning the language or improving their command of it. It was not unique to Worcester, however, although he led the way in demonstrating how resourceful it could be. Goodrich successfully did much the same thing in the Merriam 1847 edition—again as with *come*: *come about, come after, come again, come at, come away, come back, come by, come for, come into, come off from, come on, come over, come out, come out of, come out with, come short, come to, come together, come to pass, come up, come upon.*[5]

It was apparent that the competition between Worcester and Goodrich was proving to be fruitful in encouraging the development and raising the quality of dictionaries in America. The increasing role of newspapers during the 1850s in keeping track of the dictionary wars suggests that the public was well aware of what was going on in the American world of lexicography. What was at stake for the American language was far more important, of course, than the outcome of a sporting match like boxing, but there is evidence that the public viewed it as a comparable type of contest, where the competitors were slugging it out to win before time ran out for them.

After a lull of a few months in the hostilities, another prominent figure to enter the fray, on the Merriams' side, was Professor Calvin Ellis Stowe, a biblical and Greek scholar who taught at Bowdoin and Dartmouth colleges. Stowe showed himself at the behest of the Merriams, who were now in high gear with their "standard language" theme. Without mentioning

Worcester, Stowe argued in a letter in March 1855 to an unnamed Boston publishing house that Webster's dictionary was the unmatched American standard. Stowe's name was a highly desirable one to have on your side—at least in the northern states and in Britain. He was the husband of the author Harriet Beecher Stowe, whose abolitionist novel, *Uncle Tom's Cabin* (1852), was a huge international publishing success. In a letter to the *Boston Post* on March 22, 1855, the Merriams railed against Worcester's publishers for their denunciation of Stowe's letter, repeating their claims that Webster was the unrivalled national standard. Resorting to hyperbole, and stressing the word *one*, they announced that Webster was "the great American philologist, the most learned and devoted scholar . . . that the English language knows . . . and in the United States he is *the authority* everywhere except in Boston; and even there, more than any other *one*. In England he has more authority than any other *one* and is continually gaining. . . . If we would have uniformity, we must adopt Webster, for he cannot be displaced, but others may be." What they really meant, of course, was that it was Goodrich who could not be replaced.[6]

3

Stowe's endorsement gave the Merriams the opportunity to reprint in the *Post*, along with their indignant letter, a colorful piece celebrating Webster that had been published earlier that month in the *Mercantile Library Reporter*, titled "The Battle of the Dictionaries" by William Frederick Poole. Poole was no insignificant personality in Boston, where he was the distinguished librarian of the Mercantile Library. He later helped establish the Newberry Library in Chicago and became famous for library reform across the country, as well as for a standard reference work, *Poole's Index to Periodical Literature*. He was an ideal spokesman for the Merriams in Boston. The Merriams knew nothing of him, they said, except that he was "an intelligent gentleman of liberal education, a resident of Boston, who through his connection with the Mercantile Library Association was fully competent to judge" the relative popularity of the two rival dictionaries.[7]

In his article, Poole invokes the old standoff between the so-called conservatives like Johnson and Worcester and fresh-faced Americans who are living in America as it is, not as it used to be; also between the common people of the future and the American "aristocracy" of the past, still lurking in some urban centers like Boston and New York. If the future of the language were left up to Worcester, Poole writes, he would preside over the "absolute petrifaction of the orthography of our language in its present form, that is, as Mr. Worcester gives it," whereas the Goodrich-Merriam-Webster was attempting to keep up with the times by trying to record language change. The English are more receptive to change than Worcester's conservative supporters, he adds, and strongly approve of Webster: "[I]f you step into a bookstore in London and ask for the best dictionary of the English language, the American Dictionary in quarto is handed to you. At Paris, Leipsic [Leipzig], and Hamburg, it has no rival. The success of Dr. Webster in reforming many of the absurd philological anomalies of our language—which so excites the ire of fogy [old-fashioned] critics in this vicinity—is its highest recommendation in foreign countries." And yet Worcester's supporters depict Webster as "a quack and an ignoramus." This sketch of the European reception of Webster, as we have seen, was not at all as clear as Poole makes it out to be.

Poole's goal was also to put to rest the impression circulating of late that Worcester was the accepted authority in Boston and "has carried the pickets on several outposts of the enemy's camp in other sections of the country." The copy of Worcester's 1846 *Universal and Critical Dictionary* that had been sitting on a table in the Boston Mercantile Library since 1848 is looking brand new, he states, as if it has scarcely ever been touched, whereas the Merriams' large 1847 edition next to it is pretty ragged from having been consulted sometimes twenty times per day.

Poole's emphasis on the use of a dictionary to aid in reading and writing is effective, and in this regard his connection to the Mercantile Library Association or Company is particularly useful. The Mercantile Library was an institutional manifestation of the access to reading and "useful knowledge" that accompanied the growth and spread of the public school movement in the first half of the nineteenth century. By announcing that in the Mercantile Library in Boston, of all cities, the public was wearing out Webster's dictionary from heavy use and fairly ignoring Worcester's, Poole is pushing the powerful argument that Webster's dictionary better served the cause of democracy and education in America. He invites people to visit the Mercantile Library to see these dictionaries for themselves. It would be instructive to come upon similar comments about the uses of these dictionaries in other libraries at that time.[8]

Any pretense to disinterested objectivity on the Merriams' part in republishing Poole's article, however, vanished right away with an overweening encomium on Webster titled "Schoolmaster of Our Republic" that they added as a preface to Poole's article in their pamphlet, *A Summary Summing of the Charges, with Their Refutations* (1854). They plucked the essay out of *Glances at the Metropolis: A Hundred Illustrated Gems*, originally a foreword to Poole's catalog of the Mercantile Library, *Dictionaries in the Boston Mercantile Library and Boston Athenaeum*. The tribute also appeared in the *Mercantile Library Reporter* in 1854, not exactly an unbiased periodical, because Poole, an adamant supporter of Webster, was the librarian of the Mercantile Library from 1852 to 1856 and edited the journal. That connection between Poole, Webster, and the Mercantile Library Association again illustrates that the "patriotic" forces of "democracy" and the common people embodied in the Mercantile Library and central to the spread of public libraries in the country were definitely on Webster's side in defining language as they saw it championed by Webster. The *Glances* portrays Webster as a paragon of morality—which served the Merriams beautifully, since one of the major themes in their advertising campaign involved depicting Webster's reputation as an unassailably worthy human being and American—an international "gem," almost sacred, America's "great teacher," and one of America's "trinity of fame." He is lauded as

> the all-shaping, all-controlling mind of this hemisphere. He grew up with his country, and he moulded the intellectual character of her people. . . . His principles of Language have tinged every sentence that is now, or will ever be uttered by an American tongue. His genius has presided over every scene in the Nation. It is universal, omnipotent, omnipresent. No man can breathe the air of the continent, and escape it. . . . He has done for us more than Alfred did for England, or Cadmus for Greece. . . . Only two men have stood on the New World, whose fame is so sure to last—Columbus, its Discoverer, and Washington, its Savior. Webster is, and will be its great Teacher; and these three make our Trinity of Fame.

One may be reminded by this of Abigail Adams's note to her sister, Mary Smith Cranch, in January 1800, about the public's glorification of George Washington, "To no one Man in America belongs the Epithet of *Saviour* of his Country.[9]

4

For Worcester to remain competitive even as the Bohn controversy and its exploitation by the Merriams made him somewhat bitter in spite of himself, it was crucial that while this dictionary war kept thundering on he should not fail to appear in print with a fresh and timely edition. It so happened he had one ready that grew out of the importance he had always placed on the role of synonyms in defining words. In 1855, his 565-page octavo, *A Pronouncing, Explanatory and Synonymous Dictionary of the English Language*, was published by Worcester's new publishing team, Hickling, Swan, and Brown. "Substantially an enlargement of the *Comprehensive Dictionary*," he states in his preface, it was intended for high schools, institutions of higher education, and families. It contained three thousand more entry words than his 1846 *Universal* and sharper and more complete, though still relatively concise, definitions.[10]

Like all of Worcester's dictionaries intended for educational use, this book was commercially successful. Its most significant contribution was a pioneering effort to make more extensive use of discriminating synonymy than he or even any lexicographer in England had ever attempted before. He writes in his preface: "A new and peculiar feature has been given to this Dictionary by bringing into view the principal *Synonymes* of the language; . . . more useful instruction can be given in this way respecting the meaning and use of the several words classed together, and the manner in which they are to be discriminated from each other, than can be presented by any other method."[11]

He advises the reader to look at the entries for *abbey, axiom, clergyman, insanity, language*, and *lawyer* for examples of his use of synonymy, but a briefer illustration is the entry for *hint*, which he defines as "slight mention; remote allusion; intimation; suggestion; insinuation. . . . *Hint* is used in an indifferent sense, and often in a bad sense, for something thrown out against one's character; *allusion* is used in an indifferent sense; an *allusion* is commonly used in a good sense for a useful *intimation*; *insinuation* is used in a bad sense for something intimated against some person. A person is said to take, or to throw out, a *hint*; to make an *allusion*; to offer or to follow a *suggestion*; to receive or to give an *intimation*; to make or to disregard an *insinuation*."[12]

He acknowledges his debt to earlier English books of synonymy. There was, for example, *British Synonymy; or, An Attempt at Regulating the Choice of Words in Familiar Conversation* (1794) by Dr. Johnson's longtime friend Hester Lynch [Thrale] Piozzi, and William Taylor's small volume, *English Synonyms Discriminated* (1813). According to Sidney Landau, author of *Dictionaries: The Art and Craft of Lexicography* (1989), Worcester's book "can be said to have established synonym discrimination as a standard feature of larger dictionaries. . . . It was not until the word stock of English was sufficiently developed to embrace thousands of near synonyms that dictionaries of synonyms could be written with much effect."[13]

Worcester in his preface also reminds readers that he is no innovator and that his new dictionary does not set out to reform the language. His orthography is grounded on usage, etymology, and analogy, which "have been consulted in deciding disputable points; but no innovation has been attempted in relation to matters of invariable and settled usage." There is no simple way of regularizing English orthography in order to make it consistent and easy to learn. There has never been a "fixed standard" of usage by which to control spelling. In his view, it is useless and damaging to try to force English, or any language for that matter, into such a box: "This unsettled state of orthography has been regarded as a reproach to the language. It is an evil, however, which is unavoidable. . . . Some ingenious men have attempted to introduce a uniformity, and establish an invariable standard; but these attempts have been attended with little success." He intends, he says, for his dedicated sections, "Remarks on Orthography" and "Vocabulary of Words of Various or Doubtful Orthography," to constitute an authoritative statement, "a notice of nearly all the diversities of orthography in the English Language now often met with." He includes a list of no fewer than about 3,600 words that currently were spelled at least two ways in England as well as America.[14]

"In the preparation of this work," he continues in his preface, repeating what he had said in the preface to his 1846 *Universal and Critical Dictionary*, "*pronunciation* has been made a special object, and has received particular attention. . . . [T]he number of English words respecting the pronunciation of which there is any important difference, may be stated at about two thousand"—a considerable underestimate, in fact. "There is much difference in the pronunciation of many of these words, both among the best orthoëpists, and the best speakers of the language. . . . [N]o one who is scrupulous about his pronunciation, will be willing to place implicit reliance on any single orthoëpist, but he will wish to know . . . the different modes adopted by all who are entitled to be regarded as of much authority."[15]

Nonetheless, beyond regional dialects and language habits, Worcester was not alone in believing there had to be some overarching model for how educated and literate Americans spoke. "The standard of pronunciation is not the authority of any dictionary, or of any orthoëpist," he insists, which is another allusion to Webster and the Merriams' claim that their editions were the "national standard." If a "standard" does exist, as he had written in the past, it is in the "present usage of a literate and well-bred society." And where was that society? "London is the great metropolis of English literature," he declares, echoing Dr. Johnson, because it has "incomparably" a greater influence on "the many millions who write and speak the language" than any other city in the English-speaking world—although even in London the usage of "good society" is not uniform, and not even English orthoëpists agree on a so-called London standard. But as long as London "holds its rank as the great metropolis of the literature of the English language," Worcester argues, it must be the predominant influence on the language itself. By 1855, no city, no "center of intelligence and fashion" in America, neither New York, nor Boston, nor Philadelphia, had yet established itself as "the undisputed center of Anglo-American literature, as London is of English literature." Having said all that, Worcester allows that provincial rusticity is preferable to excessive, affected "precision"—the very point Porter had made—and that people need to be responsive to their linguistic environments.[16]

Worcester sent a copy of his *Pronouncing, Explanatory, and Synonymous Dictionary*, together with his pamphlet *A Gross Literary Fraud*, to a friend in London, the orthoepist Benjamin Humphrey Smart, in December 1856. Twenty years earlier, Smart had published his own important advance on Walker regarding pronunciation, *The New Critical Pronouncing Dictionary of the English Language* (styled "Walker remodeled"), which along with Walker had been a major influence on Worcester and anathema to Webster. Worcester particularly wanted from Smart some sense of English attitudes toward the Bohn fraud and the commercial and media spectacle of dictionary warfare then rife in America.

Smart wrote back several days later from the Athenaeum Club in London with a hearty personal endorsement that, surprisingly, neither Worcester nor Swan ever used. It was a lost opportunity. Smart's letter provided at least one authoritative English perspective on the American lexicographical strife: "I certainly think you have just cause of complaint both against misrepresentation at home, and unfair mercantile maneuvering here." He wrote that he had taken the copy of Worcester's latest dictionary pamphlet to his friend Charles Richardson, the author of *A New Dictionary of the English Language* (1836), no friend to Johnson's dictionary but who more than once had written scathingly of Webster. They had agreed with each other, Smart noted, "on being on better terms . . . than our lexicographical brethren appear to be with each other, beyond the Atlantic." He had tracked down Bohn in London and confronted him face-to-face: "I saw Mr. Bohn, put your pamphlet into his hands, and declared in your name that you felt he had injured you. He entered on a defense, which I could not follow, as, unfortunately, I had not had time to read the pamphlet attentively. . . . Thus much, however, I caught from him, that he thinks himself on the legal side of the hedge, and that if anyone has been wronged, it is himself."[17]

5

Swan kept up the pressure with a high-profile article by Edward S. Gould in the conservative *Democratic Review* in March 1856, which was reprinted in several of the daily newspapers. Gould writes as a man of letters who voiced among the strongest objections to Webster in the entire saga of the dictionary wars. Eleven years later he would publish a book, *Good English; or Popular Errors in Language* (1867), in which he would include several of his past essays bombarding what and whom he regarded as enemies of the English language in America. Gould's earlier hostile sentiments about Webster had been cited by Bryant in the *New York Evening Post* for June 20, 1851, of which he was editor alongside Gould, one of his contributors. Later (in 1854) Swan snuck that early attack on Webster into his *A Reply to Messrs. G. and C. Merriam's Attack upon the Character of Dr. Worcester and His Dictionaries*—as part of a letter from a state official to James W. Beekman, chairman of the Senate Committee of Literature in the State of New York. Gould writes: "Webster's career was a mistake because based on false assumptions. He *assumed* that the language needed reformation, and that he was able to reform it; the latter blunder being far the greater of the two." Webster's further blunder was "to mistake the duties of a lexicographer, whose province is to *record*, not to *legislate*."[18]

In his *Democratic Review* essay, Gould does not err on the side of nuance, modesty, or even good taste in his sweeping indictment of Webster's orthography and general incompetence to write a dictionary. He works himself up almost into a paroxysm. The language of blame and the descent to ad hominem tactics in literary battles does not get much more extreme than this: "The sum of the matter is, that Webster was a vain, weak, plodding Yankee, ambitious to be an American Johnson, without one substantial qualification for the undertaking, and the American public have ignored his pretensions." He hones in on the orthographical dispute—never mind that by now it had been tediously overworked and showed no signs of abating—and provides the public with the most devastating and thorough analysis of Webster's spelling since Lyman Cobb. Gould scoffs that one publisher, the G. and C. Merriam Company, has adopted Webster's orthography simply because it publishes his dictionary: "I hardly know how our [Massachusetts] Legislature could do a greater wrong to popular education than by inflicting Webster's radicalism on the rising generation. . . ." "[N]o man in his senses would undertake to reform" the inconsistencies in English spelling, Gould claims, because "the game would not pay for the candle"; "*no* radicalism is without its followers, and he [Webster] has his." Webster's "*Esprit-Americaine*" had led him astray, "like many other men, priding himself most on what he was least fitted for, and assuming a character for which few men *are* fitted—that of a reformer." There never has been, and never will be, an "absolute standard" of English orthography, Gould insists. Webster "changes a termination, or adds or takes away a letter, because the primitive [usage] requires it—because it endangers the pronunciation, when it does not—because it secures the pronunciation, when it does not—because the word is a noun—because it isn't a noun—because it is an exception—because it is so pronounced (by ignorant people)—because Milton spelled it so—in short, 'because' *any thing* that fits the caprice of the moment."[19]

A better witness for the prosecution of Webster's dictionaries was Lyman Cobb himself—at the moment living quietly in Yonkers, New York, but still potentially dangerous—so the Merriams reasoned, why not get him on their side by paying him to go through the High School Dictionary and the Primary Dictionary, as well as the recent 1856 edition of the Unabridged, to find and correct errors? To that end, might he not be almost as good as Goodrich? It is a sign of how determined and nervous the Merriams were that on

September 7, 1856, they ventured into enemy territory and asked Cobb to go through the three dictionaries to catch lurking spelling aberrations and inconsistencies of spelling and pronunciation, and suggest an efficient system of revision. This was rather late in the day to get someone like Cobb on board for that kind of thorough revision, but never mind. Cobb apparently was short of money, and he might be helpful in spite of his animosity toward Webster. Webster, at any rate, was not there to protest, as he surely would have done. On September 11, Cobb replied: for editing the High School dictionary, he asked for $40, for the Primary $30, and for the Unabridged $125. He could not possibly "afford to read and mark" all three dictionaries for less than $195 (around $4,900 today). There was plenty wrong with all three, he told them, but especially the Unabridged: errors and inconsistencies in the notation, egregious contradictions in all departments between the "rules" specified in the introduction and the body of the work, discrepancies in syllabication, and differences of spelling between the entry words and in definitions. He could list more problems. If the Merriams could pay him enough, he assures them the dictionary would be "vastly improved." The Merriams, however, did not want to pay that much. It is also likely that Goodrich, who had had his fill of Cobb in the 1830s, did not want him to play any part in the Webster future. No more was heard of Cobb, and he died in 1864.[20]

6

To push back against Gould, the Merriams commissioned a reply by Epes Sargent, whose short pamphlet in March 1856 had first appeared as part of an earlier pamphlet, *The Critic Criticized: A Reply to a Review of Webster's System*, and then resurfaced in the *Democratic Review* in June, the same venue as Gould's piece. Sargent was a well-known and popular journalist in Boston, biographer, novelist, poet, and dramatist, as well the author of schoolbooks and a dabbler in Spiritualism—a religion or system of beliefs based on the idea that the spirits of the dead can communicate with the living. He was a member of the Knickerbocker Group, a group of authors based in New York City, including Washington Irving, James Fenimore Cooper, and William Cullen Bryant, which took its name from Irving's *Knickerbocker History of New York* (1809) and sought to promote American national culture. He served as editor of the *Boston Daily Advertiser* in his early career and worked as well for several other Boston newspapers. His series of schoolbooks, *The Standard*

Reader (1854), *The Standard Speaker* (1857), and *The Etymological Reader* (1872), showed he had the credentials to enter the dictionary debates. He had been following closely the turmoil they generated and was eager to jump in. Sargent's membership in the Knickerbocker Group (not to be confused with the Knickerbocker Club, founded in 1871), however, where Worcester's and Webster's relationships to the English language was concerned, was at odds with the likes of Cooper, Irving, and Bryant.

Taking the high moral road, Sargent first accuses Gould of pressing his points with insulting language that one would have to search long to find equaled "in the pages of a scholar and a gentleman." He then proceeds to dismember Gould's objections to Webster's linguistic principles, accusing Gould of "the critic's disingenuous abstract of them" and "harlequin dexterity." Epes was perhaps the most distinguished and popular literary personality the Merriams ever had in their stable of supporting authors. They leaned on him in the ensuing years.[21]

7

Surfeited with this war of words as the American public was by now—the war still had a few years to run—at least several newspapers and widely circulated pamphlets had broadcast the issues, and the people were listening. An article in *Vanity Fair* in March 1860, which significantly used the word *schoolmen* to identify where much of the fury in the dictionary wars was then located, observed: "The schoolmen have been much exercised of late by the Dictionary war. 'A Webster!' 'A Webster!' and 'Worcester to the rescue!' have been the battle-cries heard even above the cannon of Napoleon III." While one article in *The Old Guard*, a magazine published in New York by Charles Chauncey Burr, a close friend of Edgar Allan Poe's, violently attacked Webster as an "immense monument of ignorance, folly and fraud," the *Knickerbocker* magazine took a more measured view that perhaps more widely reflected public opinion: "Worcester or Webster? Well, they are both stirring books, and if t'other dear charmer were away we could be perfectly happy with either"—an allusion to John Gay's *Beggar's Opera*, act 2, scene 2.[22]

While these paper bullets were whizzing back and forth, chiefly between the newspapers and magazines of Boston and New York, Worcester continued to work on his quarto, his magnum opus, reaching the letter *P* by 1858. He remained aloof, worrying about his "health and eyesight," as he confided to his brother Samuel on January 24, 1859: "I have worked about as hard of late, as I used to do before I was superannuated; and my eyes, I am happy, and I ought to be thankful, to say hold and thus far better than I expected they would. . . . much remains to be done, yet I hope, should nothing happen to prevent [it], that the work may be completed in the course of the next summer. How it will be received, or what success may attend its publication I cannot say; the publishers are more sanguine about it than I am." His eyes had recovered enough to enable him to work, but his wife, Amy Elizabeth, was ill and could not help him with the reading of proofs, as she had done many times, "which makes my situation and labors more difficult." Five months later he was further behind in his "alphabetical journey," now with no prospect of reaching the end until after the end of the summer. In October he had reached halfway through the letter *U* and hoped to finish by the end of the year, which he did.[23]

Meanwhile, Goodrich was annoyed that while his old friend Worcester was getting on valiantly with his great work, he himself was bedeviled yet again by the Merriams. They continued to pressure him over what they judged to be his greater loyalty to White, his octavo abridgment publisher, than to them. After some fifteen years of steady work for them in behalf of the Webster cause, they had begun to doubt his ability, partly for health reasons, to stay the course. He felt they did not completely trust him, and he admitted to them that "I have felt deeply wounded by many things which have taken place, and have certainly lost the alacrity I once had for making improvements in the dictionary."[24]

He was burned out by dictionary-making in general: "I must say, in all frankness, that no pecuniary recompense which any man can offer could tempt me [again] for a moment to do any thing of this kind. Nor do I feel that I am personally called upon to do anything more in behalf of the Renewers [of copyright, the Webster family] for the protection of this literary property." His "accumulation of knowledge" over the past few years had placed him in great demand, and he regularly received offers from Harpers and other publishers to author books more pleasing to himself and "wholly independent of any dictionary." Tired and dropping his guard, he acknowledged to the Merriams that they were right—his main loyalty was and always had been to White and the octavo abridgment, "the chief bond which holds me to any further labor in lexicography." He had never had an easy relationship with them: "[W]ithout some adjustment between us which shall create confidence in the future, it is better for you and me to attempt nothing more in common." He was aware Noah Porter was their "warm friend," and that they might want him to take over. "I have never communicated with him on the subject since last July," Goodrich told them, but Porter might help to restore "kindly relations" between them.[25]

Goodrich's letter shocked the Merriams. Porter was indeed in the wings, able (but also not entirely willing) to take center stage if asked. They flirted with the idea of hiring him but were not yet ready to do without Goodrich's unmatchable knowledge of the dictionary, especially in the face of the threat posed by Worcester's imminent quarto. Goodrich was still the central player, in other words, linking together the whole enterprise with his family contacts and the leverage of the octavo abridgment. He leveled with them: "Nothing would be more disastrous to your own interests than to have me break down under these labors through superinduced care and anxiety." It is hard to say what Goodrich wanted in making such a remark. Perhaps he simply sought greater appreciation from them.[26]

So once more they patched up their differences. On October 27, 1858, Charles Merriam told Goodrich that the "great and important labor" needing to be done, far more important than grumbling to each other, was "passing critically over the body of the work, reconstructing the definitions where required, correcting them where inaccurate. . . . There remains seeing the work through the press and . . . later labor after Worcester is out, collating recent English dictionaries, giving our work in general a superiority in its final revision to anything else of the kind then before the public. . . . Your seeing the specimen of Worcester we are led to feel the desirableness of having the stereotyping of our revision commence as early as consistent after that [edition] appears." They thought Worcester would publish in August or September 1859, perhaps earlier. A mountain of work remained for Goodrich, or whoever took his place, to plow through—much more than the Merriams realized.[27]

16

The "Terrible Rival"

Worcesterian Resurgence

In their advertising for the forthcoming quarto, Worcester's publishers, now Swan, Brewer, and Tileson, with Swan very much in charge, made a tactical error that cost them monumentally. Swan was responsible for a statement that suggests, when it got down to intrigue and strategies, he may not have been quite as nuanced and cunning as the Merriams in the race for dictionary supremacy. Swan announced in mid-1858 that Worcester's next quarto would contain thousands of helpful woodcut illustrations appearing next to the definitions of the words to which they referred. The publishers declared it would be the first illustrated English dictionary ever to be published. That was not true, since several dictionaries in England had been illustrated, going right back to Thomas Blount's *Glossographia* and Nathan Bailey's in the eighteenth century, but it would be America's first, and that was bad news for the Merriams.

Illustrations in Worcester's dictionary would be a bold achievement the Merriams could never match or easily dismiss because even if they published their own illustrated dictionary later, Worcester would forever after be known as the man who had again changed the face of the American dictionary. He had done it before with what he called "discriminating" synonymy, the practice of including in his definitions the study, often extended, of words with the same or similar meaning, or having the quality of being similar. It would be a distinction that Worcester's publishers could advertise effectively to sell their dictionary for decades ahead. The Merriams realized they had to publish a new edition immediately, with illustrations, before Worcester's appeared, but how could they do that? There simply was no time. A huge amount of work remained to be done on the large quarto they had under way. Recently, they had made it publicly known that at their invitation a German philologist, Carl August Friedrich Mahn, was working on a complete overhaul of Webster's etymology in order to bring it in line with the latest scholarship. And a team of scholars, ever expanding, was just then beginning to revise every other aspect of the dictionary. Several of these scholars were drawn by Goodrich from Yale's faculty. All of this would take at least five years to complete. If the Merriams had any hope of publishing a large quarto with illustrations before Worcester's, they would have to take a dramatic shortcut, piecing together a rushed hybrid of the 1847 edition with woodcut illustrations and other features added so as to make it look like a brand new revision. The hitch was that since they would have to use the 1847 stereotyped plates, they could not include the woodcuts in the text, as Worcester was doing, since that would involve having to remake the whole book at great expense.

Goodrich outlined for William Webster the "able and far reaching plan" the Merriams, in their extremity, had up their sleeves to "meet the exigency at the time of Worcester's appearance":

> They have had 1500 [wood]cuts engraved, classifying the subjects to some extent. These will occupy nearly one hundred pages of the appendix, and can be printed in a superior style by the use of appropriate paper. These cuts have references to the words in the vocabulary to which they belong, and a mark of reference will be cut into the existing plates pointing to the fact that the word thus noted has an engraving to illustrate it. . . . The Merriams are also very urgent that I should enlarge the discriminations of synonyms . . . and have this inserted in this appendix.

The Merriams would saturate the market with this edition, "throw it into market from Maine to California a month or two *in advance* of Worcester, with a view to 'take out the wind from his sails.'" They would be able to deal Worcester a coup de grâce by undercutting the price of his book by as much as $2 per copy, because the illustrations, and the special paper needed for them, would be limited to the appendix. Worcester's book would integrate the woodcuts with the text, requiring special paper for the entire work. Grouping the illustrations as an appendix, under various subjects, Goodrich adds, would "make the greater show" and enable the public to compare the images more efficiently. "Determined to fight the battle to the utmost of their strength," they were put to great expense by their scheme, but from it they hoped "to continue their hold on the market." Above all, Goodrich implored William not to tell anybody about this plan: "[T]he whole matter is [to be] kept as much as possible a secret. It would be desirable therefore that *nothing of what has here been stated should be mentioned to anyone.*"[1]

2

In the meantime, the newspaper and magazine skirmishes revived again with the news that C.A.F. Mahn was getting rid of virtually all of Webster's etymology, sensational news in the current media environment that threatened Webster's reputation, especially as he had repeatedly reminded the public that he had spent ten long years on his etymology. In a pretense of impartiality, in an article titled "Webster's Dictionary" that appeared in a New York magazine, the *Home Journal*, in March 1859, Edward Gould again led the charge against Webster. What continued to irritate him and many others was the emphasis on Americanness in the title of Webster's dictionary. It is "provocative of controversy," he claims: "It is an assumption of originality and of superiority on the part of the author, which could not escape dispute on either side of the Atlantic. And, indeed, a warfare has followed the publication of the work exceeding, both in intensity and duration, almost any strife in the annals of bibliography." Taking note of Mahn's new job, Gould adds that it was about time Goodrich and the Merriams threw out the fruits of Webster's misguided etymological research.

Gould turned up the heat when he returned to the orthography, "the stumbling-block of the dictionary through its whole history," that has made it "permanently mischievous." He concedes that by this woefully late date the number of offending words had become small, a *petite misère*, bearing "the same proportion to the whole work as a mosquito bears to the bulk of a man he is tormenting." Mosquito-like or not, the *petite misère* remains: Webster "has managed to perplex and confuse the orthography of our vernacular for (past, present, and future) perhaps three generations. That is the actual evil he has done. The good he has done in this behalf, is best expressed by a figure 9 with the tail cut off." If the Merriam team of scholars is able to banish all traces of Webster's lexicography, he adds, one day he might just be able to recommend their dictionary to his friends. But he strongly doubts that would ever happen. Gould had many eager supporters, one of whom wrote to the *Home Journal* in April under the name "Jonathan," declaring that the Merriams had no choice but to rid themselves and the nation of all of Webster's odd orthography, otherwise Worcester, "a terrible rival," would consign the old lexicographer to deserved oblivion.[2]

One anonymous article deserved another, and before long, infuriated by this latest flurry, Poole sent the *Home Journal* another defense of Webster, signing it "Philorthos," a simple Greek compound meaning "lover of correctness." The editors, fed up with the controversy, declined to publish it. But when the *New York Daily Tribune* picked it up instead, the Merriams took notice and a few weeks later published it themselves as a pamphlet, attempting to neutralize the spelling spook by deftly renaming Poole's article *The Orthographical Hobgoblin*. They prefaced it by agreeing with Gould that the differences of spelling between Worcester's last series of dictionaries and the Goodrich-Merriam-Webster editions are "very slight." Portraying Gould as an essentially uninformed troublemaker, Poole dismisses Webster's critics as desperately belligerent, depicting them as mere conjurers of orthographical phantoms dedicated to "frightening timid and conservative people." These critics have identified Webster as the "Vandal," and "all fogeydom is therefore summoned to the rescue." And yet, he adds, twenty copies of this vandal's dictionary are sold for every one by any other author—a pretty accurate estimate. For good measure, Poole goes on to malign Worcester, falsely and vaguely, reviving the old lie that Worcester continued to be guided by Goodrich-Merriam-Webster editions: "Worcester's orthography is neither American nor English, but is a mongrel, vacillating compilation, without purpose or system. . . . Each succeeding edition improves, and conforms more and more to Webster."[3]

Poole cites Gould's four classes of orthography and provides comparative analyses to demonstrate that the specter of continuing confusion raised by critics of Webster's spelling amounts now merely (or mostly) to a regurgitation of egregiously outdated but oft-repeated complaints; and that they do not take into account the hundreds of orthographical corrections made by Webster himself and other lexicographers (almost entirely Goodrich) since his first unabridged edition in 1828. In Poole's first class of twenty "miscellaneous" words, nine that he identifies as "correct orthography" he maintains are exactly as Webster had them in his last 1843 edition; for six, he adds, Webster gave two spellings; and two are not to be found in any of his dictionaries. The important and dizzying fact to keep in mind in the middle of all this scrapping about orthography in the late 1850s, apart from the commercial imperatives, is that American spelling was still in transition and therefore exceedingly complex—something to quarrel over endlessly. In any case, Poole's strictures illustrate the kind of debates that were being aired before the public.

Here are a few of Gould's twenty examples with Poole's comments:

"Correct" Orthography	*Webster's Orthography*

1. axe   ax

POOLE: "*ax* has been the English spelling for over 200 years, and Webster wanted to keep it because it is consistent with monosyllables like *wax, tax,* and *lax.*"

2. comptroller   controller

POOLE: "for over 200 years lexicographers had *controller.*"

3. contemporary   cotemporary

POOLE: "both have long been in use but Webster prefers *cotemporary* because it is shorter and easier to pronounce."

4, 5, 6. defence, offence, pretence   defense, offense, pretense

POOLE: "French precedent, analogy, and wide usage demand 's,' not 'c.'"

7. ambassador   embassador

POOLE: "many lexicographers, including Dr. Johnson, give both; Webster prefers *embassador,* for it is consistent with *embassy.*"

8. height   hight

POOLE: "Webster gives both, prefers *hight,* consistent with *high, highly.*"

9. practise (verb)   practice

POOLE: "he [Gould] wrongly censures Webster for [not making] the distinction between the verb and the noun ('practice'). Webster refuses the difference. 'No possible advantage can be claimed for it, unless it be to puzzle the school boy and the foreigner, who, in learning to spell, are already sufficiently bewildered in the existing mazes of orthographical anomalies.'"

10. wo   woe

POOLE: "analogy warrants *woe,* as in *doe, hoe, foe, toe.*"

Poole takes up the three other classes to illustrate the range of complexity inherent in English spelling and how Webster has succeeded in simplifying it to accommodate American usage: (1) words Gould says are "properly" spelled with two *l*'s that Webster spells with one; (2) words Gould says are "properly" spelled with one *l*, which Webster spells with two; and (3) hundreds of words ending with *re* that Webster spells *er*. There is no mystery in any of this, Poole writes, ending his survey by quoting from *Hamlet*: "There needs no ghost, my lord, come from the grave, / To tell us this."[4]

3

The Merriams' Pictorial Edition of *An American Dictionary of the English Language* was published in 1859, with the eighty-one-page section containing the woodcuts placed prominently at the beginning of the book, not in an appendix at the end as Goodrich thought would happen. The *Atlantic Monthly* in 1859 scoffed at the illustrations, calling them "primer-pictures . . . fitted for a child's scrap-book [more] than for a volume intended to go into a student's library." There were some amusing responses to the illustrations, such as one in the *Christian Advocate*, reprinted by Swan: "The picture of a 'lady attired in hooped dress' was intended doubtless for posterity, so that our descendants may see what was the fashion in this year of grace 1860. We are bound to say, however, that the thing is a vile caricature. The publishers ought to be ashamed of thus slandering the sex." Nevertheless, the Pictorial Edition sold so well that the Merriams reprinted it in 1860. It achieved exactly what they had hoped for by snatching much of the public's attention from Worcester's expectant hands and dulling somewhat the public impact of his first unabridged, illustrated quarto when it appeared a few months later. More personally, it also dimmed the personal glow of satisfaction Worcester anticipated in completing his great work. As Charles Merriam put it in his "Recollections," "Worcester after that fell comparatively harmless to the ground." The Merriams sent the edition to a few English experts in England, one of whom was B. H. Smart, hoping for influential endorsements. Smart did not oblige them. He thanked them but stated a fact that disputed their advertising pitch over the years that Webster was by far the preferred lexicographer in England. Not true, wrote Smart: "Take it all together, it must be considered, in America, at least, as the surpassing work of its kind [the nation's first pictorial edition]. I say in America, because Webster's name no doubt there carries an authority with it which our English public are not willing to yield when difference of opinion or practice exists—e.g., in the spelling of honour, favour, etc." All was not lost, however. Herbert Coleridge, president of the London Philological Society and grandson of the poet Samuel Taylor Coleridge, on August 7, 1860, gave the Merriams what they wanted: "As a general book of reference, adapted to the wants of that enormous majority of educated persons who are not linguistic scholars, it would, I think, be difficult to frame a better or more serviceable Dictionary than that of Webster *in its later* editions."[5]

Early in January 1860, when Worcester was seventy-five, his magnum opus, two-volume, unabridged quarto (copyrighted 1859)—his first quarto—finally appeared with the straightforward title *A Dictionary of the English Language*. It was priced at $7.50 (about $150 today). Goodrich thought it overpriced because of the expensive woodcuts, though Professor Joseph Bosworth, Rawlinson Professor of Anglo-Saxon at Oxford, wrote to Worcester that it was "the most complete & practical—the very best, as well as the cheapest English Dictionary, that I know, & I have, therefore, no doubt of its success." Once the printed pages were available, the publishers sent more than six thousand copies to subscribers and booksellers throughout the country as fast as they could get them bound, as well as several thousand more to England.[6]

The dictionary's publication in London by Samson Low, Son & Co. after Worcester's death is particularly interesting because it included an "Advertisement," written by Worcester in Cambridge in 1859, as well as a picture and a two-page biography of him, that do not appear in the Boston edition in 1860, or ever had appeared in any one of his dictionaries while he was alive. The "Advertisement" can be read as a final word on Webster and the Merriam's relentless accusations against him of complicity in the Bohn affair and charges of plagiarism during his entire career as a lexicographer. Placed in the dictionary, his supreme effort as a lexicographer, it gave him a chance to get that message out to a wider public than ever before. In fact, the positive and celebrative way Worcester is introduced to the British public in this prefatory material reflects an English influence and determination to set the record straight about Worcester's stellar career. What is curious is that all this should be included in the London but not the American edition. The Bohn affair occurred in London, however, and this may partly explain the need to include the facts for the British public in a legitimate edition of Worcester.

[i. EXULCERATED; pp. EXULCERATING, EXUL-
CERATED.]
1. To make sore with an ulcer; to ulcerate.
Cantharides applied to any part of the body *exulcerate* it.
Bacon.

2. To irritate; to fret; to exasperate.
Froward, *exulcerated*, and seditious spirits. *Bp. Reynolds.*

EX-ŬL′CER-ĀTE, v. n.　To ulcerate.　*Bacon.*

† EX-ŬL′CER-ĀTE, a.　Vexed; ulcerated. *Bacon.*

EX-ŬL-CER-Ā′TIQN, n.　[L. *exulceratio*; It. *esul-
cerazione*; Sp. *exulceracion*; Fr. *exulcération.*]
1. (*Med.*) Superficial ulceration.　*Palmer.*
2. Irritation; exacerbation; exasperation.
"This *ulceration* of mind."　*Hooker.*

EX-ŬL′CER-A-TIVE, a.　[It. *esulcerativo*; Fr.
exulcératif.]　That exulcerates or makes ulcer-
ous.　*Holland.*

EX-ŬL′CER-A-TQ-RY, a.　[Sp. *exulceratorio.*]
Causing ulcers; exulcerative. [R.]　*Hulœt.*

EX-ŬLT′ (ęgz-ŭlt′), v. n.　[L. *exulto*; *ex*, from,
and *salto*, to leap; It. *esultare*; Fr. *exulter.*] [i.
EXULTED; pp. EXULTING, EXULTED.] To re-
joice exceedingly; to rejoice in triumph; to
be in transport; to triumph.
The goddess goes *exulting* from his sight.　*Dryden.*

EX-ŬLT′ANCE, n.　Transport; exceeding joy;
triumph; exultation; exultancy. "We have
great cause of *exultance*."　*Gov. of the Tongue.*

EX-ŬLT′AN-CY, n.　Transport; exultation; triumph; rapture; exultance. [R.]　*Hammond.*

EX-ŬLT′ANT, a.　That exults; rejoicing exceedingly; triumphing; exulting. "With such *ex-
ultant* sympathy and joy."　*More.*

EX-UL-TĀ′TIQN, n.　[L. *exultatio*; It. *esultazione*;
Sp. *exultacion.*]　An act of exulting; transport
of joy; triumph; rapturous delight. "Instances
of devout *exultation.*"　*Atterbury.*

EX-ŬLT′ING, p. a.　Triumphing; rejoicing greatly.

EX-ŬLT′ING-LY, ad.　In an exulting manner.

† EX-ŬN′DĀTE, v. a.　[L. *exundo, exundatus.*]
To overflow; to abound; to inundate.　*Bailey.*

EX-UN-DĀ′TIQN, n.　Overflow; inundation. "The
regular *exundation* of the Nile."　*Geddes.*

EX-ŬN′GU-LĀTE, v. a.　[L. *ex*, from, and *ungula*,
a claw, a hoof.]　To pare off, as nails or other
superfluous parts. [R.]　*Maunder.*

EX-ŬN-GU-LĀ′TIQN, n.　The act of exungulat-
ing. [R.]　*Crabb.*

† EX-Ū′PER-A-BLE, a.　[L. *exuperabilis.*] Con-
querable; superable; vincible.　*Johnson.*

† EX-Ū′PER-ANCE, n.　[L. *exuperantia.*] Over-
balance; greater proportion.　*Fotherby.*

† EX-Ū′PER-ANT, a.　Overbalancing; of greater
proportion.　*Bailey.*

† EX-Ū′PER-ĀTE, v. a.　[L. *exupero, exuperatus.*]
To excel; to surmount.　*Cockeram.*

† EX-Ū-PER-Ā′TIQN, n.　The act of exuperating,
excelling, or surmounting.　*Cockeram.*

† EX-ŬR′GENCE, n.　The act of rising or appearing.　*Baxter.*

† EX-ŬR′GENT, a.　[L. *exurgo, exurgens*, to rise
out; *ex*, out of, and *surgo*, to arise.]　Arising;
commencing.　*Dr. Favour.*

† EX-ŬS′CI-TĀTE, v. a.　[L. *exuscito, exuscitatus.*]
To stir up; to rouse; to excite.　*Bailey.*

† EX-ŬST′ (ęgz-ŭst′), v. a.　[L. *exuro, exustus.*]
To burn up; to consume.　*Cockeram.*

EX-ŬST′IQN (ęgz-ŭst′yụn), n.　A burning. *Bailey.*

EX-Ū′VI-A-BLE, a.　That may be cast off. *Clarke.*

EX-Ū-Ū′VI-Æ (ęgz-yū′ve-ę), n. pl.　[L.]
1. Whatever is put off, or shed and left, by
animals or by plants; the cast skin, shells, &c.,
of animals.　*Woodward.*
2. (*Geol.*) The spoils and remains of natural
objects deposited at some great change in the
earth, as fossil remains of animals.　*Lyell.*

EX-Ū-VI-Ā′TIQN, n.　[L. *exuvia*, the cast-off skin
of certain animals.]　(*Zoöl.*) The process by

---

which the crustaceous animals throw off their
old shell, and form a new one.　*Ogilvie.*

EX VŌ′TŌ.　[L.]　After one's wishes; according to a vow.　*Sears.*

EY, may come from A. S. *ig*, an island. — Hence
comes *eyot*, or *eyet*, a small island.　*Johnson.*

EY′A-LĔT (ī′ə-lĕt), n.　A Turkish government or
principality under the administration of a vizier
or pacha of the first class.　*Simmonds.*

† EY′AS (ī′əs), n.　[Fr. *niais*. "Our own word
was sometimes formerly written *nyas.*" *Johnson.*]　A young hawk just taken from the nest.
"Little *eyasses* that cry out."　*Shak.*

† EY′AS (ī′əs), a.　Unfledged.　*Spenser.*

EY′AS-MŪS′KĘT, n.　[It. *muschetto*; Fr. *mou-
chet.*]　A young, unfledged sparrow-hawk. *Shak.*

EYE (ī), n.; pl. EYES (īz).　[Goth. *augo*; A. S.
eage; Dut. *oog*; Ger. *auge*;
Dan. *öje*; Sw. *öga.* — Gr.
ὄκος or ὄκαλλος; L. *oculus*;
It. *ochio*; Sp. *ojo*; Fr. *œil.*]
1. The organ of vision.
And read their history in a nation's *eyes.*　*Gray.*
A beautiful *eye* makes silence eloquent; a kind *eye* makes contradic-
tion an assent; an enraged *eye* makes
beauty deformed.　This little member gives life to every other part
about us.　*Addison.*
☞ In the figure, a is the
sclerotic membrane; b the cornea; c the choroid
membrane; d the retina; e the vitreous humor; f the
crystalline humor or lens; g the aqueous humor; h
the iris; i the ciliary ligament; k the ciliary pro-
cesses; l the ora serrata of the ciliary body; m the
canal of Petit; n the foramen of Sœmmering; o the
sheath of the optic nerve; p the substance of the optic
nerve; q the central artery of the retina.　*Eng. Cyc.*

2. Ocular knowledge; sight; view.
Before whose *eyes* Jesus Christ hath been evidently set
forth.　*Gal. iii. 1.*

3. Power of perception.
The *eyes* of your understanding being enlightened. *Eph. i. 18.*

4. Aspect; regard; as, "To have an *eye* to
one's interest."

5. Notice; observation; watch; vigilance.
After this jealousy, he kept a strict *eye* upon him. *L'Estrange.*

6. Face; front.
Her shall you hear disproved to your *eyes.*　*Shak.*

7. Any thing formed like an eye.
Colors like the eye of a peacock's feather.　*Newton.*

8. A small perforation; an eyelet; as, "The
eye of a needle."

9. A small catch to receive a hook; as, "Hooks
and *eyes.*"

10. A bud of a plant.
Vine shoots to be left with three or four *eyes* of young
wood.　*Evelyn.*

11. A small shade of color.
Red .... with an *eye* of blue makes a purple.　*Boyle.*

12. A hole or whey-drop in cheese.

13. (*Naut.*) A loop or ring; — a position of
direct opposition; as, "To sail in the *eye* of the

EYE′BRŎW (ī′brŏŏ), n.　The hairy arch over the
eye; the brow.　*Ray.*

EYED (īd), a.　Having eyes; — used in composition; as, "Bright-*eyed.*"　*Shak.*

EYE′-DRŎP (ī′drŏp), n.　A tear.　*Shak.*

EYE′-FLĂP (ī′flăp), n.　A piece of leather that
covers the eye of a coach-horse; a blinder. *Ash.*

EYE′-GLANCE (ī′glȧns), n.　A glance of the eye;
quick notice of the eye.　*Spenser.*

EYE′-GLĂSS (ī′glȧs), n.　1. A glass to assist the
sight; spectacles.　*Shak.*
2. A glass in an optical instrument that is
next to the eye; eye-piece.　*Newton.*
3. (*Med.*) A small glass, porcelain, or metal-
lic vessel, used for applying lotions to the eye.
Dunglison.

EYE′-GLŬT-TING, a.　Feasting the eye to satie-
ty.　*Spenser.*

EYE′-LĂSH (ī′lăsh), n.　1. The line of hairs that
edges the eyelid.　*Johnson.*
2. One of the hairs on the edge of the eyelid.

EYE′-LĘSS (ī′lęs), a.　Wanting eyes; deprived of
sight; blind. "*Eyeless* in Gaza."　*Milton.*

EYE′-LĘT (ī′lęt), n.　[Fr. *œillet*, a little eye.]
1. A hole for the light, &c.　*Johnson.*
2. A hole to receive a small cord or lace in
parts of dress, &c.; a loop-hole.　*Wiseman.*

EYE′-LĘT-EĔR (ī-lęt-ēr′), n.　A small pointed instrument for piercing eyelet-holes; a stiletto.
Simmonds.

EYE′-LĘT-HŌLE (ī′lęt-hōl), n.　A hole in a garment in which the eye of a button or lace is put;
a hole in a sail for a rope.　*Ash.*

† EYE′-LI-AD (ī′le-ȧd), n.　[Fr. *œillade.*] An eye-
glance; an eye-beam. — See ŒILIAD.　*Shak.*

EYE′-LĬD (ī′lĭd), n.　The membrane or skin that
closes the eye. "*Sleeping eyelids.*"　*Shak.*

EYE′-QF-FĔND′ING, a.　That offends the eye.
"*Eye-offending* marks."　*Shak.*

EYE′-PIĒCE, n.　The lens, or combination of
lenses, which is nearest to the eye in a tele-
scope, or by means of which a distinct view of
an object is obtained; eye-glass.　*Brande.*

EYE′-PĬT (ī′pĭt), n.　A pit, or cavity, in the orbit
of the eye.　*Goldsmith.*

EYE′-PLĒAS-ING, a.　Pleasing the eye; gratify-
ing the sight.　*Sir J. Davies.*

EYE′R (ī′ęr), n.　One who eyes.　*Gayton.*

EYE′-SĂLVE (ī′sȧv), n.　Ointment for the eyes.
"And anoint thy eyes with *eye-salve.*" *Rev. iii. 18.*

EYE′-SĔR-VANT (ī′sĕr-vȧnt), n.　A servant that
works only while watched.　*Johnson.*

EYE′-SĔR-VICE (ī′sĕr-vis), n.　Service performed
only under inspection.
Not with *eye-service*, as men-pleasers, but as servants of
Christ.　*Eph. vi. 6.*

EYE′-SHŎT (ī′shŏt), n.　Reach of the eye; sight;

FIGURE 16. Worcester's *A Dictionary of the English Language* was published in 1860. Detail: The extensive definition of *eye* and the illustration that accompanies it might reflect
Worcester's particular interest in vision, owing to his temporary blindness. Courtesy of Indiana State University Special Collections, Cordell Collection of Dictionaries.

After laying out the facts, the "Advertisement" concludes: "It seems proper, however unpleasant, to give this statement of facts; and a bare statement is deemed sufficient, without any comment." As for the biography, even if it is only a quick summary of his life, it is the kind of attention we know he eschewed and would have vetoed.

The 1860 dictionary was a triumph, a solid piece of scholarship. Worcester's introduction contains an analysis of Americanisms, provincialisms, and archaisms; a history of the English language; a historical survey of English lexicography slightly extended from the version in his introduction to the 1846 edition; and scholarly treatments of grammar, pronunciation, and orthography. He also included a long list of American and English dictionaries, drawing on his own unmatched private collection and also Harvard's resources. Much in his preface and introduction repeats what he had written in his 1855 edition, but much in it is also new and far more both concentrated and expansive. The book was like a portable mini-library, containing "in one volume all that is necessary in a work of reference." Worcester and six "assistants" on whom he had called informally from time to time had consulted several authorities, most of them faculty at Harvard, in the sciences, medicine, and industry.

He states outright at the start of his preface his principle tenets in compiling his lexicon: "in order to be complete," a dictionary "must contain all the words of the language in their *correct orthography* [my italics], with their pronunciation and etymology, and their definitions, exemplified in their different meanings by citations from writers belonging to different periods of English literature. . . ." Among his entry words he also included many additional technical terms drawn from "the arts, architecture, astronomy, botany, chemistry, entomology, geology, ichthyology, mathematics, mechanics, mineralogy, music, ornithology, paleontology, zoology, etc." He acknowledges that the acquisition of entry words drawn from so many of the sciences had posed a large and potentially controversial problem regarding which to allow into the dictionary. A good many had been included by Webster before him in his 1828 dictionary, but Worcester added to them considerably. Several critics thought none should have been included, or at least not those so obscure as to be well outside almost everybody's interest or curiosity. Worcester maintained that not to include any would leave thousands of readers unsatisfied and render the dictionary fatally flawed in an era of rapidly expanding knowledge. And as regards the reader's ability to understand the meanings of obsolete words in old texts, he writes defensively, as he had done in 1846: "A dictionary that is designed to be a complete glossary of all English books which are now read, must contain many words which are obsolete, and many which are unworthy of being countenanced." It was pronunciation, however, his specialty, that received somewhat more of Worcester's attention. In a section titled "Principles of Pronunciation," he provides a table or "Key" to the pronunciation of vowels and consonants, followed with "Remarks on the Key" that extends to thirteen pages. There was no doubt after that where he stood on that complicated subject.[7]

The book was the largest, most comprehensive dictionary of English published to date, containing 1,000 woodcuts, 1,800 pages, and 104,000 entry words (3,000 more than in his 1846 edition and about 19,000 more than the last Goodrich-Merriam edition), "for [all of] which authorities are given." Ease of reading was a welcome feature: the pages were divided into three columns each, and different typefaces were used for the entry words, definitions, and synonyms so that at a glance the reader could tell where to look in an entry. Based on the same English authorities he had cited in his earlier dictionaries, and on what he termed "refined" or "educated" usage in the United States, Worcester's orthography, pronunciation, and etymology were still relatively conservative.

4

Virtually all the notices of Worcester's dictionary were enthusiastically positive. One of these, an anonymous review in the *New York Times* for May 26, 1860, apparently by a scholarly expert on the history of philology and lexicography, merits a close look. The reviewer chose the Goodrich-Merriam 1847 *American Dictionary* to compare with Worcester's new edition. The review is impressive for its authoritative tone and expertise, and its readiness to find fault with Worcester and Johnson as well as with Webster, although it comes down far more heavily against the role Webster's work had played in the progress of the English language in America. Except for Swan's "The Critic Criticized," it is the most complete review and analysis of Worcester's dictionary published in the lexicographer's lifetime and takes us far beyond most of the biased commentators who were being played by the publishers. It also provides a reading of linguistic attitude in the United States at midcentury.

The *New York Times* review begins by reminding readers of the growing importance and power of an English dictionary in contemporary American society: "It is hard to see how it can be otherwise than one of the main principalities and powers of the intellectual world." The reviewer wants no part in the current dictionary war, he says, and distances himself from it: "The War of the Dictionaries threatens to become as celebrated in the annals of literary controversy as [Jonathan Swift's] famous Battle of the Books. Ever since the appearance of Dr. WORCESTER'S great Quarto, the rival publishers have kept up a perpetual series of literary skirmishes, belligerent ballista filling all the journals. . . . Of course, amid this tempest of detraction and of praise, the calm voice of positive criticism is hard to hear." He believes his is a "calm voice" that places both men in the larger context of eighteenth- and early-nineteenth-century lexicography and philology. His overarching judgment, one that had hardened into a consensus over the years, is that Webster's failing had always been "his assumption that he had a mission to regulate the English language, not seeming to realize that a lexicographer's function can never legitimately go beyond recording it." Webster had forgotten, or perhaps never fully understood, that there was nothing more important "for the lexicographer to do but to accept this great living mystery of language, and be content to record the motions of its creative energy. . . . Controlling or repression is all in vain."[8]

The reviewer adds his voice to the contemporary disdain for the linguistic quackery, still lurking in the American study of etymology, of "word-compellers" who chase "a panting syllable through time and space" and in the process force English vocables into Hebrew, Ethiopian, Basque, or Chinese. They are traveling through nonsense, he asserts, perpetuating "the grotesque guesses of the old philologists, which had well nigh brought the whole study of words to be viewed with discredit and contempt." Webster was one of the worst offenders, the review argues: "The very head and front of WEBSTER'S offending" was his vain hunt for the origins of English words by tracing with analogy the radicals or roots of words in various ancient languages around the world. No surgery can save it; it is "enough to take away one's breath to read it."[9]

The reviewer is pleased with Worcester's definitions because he does not detect in them "individual whimsies." As a reviewer in the *North American Review* in April 1860 puts it, the excessive length of most of Webster's definitions is achieved by stuffing them with extraneous material. For the word, *faith*, for example, Webster gives twelve meanings while Worcester offers only five; but Webster's third meaning, "evangelical, justifying or saving faith," prompts the reviewer to remark that it "is in no sense a definition of *faith*, but the edifying statement of a fundamental principle of practical theology, such as belongs of right to a sermon, not to a dictionary." Worcester, himself devoutly religious, writes in his preface that a dictionary's "moral influence, so far as such a work should have any, should be unexceptional."[10]

5

From leading linguists and literary figures in America and England Worcester received letters of admiration, approval, and congratulation, and in the months and years to come there would be enthusiastic support from such as Thomas Carlyle, William Makepeace Thackeray, Horace Mann, Hawthorne, Holmes, Longfellow, Bryant, and many others to whom he or his publisher had sent gift copies or who wrote to him of their own accord. Many of them thought that at last America had a superb dictionary: respectable toward the history of the language, displaying Worcester's extensive and accurate knowledge of its complexity, and well-suited to serve America's needs for many years to come. Surely, they must have thought, the dictionary wars are now over. Holmes wrote to Worcester on January 10, 1860, "This [is] indeed a monumental work, and one of which our city and country may be proud as long as we have a city, a country, and a language. It gives me great satisfaction to think that your health and strength have enabled you to endure labours of so great an achievement and to see it successfully completed." Invoking Worcester as a lexicographical god, a veritable Apollo, Josiah Quincy III— former president of Harvard and mayor of Boston, after whom Quincy Market in Boston was named—waxed lyrical: "Without putting on any wing of fancy, assuming no airy stand on Parnassus, but resting on a deeply laid rock of useful labor, you have a right as much as any poet to exclaim, 'Exegi monumentum aere perennius' [I have erected a monument more lasting than bronze (Horace, *Odes* 3.30)]."[11]

A letter he received from his old student Nathaniel Hawthorne especially delighted him. Worcester had sent him a gift of this latest edition, which prompted Hawthorne to write back thanking his old schoolmaster for his "noble Dictionary" in such a way that reveals he was very much aware of the

Quincy   Everett   Sparks   Walker   Felton

FIGURE 17. Five presidents of Harvard University, 1861. *Left to right*: Josiah Quincy III (1829–45), Edward Everett (1846–49), Jared Sparks (1849–53), James Walker (1853–60), and Cornelius Conway Felton (1860–62). Courtesy of Harvard University Archives, HUPSF Presidents (15a), W418135.

dictionary wars that had been raging for about thirty years and Webster's efforts to overhaul the language: "[O]f all lexicographers, you seem to me best to combine a sense of the *sacredness* of language with a recognition of the changes which time and human vicissitude inevitably work upon it. It will be ominous of anarchy in matters moral and political, when our Dictionaries cease to be mainly conservative; and for my own part, I would not adopt a single new spelling, unless it were forced upon me by the general practice of the age and country;—not willingly, admit a new word, unless it brought a new meaning along with it." Thinking back to his school days, he added, "I well remember your kindness, my dear Sir, in my early days; and I have seen with the greatest pleasure the growth of the indestructible reputation which you have since built up." Since he was not a lexicographer, or a linguist, Hawthorne's sentiment that dictionaries must ward off "ominous" anarchy and remain "mainly conservative" is necessarily oversimplified and not entirely representative of Worcester's more nuanced views on the subject; but Worcester would have had no difficulty understanding the spirit of the remark.[12]

From England, Thomas Carlyle's approving mention of him and Dr. Johnson in the same breath must have delighted Worcester: "So far as I can examine, it is a most lucid, exact, comprehensive, altogether useful-looking dictionary; the definitions of meaning are precise, brief, correct,—the woodcuts occasionally a great help,—new fields are opened with success, everything is calculated for carrying information by the directest road. Samuel Johnson said of his work, 'Careful diligence will at last prevail'; you too I believe I can congratulate on a great mass of heavy and hard work faithfully done—a good victory, probably the only real victory possible to us in this world." Charles Dickens told Worcester that his dictionary was "a most remarkable work, of which America will be justly proud, and for which all who study the English language will long have reason to respect your name, and be grateful to you." William Makepeace Thackeray went so far as to say that he had surpassed Johnson: "I have had no dictionary all my life but an old (abridged) Johnson of my father's, and whenever I have consulted it I have been aware of its countless shortcomings. Let me thank you for giving me this useful and splendid book, and for thinking it would be acceptable to an English man of letters who holds Boston and the States in very cordial and grateful remembrance."[13]

6

Even as he struggled in the late 1850s to complete his unabridged edition, Worcester took an intelligent interest in what had been going on in America politically. Unlike Webster, however, his attention to politics was quiet and private. He shared his views on politics only with good friends and especially with his brother Samuel T. Worcester, a successful judge in Ohio. His letters to Samuel, in only a few of which he wrote about his dictionary labors, are where he opened up about the state of the country.

"You say, 'the political horizon for the future looks more hopeful to me than it has done for years before,'" he wrote to Samuel on January 24, 1859. "I think it still looks rather bad; though I hope the president [James Buchanan] and the slave-power will be checked in their worst designs." It had begun to look as if war was inevitable, that it could erupt at any time. On January 28, 1861, his pessimism seeped into another letter to Samuel: "The aspect of our public affairs is very bad. It seems doubtful whether all the States will consent to be under the government, as administered by Mr Lincoln; and if a concession or compromise should be made, what reason have we to expect that the free and slave states will get along harmoniously together, as long as slavery exists?"[14]

By February 1862, the Civil War was not yet a year old, and Worcester already was weary and despairing. "The war continues to drag, drag, drag," he wrote to Samuel, "nor does the prospect of its speedy or successful termination seem to grow brighter." Throughout the coming violent months and years of battle, he followed the progress of the war carefully, the fortunes and misfortunes of the various generals, the victories and defeats, and the politics of the government and the Lincoln administration. His remarks were always tempered, never heated, as in June 1862: "I am disposed to think well of the President, and most of the others who have the chief management of the war; but I suppose they have made some great mistakes, perhaps not more than might be expected.[15]

Compared with the bloody progress of the Civil War, the dictionary war and the strains and pressures of finishing his quarto in 1860 perhaps at times seemed to him a mite trivial. But the dictionary wars, too, seemed set to "drag, drag, drag," and for the next four years they would run—in one of those neat historical coincidences—concurrently with the great battles of the war between the states. Everything seemed in flux, from the destiny of his enormous dictionary contribution to the English language, to the future of America.

7

Worcester still avoided taking any part in the publishers' press campaigns, fearing they would entangle him in yet another soul-destroying public quarrel with the perfidious Merriams just when he was enjoying the sensations of magnificent success. Glad to be out of his "box," he traveled instead, visiting friends and family in New England and the Midwest, including his brother Samuel in Ohio and several siblings and cousins scattered around the country. The Merriams were determined to raise the temperature again, however, even as they watched the progress of the intense editorial work for the final stages of their own quarto, which they hoped would establish it as indisputably the nation's "standard" dictionary and finish off Worcester. Trouble came sooner than Worcester expected.[16]

Rev. Henry M. Dexter, the controversial historian of the Congregational Church, provided some immediate and immoderate provocation when he attacked Worcester's quarto on January 27, 1860, in a biting editorial that appeared in the religious Boston newspaper, the *Congregationalist*, of which he was editor (1851–66). In it he warns readers that buying Worcester's book would damage, or at least retard, their spiritual as well as linguistic development— that is, Worcester's dictionary supposedly lacked the religious dimensions that had always clung to Webster's lexicon. This was the first prominent attack to emphasize religion in comparing the dictionaries. After Dexter's editorial, the brilliant linguist and philologist George P. Marsh felt compelled to speak out. A Vermonter who served Presidents Zachary Taylor and Abraham Lincoln as minister to the Ottoman Empire and Italy, Marsh was a pioneer environmentalist and lectured extensively on the history of the English language at Columbia University and the Lowell Institute in Boston. He was about to publish his *Origins and History of the English Language* (1862) and would contribute substantially to the *New English Dictionary*, which later became the *Oxford English Dictionary*. (Oxford University Press did not begin as its publisher until 1879, the *OED* having struggled for more than a decade to gain momentum through a change of editors and sundry other interruptions.)

With some experience himself as a lexicographer, Marsh elevated the discourse of the dictionary wars, in this final stage of the conflict, to the highest scholarly and analytical level they had yet attained. A staunch supporter of Worcester, whose command of the lexicographical history and progress of the language he believed was unmatched in America, Marsh in the June 15, 1860, issue of the *New York World* compares Worcester's quarto with the Merriams' hastily assembled Pictorial Edition in 1859. He finds fault with Webster for his "unscholarlike and unsound" etymology, his narrow representation of the language in restricting the number of obsolete words, his failure to record sufficiently the language of cultivated English in both America and England, the lingering arbitrariness (even after Goodrich's many revisions) of his spelling and pronunciation, and what he regarded as his general unreliability.[17]

Marsh's review inevitably ignited a new round of fighting. An anonymous author, signing himself "Equal Justice," hit back in the September 1859 issue of the *New York World* with an article, "The Two Dictionaries, or the Reviewer

Reviewed." The savagery of this hard-hitting assault reopened wide old wounds. The author replies to Marsh by taking what was meant to look like a similarly scholarly line. He chronicles the reactionary progress of Webster haters and the nobler motives of Webster lovers: "'The War of the Dictionaries,' as it has been termed, began with an ill-tempered and vituperative attack upon Webster. These assaults have been from time to time renewed in a like spirit. . . . Pecuniary interests; a desire for the notoriety supposed to result from attacking a distinguished man, or work; display of lore; an aversion to changes, even if salutary; and an inordinate attachment to old forms, and true and scholarly criticism, have all, at one time or another, been apparent." "Yielding indiscriminate laudation to Worcester at nearly every step," "Equal Justice" continues, "and visiting, as universally, disparagement upon Webster, the *animus* of [Marsh's] paper does not, we confess, strike us favorably." He sums up, "In the *vocabulary* there is not much to choose. In *pronunciation* and *orthography*, not stuff enough to make an argument. In *etymology*, Webster is an original with the errors of his time, still instructive and inspiring, often sagacious, and always full. Worcester is meager, unscholarlike, and of little worth, and altogether behind the means at command. In *definitions* Webster maintains his unquestioned supremacy, as also in the *synonyms* and *pictorial illustrations*." The superiority of Worcester's pronunciation and orthography had been widely and long acknowledged, so there was, in fact, plenty there to "make an argument." In his definitions Webster, indeed, had the upper hand in public opinion. But the absurdity of the remarks about Webster's etymology is obvious, especially given that the Merriams had retained, back in 1854, C.A.F. Mahn from Germany to mostly banish Webster's entire etymology.[18]

This was just the return to dictionary warfare Worcester feared. He wanted no part of it. He wrote to his brother on August 6, 1860, eight months after his unabridged quarto appeared, about a belligerent pamphlet Swan had released earlier in the year: "I suppose you may have seen [Swan's] *Critic Criticized*. I took no part in the preparation of it, and advised to do nothing of the sort at present at least. If the battle contrives to rage, I do not intend to take any part in it, unless I am compelled." "It is not as I could wish," Worcester told his brother, "and I am sorry that they have made a comparison with Webster's."[19] He was referring to Swan's new contribution in March, *The Critic Criticized and Worcester Vindicated . . . Comparative Merits of Worcester's and Webster's*

Figure 18. "Spring Intelligence: The Battle of the Dictionaries," from a cartoon in *Vanity Fair*, March 10, 1860. Courtesy of *Vanity Fair*.

Dictionaries. Swan's essay is a rousing indictment of the Merriams' lack of modesty and undeserved claims to "a patent right to sit in judgment and dictate to the literary world." It is a stinging attack on Webster by a very angry man offended by the religious complexion of Dexter's recent editorial and the spectacle he depicted of America hoodwinked, as he thought, for so long by a former schoolteacher whom he regarded as inferior to Worcester as a person, intellect, and philologist.[20] Worcester, for a variety of personal reasons, might have regretted the pamphlet, but it was (putting aside Swan's bias) up to this point in the history of the dictionary "wars" the most thorough and well-documented and illustrated analysis of the Worcester and Webster dictionaries that had yet appeared before the public.

Following on the publication of Worcester's 1860 quarto, the combative Swan offered up another rebuke of the Merriams with *A Comparison of Worcester's and Webster's Quarto Dictionaries* (1860). He parades a host of Worcester's testimonials from England and America, arguing that pre-1860 quarto comparisons of the two dictionaries by the Merriams are now hopelessly out of date and of no value in current comparisons. Worcester's testimonials, on the other hand, are fresh and on the cutting edge of lexicographical progress. He provides the resoundingly enthusiastic endorsement from Louis Agassiz, for example, Harvard's famous professor of zoology and geology, on Worcester's state-of-the-art coverage of the sciences:

> I have looked over your great edition of Worcester's Dictionary, chiefly with the view of ascertaining how far it covers the ground in which I am particularly interested. It is of great importance, in our days, when the nomenclature of science is gradually creeping into common use, that an English Lexicon should embrace as much of it as is consistent with the language we speak. I am truly surprised and highly delighted to find that you have succeeded far beyond my expectation in making the proper selection, and combined with it a remarkable degree of accuracy. More could hardly be given, except in a scientific Cyclopaedia.[21]

8

It remained for the periodicals to weigh in on the final campaigns of this dictionary war, at this point giving the verdict largely in favor of Worcester. In his recently established *Atlantic Monthly*, James Russell Lowell had no doubts:

> From this long conflict Dr. Worcester has unquestionably come off victorious. . . . A conclusive reason with us for preferring Dr. Worcester's dictionary is, that its author has properly understood his functions, and has aimed to give us a true view of English as it is and not as he himself may have wished it should be or thought it ought to be. . . . He intrudes no theories of his own . . . but cites the opinions of the best authorities, and briefly adds his own where there is occasion. . . . For ourselves we

shall wish to own both Webster and Worcester, but if we could only possess one, we would choose the latter.

In Britain the reviews of Worcester continued unfailingly positive and seemed likely to silence the Merriams' claims that Webster was the preferred choice there. The eminent English historian and editor Henry B. Wheatley wrote in 1865 that Worcester's dictionary was "the work upon which his fame will rest" and that it was "a most admirable dictionary." And the *Athenaeum*, a London literary magazine, declared, "The volumes before us show a vast amount of diligence; but with Webster it is diligence in combination with fancifulness,—with Worcester in combination with good sense and judgment. Worcester's is the soberer and safer book, and may be pronounced the best existing English Lexicon."[22]

Jonathon Green, however, the modern historian of British and American lexicography, notices a dark cloud for Worcester in English blessings: "A clue to Worcester's demise can be seen, perhaps, in his particular success in England."[23] While those and many other British reviews might have been a blessing for the British market, they probably would prove to be a curse for the American. For America, with its own unique language needs and a diverse population still mushrooming with legions of immigrants, as well as a persistent cultural need to identify its language as American and its dictionaries as homegrown, these identifications of Worcester's dictionary with Britain sounded a discordant un-American note. Never mind that in this dictionary, as in his earlier editions, Worcester had included as many American words as appear in Goodrich-Merriam, had contributed American senses for many traditional words, and had scrupulously recorded the present state of American orthography and orthoepy.

For an unbridged quarto, Worcester's sales were robust. From 1860 to September 1863, twenty-seven thousand copies were printed, greatly exceeding sales of Webster's quarto in 1828 and the editions of 1841, 1847, and 1859. The far more popular Goodrich/Worcester octavo revision of 1829 was the exception. These figures for their unabridged edition were promising enough for Swan to boast that the American market was witnessing a Worcesterian resurgence that would soon overtake the sales of the Merriam-Webster dictionaries. The Merriams knew they had triumphed in the schools market and that sales figures put them well in the lead with the general public, but

Worcester's success did worry them. They needed to remind the public who was winning this war. In May 1861, they put the current state of sales figures on the record in a pamphlet titled *The Two Dictionaries*. On the final page, they boasted about the results of a survey of booksellers in Cincinnati, New York, Boston, Philadelphia, New Haven, St. Louis, Chicago, and several other cities, conducted by the Merriams themselves in August and September 1860. The survey showed for all to see, at least from these dealers chosen by the Merriams, that Webster's Pictorial Edition for those months outsold Worcester 5,787 to 786, or at a ratio of about seven-to-one. Even in Boston, the ratio was six-to-one in Webster's favor.[24]

There was still nothing certain about how this civil war of words might turn out, but halfway through 1861, Worcester knew in his heart that in spite of the healthy sales of his quarto, the praise the critics were showering on his dictionary, and what many judged to be the superiority of his dictionary to what the Merriams thus far had produced, the momentum of sales unmistakably put them in the winner's column. As always, the Webster brand seemed poised to prevail, provided the new Merriam quarto, when it arrived, did not stumble badly.

Unsettled as the Merriams were by the strong praise for Worcester, the appearance of his dictionary more than four years before the publication of their thoroughly revised quarto was a strategic advantage for them. They and their editors could take full advantage of what Worcester had wrought by using his edition as a benchmark and source. As Charles Merriam would write in his "Recollections" in 1883, "Thank God for Worcester."

Worcester had taken himself out of the dictionary wars after the publication of his quarto, but to remain scholarly idle was not in his blood. As he waited for the new Merriam edition, he continued to work on revising and adding to his own dictionary. He had his book reprinted and bound in seven volumes, with interleaved blank pages in each so he could add and revise text uncramped for space and at an unpressured pace. He never said so, as far as anyone knows, but appearances suggested he intended to publish another edition that he could hope would once more outshine the Goodrich-Merriam editions. Had he lived long enough, and with the massive help of top linguists and scholars from different fields he would have sought out at Harvard and elsewhere, he might still have shifted the balance permanently in his favor. But the signs were not good.

9

The Civil War ended in the spring of 1865, just after the assassination of Lincoln on April 14. More than six hundred thousand soldiers were dead. On Harvard's campus, the enormous campaign to raise money for the construction of Memorial Hall (to memorialize those Harvard men who died fighting for the Union cause) was just getting under way. For Worcester, his own battles were coming to an end. He wrote to brother Samuel on April 16 that he was not well and felt "old" and "decrepit": "I cannot expect to live a great while. I have myself had a cold, for five or six weeks past; but it is much better now than it has been."[25]

After a brief illness, at the age of eighty-one, Worcester died peacefully in Cambridge on October 27, 1865—the same year Edward Everett died—at the large home he had built next to Longfellow on Brattle Street in which he and his wife, Amy Elizabeth, had lived for more than twenty years. It may have been complications from that protracted cold that eventually ended his life. No known record of his last days has survived. He had no family nearby except his wife to write about them, and she seems not to have done so. He was buried in Mount Auburn Cemetery in Cambridge. Friends from the Harvard faculty, old and new, raised a prominent cenotaph as a memorial to him, on which he is identified simply as "geographer, historian, lexicographer." Worcester's funeral was, like his private life, a quiet affair.

A short time before his death, he donated $1,000 toward a $30,000 fund for the benefit of the American Peace Society, in whose principles he deeply believed. He left his considerable estate, including his house on Brattle Street, to Amy Elizabeth, specifying in his will that on her death (1881) half of the proceeds of his quarto would be left to the same society and half to the American Bible Society, which was committed to the cause of ending slavery and preventing the corruption of biblical text.

10

If Worcester had lived long enough to look into the Merriams' new quarto, he would have recognized that his own great work would certainly be eclipsed. As it happened, Swan had died in 1864, and with him no longer leading the charge against the Merriams, the fight in behalf of Worcester evaporated quickly. J. B. Lippincott Company of Philadelphia, who had purchased the copyright to all of Worcester's dictionaries in 1877, put up a good fight in the twilight history of Worcester's dictionaries by publishing a new Worcester quarto in 1881. It contained more than twelve thousand new words and synonyms, probably drawn from Worcester's notes in his interleaved volumes, but otherwise it was only slightly revised from the 1860 edition. Lippincott also brought out *A New Etymological Dictionary of the English Language* in 1888 based on recent updates of Worcester's etymologies by the eminent English philologist Walter William Skeat and others, another edition in 1891, and a school edition in 1908. By then, sadly, the life had gone out of Worcester's dictionary, and Lippincott decided it would be a waste of money to continue competing with the Merriam dictionary-publishing machine.[26] Writing in 1913 to an early chronicler of the Worcester-Webster saga, Lippincott explained, "Worcester's quarto dictionary has not been revised for twenty years or more, and while in its essential features it is an excellent book for the average man, yet it will not meet the requirements of those who desire the up-to-date terms, for it is deficient in this particular. We have long since ceased to send out particulars of this book."[27]

A contentious American era of lexicography had ended, and a new one, in which Worcester's great dictionary would play little part, was beginning in both America and Britain. Nevertheless, the formidable reputation of Worcester's large 1860 quarto edition at the time of his death was fairly captured by Ezra Abbot, later Bussey Professor of New Testament Criticism and Interpretation in the Harvard Divinity School, who in his memorial address at the American Academy of Arts and Sciences a few months after Worcester's death could not resist an oblique reference to Webster's "wild aberrations and extravagances":

It will not be deemed invidious to say, that, at the time of its [Worcester's] publication, notwithstanding the great merits of its chief competitor, the general verdict of scholars at home and abroad placed it at the head of English lexicographical literature; and if it has since been equaled or surpassed, we may indulge a pardonable pride in the fact that the only dictionary of the English language which even now can pretend to rival it in fullness and accuracy is also the product of American enterprise, industry, and scholarship. . . .

All the works of Dr. Worcester give evidence of sound judgment and good taste, combined with indefatigable industry and a conscientious solicitude for accuracy in the statement of facts. The tendency of his mind was practical rather than speculative. As a lexicographer, he did not undertake to reform long-established anomalies in the English language. . . . In the mazy paths of etymology, if he cannot claim the merit of an original explorer, his good sense preserved him from the wild aberrations and extravagances into which many have been misled.[28]

The president of the Massachusetts Historical Society announced at its November 1865 meeting, "No lexicographer of the English tongue, of equal merit and equal accomplishment, survives him on either continent." Worcester's 1860 masterpiece, he continued, "is inferior, to say the least, to no English dictionary ever published." He added, "By a striking coincidence, a late steamer from England brings word, that Dr. Charles Richardson, whose labors in the same field might perhaps have been compared with those of Dr. Worcester, died a few weeks before him."[29] With the death of those two men and the Merriams' promotion of editorial methods involving a large team of scholars for the production of their next unabridged edition, the old order of the single lexicographer working mostly on his own vanished forever.

17

The Merriams Triumphant

"Worcester! Worcester!

All Change for Webster!"

Goodrich's health was failing. His wife, Julia, never stopped pleading with him to give up lexicography. His spirits were depressed. "I sincerely wish I could find someone who could take my place," he told the Merriams in January 1860. "It involves so much care, that is increasing, and such constant liability to driving work in all my working hours, so much setting aside of my appropriate studies that I should not for an instant be tempted to think of it could I think of anyone who would command the confidence of the parties."[1] He could think of one: he was still getting the distinct feeling that the Merriams preferred to have the younger Noah Porter as chief editor.

As Porter had already shown himself to be fully sympathetic to Goodrich's ongoing efforts to improve Webster's dictionary, the Merriams concluded that with his Yale connection he would be the logical successor to Goodrich. Just days after receiving Goodrich's letter in January, they asked Porter to assume editorial control of the dictionaries, perhaps initially as coeditor. But for personal reasons Porter, too, was apprehensive about slipping into the Merriam harness. He was fond more than ever of hiking in the Adirondacks and preferred teaching philosophy, rhetoric, and philology at Yale to drudging through the endless labyrinths of lexicography. The Merriams pressed him to accept their offer, however, and at last he agreed. With that, Goodrich finally had shaken off the lexicographical albatross that had clung to his neck for over thirty years.

As a condition to accepting the job, Porter told the Merriams on February 3, 1860, that there had to be a clear understanding with Goodrich: "I have no wish that Mr. Goodrich should not exercise his judgment and his research and his experience to bring all the original contributions to the work which he can. But if you hold me responsible I must ask that he give me information of all material alterations and suggestions before they go into the copy. . . . Mr. Goodrich as the representative of the family and as one trained under his father's [i.e., Webster's] eye and familiar with his principles will of course be expected to give his views at all times—with entire freedom and I shall be very slow to oppose his fixed opinions, but as the cases are numerous and decisions must be promptly made, he must see the necessity of a final decision without long debate." Having himself successfully and firmly shut the door against his brother-in-law Fowler's wasteful editorial meddling back in the 1840s, Goodrich understood Porter's concern, although surely he objected to the notion that he was "trained" by Webster. His role from now on would be strictly advisory.[2]

Goodrich already had enlisted his colleagues Professors William Dwight Whitney (professor of Sanskrit at Yale and later editor of the rival *Century Dictionary and Cyclopedia* (1889–91) and Daniel C. Gilman (later the first president of Johns Hopkins University, where he established the first program of advanced graduate education in America) to assume joint control of revising all the nontechnical definitions. Webster's definitions had been particularly on Goodrich's mind. Many of them would have to be overhauled or completely rewritten because after Worcester's edition it was obvious they could not compete. He stressed to the Merriams on January 26, 1860, that in order to bring them into line with C.A.F. Mahn's new etymologies, they would require a new arrangement: "New senses have come into use, and must be brought in, and to do this in the right way and place requires rearrangements to a greater or less extent. Sometimes definitions or parts of them are clumsy, unscholarlike, and have been much found fault with—and these must undergo modification. In [the vocabulary] of science, many changes [to the definitions] are requisite, for accuracy, for introduction of later facts, and for conciseness. . . . [A] certain amount of reconstruction is requisite."[3]

None of that would ever again be Goodrich's concern. After a long and heroic career of unending revisions that repeatedly rescued Webster's dictionaries from the ignominy of lexicographical and commercial failure, he died in New Haven on February 25, 1860. Suffering from migraines for most of his Yale career, he possessed a nervous energy that made him capable of an immense amount of work but which was often physically debilitating. He was buried in Grove Street Cemetery in New Haven, and his memorial stone reads, "Professor of the Pastoral Charge Yale College, died Feb. 25, 1860, aged 70."

In a brief testimony to Goodrich's religious presence at Yale for more than forty years, the college secretary, Franklin B. Dexter, noted in 1861 that Goodrich provided "unquestionably the most efficient religious influence in the College." And in his lengthy memorial address for Goodrich at Center Church, New Haven, Theodore Dwight Woolsey, president of Yale between 1846 and 1871, remarked that people often had come from outside Yale to seek Goodrich's pastoral help: "Probably no man in New Haven was more resorted to as a counselor than he was in the last twenty or twenty-five years of his life." There is no mention on his monument in Grove Street Cemetery of his academic career or his historically important lexicographical achievements.[4]

2

Porter now was in charge of overseeing the editorial work for the edition, with William Webster as a token presence to keep the Webster family happy and informed. Porter had already provided some ancillary help with this edition. It was he who, while on a year's sabbatical in Germany, had looked in on Mahn and, with Goodrich's approval, hired him to eliminate Webster's etymology. Now, with Porter's agreement and advice, the Merriams set about assembling their large team of editors and assistants. They hired William Wheeler, a writer and editor with special expertise in orthoepy; he had assisted Worcester for four years in the treatment of pronunciation and now snatched the opportunity to work for the Merriams. He did not distinguish himself for modesty. "The assistance I furnished [to Worcester]," Wheeler wrote in his job application letter to the Merriams on November 29, 1860, "extended to every department of the work, *except synonyms*. I think I may justly, and I hope without vanity, lay claim to a considerable share of the merits" of Worcester's 1860 unabridged quarto. "I certainly am not responsible for many of its defects," he added vaguely and ungraciously. They hired him annually to import and modify Worcester's system of pronunciation and spare Porter from some of the general editorial labor.[5]

In a letter to Wheeler on February 20, 1862, two years after the publication of Worcester's book, the Merriams reviewed the progress they had made thus far and listed something like thirty professors, scientists, and general

FIGURE 19. Noah Porter, professor of moral philosophy and metaphysics at Yale University, succeeded Chauncey Allen Goodrich in 1860 as editor of Webster's dictionaries and was the principal editor for the triumphant 1864 edition. Courtesy of *Appleton's Cyclopaedia of American Biography*, ed. James Grant Wilson, 1888.

assistants who now made up their team. Whitney and Gilman had under their control "the general literary reconstructing and recasting of the definitions. . . . It involves throwing two or more definitions into one, where desirable, giving the definitions in a better, or historical, order . . . correcting, giving literary finish, adopting illustrative citations etc." Pronunciations were being completely reviewed and given a new set of diacritical notations. Of the thirty researchers at work, remarkably, about half of Yale's twenty faculty members were among them, several recruited first by Goodrich and the rest later by Porter, in effect making the projected dictionary very much a Yale product. In addition to Whitney and Gilman, who were focusing on definitions pertaining to the arts and literature, other experts were revising the vocabulary of the natural and applied sciences, engineering, the military, legal professions, mathematics, medicine, astronomy, and archaeology. Classical, scriptural, geographical, and biographical tables were being completed; and the collection and engraving of illustrations were well in hand—"we shall make this department pretty full." "Don't you think we have a pretty good team?" the Merriams asked Wheeler.[6]

When one of the Yale researchers, the eminent geologist and zoologist James Dwight Dana, had to retire from the project because of illness, Porter recruited a young medical student at Yale to take his place. His name was William Chester Minor, featured in Simon Winchester's best seller *The Professor and the Madman* (1998), who later, as a convicted murderer, would take up a major, tireless, and sensational role as contributor to the *Oxford English Dictionary* while an inmate of a psychiatric hospital in England.[7] Goodrich's son, another Chauncey, was also among the assistants, as were a number of literary men who helped with the writing. The Merriams even enlisted the services of George Perkins Marsh, Worcester's staunch advocate. "We have a long written statement," Charles Merriam wrote to Wheeler, "for which we paid, from Hon. George P. Marsh, of his views of what a Dictionary should be, and the points of improvement." One point was a strong urging of "reading the old writers, for obsolescent words—now returning to use, as he [Marsh] thinks—verified by citations. . . . Prof. Porter has also employed several readers with like objectives."

Courageously and ambitiously, then, while the Civil War was convulsing the nation, throwing the economy into disarray with financial panic and widespread bankruptcies damaging the book trade, the Merriams were spending a lot of money with little certainty of ultimate success in a chaotic market. They were also losing money dramatically, as Charles Merriam recollected about twenty years later: "When the civil war of 1860 broke out, it seriously affected the Book trade. The sales of the speller, fell off greatly. In 1859, the sales were 1,104,948. In 1860, 958,108. But in 1862 they fell off to 308,147. Now the Dictionaries also fell largely off." George Merriam was determined to forge head, however, whatever was in his way. Paper and bookbinding, for example, right away became expensive for the publication of books, but he made sure enough paper was available to prevent the interruption of the printing of the dictionary. He and his brother had set in motion an expensive and well-tuned engine of laborers and could not afford to wait for economic conditions to improve. Usually three pages of prepared copy were daily given to the compositor, with the proofreading just managing to keep up. The Boston Stereotype Foundry, a typesetting company that since 1859 had been producing the high-quality electroplates from which the edition was to be printed by Henry Houghton in Boston (the founder of what eventually became the publishing firm Houghton, Mifflin and Company) complained to the Merriams that it was losing money waiting for copy that was not being sent promptly and regularly enough to keep up with the established schedule. The root of the problem was annoying delays in the work of several of the scholars, especially regarding the tables. The engraved illustrations were slow coming in as well. Moreover, the foundry was dismayed by the "shocking" quality of the proofs it was receiving, "full as bad as Worcester," was the complaint (Boston Stereotype had provided plates for Worcester's 1860 edition). Nonetheless, by May 1864, Houghton was about to begin printing, and by August he was binding about two hundred copies per day. The great dictionary was on target for release before the end of the year.[8]

Virtually every one of the editors and contributors worked with a copy of Worcester's celebrated quarto open on his desk. (During the long period when James Murray was editor of the *Oxford English Dictionary*, called originally the *New English Dictionary*, he had all his team keep an open copy on their desks of the edition the Merriams were now preparing.) Wheeler's letters are filled with references to Worcester and how the editorial team was harvesting his work and using him as a standard and benchmark. In light of the Merriams' hostility toward Worcester and his dictionaries and their carefully orchestrated campaigns against him over a period of twenty years, their reliance on him at this stage has to be regarded as one of the greater ironies in the history of lexicography—not merely that they had Worcester's dictionary on their desks, but also that they used his work to such an extent, although Webster and they had persistently accused Worcester of doing exactly that to them.

3

An American Dictionary of the English Language, Royal Quarto Edition (10 by 12.5 inches, noticeably larger than a regular quarto) appeared in late September 1864. It contained a massive 114,000 entry words, about 35,000 more than Webster's original 1828 edition. Mahn's etymology incorporated the latest Continental philological research. The editors had made every effort to make the pronunciation and spelling (on the back of Worcester) still more respectable and reliable. Diacritic symbols were simplified beyond even what

Worcester had done in order to guide the reader toward, especially, current and widely practiced American pronunciation. The definitions were modernized, sharpened, and purged of remnants of Websterian elaboration. In spite of Goodrich and the Merriams' denigration of Worcester's synonymy, this edition kept to Worcester's model of offering numbers of synonyms for each word and the careful discrimination of their meaning. Synonymy took up a good deal of space, but on this matter they were determined not to be outdone by their great rival.

The Merriams and all the contributors knew that the success of the new edition was due in no small measure to the efficient way they took advantage of Worcester's work. "Thank God for Worcester," indeed. While not specifying just how extensive the debt to Worcester was, Porter does acknowledge his influence, grouping his dictionary with a clutch of others: "As this Dictionary was designed to be not merely a compilation, but a digest of results obtained by independent research, comparatively few references are made to other Dictionaries and Encyclopedias. But the best works of this kind have been freely consulted, and, among them, the well-known dictionary of Dr. Joseph E. Worcester, which is so honorable to the industry of the author and the scholarship of the country."[9]

In his preface, Porter provides some additional perspective on the history and scope of the new quarto. He wants to make sure the reader understands that Noah Webster's lexicography is scarcely to be seen in this edition except mostly in some lingering definitions. "The work of revising the definitions of the principal words," Porter writes, "occasioned great and perplexing difficulties to Professor Goodrich and those with whom he conferred." Even Webster's introductions to his several editions were eliminated, according to "the wants of the present generation." Along with all other post-Johnson lexicographers of the language, Porter candidly says that Webster had been trapped by the influence of Johnson's definitions in spite of his protestations against them: "[H]e had not emancipated himself entirely from the influence of Johnson's example in accumulating definitions that are really the same, though at first sight they may appear to be different." Webster's "theory . . . was better than his practice." As for the orthography, "to remove every reasonable ground of complaint against the Dictionary . . . an alternative orthography is now given in almost every case, the old style of spelling being subjoined to the reformed or new."[10]

4

This new, large, unabridged quarto effectually ended the American dictionary wars of the first half of the nineteenth century. The conductors on trains from Boston to outlying towns were wont to shout out as they pulled into the town of Worcester, "Worcester! Worcester! All change for Webster!" unaware perhaps of a larger meaning of their cries.[11]

Critical opinion in the United States changed almost overnight. Leading authors who had long preferred Worcester acknowledged the superior fruits of the research of Porter's team, especially the important etymological contribution of Mahn. Although Holmes remained faithful to Worcester, even he spoke well of the new quarto and admitted he made use of it. Ralph Waldo Emerson assured the Merriams in August, "On my return home from the seashore a few days ago, I found the stately gift you had sent me to my great delight. In my youth my father gave me Johnson's Dictionary; long after in Cambridge I became acquainted with Mr. Worcester, and bought his book. In the meantime, I have learned from good judges the superiority of Webster's Dictionary, and am very grateful to you for the gift." When Longfellow received a new issue of the Merriam quarto in 1878, and was asked for an endorsement, he struggled against an allegiance to the memory of his old neighbor, realizing that the Merriams had won the war at last: "I have a copy of a previous edition of this valuable work, but the one you now send me seems in many respects more complete." Although Longfellow still declined to let Merriam use his name and any remarks he might make about the dictionary as part of their advertising, many others did not. John Greenleaf Whittier extolled the dictionary's "great literary excellence, the unmistakable clearness of its definitions, and the thoroughness and accuracy of its etymology. I have learned to trust implicitly its authority."[12]

Even Mark Twain, who had amused himself over the size and weight of Goodrich's hefty 1847 quarto, added his testimonial. In a letter of appreciation in March 1891 for the gift of a new (third) issue fresh off the press, he was uncharacteristically effusive: "A Dictionary *is* the most awe-inspiring of all books, it knows so much: and to me this one is the most awe-inspiring of all dictionaries because it exhausts knowledge, apparently. It has gone around like a sun, and spied out everything and lit it up. This is a wonderful book— the most wonderful that I know of, when I think over the impressive fact that

An-tit′ro-pal, *a.* [Gr. ἀντί, against, and τρέπειν,
An-tit′ro-poüs, to turn; τρόπος, turn.] (*Bot.*)
At the extremity most remote from the hilum, as
the embryo, or inverted with respect to the seed,
as the radicle.   *Lindley.*

An′ti-type, *n.* [Gr. ἀντίτυπος, of corresponding
form, from ἀντί, against, corresponding, and τύπος,
type, figure. See TYPE.] That which is shadowed
out by the type, and so is correlative to it. Thus
the paschal lamb, in Scripture, is the type of which
Christ is the *antitype.*

An-ti-typ′ic-al, *a.* Pertaining to an antitype; explaining the type.

An-ti-typ′ous, *a.* Pertaining to a type; antityp-
ical. [*Obs.*]   *Cudworth.*

An-ti-vac′ci-nist, *n.* [See ANTI and VACCINIST.]
One who is opposed to vaccination.

An′ti-va-ri′o-loüs, *a.* [From *anti* and *variolous,*
q. v.] Preventing the contagion of the small-pox.

An′ti-ve-ne′re-al, *a.* [From *anti* and *venereal,*
q. v.] Resisting venereal poison.

An′ti-zym′ic, *n.* [Gr. ἀντί, against, and ζύμη,
leaven.] Preventing fermentation.   *Craig.*

Ant′ler, *n.* [O. Fr.
antoillier, andoil-
ler, endouiller, N.
Fr. andouiller.] A
start or branch of
a horn of a cervine
animal, as of the
stag or mouse. The
branch next to the
head is called the
brow-antler, and
the branch next
above, the *bes-antler.*

Ant′lered, *a.* Furnished with antlers. "The
antlered stag."   *Cowper.*

Ant′-li′on, *n.* (*Entom.*) An insect or fly (*Myrmeleon
formicarius*), which prepares a kind of pitfall for
ants, &c.   *McMurtrie.*

An-to-e′ci, n. pl. See ANTISCII.

An-to-no-ma′si-a (Synop., § 130), *n.* [Lat. antonomasia, Gr. ἀντονομασία, from ἀντονομάζειν, to name
instead, from ἀντί, instead, and ὀνομάζειν, to name,
ὄνομα, name.] (*Rhet.*) The use of the name of some
office, dignity, profession, science, or trade, instead
of the proper name of the person; as when *his maj-
esty* is used for a king, or *his lordship* for a noble-
man, or when, instead of Aristotle, we say, *the
philosopher* ; or, conversely, the use of a proper
name instead of an appellative, as when a wise man
is called a *Cato,* or an eminent orator a *Cicero,* the
application being supported by a resemblance in
character.

An-to-no-mas′tic-al-ly, *adv.* By means, or in
the manner, of the figure antonomasia.

Ant-or′bit-al, *a.* [Lat. *ante,* before, and *orbitus,*
an orbit.] Anterior to the orbit.

An′tre (än′tẽr), *n.* [Fr. & Pr. an-
tre, Lat. antrum, Gr. ἄντρον.] A
cavern. [*Obs.*]   *Shak.*

An-tro′rse, *a.* [Lat., as if antror-
sum, forward, for anteroversum,
from ante, before, and versum,
turned.] (*Bot.*) Forward or up-
ward in direction.   *Gray.*

A-nū′bis, *n.* An Egyptian deity,
the conductor of departed spirits,
and represented by a human figure with the head of a dog or fox.

Ā′nus, *n.* [Lat. *anus, gen. oni.*]
(*Anat.*) The circular opening at
the lower extremity of the alimen-
tary canal, through which the ex-
crement are expelled. *Dunglison.*

An′vil, *n.* [O. Eng. *anvelt, anvild,*
anvile, A-S. anfilt, anfilt, onfilt, O. H. Ger. ana-
falz, D. aanbeld.]
1. An iron block,
usually with a steel
face, upon which met-
als are hammered and
shaped.
2. (*Fig.*) Any thing
on which blows are
laid.
To be on the anvil, to
be in a state of discus-
sion, formation, or prep-
aration, as when a
scheme or measure is forming, but not matured.

An′vil, *v. t.* To form or shape on an anvil; as, *an-
viled* armor. [*Rare.*]   *Beau. & Fl.*

Anx-Ī′e-tûde, *n.* Anxiety. [*Rare.*]

Anx-Ī′e-ty (ang-zī′e-tỹ), *n.* [Fr. *anxiété,* Pr. anxie-
tat, Lat. anxietas, from anxius. See ANXIOUS.]
Concern or solicitude respecting some event, future
or uncertain, which disturbs the mind, and keeps it
in a state of painful uneasiness.

Syn.—Care; solicitude; foreboding; uneasiness; per-
plexity; disquietude; disquiet; watchfulness; restless-
ness. See CARE.

Anx′ioüs (ănk′shŭs, 82), *a.* [Lat. *anxius,* from
angere, to cause pain, to torture. See ANGER.]
1. Full of anxiety or disquietude; greatly concerned or solicitous, especially respecting something

future or unknown; being in painful suspense;—
applied to persons; as, *anxious* to please; *anxious*
for the issue of a battle.
2. Accompanied with anxiety;—applied to
things; as, *anxious* labor.

The sweat of life, from which
God hath bid dwell far off all *anxious* cares.   *Milton.*

☞ It is followed by *for* or *about* before the object.

Syn.—Solicitous; careful; uneasy; unquiet; restless; concerned; disturbed; watchful.

Anx′ioüs-ly, *adv.* In an anxious manner; solici-
tously; with painful uncertainty.

Anx′ioüs-ness, *n.* The quality or state of being
anxious; great solicitude.

A′ny (ĕn′nỹ), *a.* [A-S. ænig, from an, one,
O. H. Ger. einic, einig, D. eenig.] One indefinitely;
is derived from the word *one,* and, in the plural,
is, ic, which signifies abounding with, full of, like
the Latin *-osus.*
1. One indifferently, out of an indefinite number.
Nor knowing whom I ask, of *any* I can meet. *Milton.*

If a soul shall sin against *any* of the
commandments of the Lord.   *Levit. iv. 2.*
2. Some; indefinitely; when used where there
are there may be few or many.

☞ Its derivative significations are the same, but it
differs but little from *some.* The idea of one indefinite
thing better. [*Colloq.*]

A′ny-how, *adv.* In any way; at any rate; in any
event. [*Colloq.*]
A′ny-where, *adv.* In any place.   *Udal.*
A′ny-whith′er, *adv.* To any place.
A′ny-wise, *adv.* In any way. "*Anywise* a good
relative."   *Barrow.*

A-ō′ni-an, *a.* [From *Aonia,* a part of Bœotia, in
Greece.] Pertaining to Aonia, in Bœotia, or to the
Muses who were supposed to dwell there.
Aonian fount, the fountain of Aganippe, at the foot of
Mount Helicon, not far from Thebes, and sacred to the
muses.

A-ō′rist, *n.* [Gr. ἀόριστος, without boundaries, indefinite, from *a* priv. and ὁρίζειν, to mark out boundaries, ὅρος, boundary, limit.] (*Gram.*) A tense in
the Greek language, which expresses an action as
completed in past time, but leaves it, in other respects, wholly indeterminate.

A-ō′rist, *a.* Indefinite or indeterminate as to past
time.   *Harris.*

A-ō-rist′ic, *a.* [Gr. ἀοριστικός.] Pertaining to an
aorist, or indefinite tense; indefinite.

A-ōr′ta, *n.* [N. Lat. *aorta,* Gr.
ἀορτή, from ἀείρειν, to lift, heave.]
(*Anat.*) The great artery, or trunk
of the arterial system, proceeding
from the left ventricle of the heart,
and giving origin to all the arte-
ries, except the pulmonary arte-
ries.

☞ It first rises, when it is called
the *ascending aorta;* then makes a
great curve, when it gives off branches
to the head and upper extremities;
then proceeds downward, and is
called the *descending aorta,* giving off
branches to the trunk. It finally divides into the two iliacs, which supply
the pelvis and lower extremities.

A-ōr′tal, *a.* Pertaining to the aorta, or great
A-ōr′tic, artery.   *Darwin.*
His dewy locks did drop with brine *apace.* *Spenser.*
A wide diffusion and visible triumph of the gospel draws on
apace.   *I. Taylor.*

Ap-a-gō′ge, *n.* [Gr. ἀπαγωγή, a leading away,
from ἀπάγειν, to lead away, from ἀπό, from, and
ἄγειν, to lead, drive.]
1. (*Logic.*) An indirect argument which proves a
thing by showing the impossibility or absurdity of
the contrary thing. It corresponds to the *reductio
ad absurdum.*   *Ernesti.*
2. (*Math.*) A progress or passage from one proposition to another, when the first, having been demonstrated, is employed in proving others.

Ap-a-gōg′ic-al, *a.* Proving indirectly, by showing
the absurdity or impossibility of the contrary; as,
an *apagogical* demonstration.   *Darwin.*

A-pā′gy-noüs, *a.* [Gr. ἀπαί, once, and γυνή, a female.] (*Bot.*) Fructifying at once; perishing immediately after flowering; monocarpous.   *Brande.*

A-pāid′, *a.* [O. Fr. *apaié.*] Appaid; satisfied. [*Obs.*] *Chapman.*

Ap-a-lā′chi-an, *a.* See APPALACHIAN.

Ap′an-age, *n.* See APPANAGE.

A-pān′thro-py, *n.* [Gr. ἀπανθρωπία, from ἀπό,
from, away from, and ἄνθρωπος, man.] An aversion
to the company of men; a love of solitude.

Ap-a-rith′me-sis (Synop., § 130), *n.* [Gr. ἀπαρίθ-
μησις, from ἀπαριθμεῖν, to count off or over, from
ἀπό, from, and ἀριθμεῖν, to count, ἀριθμός, number.]
(*Rhet.*) Enumeration of parts, or particulars.

Ap′a-thy, *n.* [Fr. *apathie,* Lat. *apathia,* Gr. ἀπάθεια,
from *a* priv. and πάθος, from παθεῖν, πάσχειν, to
suffer.] Want, or a low degree, of feeling; priva-
tion of passion, or insensibility to pain;—applied
either to the body or the mind. As applied to the
mind, it is stoicism, a calmness of mind incapable
of being ruffled by pleasure, pain, or passion.
According to the Stoics, *apathy* meant the extinction of the
passions by the ascendency of reason.   *Fleming.*

☞ In the first ages of the church, the Christians
adopted the term to express a contempt of earthly con-
cerns.

Syn.—Insensibility; unfeelingness; indifference; un-
concern.

Ap′a-thist′ic-al, *a.* Apathetic. [*Rare.*]   *Seward.*

Ap′a-thy, *n.* [Fr. *apathie,* Lat. *apathia,* Gr. ἀπάθεια,
from *a* priv. and πάθος, from παθεῖν, πάσχειν, to
suffer.] Want, or a low degree, of feeling; priva-
tion of passion, or insensibility to pain;—applied
either to the body or the mind. As applied to the
mind, it is stoicism, a calmness of mind incapable
of being ruffled by pleasure, pain, or passion.
According to the Stoics, *apathy* meant the extinction of the
passions by the ascendency of reason.   *Fleming.*
☞ In the first ages of the church, the Christians
adopted the term to express a contempt of earthly con-
cerns.
Syn.—Insensibility; unfeelingness; indifference; un-
concern.

Ap′a-tite, *n.* [From Gr. ἀπάτη, deceit, ἀπατάν, to
deceive; it having been often mistaken for other
minerals.] (*Min.*) Native phosphate of lime, oc-
curring usually in six-sided prisms, of a green or
greenish color, and resembling beryl, but much
softer.   *Dana.*

A-pau′mee, *n.* See APPAUMEE.

Ape, *n.* [A-S. *apa,* Icel. *api,*
Sw. *apa,* Dan. *abe,* N. Fr.
apa, W. *epa,* O. H. Ger. *affo,*
M. H. Ger. & N. H. Ger. *affe,*
Skr. *kapi,* Gr. κῆπος, κέβος.]
1. (*Zoöl.*) A quadrumanous
mammal of the genus *Pithecus,*
having teeth of the same number and form as in man, and
possessing neither a tail nor
cheek pouches.
2. One who imitates servilely,
in allusion to the manners of the
ape; a silly fellow.   *Nabbes.*

Ape, *v. t.* [imp. & p. p. APED; *p. pr. & vb. n.* APING.]
To mimic, as an ape imitates human actions; to
imitate servilely.
The people of England only *ape* the fashions they have
never tried.   *Burke.*

A-pēak′, *adv.* [Prefix *a* and *peak.*]
1. On the point; in a posture to pierce. *Johnson.*
2. (*Naut.*) Perpendicular. The anchor is *apeak,*
when the cable is drawn so as to bring the ship's
bowl directly over it. Synb. also *apeek.*] *Totten.*

A-pēl′loüs, *a.* [Gr. *a* priv. and Lat. *pellis,* skin.]
Destitute of skin.   *Brande.*

Ap′en-nine, *a.* [Lat. *Apenninus: ad* and *penninus,*
an epithet applied to a peak or ridge of the Alps.
Livy. Celtic *pen,* or *ben,* the peak of a mountain, or,
in general, a mountain.] Pertaining to, or desig-
nating, a chain of mountains extending from the
Alps, south of the plains of Piedmont, and around
the Gulf of Genoa, to the center of Italy, and thence
south-east to the extremity;—used in the *pl.* as a n.

A-pēp′sy (Synop., § 130), *n.* [N. Lat. *apepsia,* Gr.
ἀπεψία, from ἄπεπτος, uncooked, undigested, from *a*
priv. and πέπτειν, to cook, concoct, κιττειν, to cook, to digest,]
(*Med.*) Defective digestion; Indigestion. *Coxe.*

Ap′er, *n.* [From *ape.*] One who apes.

A-pēr′i-ent (89), *a.* [Lat. *aperiens, p. pr.* of *aperire,*
to uncover, open, from *ab* and *parire, parere,* to
bring forth, produce.] (*Med.*) Having the quality
of opening; laxative.   *Arbuthnot.*

A-pēr′i-ent, *n.* (*Med.*) A remedy that promotes ex-
cretion; a laxative.

A-pēr′i-tive, *a.* [Fr. *apéritif,* from Lat. *aperire.*]
Serving to open; deobstruent; aperient.   *Harvey.*

A-pert′ (14), *a.* [Lat. *apertus, p. p.* of *aperire.*]
Open; evident; undisguised. [*Obs.*]   *Fotherby.*

A-pēr′tion, *n.* [From *aperire.*] The
act of opening, or the state of being opened; an opening, a gap, aperture, or passage. [*Rare.*] *Wiseman.*

---

fûrl, rŭde, push; e, i, o, silent; ç as s; çh as sh; e, ch, as k; ġ as j, ġ as in ġet; ẓ as z; x as gz; n as in linger, link; th as in thine.

FIGURE 20. The American dictionary wars effectively ended with the publication of the 1864 unabridged Webster's dictionary, a page of which is shown here. Detail: The definition of *apathy* includes notations on pronunciation and etymology, an illustrative quotation, a note on its usage in an early Christian context, and several synonyms. Courtesy of Indiana State University Special Collections, Cordell Collection of Dictionaries.

if it had been builded by one man instead of a hundred he would have had to begin it a thousand years ago in order to have it ready for publication today." Twain does not in this passage point out that the large team who produced this marvelous dictionary had made it into something quite different from what Webster wrote. He also may not have been thinking of it at the time, but with that remark Twain does remind us that Worcester and Webster, as well as Johnson, Richardson, Bailey, and a host of lexicographical ghosts reaching back to the seventeenth century and further, did produce their dictionaries practically single-handedly.[13]

Walt Whitman can have the last word among America's distinguished authors. He had mixed feelings. In his notes on the American language collected into *An American Primer*, he expresses his reverence for the language: "America owes immeasurable respect and love to the past, and to many ancestries, for many inheritances—but of all that America has received from the past, from the mothers and fathers of laws, arts, letters, etc., by far the greatest inheritance is the English Language—so long in growing—so fitted." He had kept close track of the dictionary controversies, though, and there he felt America still did not have "a Perfect English Dictionary": "Dr. Johnson did well; Sheridan, Walker, Perry, Ash, Bailey, Kenrick, Smart, and the rest, all assisted." Webster and Worcester "have done well"; "and yet the Dictionary, rising stately and complete, out of a full appreciation of the philosophy of language, and the unspeakable grandeur of the English dialect, has still to be made—and to be made by some coming American worthy of the sublime work. The English language seems curiously to have flowed through the ages, especially toward America. . . ."[14]

5

In their advertisements, the Merriams heaped endorsements upon endorsements from school and university administrators, government officials, law courts, libraries, and institutions of all kinds across the country, repeatedly publishing them for the next thirteen years, while they remained the "Webster" publishers, in one form or another. They took no chances that at the eleventh hour a Worcester revival launched by J. B. Lippincott, the "largest book jobbers in the United States," might yet defeat them. Still looking over their shoulders at Worcester, as they had done for more than twenty years, they saturated the country with promotions, publicity pamphlets, and

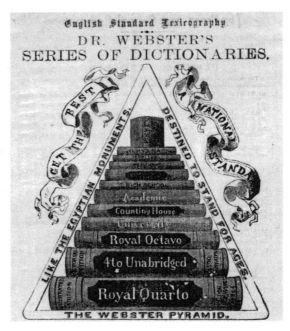

FIGURE 21. In this Merriam advertisement, Webster's dictionaries, "like the Egyptian monuments," are "destined to stand for ages." Courtesy of the Beinecke Rare Book and Manuscript Library, Yale University, G. and C. Merriam Company Papers.

slogans such as "an old sun rising with new splendor," "get the best," "a national standard," "the highest authority in Great Britain, as well as in the United States," "the only complete English dictionary," and "like the Egyptian monuments, destined to stand for ages." They continued to publish innumerable little booklets containing copious reports of sales figures from cities all over the country, with comparisons supporting their contention that Worcester was getting clobbered on all fronts. Even President Ulysses Grant confirmed the Merriams' claim that their dictionary was the "national standard" in both America and Britain by declaring in a letter to them that this was now "the best Dictionary of the English language ever published at any time in any country." They correctly claimed it was the largest-selling, single-volume dictionary on the market.[15]

The *New York Tribune* announced in 1870, only six years after publication, that the Merriam unabridged was becoming something of a national treasure: "The *Unabridged* is generally regarded as the Dictionary of the highest authority in the language, and has a sale all over the civilized world. It is regularly issued in London, and in English as well as American Courts of Justice is considered as the leading authority on the meaning of words." The Merriams were particularly keen to demonstrate that their book was international in scope, the standard English dictionary globally. The English publishing firm George Bell & Sons helped them achieve this by acquiring British distribution rights in the 1850s and publishing editions in Britain through the late nineteenth century and well into the twentieth. In their 1886 edition, interestingly, they did away with the word "American" in the title, preferring, *Webster's Complete Dictionary of the English Language*. They appeared to think that "American" would be more likely to lose than gain sales in England. They continued to leave off "American" in their later English editions. The American spelling in their editions would not have disturbed English readers as much as the obtrusive word "American" title because by then they were used to it in the lexicon of Worcester and Webster's dictionaries.

The Merriams' claim that since the Goodrich-Merriam edition in 1847 they had dominated the British dictionary market seemed at last beyond doubt. The claim was strengthened by an eighteen-page article in the *London Quarterly Review* for October 1873, "English Dictionaries," by the Englishman Edward Burnett Tylor, regarded by many as the founder of cultural anthropology. The article was the latest attempt at a history of English lexicography in a country that had come to feel awkward, even ashamed, over how American dictionaries had effectively replaced homegrown ones, except for Walker, who "scrupulously followed Johnson." Not mentioning Worcester at all, Tylor states the case with a sensible directness that would have further exasperated the English philological world in general and in particular the London Philological Society, which had recently begun work on what became known as the *Oxford English Dictionary*:

> Seventy years passed before Johnson was followed by Webster, an American writer, who faced the task of the English Dictionary with a full appreciation of its requirements, leading to better practical results. . . . Webster's *American Dictionary of the English Language* . . . appeared at once in England, where successive re-editing *has as yet kept it in the highest place as a practical dictionary.* . . .

The good average business-like character of Webster's Dictionary, both in style and matter, made it as distinctly suited as Johnson's was distinctly unsuited to be expanded and re-edited by other hands. Professor Goodrich's edition of 1847 is not much more than enlarged and amended, but other revisions since have so much novelty of plan as to be described as distinct works. . . . The American revised Webster's Dictionary of 1864, published in America and England, is of an altogether higher order. . . . On the whole . . . as it stands [it] is the most respectable, and CERTAINLY THE BEST PRACTICAL ENGLISH DICTIONARY EXTANT.[16]

If "average business-like character" was the reputation of Webster's legacy in England, it was a price the Merriams were happy to pay for such praise. They described this article as "an intelligent and most impartial source" and plugged it into several of their advertisements.

6

George and Charles Merriam's entrepreneurial drive had been commercially successful beyond their dreams. Their sometimes ruthless determination had triumphed. Irked by distractions, they had not tolerated delay—as George Merriam once remarked back in 1844, when he and his brother were struggling to get started with their publishing of Webster's dictionary, "Don't let anxieties for progress trouble you, a business man's fidgets are not always wise. . . . We cannot & will not at this stage resort to delay."[17] It was he who boldly had decided to push on with their final major edition even though the start of the Civil War had complicated the economics of publishing. He and Charles complemented each other well. George was the strategist. Charles was more the diplomat with a literary bent. While George held the title of president of the firm, Charles's job had always been to correspond with members of the Webster family, several of the dictionary's editors (mostly Goodrich), and newspaper and magazine editors, forging solutions to the many awkward and potentially damaging complications of family, editors, legal issues, publicity, and the ever-present competition from Worcester.

After thirty-three years on the firing line, in 1877 Charles Merriam sold his interest in the company to the publishers Ivison, Blakeman, Taylor & Company. He died ten years later at the age of eighty-one. George Merriam died

CHARLES MERRIAM.

FIGURE 22. Charles Merriam, ca. 1870s. He and his brother George purchased the rights to Webster's dictionaries in 1844 and, with great determination and skill, made a fortune from them. Courtesy of the Beinecke Rare Book and Manuscript Library, Yale University, G. and C. Merriam Company Papers.

in 1880, at age seventy-seven. Their younger brother, Homer, who had taken over as president in 1880 on the death of George, held that post until he was ninety-one in 1904. That ended sixty years of the Merriam family's control of the Webster lexicons, during which—chiefly with Goodrich's help—they took Webster's almost defunct dictionary to world-class fame.

Conclusion

Who were winners and losers of the dictionary wars? In an extended, complicated, and comprehensive conflict such as this, lasting some thirty-five years, there were many victories and defeats for all the main participants along the way, with huge implications for the course of the American language and American nationhood.

If we consider the results in personal as well as historical terms, one answer to the victory question is that neither Worcester nor Webster emerged victorious. Not Worcester, because unquestionably the Merriams defeated him, and soon enough his dictionary was sidelined, if not ignored, by the public. Although his dictionaries incited Webster, and later the Merriams, to make war against him, causing him virtually uninterrupted anguish during the second half of his life, it is true he found solace in the knowledge that his judicious and widely respected linguistic scholarship to the end of his lexicographical career was the most respected and valued by the majority of the nation's leading authors, critics, professors, and major institutions. He also knew that his work, chiefly through the efforts of Goodrich, benefited the progression and quality of Webster dictionaries published by the Merriams, pushing back against Webster's radicalism and thereby influencing the progress of the American language. Still, his great disappointment was not that he did not succeed in the marketplace as much as his rivals—he had plenty of commercial success with his other books to satisfy him—but that the long-term influence his dictionary might have exerted on American culture, had he won, was far less than it might have been.

Webster was not victorious in his lifetime, either, because his dream of the evolution of American English guided by his radical linguistic and lexicographical reforms was never realized. Indeed, his efforts brought him the pain of ridicule, which he seemed never able to comprehend. He had abandoned his hopes for a language-based national unity long before his death.

Afterward, the Merriams tried to keep it alive for mainly commercial reasons, but they and their editors went about this by progressively suppressing and eliminating his lexicography. If he had come back in 1864, just twenty-one years after his death, and read the celebrated 1864 Merriam quarto, the title of which bore his name, it would have shattered him to see what had become of his work, just as the Goodrich/Worcester abridgment had horrified him in 1829. He would not have recognized it. He had hoped his final lexicographical effort, his 1841 edition, had set his dictionary on the right track and would silence most of his critics. It did not. Much, or most, of what he stood for as a lexicographer, except for a handful of his spelling reforms and his reputation as a definer of words, vanished in the 1864 edition. The betrayal he first felt at the hands of Goodrich would have struck him as compounded a thousand times by the multitude of hands that created that triumphant edition. Still, his solace was that his pioneering 1828 *American Dictionary* had shown the English that the Americans were capable of writing their own dictionaries, independent of Johnson—although, as we have seen, he depended heavily on Johnson in that edition, in spite of what he claimed; and that dependency continued long after his death in 1843. His dictionary registered Americans' pride in their own language, that they were eager to follow it wherever it took them. His personal dictionary wars, he argued, were America's wars.

Goodrich was one of the winners, for himself and in behalf of the Webster family and the brand name of Webster. With his octavo abridgment he rescued Webster's dictionary from early commercial failure, and for twenty years after the Merriams came on the scene, more than anyone else he helped perpetuate and ensure the Webster legacy through his superb lexicography. His work brought him well-earned, if only temporary, fame in that field of scholarship. The protracted disputes also brought him residual disillusionment and frustration, however. Lexicography in the service of his father-in-law had detoured and devoured his scholarly career. What other books might this highly intelligent and dynamic man have written, ones that could have brought him before the public in a more accessible and popular vein in his own right? Might he have spared himself thousands of days of worry and fret by staying clear of the dictionary wars entirely? His angst was that of centuries of lexicographers before him. Essentially a literary man, he discovered firsthand what Samuel Johnson meant when he moaned over the drudgery of lexicography; but Johnson did not have to deal for decades with personalities and forces vying for lexicographical advantage in a fiercely competitive publishing world.

The real winners of the final stage of the dictionary wars were the Merriams and the newspapers. It was the Merriams, not a national academy as in France and Italy, who reaped the rewards of their victory. When they took over, the Webster unabridged dictionary was almost defunct. With industry, imagination, and no small portion of commercial ruthlessness, they carried it to unimagined success, in the process earning a fortune for themselves and creating one of the more powerful publishing houses in America.

As for the newspapers, the dictionary wars, principally in the 1840s and 1850s, gave them (and the pamphleteering that kept pace with them) a bonanza of sensational journalism. Journalism, to a degree unprecedented internationally, had become a major factor in American life just in time to take advantage of this. Hundreds of newspapers across the country participated in the wars, monopolizing public opinion about the debate. The papers not only reflected the growing self-consciousness of Americans about their language and how they used it but also heightened various cultural conflicts that were inherent in these clashes. Education was one battlefield. Others were literacy, linguistic norms and standards, styles of speech, populism versus traditional standards, and even religion and morality. One can regret the ill-nature of much of this "inky war" and its parade of insults and declamatory misrepresentation, but the newspapers provided the general public with a knowledge of many such issues pertaining to their language and the dictionaries that described and recorded it. It was a raised consciousness that could not have been achieved as conveniently in any other way. The intense dictionary competition and controversies that the newspapers broadcast gave the burgeoning American public a better product, better dictionaries, and a clearer sense of themselves, so in that respect the people were also major winners.

APPENDIX A

The "Webster" Brand

The brand name "Webster" involved another dictionary conflict that was fought in the late nineteenth and early twentieth centuries. Because the Merriam copyright expired in 1889, G. & C. Merriam was forced by the publication of a number of non-Merriam "Webster" dictionaries to pursue lawsuits in order to prevent any other company from using the name in the title of a dictionary. By 1909, the company had lost a string of these lawsuits, and the name was judged to be in the public domain, a genericized trademark for any American English dictionary. A judge that year ruled on what had become an ongoing, complicated, legal battleground: the Merriam company "is in no position to deny a purely descriptive use of the word to any other dictionary which is as legitimate as its own. The constant iteration that all such are 'bogus' or not 'genuine' is merely a childish extravagance." The one qualification was that a non-Merriam dictionary had to carry a disclaimer: "This dictionary is not published by the original publishers of Webster's dictionary or their successors."[1]

One of the first non-Merriam dictionaries to be well known as "Webster's" was *Webster's Universal Dictionary*, published by the World Syndicate Publishing Company in 1937. After that, such titles multiplied. *Webster's New Universal*, for example, is a new version of the unabridged *Random House Dictionary of the English Language* (1966), which is unrelated to the Merriam editions or to the literary content of dictionaries in the Websterian line of descent. To name a few others: the World Publishing Company's *Webster's New World Dictionary of the American Language* (1951) and its college-size *Webster's New World Dictionary of the American Language* (1953), Simon and Schuster's *Webster's New Twentieth Century Dictionary* (1979), and Microsoft's

Encarta Webster's Dictionary, formerly called the *Encarta World English Dictionary* (1999; 2nd edition, 2004).

A later legal battle was fought in 1991, when Random House added *Webster* to the title of its college dictionary. Merriam-Webster, Inc. interpreted this as an aggressive move on its lucrative Webster-brand college dictionaries and took Random House to court. Merriam-Webster won, but in September 1994, the verdict was overturned on appeal. This put the issue beyond any doubt. The name "Webster" legally does not now necessarily have a connection with either Merriam or Noah Webster himself. Indeed, as David Micklethwait explains, "there are now so many non-Merriam Webster dictionaries on the market in America that it can no longer be said that, without a disclaimer, people will assume any Webster dictionary to be a Merriam." Because of that reality of American dictionary publishing, the Merriam company now publishes its "Webster" dictionaries with its own disclaimer:

> The name *Webster* is no guarantee of excellence. It is used by a number of publishers and may serve mainly to mislead an unwary buyer.
>
> *Merriam-Webster*™ is the name you should look for when you consider the purchase of dictionaries or other fine reference books. It carries the reputation of a company that has been publishing since 1831 and is your assurance of quality and authority.[2]

In *Webster's New World Dictionary of the American Language, College Edition* (1957), incidentally, the World Publishing Company makes a point of saying its dictionary has nothing at all to do with Noah Webster, Merriam, or any edition deriving from Merriam dictionaries. In spite of paying oblique lip service to Webster—because that always has been where the commercial leverage is—as having laid the foundations of American lexicography, it instead credits Worcester's *Comprehensive, Pronouncing, and Explanatory Dictionary of the English Language* of 1830 with having laid down the "broad foundations for American dictionaries" with "new words, a more conservative spelling, brief, well-phrased definitions, full indication of pronunciation by means of diacritics, use of stress marks to divide syllables, and lists of synonyms." Webster's 1828 dictionary, it continues, "was not, as is often claimed, the real parent of the modern American dictionary; it was merely the foster-parent. . . . The first American lexicographer to hit upon the particular pattern that distinguished the American dictionary was Webster's lifelong rival,

Joseph E. Worcester. . . . Because it was compact and low-priced, it immediately became popular—far more popular, in fact, than any of Webster's own dictionaries *in his own lifetime* [my italics]"—that is, before the Merriams came on to the scene.[3]

That point about popularity is an oversight if one regards the Goodrich octavo as one of Webster's dictionaries. Nonetheless, the historical point is well taken. It's not just a matter of whether a dictionary bearing the name "Webster" relates to the Merriam company, but whether (or how much) it, or any Merriam company dictionary from the 1850s onward, relates textually to Webster himself.

In any case, thanks to Chauncey Allen Goodrich, George and Charles Merriam, Noah Porter, and the Merriam editors who followed, the prestigious label "Webster" remains iconic in America. It sells dictionaries because the distinguished publishing quality historically attached to the name—its American origin, ingenuity, and even moral or Christian basis, and its long identification as the alleged "standard" in America—gives people confidence that by buying a book with that name in the title they are on reliable ground.

Four Centuries of Selected Dictionaries of the English Language

The following list is limited to general-purpose, monolingual dictionaries.

Date	Author	Dictionary Title / Description
		17th CENTURY
1604 (1609, 1613, 1617)	Robert Cawdrey	*A Table Alphabeticall . . . of Hard Usuall English Wordes* Ca. 3,000–3,200 entry words; believed to be the first monolingual English dictionary. London: T. S. for Edmund Weauer. (*Note*: Richard Mulcaster's, *Elementarie* in 1582 is an effort to organize the English language with a list of 8,000 words. London: T. Vautroullier.)
1616	John Bullokar	*An English Expositor: Teaching the Interpretation of the Hardest Words Used in Our Language* Ca. 5,000 entry words; the second monolingual English dictionary. London: Printed by Iohn Legatt.
1623	Henry Cockeram	*The English Dictionarie; or, An Interpreter of Hard English Words* First to use *dictionarie* in its title; in three parts. London: Printed for Edmund Weauer.
1656	Thomas Blount	*Glossographia; or, A Dictionary Interpreting the Hard Words . . .* Ca. 11,000 entry words. London: Printed by Tho. Newcomb.

1658 (1696)	Edward Phillips	*The New World of English Words* Ca. 4,000 entry words expanded to ca. 17,000 in 1696 5th ed. London: Printed for J. Phillips at the Kings Arms, London.
1673	Thomas Blount	*A World of Errors Discovered in the New World of Words &c.* An attack on Phillips. London: Printed by T. N. for Abel Roper, John Martin, and Henry Herringman.
1676	Elisha Coles	*An English Dictionary Explaining the Difficult Terms That Are Used in Divinity, Husbandry . . .* Ca. 26,000 entry words, including regional dialect words, 330 pp. London: Printed for Samuel Crouch.

18th CENTURY

1702	John Kersey the Younger	*A New English Dictionary* Ca. 28,000 entry words "commonly used in the language." London: Printed for E. Bell . . .
1704	John Harris	*Lexicon Technicum; or, An Universal English Dictionary of Arts and Sciences* Emphasizes science. London: Printed for D. Brown [and nine others].
1706	John Kersey, ed.	Edward Phillips's *The New World of English Words* Ca. 38,000 entry words. London: Printed for J. Phillips, [etc.].
1721	Nathan Bailey	*An Universal Etymological English Dictionary* Ca. 40,000 entry words. London: Printed for E. Bell; vol. 2 in two parts (1727).
1730	Nathan Bailey	*Dictionarium Britannicum* Ca. 48,000 entry words; nearly 30 editions. London: Printed for T. Cox.
1747	Samuel Johnson	*Plan of a Dictionary of the English Language*
1749	Benjamin Martin	*Lingua Britannica Reformata or a New English Dictionary* Ca. 24,500 entry words. London: Printed for J. Hodges.
1755	Samuel Johnson	*A Dictionary of the English Language* Ca. 40,000 entry words, in 2 vols. London: Printed by W. Strahan.
1755	Joseph Nicoll Scott, ed.	*A New Universal Etymological English Dictionary* Edition of Bailey's *Dictionarium*, known as Scott-Bailey. London: Printed for E. Bell.

1757	James Buchanan	*Linguae Britannicae Vera Pronunciato or, A New English Dictionary . . . Designed for the Use of Schools, and of Foreigners, as Well as Natives Who Would Speak, Read, and Write English with Propriety and Accuracy* Sometimes referred to as the first English pronouncing dictionary. 1 vol., 463 pp. London, Middlesex.
1764	John Entick	*The New Spelling Dictionary* Attaches Buchanan's Scottish pronunciation reform. London: Printed for C. Dilly.
1773	William Kenrick	*A New Dictionary of the English Language* Uses diacritical marks to indicate pronunciation; divides words into syllables. London: Printed for John & Francis Rivington [and four others].
1775	William Perry	*The Royal Standard English Dictionary* Numbers the sounds of each vowel. Edinburgh: Printed by David Willison; . . . London: J. Bell. . . .
1780	Thomas Sheridan	*A General Dictionary of the English Language* "To establish a plain and permanent standard of pronunciation." London: Printed for J. Dodsley, C. Dilly, and J. Wilkie.
1791	John Walker	*A Critical Pronouncing Dictionary and Expositor of the English Language* London: Sold by J. Robinson. . . . In the Strand. (Worcester thought this was the best edition of Walker.)
1797–98	Samuel Johnson Jr.	*A School Dictionary, Being a Compendium of the Latest and Most Improved Dictionaries* Ca. 4,500 entry words; thought to be the first English dictionary written in America. New Haven, [CT]: Printed & sold by Edward O'Brien who holds the copyright for the state of Connecticut and New York.

19th CENTURY

1800	Caleb Alexander	*The Columbian Dictionary of the English Language* Considered the second English dictionary written in America, with "many new words peculiar to the United States." Boston: Isaiah Thomas & Ebnezer T. Andrews. Mostly recycled material from Johnson.
1806	Noah Webster	*A Compendious Dictionary of the English Language* Ca. 40,000 entry words; Webster's first dictionary; his abridgment of this for schools followed quickly. New Haven, CT: Sidney Press.

1818	Charles Richardson	*A New Dictionary of the English Language* London: William Pickering.
1818	Rev. Henry J. Todd, ed.	*Johnson's Dictionary of the English Language* Known as Todd-Johnson. With "numerous corrections and the addition of several thousand [head]words." This edition was widely used in America well into the nineteenth century. London: Printed for Longman, Hurst, Rees, Orme, and Brown.
1820	Samuel Johnson; Albert Chalmers, ed.	*A Dictionary of the English Language: New Edition, Corrected and Revised* An abridgment of Todd-Johnson, using many new entry words and definitions contributed by Johnson's friend, the Shakespearean Edmond Malone. London: Thomas Tegg.
1827	Joseph Emerson Worcester, ed.	*Johnson's English Dictionary, as Improved by Todd and Abridged by Chalmers* The first edition of an English dictionary (Todd-Johnson) edited by Worcester. Up to 1863, it sold an average of 12,000 copies annually. Boston: Charles Eiver and T. Harrington; an 1830 edition was published in Boston by Perkins and Marvin, and Hilliard, Gray, Little, and Wilkins.
1828	Noah Webster	*An American Dictionary of the English Language* Unabridged quarto, ca. 70,000 entry words; ca. 12,000 more than the most recent Todd-Johnson. New York: Sherman Converse.
1829–31	Noah Webster	*A Dictionary of the English Language, for the Use of Primary Schools and the Counting-House* 532 pp. New York: White, Gallaher, and White.
1829	Noah Webster; Joseph E. Worcester and Chauncey A. Goodrich, eds.	*An American Dictionary of the English Language* Octavo abridgment of Webster's 1828 quarto, edited by Joseph E. Worcester, supervised by Chauncey Allen Goodrich; ca. 83,000 entry words, 940 pp. Contains the first appearance of John Walker's *A Key to the Classical Pronunciation of Greek, Latin, and Scripture Proper Names* in a Webster dictionary. New York: Sherman Converse.
1830 (1831, 1835)	Joseph Emerson Worcester	*Comprehensive Pronouncing and Explanatory Dictionary of the English Language* Ca. 43,000 entry words, 343 pp.; small and intended for schools; 57,000 copies printed up to 1863 (Allibone). Boston: Hilliard, Gray, Little & Wilkins.

1831–32	Noah Webster	*A Dictionary of the English Language / to Which Are Prefixed an Introductory Dissertation on the Origin, History, and Connection of the Languages of Western Asia and of Europe, and a Concise Grammar, Philosophical and Practical, of the English Language* 2 vols., no pagination. 1st British edition. Reprinted by Edmund H. Barker. London: Black, Young & Young, 1832.
1832–33	Jonathan Boucher, James Odell, and Joseph Hunter, eds.	*Glossary of Archaic and Provincial Words: A Supplement to the Dictionaries of the English Language, Particularly Those of Dr. Johnson and Dr. Webster* London: Black, Young & Young.
1835 (2nd ed., 1843)	Joseph Emerson Worcester	*An Elementary Dictionary for Common Schools with Pronouncing Vocabularies of Classical, Scripture, and Modern Geographical Names* 324 pp. Boston: G. W. Palmer (both editions).
1841	Noah Webster	*An American Dictionary of the English Language* A new, abridged, royal octavo edition, 2 vols., 1,008 pp. Revised and expanded 2nd ed. of the quarto, edited by Chauncey Allen Goodrich with Webster's assistance; 3,000 copies printed. New York: White and Sheffield.
1846–47	Joseph Emerson Worcester	*A Universal and Critical Dictionary of the English Language* Large octavo, 956 pp., over 80,000 entry words (27,000 more than in his 1830 dictionary); includes Walker's *Key*. Boston: Wilkins, Carter & Co.
1847	Noah Webster	*An American Dictionary of the English Language* Popular new and revised edition, one-volume royal octavo, edited by Chauncey Allen Goodrich. The first Webster dictionary published by Merriam, priced at $6, one-third the cost of the original 1828 quarto; 1,367 pp.; 13,500 copies printed from 1856 to 1863 (Allibone). Springfield, MA: G. & C. Merriam.
1848	Noah Webster	*An American Dictionary of the English Language* Octavo abridgment, edited by Chauncey Allen Goodrich. New York: Harper & Bros.
1850	Rev. John Ogilvie	*The Imperial Dictionary of the English Language* 2 vols., heavily borrowed from Merriam-Webster. A Supplement in 1855 increased the number of entry words to 100,000; 2,000 woodcut illustrations. London: Blackie & Sons.

1855	Joseph Emerson Worcester	*A Pronouncing, Explanatory and Synonymous Dictionary of the English Language* Octavo, 565 pp. An extensive enlargement of the *Comprehensive Dictionary* (1830). Boston: Hickling, Swan, and Brown.
1859	Noah Webster	*An American Dictionary of the English language, Pictorial Edition* Revised and enlarged, quarto, 2 vols. A rush job by Merriam to prevent Worcester's 1860 ed. from being the first illustrated American edition. Springfield, MA: G. & C. Merriam.
1860	Joseph Emerson Worcester	*A Dictionary of the English Language* Quarto, 2 vols., 104,000 entry words, 1,800 pp., 1,000 woodcut illustrations; 27,000 copies printed up to 1863 (Allibone). Boston: Hickling, Swan & Brewer.
1864 (1878, 1884, 1886)	Noah Webster, Noah Porter, and Chauncey Allen Goodrich, eds.	*An American Dictionary of the English Language by Noah Webster, LL.D. / Thoroughly Revised, and Greatly Enlarged and Improved by Chauncey A. Goodrich, D.D., and Noah Porter, D.D.* Unabridged, royal quarto, 2 vols., 1,766 pp., illustrated; so-called Webster-Mahn edition. Springfield, MA: G. & C. Merriam.
1886	Noah Webster, Chauncey A. Goodrich, Noah Porter, and C. A. Mahn, eds.	*Webster's Complete Dictionary of the English Language / Thoroughly Revised and Improved by Chauncey A. Goodrich, Noah Porter, Assisted by C. A. Mahn, and Others* "Authorized and Unabridged." London: George Bell & Sons.
1889–91 (last ed. 1927)	William Dwight Whitney, ed.	*The Century Dictionary and Cyclopedia* Published by the Century Company, New York: 6 vols., ca. 500,000 entry words, 7,046 pp., ca. 10,000 woodcut illustrations. In scope, potential rival to the *Oxford English Dictionary*. New York: Century Co.
1890	Noah Webster; Noah Porter, ed.	*Webster's International Dictionary of the English Language: Being the Authentic Edition of Webster's Unabridged Dictionary, Comprising the Issues of 1864, 1879 and 1884 / Thoroughly Revised and Much Enlarged under the Supervision of Noah Porter* 175,000 entry words (56,000 more than the 1864 ed.). Springfield, MA: G. & C. Merriam.
1893	Funk & Wagnalls	*A Standard Dictionary of the English Language* Definitions arranged according to order of importance (user convenience) rather than historical order; compiled by a team of 740 people. New York: Funk & Wagnalls.

1898	G. and C. Merriam	*Webster's Collegiate Dictionary*
		Compact edition of Webster's *International Dictionary.* Springfield, MA: G. & C. Merriam; editions followed in 1910, 1916, 1936, 1946, 1963, 1973, 1983, 1993, 2004, 2012 (11th ed.).

20th CENTURY

1900	Noah Porter, ed.	*Webster's International Dictionary*
		With supplement adding 25,000 entry words. Springfield, MA: G. & C. Merriam.
1909	William Torrey Harris and F. Sturges Allen, eds.	*Webster's New International Dictionary* More than 400,000 word entries. Springfield, MA: G. & C. Merriam.
1913	Funk & Wagnalls; Isaac K. Funk, chief ed.	*New Standard Unabridged Dictionary of the English Language* 450,000 entry words. New York: Funk & Wagnalls.
1928 (published in fascicles, beginning in 1884)	James A. H. Murray et al., eds.	*Oxford English Dictionary* 400,000 entry words and phrases, 10 vols., one-volume supplement, 1933. Oxford, Clarendon Press; London: H. Milford; New York: Oxford University Press.
1934	William Allan Neilson and Thomas A. Knott, eds.	*Webster's New International Dictionary* 2nd ed., known as "Webster's Second"; 600,000 entry words, 3,214 pp. Springfield, MA: G. & C. Merriam.
1946	Funk & Wagnalls	*College Standard Dictionary of the English Language* 145,000 entry words. New York: Funk & Wagnalls.
1947	Clarence Barnhart, ed.	*American College Dictionary* 132,000 entry words; based on the 1927 *New Century Dictionary*; later expanded to the *Random House Dictionary of the English Language* (1966). New York: Random House.
1951	World Publishing Company	*Webster's New World Dictionary of the American Language* 2 vols.; full etymology; unrelated to the Merriam line of Webster dictionaries. Cleveland, OH: World Publishing Co.
1953	World Publishing Company; David Guralnik and Joseph Friend, eds.	*Webster's New World Dictionary of the American Language, College Edition* Ca. 142,000 entry words, considered at the time the largest desktop dictionary. The 1957 ed. mentions that the dictionary is totally unrelated to the Merriam-Webster dictionary series. Cleveland, OH: World Publishing Co.

1961	G. and C. Merriam; Philip Babcock Gove, ed.	*Webster's Third New International Dictionary, Unabridged* Known as "W3"; over 450,000 entry words (ca. 100,000 new). Springfield, MA: G. & C. Merriam.
1963	G. and C. Merriam Philip Babcock Gove, ed.	*Webster's Seventh New Collegiate Dictionary* The first Merriam *Collegiate Dictionary* based on *Webster's Third*. Springfield, MA: G. & C. Merriam.
1966	Random House; Jess M. Stein, ed.	*The Random House Dictionary of the English Language: The Unabridged Edition* Later published with the title *Random House Webster's Dictionary of the English Language*. Computerized by Laurence Urdang. New York: Random House.
1968	Random House; Laurence Urdang, ed.	*Random House Dictionary of the English Language, College Edition* 155,000 entry words. New York: Random House.
1969	Houghton Mifflin; William Morris, ed.	*American Heritage Dictionary of the English Language* This dictionary was a response to the controversy raised by *Webster's Third International Dictionary* in 1961. New York: American Heritage Publishing Co.; Boston: Houghton Mifflin; editions have followed in 1980, 1992, 2000, 2011.
1979	Harper Collins; Patrick Hanks, ed.	*Collins English Dictionary* 1st ed., unabridged (12th ed., 2014). London: Collins.
From the mid-1990s	electronic dictionaries	Print dictionaries available in digital form, with access through download or CD-ROM.
The present	online dictionaries	Some of the following are compiled by professional lexicographers, and others are crowd-sourced with no editorial oversight. Among the websites are The Cambridge Dictionary, http://dictionary.cambridge.org; Dictionary.com, http://dictionary.com; Macmillan Dictionary, http://macmillandictionary.com; Dictionary by Merriam-Webster, http://merriam-webster.com; OneLook, http://onelook.com; Oxford Dictionaries, http://oxforddictionaries.com; Urban Dictionary, http://urbandictionary.com; Wiktionary, http://wiktionary.org; Word Spy, http://wordspy.com; Wordnik, http://wordnik.com. The list continues to grow.

APPENDIX C

Publishing Terms

abridged dictionary: An unabridged dictionary that has been reduced in size and scope by a variety of omissions or reductions of elements such as the number of entry words (for example, obsolete and technical terms), definitions of a word, textual illustrations, synonyms and synonym discussions, etymology, symbols of pronunciation, and abbreviations. It also contains revisions of the unabridged "parent" dictionary with the addition of new senses of words and the addition of new entry words.

book sizes
> folio: A book format produced by folding a large printer's sheet once, making two leaves or four pages that form the individual sections (gatherings) of the book.
>
> quarto: A book format (abbreviated 4to or 4°) produced by folding a large printer's sheet twice, making four leaves or eight pages, each leaf one-quarter the size of the original sheet. This is the most common format of unabridged dictionaries discussed in this book.
>
> octavo: A book format (abbreviated 8to or 8vo) produced by folding a large printer's sheet three times, making eight leaves or sixteen pages, each one-eighth the size of the original sheet. This is the format commonly used for abridgments of dictionaries discussed in this book. It is the average size of a hardcover book today.
>
> royal octavo: A book only slightly larger than a regular octavo, printed from a royal sheet rather than from the slightly smaller sheet from which a regular octavo is produced.
>
> duodecimo: A book format (abbreviated 12to or 12mo) produced by folding a large printer's sheet four times, making twelve leaves or twenty-four pages, used for some smaller abridged dictionaries. It is the size of a popular paperback book today.

diacritic: A sign or mark used to indicate special sounds or phonetic values of a letter.

entry word or headword: The word under which definitions and other explanations of that word appear.

fascicle: A section of a book or set of books being published in installments as separate pamphlets or volumes.

hard word: Earliest term for a foreign word (chiefly Latin) entering the language.

neologism: A new word, usage, phrase, or expression entering the language.

notation: Symbols, characters, and numbers used to indicate pronunciation.

orthoepy: The study of the correct pronunciation of words and its relationship to spelling.

orthography: The study of correct spelling.

stereotype printing: Increasingly from the late eighteenth century onward, stereotyping re-placed the hand-cast type form that was used in the traditional method of printing. It involved making a papier-mâché or plaster mold from the surface of the typeset form, onto which (when the mold cooled) hot metal would be poured to create the stereotype plate. Printing would then be done from that plate instead of from the original typeset form. There were several advantages to this method, among which were the superior mo-bility of the stereotype plates, ease of storage for future and frequent use, and longevity, since the original forms wore out far more quickly. The plates could also be purchased by and sold to other printers and publishers. Printers/publishers, or anyone owning the plates, possessed great leverage over the publishing fortunes of, for example, a dictionary, especially if they could acquire the copyright as well.

synonymy: A list or collection of synonyms for an entry word in a dictionary, especially one in which their meanings are carefully distinguished from each other.

unabridged dictionary: The most comprehensive version of a dictionary, not reduced in size; a dictionary that gives "full coverage to the lexicon in general use at a particular time in the history of the language and substantial coverage to specialized lexicons . . . with quo-tations given to support its definitions, illustrate context, and suggest typical varieties of usage" (Landau, *Dictionaries: The Art and Craft of Lexicography*, 17–18).

word count: The number of entry words in a dictionary. These figures are variously reckoned in different dictionaries, which sometimes complicates direct comparisons.

"The Spelling Bee at Angels

(Reported by Truthful James)"

Waltz in, waltz in, ye little kids, and gather round my knee,
And drop them books and first pot-hooks, and hear a yarn from me.
I kin not sling a fairy tale of Jinnys fierce and wild,
For I hold it is unchristian to deceive a simple child;
But as from school yer driftin' by, I thowt ye'd like to hear
Of a "Spelling Bee" at Angels that we organized last year.

It warn't made up of gentle kids, of pretty kids, like you,
But gents ez hed their reg'lar growth, and some enough for two.
There woz Lanky Jim of Sutter's Fork and Bilson of Lagrange,
And "Pistol Bob," who wore that day a knife by way of change.
You start, you little kids, you think these are not pretty names,
But each had a man behind it, and—my name is Truthful James.

There was Poker Dick from Whisky Flat, and Smith of Shooter's Bend,
And Brown of Calaveras—which I want no better friend;
Three-fingered Jack—yes, pretty dears, three fingers—*you* have five.
Clapp cut off two—it's sing'lar, too, that Clapp ain't now alive.
'Twas very wrong indeed, my dears, and Clapp was much to blame;
Likewise was Jack, in after-years, for shootin' of that same.

The nights was kinder lengthenin' out, the rains had jest begun,
When all the camp came up to Pete's to have their usual fun;
But we all sot kinder sad-like around the bar-room stove
Till Smith got up, permiskiss-like, and this remark he hove:

"Thar's a new game down in Frisco, that ez far ez I can see
Beats euchre, poker, and van-toon, they calls the 'Spellin' Bee.'"

Then Brown of Calaveras simply hitched his chair and spake,
"Poker is good enough for me," and Lanky Jim sez, "Shake!"
And Bob allowed he warn't proud, but he "must say right thar
That the man who tackled euchre hed his education squar."
This brought up Lenny Fairchild, the schoolmaster, who said
He knew the game, and he would give instructions on that head.

"For instance, take some simple word," sez he, "like 'separate:'
Now who can spell it?" Dog my skin, ef thar was one in eight.
This set the boys all wild at once. The chairs was put in row,
And at the head was Lanky Jim, and at the foot was Joe,
And high upon the bar itself the schoolmaster was raised,
And the bar-keep put his glasses down, and sat and silent gazed.

The first word out was "parallel," and seven let it be,
Till Joe waltzed in his "double l" betwixt the "a" and "e,"
For since he drilled them Mexicans in San Jacinto's fight
Thar warn't no prouder man got up than Pistol Joe that night—
Till "rhythm" come! He tried to smile, then said "they had him there,"
And Lanky Jim, with one long stride, got up and took his chair.

O little kids, my pretty kids, 't was touchin' to survey
These bearded men, with weppings on, like schoolboys at their play.
They'd laugh with glee, and shout to see each other lead the van,
And Bob sat up as monitor with a cue for a rattan,
Till the Chair gave out "incinerate," and Brown said he'd be durned
If any such blamed word as that in school was ever learned.

When "phthisis" came they all sprag up, and vowed the man who rung
Another blamed Greek word on them be taken out and hung.
As they sat down again I saw in Bilson's eye a flash,
And Brown of Calaveras was a-twistin' his moustache,
And when at last Brown slipped on "gneiss," and Bilson took his chair,
He dropped some casual words about some folks who dyed their hair.

And then the Chair grew very white, and the Chair said he'd adjourn,
But Poker Dick remarked that he would wait and get his turn;
Then with a tremblin' voice and hand, and with a wanderin' eye,
The Chair next offered "eider-duck," and Dick began with "I,"
And Bilson smiled—then Bilson shrieked! Just how the fight begun
I never knowed, for Bilson dropped, and Dick, he moved up one.

Then certain gents arose and said "they'd business down in camp,"
And "ez the road was rather dark, and ez the night was damp,
They'd"—here got up Three-fingered Jack and locked the
door and yelled:
"No, not one mother's son goes out till that thar word is spelled!"
But while the words were on his lips, he groaned and sank in pain,
And sank with Webster on his chest and Worcester on his brain.

Below the bar dodged Poker Dick, and tried to look ez he
Was huntin' up authorities thet no one else could see;
And Brown got down behind the stove, allowin' he "was cold,"
Till it upsot and down his legs the cinders freely rolled,
And several gents called "Order!" till in his simple way
Poor Smith, began with "O-r"—"Or"—and he was dragged away.

O little kids, my pretty kids, down on your knees and pray!
You've got your eddication in a peaceful sort of way;
And bear in mind thar may be sharps ez slings their spellin' square,
But likewise slings their bowie-knives without a thought or care.
You wants to know the rest, my dears? Thet's all! In me you see
The only gent that lived to tell about the Spellin' Bee!

**

He ceased and passed, that truthful man; the children went their way
With downcast heads and downcast hearts—but not to sport or play.
For when at eve the lamps were lit, and supperless to bed,
Each child was sent, with tasks undone and lessons all unsaid,
No man might know the awful woe that thrilled their youthful frames,
As they dreamed of Angels Spelling Bee and thought of Truthful James.

Bret Harte (1878)

Acknowledgments

First, my everlasting gratitude to my wife, Maureen, who skillfully read the manuscript many times, organized aspects of the process along the way, and sustained me creatively, practically, and steadily. Her resilience and accuracy have been invaluable. I dedicate this book to her. My son, Andrew, and daughter, Claire, and their families, as always, have in their ways been encouraging witnesses to the progress of this book.

My literary agent in London, David Godwin, through the years has been a source of encouragement, good ideas, friendship, and guidance; and I proffer thanks also to Laura Mamelok, my literary agent in New York, whose careful and practical guidance in later stages has been wonderful.

I could not be more fortunate than I have been in having Anne Savarese as my editor at Princeton University Press, whose support and imagination with so many aspects of the publication process, from beginning to end, has made the whole process go smoothly. I cannot express enough my gratitude to her. This book also benefited hugely from the endlessly discerning thoroughness, accuracy, and sensitivity of Beth Gianfagna, my copy editor, who is surely one of the best. The combined help of Ali Parrington, Thalia Leaf, and Theresa Liu at Princeton University Press has also smoothed the way considerably.

In researching and writing about the dictionary wars, I have benefited from the assistance of the staffs of libraries and archives, and several other institutions and museums. My thanks to the British Academy for a grant enabling me to spend valuable time in the United States at the Beinecke Rare Book and Manuscript Library at Yale University; Yale University Manuscripts and Archives, Sterling Library; New Haven Museum and Historical Society; Houghton Library at Harvard University; Harvard University Archives; New York Public Library; Special Collections, Indiana State University Library; Special Collections, Connecticut Historical Society in Hartford,

Connecticut; Jones Library, Amherst, Massachusetts; Craigie-Longfellow House in Cambridge, Massachusetts; Boston Public Library; Massachusetts Historical Society in Boston; Cambridge (Massachusetts) Historical Society; and the British Library. My thanks go also to several of those libraries and institutions for permission to quote from material and include in this book certain images as illustrations. In addition, I extend my gratitude to Anita Israel at the Craigie-Longfellow House; Leah Jehan, Anne Marie Menta, and Moira Ann Fitzgerald at the Beinecke at Yale; James W. Campbell, Librarian and Curator of Manuscripts, and Jason Bischoff-Wurstle, Director of Photo Archives, at the New Haven Museum; Sierra Dixon and Karen Li Miller, Connecticut Historical Society; Fred Burchsted, Research Library, Widener Library, Harvard; Dennis Vetrovec and Joshua Stabler, Special Collections, Indiana State University; and Tevis Kimball, Curator of Special Collections at the Jones Library in Amherst. My gratitude and thanks, too, to John Kulka. For a good deal of information on Lyman Cobb, I am indebted to Charles Monaghan, who sent me several notes and an essay on Cobb without which chapter 7 would have been undernourished. I could mention many more research debts, of course, and readers can find references to them in the text and notes.

Abbreviations

CHS: Connecticut Historical Society, G. & C. Merriam Co., records and correspondence, 1833–79, Ms. 62433.

Ford Notes: Emily Ellsworth Fowler Ford, *Notes on the Life of Noah Webster*, ed. Emily Ellsworth Ford Skeel, 2 vols. (New York: privately printed, 1912).

GFP: Goodrich Family Papers, Department of Manuscripts and Archives, Sterling Memorial Library, Yale University, series 1, Ms. 242.

Merriam Papers: G. & C. Merriam Company Archive, General Collection, Beinecke Rare Book and Manuscript Library, Yale University, GEN MSS 370.

Webster Letter-Book: Beinecke Rare Book and Manuscript Library, Yale University, Uncat. Ms. 653, box 10.

Webster Letters: *Letters of Noah Webster*, ed. Harry R. Warfel (New York: Library Publishers, 1953).

Worcester Letters: Special Collections, Cunningham Memorial Library, Indiana State University.

Notes

Chapter 1

1. Paine, "A Letter Addressed to the Abbe Raynal, on the Affairs of North-America," 38; Anthony Trollope, *North America*, chap. 15, "Literature," 1:295; Krapp, *The English Language in America*, 1:20.
2. Boswell, *The Life of Samuel Johnson*, 3:290, entry for April 15, 1778; Samuel Johnson, review of Lewis Evans, *Map and Account of the English Colonies in America*.
3. Jefferson to Waldo, August 16, 1813, in *The Writings of Thomas Jefferson*, ed. Lipscomb and Bergh, 6:188; Simpson, *The Politics of American English, 1776–1850*, 33. See also Basker, "Samuel Johnson and the American Common Reader," *Age of Johnson*, 6:3, from which I draw in this section on Johnson and America. See also Basker, *Samuel Johnson in the Mind of Thomas Jefferson* (Charlottesville, VA: The Johnsonians, 1999).
4. Hawthorne, *Passages from English Note-Books*.
5. Melville, *Moby Dick*, chap. 104, "The Fossil Whale"; Fischer, *Abroad with Mark Twain and Eugene Field*, 150–51.
6. Jefferson to Waldo, August 16, 1813, *The Writings of Thomas Jefferson*, ed. Lipscomb and Bergh, 6:188. On Jefferson's relationship to American English and dictionaries, see Percy, "Political Perspectives on Linguistic Innovation in Independent America." I have taken a few of Jefferson's remarks from her citations. See also Micklethwait, *Noah Webster and the American Dictionary*, 133–36; and Krapp, *The English Language in America*, 1:9. See also Lynch, *The Lexicographer's Dilemma*, 116–38.
7. *European Magazine and London Review* 12 (August 1787): 114.
8. Jefferson to Waldo, August 16, 1813, *The Writings of Thomas Jefferson*, ed. Lipscomb and Bergh, 6:188.
9. Jefferson to Adams, August 15, 1820; Jefferson to William S. Cardell, January 27, 1821 (both cited by Percy in "Political Perspectives on Linguistic Innovation in Independent America," 50).
10. Adams to Edmund Jenings, September 23, 1780, in *The Works of John Adams*, ed. Charles Francis Adams, 9:510. Also cited in Krapp, *The English Language in America*, 7.
11. John Witherspoon, *Pennsylvania Journal and Weekly Advertiser*, nos. 5–7 (May 9, 16, 23, and 30, 1781), under the heading "Druid," reprinted in Mathews, *The Beginnings of American English*, 13–30.
12. Frances Trollope, *Domestic Manners of the Americans*, appendix C.
13. On Walsh's "Appeal," see Eaton, "From Anglophile to Nationalist." Irving, "English Writers on America," in *The Sketch-Book of Geoffrey Crayon, Gent*.

14. Nevins, *American Social History as Recorded by British Travelers*, 3; Lodge, "Colonialism in the United States"; Mencken, *The American Language* (2nd rev. and enl. ed., 1921), 19–21, 24, 285 (see pp. 14–20 in the section, "The English Attack," for a few of the more lurid examples of British condemnations); Hamilton, *Men and Manners in America*, 1:128.

15. *Edinburgh Review* 15 (October–January 1809–10): 446; Sydney Smith, review of Adam Sybert, *Statistical Annals of the United States*, *Edinburgh Review* 33 (1820): 80; Martineau, *Society in America*, 2:206–7.

16. Pickering is cited by Mencken, *The American Language* (1937), 17; Channing, *The Importance and Means of a National Literature*, 2, 15–16. A few of these and other citations that follow are drawn from Mesick's book, *The English Traveller in America*.

17. See Matthiesen's landmark study, *American Renaissance*, which examines the first "flowering" of American literature in the 1850s. See also Volo and Volo, *The Antebellum Period*, chap. 8, for a perspective on the efforts of early American authors to define and raise the status of American literature.

18. Emerson, *The American Scholar* and "Nature," in *The Collected Works of Ralph Waldo Emerson*, ed. Spiller and Ferguson, vol. 1.

19. Landor, *Charles James Fox: A Commentary on His Life and Character*, ed. Stephen Wheeler (London, 1907), 146ff.; Dwight, *Remarks on the Review of Inchiquin's Letters*, iv.

20. John Mactaggart, *Three Years in Canada*, 2:325–26.

21. Boucher, *Glossary of Archaic and Provincial Words*, xxiii; Hamilton, *Men and Manners in America*, 127–29. Boucher's *Glossary* was unpublished in his lifetime.

22. Read, "Amphi-Atlantic English," 59, 81–82; Martineau, *Society in America*, cited by Mary Orne Pickering, *Life of John Pickering*, 432.

23. Read, "British Recognition of American Speech in the Eighteenth Century," 43–50; Cresswell, *The Journal of Nicholas Cresswell, 1774–77*, 271, 80.

24. Boorstin, *The Americans*, 276, 284–89.

25. Willis on Everett, *Pencillings by the Way*, 395; Emerson, *Selected Lectures*, 104; Everett to Lincoln, November 20, 1863, in James W. Matthews, "Fallen Angel."

26. Everett, "Mr. Walsh's Appeal," *North American Review* 10 (1820): 363–64, and "England and America," *North American Review* 13 (1821): 35, both cited in Mencken, *The American Language*, 4th ed., chap. 1, sec. 6, "The Views of Writing Men," 67–68.

27. Edward Everett Papers, Massachusetts Historical Society, Boston, Ms. N-1201. Everett on American and British spoken and written English: letter to Pickering, April 12, 1817, in the John Pickering correspondence; Everett Ms. Journal, May 20, 1818 (microfilm reel 35), vol. 131; Everett to Pickering August 14, 1818, in Pickering correspondence; Everett, untitled article, *North American Review* 10 (April 1820): 207. See Allen Walker Read, "Edward Everett's Attitude towards American English," 112–29, where these Everett passages are cited; see also Long, *Literary Pioneers*.

28. Ticknor, *Life, Letters, and Journals of George Ticknor*, ed. Hillard et al., 1:58; White, *England without and Within*, 366 ("my tribe"); Frederick Marryat, *A Diary in America*, 2:222 ("drawl"); *Literary Gazette*, published in London by H. Colburn (2nd ed., 1818–36), 456–57. See also Paul K. Longmore, "'They . . . Speak Better English Than the English Do.'"

29. Cooper, *Notions of the Americans*, 2:122–36, 161ff.; Cooper, *Satanstoe; or, The Littlepage Manuscripts*, chap. 14; Cooper, *The American Democrat*, ed. Dekker and Johnston, 167–72.

30. Andrew Lang, "Americanisms," *Academy*, March 2, 1895, 193.

31. John Ruskin, *Fors Clavigera: Letters to the Workmen and Labourers of Great Britain* (1890), 4:75 (cited by Read in "Amphi-Atlantic English," 64–65); Mencken, *The American Language* (1919 ed.), 23 ("last drops"). See also Simpson, *The Politics of American English, 1776–1850*, 151–53, 183–84.

32. *Gentleman's Magazine* 57, pt. 2 (November 1787): 978.

Chapter 2

1. Noah Webster, *Dissertations on the English Language*, with an appendix, "An Essay on the Necessity, Advantages and Practicability of Reforming the Mode of Spelling, and of Rendering the Orthography of Words Correspondent to the Pronunciation," 20, 398, 406.

2. John Adams, "On Education," in *The Works of John Adams*, ed. Charles F. Adams, 9:510.

3. Brackenridge, *Modern Chivalry, Containing the Adventures of Captain Farrago and Teague O'Regan*, 1:xv; Ladd, *The Literary Remains of Joseph Brown Ladd, M.D.*, 186; Webster, *Dissertations on the English Language*, 171.

4. Jefferson to Madison, August 12, 1801, cited by Warfel, *Noah Webster: Schoolmaster to America*, 272.

5. See Taylor, *Writing Early American History*, chap. 10, on Jill Lepore's book, *A Is for American*, which cites Pickering's description of Webster here (58) and others in her *The Story of America*, chap. 7, "A Nue Merrykin Dikshunary," 111–29; and her *New Yorker* article, "Noah's Mark," 78–87.

6. Ford Notes, 1:10–11.

7. Webster, *Instructive and Entertaining Lessons for Youth*, chap. 64 (Dwight quoted on 197).

8. Buckminster to Webster, October 30, 1779, fragment, Noah Webster Papers, Manuscripts and Archives Division, New York Public Library, box 2 (Ford Notes, 1:20–21). For Webster at Yale, see Ford Notes, 1:11–21; and Memoirs Nos. 4 and 5, in Rollins, *The Autobiographies of Noah Webster*, 123–33.

9. Memoir No. 5, in Rollins, *Autobiographies*, 133–34; letter to Thomas Dawes, December 20, 1808, Webster Letters, p. 310.

10. Memoir No. 6, in Rollins, *Autobiographies*, 134–36; Ford Notes, 1:23; *Collections of the Huguenot Society of America* 1 (1886): lxvii, 60.

11. Memoirs Nos. 7 and 8, in Rollins, *Autobiographies*, 136–37; Barlow to Webster, August 1782, Ford Notes, 1:30 (cited from Todd, *Life and Letters of Joel Barlow, LL.D.*, 42).

12. Webster, Introduction to "Blue-Back Speller," in Rollins, *Autobiographies*, 70–71. The best study of the speller is by E. Jennifer Monaghan, *A Common Heritage: Noah Webster's Blue-Back Speller*.

13. Webster, *The American Spelling Book*, lesson 5, p. 19.

14. Webster cited by Horace E. Scudder, *Noah Webster*, 20–21; Webster, *A Collection of Essays and Fugitiv Writings*, 96.

15. For background on British and American grammar schoolbooks, see Cmiel, *Democratic Eloquence*, 31–34, 74–77; and Schweiger, "A Social History of English Grammar in the Early United States." Cmiel mentions several other American grammars that had their day in the sun in the first half of the nineteenth century.

16. Kirkman, *English Grammar in Familiar Lessons*, lecture 1, p. 13. See Schweiger, "A Social History of English Grammar," 533.
17. Lindley Murray has been the subject of a book-length study by Charles Monaghan, *The Murrays of Murray Hill*.
18. Webster, *A Grammatical Institute of the English Language*, pt. 1, p. 14 (included in Rollins, *Autobiographies*, 69–79).
19. *Papers of the Continental Congress, 1774–1789* (no. 78), 4:369–71. For some additional legal background on the American search for copyright, see Buinicki, *Negotiating Copyright*; and Bracha, "The Ideology of Authorship Revisited."
20. Webster, "To the General Assembly of Connecticut," Webster Letters, 1–3; Memoir No. 8, in Rollins, *Autobiographies*, 137; William Stanhope Smith to Webster, September 27, 1782, cited in Warfel, *Noah Webster: Schoolmaster to America*, 56, 58–59. See also Pelanda, "Declarations of Cultural Independence."
21. Micklethwait, *Noah Webster and the American Dictionary*, chap. 5, "Origin of the Copy-Right Laws in the United States," 74–80; Warfel, *Noah Webster: Schoolmaster to America*, 58.
22. See "Memorial to the Legislature of New York" and Webster to John Canfield, January 6, 1783, Webster Letters, 5–7 and 4.
23. Webster, *American Selection of Lessons of Reading and Speaking . . . Being the Third Part of A GRAMMATICAL INSTITUTE of the English Language*" (New York, 1802), preface; Webster to Timothy Pickering, October 28, 1785, Webster Letters, 39. See Cmiel *Democratic Eloquence*, chap. 1, "The Best Speech of the Best Soul," 31–49, to which I am indebted for some of this discussion of British and American grammar and rhetoric.
24. Webster, "Essay on the Necessity . . . ," *Grammatical Institute* (1783), pt. 1, pp. 393–98. See also Mencken, *The American Language*, chap. 8, "The Influence of Webster."
25. E. Jennifer Monaghan, *A Common Heritage*, 31–33.
26. See Rollins, *The Long Journey of Noah Webster*, 50–53, on Webster's months in Philadelphia.
27. Webster to Rebecca Greenleaf, January 27 and February 10, 1788, Webster Letters, pp. 73–74, 76.
28. Pickering to his nephew John Gardner, July 4, 1786, in *The Life of Timothy Pickering* by his son Octavius Pickering, 1:535; Hazard to Belknap, March 5, 1788, *Correspondence between Jeremy Belknap and Ebenezer Hazard*, vol. 3, pt. 2, p. 23.
29. See Rollins, *The Long Journey of Noah Webster*, 58–60, for Webster's mental state when he returned to Hartford.
30. Webster, *Dissertations on the English Language*, appendix (406); preface (ix).
31. Webster, *Dissertations*, 25, 26, 28, 171, 179.
32. Webster, *A Collection of Essays and Fugitiv Writings*, ix–xi.
33. Cobbett on Webster, cited in Warfel, *Noah Webster: Schoolmaster to America*, 224. For a selection of Webster's writing in the *Minerva*, see Rollins, *The Long Journey of Noah Webster*, 76–83; also Warfel, *Noah Webster: Schoolmaster to America*, 223–41.
34. Webster, *American Minerva*, July 12, 1797.
35. Ford Notes, 1:479; Webster, "Revolution in France" (1794), reprinted in *A Collection of Papers on Political, Literary, and Moral Subjects*, 35.
36. Bynack, "Noah Webster's Linguistic Thought and the Idea of a National Culture," 102–4. Among German linguistic philosophers, Webster appears to have been influenced chiefly

by Pierre Louis Moreau de Maupertius, Johann David Michaelis, and Johann Gottfried Herder. Herder's essay "On the Origin of Language" was particularly influential, with its focus on the role that national rather than universal factors play in the evolution of language. See Vincent P. Bynack, "Noah Webster's Linguistic Thought and the Idea of a National Culture," 104–7.

Chapter 3

1. Webster to Dennie, September 30, 1796, Webster Letters, 141–42.
2. Webster, preface to *An American Dictionary of the English Language* (New York, 1828); Rollins, *The Journey of Noah Webster*, 95.
3. Lepore, *The Story of America*, 111–12.
4. "To the Governors, Instructors, and Trustees of the Universities, and Other Seminaries of Learning, in the United States," January 1798, Webster Letters, 173–77.
5. "A Letter to Dr. Ramsay, of Charleston, S.C., Respecting the Errors in Johnson's Dictionary, and Other Lexicons," October 1807, Webster Letters, 282–92. See also Webster to Dawes, August 5, 1809, Webster Letters, 330. See also Lynch, *The Lexicographer's Dilemma*.
6. Webster to Timothy Pickering, July 17, 1798, Webster Letters, 183–84; *Connecticut Herald*, June 4, 1800.
7. Warren Dutton, articles in the *New England Palladium*, October 2 and November 6, 1801, cited in Wells, *Dictionaries and the Authoritarian Tradition*, 64–65, and Warfel, *Noah Webster: Schoolmaster to America*, 293–97.
8. Webster, "To the New England Palladium," November 10, 1801, Webster Letters, 246.
9. *The Philadelphia Aurora* (1800), quoted by E. Jennifer Monaghan, *A Common Heritage*, 119; *Portfolio*, November 28, 1801, quoted in Andresen, *Linguistics in America 1769–1924*, 67; and see Warfel, *Noah Webster: Schoolmaster to America*, 291–94 for other pertinent citations.
10. *Papers of Benjamin Franklin*, 4:102–8. See Allen Walker Read, "Dictionaries," *The New Encyclopedia Britannica*, 2007 ed. The first version of this article was published in the 15th edition (1974), 5:713–22. Passages cited here are from both editions. See Micklethwait, *Noah Webster and the American Dictionary*, 133, on the pre-Webster American dictionaries; and Percy, "Political Perspectives on Linguistic Innovation," 43, 45 (from which I have borrowed examples).
11. Joshua Kendall discusses Johnson Jr.'s and John Elliott's dictionaries in *The Forgotten Founding Father*, 229–31. There is a quaint article on Samuel Johnson Jr. of New Haven, Connecticut, in the *Connecticut Magazine: An Illustrated Monthly* (Hartford, CT) 5 (December 1899), in which Webster's letter is quoted. I am not aware that any evidence has turned up of a meeting between this Johnson and Webster.
12. Webster to Carey and John West, June 14 and August 18, 1805, Webster Letters, 262–64.
13. See the following studies on Webster's early lexicography: Burkett, *American Dictionaries of the English Language before 1861*, 124–32; Friend, *The Development of American Lexicography, 1798–1864*, 14–24; Sidney Landau, *Dictionaries: The Art and Craft of Lexicography*, 59–64; Green, *Chasing the Sun*, 256–59; and Micklethwait, *Noah Webster and the American Dictionary*, 142–49.
14. Preface, *Compendious Dictionary*, section on orthography, vi–x.

15. See Krapp, *The English Language in America*, 1:341–43. I have drawn several of my spelling examples from these pages.
16. Webster to John Pickering, December 1816, Webster Letters, 372–73; Krapp, *The English Language in America*, 1:332–33.
17. Preface, *Compendious Dictionary*, xi, xiv.
18. Letters from Quincy, Dawes, and Adams, June 30, August 14, and November 5, 1806, Ford Notes, 2:6, 8–9, 9–12.
19. Webster to Barlow, November 12, 1807, Webster Letters, 299; *Monthly Anthology and Boston Review* 7 (1809): 247–64.
20. Webster to Samuel Latham Mitchill, June 15, 1807, Webster Letters, 276.

Chapter 4

1. Webster to Barlow, November 12, 1807, Webster Letters, 294–300.
2. Dawes to Webster, August 5, 1807, Noah Webster Papers, Manuscripts and Archives Division, New York Public Library (bracketed phrase is in the original); Krapp, *The English Language in America*, 2:365. Webster described at length his religious conversion in a letter to Dawes, December 20, 1808, Webster Letters, 309–15.
3. Webster to Ramsay, October 1807, Webster Letters, 282, 291, 286, 287; Webster to Dawes, August 5, 1807, Webster Letters, 330; Madison to Webster, May 31, 1813, Ford Notes, 2:119–20; John Jay to Webster, May 31, 1813, Ford Notes, 2:120.
4. Dawes to Webster, January 12, 1811, Ford Notes, 2:82; Wolcott to Webster, September 19, 1807, Ford Notes, 2:26–27; "To the Friends of Literature in the United States," February 25, 1807, Webster Letters, 279–81; Noah Webster Sr. to Webster, June 9, 1807, Ford Notes, 2:20; Webster to Madison, February 20, 1809, Webster Letters, 315.
5. Webster to Dawes, July 25, 1809, Ford Notes, 2:323.
6. Webster to Quincy, February 12, 1811, Ford Notes, 2:102.
7. Eliza Webster reminiscence, Ford Notes, 2:116.
8. Webster to Jay, June 9, 1813, Ford Notes, 2:121. See also Webster to Quincy, February 12, 1811, Ford Notes, 2:102.
9. On Jones, Schlegel, Bopp, and the Grimm brothers, see Béjoint, *The Lexicography of English*, 97; and Green, *Chasing the Sun*, 277–85.
10. Webster, *An American Dictionary of the English Language* (1841), introduction, xx; Jones, *The Works of Sir William Jones*, 3:199–200; Webster, *Observations on Language, Addressed to the Members of the Mercantile Library Association*, 5–6. See also Read, "The Spread of German Linguistic Learning in New England during the Lifetime of Noah Webster." For Webster's etymological principle of radicals and roots, see Krapp, *The English Language in America*, 1:363–65. On Webster's etymology, see also Laird, "Etymology, Anglo-Saxon, and Noah Webster"; and Bivens, "Noah Webster's Etymological Principles."
11. Sledd and Kolb, *Dr. Johnson's Dictionary*, 183; Webster, *Dissertations on the English Language*, 287; Butler, *John Horne Tooke, Burke, Paine, Godwin, and the Revolution Controversy*, 18–19. See also Simpson, *The Politics of American English, 1776–1850*, 81–90.
12. Pickering to Horace Binney, July 1816, cited in Mary Orne Pickering, *Life of John Pickering*, 258–60.

13. Webster's attack in his *Letter* to Pickering, December 1816, is included in Webster Letters, 341–94; citations are listed here in the order they appear: 367, 383, 382, 372, 367.

14. Webster, *Letter to the Honorable John Pickering*, in Webster Letters, 382, 393, 394. On Pickering, see also Burkett, *American Dictionaries of the English Language before 1861*, 84–94; and Micklethwait, *Noah Webster and the American Dictionary*, 172–73.

15. Webster to Stephen Van Rensselaer, November 5, 1821, Webster Letters, 405–6.

16. Ford Notes, appendix 32, 506.

17. From Dawes (February 14, 1824) and Cranch (March 1, 1824) to Webster, cited in Ford Notes, 2:195, 196.

18. Goodrich, *Recollections of a Lifetime*, 2:18–19.

19. William Webster to Rebecca Webster, September 24, 1824, Ford Notes, 2:246–47.

20. Ford Notes, 2:292n1; Webster to Samuel Lee, December 20, 1824, Webster Letters, 413, cited by Webster himself in the preface to his 1828 *American Dictionary*; Webster to Rebecca Webster, December 6, 1824, Ford Notes, 2:267.

21. Webster to Rebecca, December 26, 1824, Ford Notes, 2:275.

22. Ford Notes, 2:293; Webster to Madison, March 17, 1826, Ford Notes, 2:294–95.

23. *Report of the Case of Joshua Stowe vs. Sherman Converse, for a Libel . . .* (County of New Haven: S. Converse, 1822), 13.

24. Converse to Jefferson, February 6, 1826, and Jefferson to Converse, February 20, 1826, Thomas Jefferson Papers, Library of Congress, Manuscript Division, series 1, General Correspondence, 1751–1827 (cited in Micklethwait, *Noah Webster and the American Dictionary*, 194, 195).

25. Julius H. Ward, *The Life and Letters of James Gates Percival*, 80, 36, 80. Eulogies of Percival in 1856, ed. Draper, were published in *Collections of the Historical Society of Wisconsin* 3 (1904): 66–80.

26. Webster to Daniel Webster, September 30, 1826, Webster Letters, 417–20; Noah Webster to William Chauncey Fowler, January 29, 1831, Webster Letters, 424–25. For an account of Webster's new copyright initiatives, I am indebted to Micklethwait, *Noah Webster and the American Dictionary*, 211–21.

27. Ward, *The Life and Letters of James Gates Percival*, 475.

28. Ward, *The Life and Letters of James Gates Percival*, 286–87, 475.

29. Ward, *The Life and Letters of James Gates Percival*, 286.

30. Webster to Converse, May 23, 1828. Nate D. Sanders, Inc., in Los Angeles put up Webster's letter to Converse for auction in 2010, but it remains a mystery who purchased it and where it is now.

31. *American Quarterly Review* 4 (1828): 204; letter to editor, *Albany Argus*, December 1827, Webster Letters, 422; Richardson, "An American Dictionary of the English Language," 82; Green, *Chasing the Sun*, 264.

32. Everett to Webster, June 19, 1827, Noah Webster Papers, Manuscripts and Archives Division, New York Public Library, cited by Read, "Edward Everett's Attitude towards American English," 124–27; Everett, review in the *North American Review* 29 (October 1829): 536.

33. Samuel Johnson, *Rambler*, no. 51, September 7, 1751. A full and most carefully researched examination (much of it among archives in the New York Public Library) of the 1828

edition is by Micklethwait, *Noah Webster and the American Dictionary*, 171–98. See also Friend, *The Development of American Lexicography, 1798–1864*, chap. 2; Burkett, *American Dictionaries of the English Language before 1861*, 153–60; Krapp, *The English Language in America*, 1:362–69; and Scudder, *Noah Webster*, 82–93.

34. Webster, preface to 1828 quarto, viii. Miyoshi has interesting things to say about the American character of the 1828 edition in *Johnson and Webster's Verbal Examples*, 60.

35. Sledd and Kolb, *Dr. Johnson's Dictionary*, 155, 191–92, quote Richardson's "original prospectus" from "The Address to the Public, from the American Publisher," p. 2 ("elders of English lexicography"); Burkett, *American Dictionaries of the English Language before 1861*, 153 ("oriental readings), quotes from Richardson in the *Westminster Review* (1828); Webster, *Mistakes and Corrections* (1837). On Horne Tooke's influence on Webster, see Simpson, *The Politics of American English*, 81–90.

36. For a quick assessment of Webster's influence on American spelling, see Conrad T. Logan, "Noah Webster's Influence on American Spelling"; and Percy, "*Plane* English; or, The Orthography of Opposition in Mid-Eighteenth-Century Britain."

37. Murray, "The Evolution of English Lexicography," the Romanes Lecture, delivered in the Sheldonian Theatre, Oxford, June 22, 1900, cited by Krapp, *The English Language in America*, 1:367.

38. Joseph W. Reed, "Noah Webster's Debt to Samuel Johnson," *American Speech*, vol. 37 (May 1962), 95–105.

39. Micklethwait, *Noah Webster and the American Dictionary*, 188. See Cynthia L. Hallen and Tracy B. Spackman, "Biblical Citations as a Stylistic Standard in Johnson's and Webster's Dictionaries, *Lexis*, vol. 5 (2010). See also Reed, "Noah Webster's Debt to Samuel Johnson."

40. Kent, "Anniversary Address to the Phi Beta Kappa Society Chapter of Connecticut," 2.

41. Richard Garnett, "English Lexicography," *Quarterly Review* 54 (July–September 1835): 304–5 (later published in *The Philological Essays of the Late Rev. Richard Garnett*); Micklethwait, *Noah Webster and the American Dictionary*, 276.

Chapter 5

1. Jefferson to Yancey, January 6, 1816, *The Papers of Thomas Jefferson*, Retirement Series, 19:328. For a historical account of eighteenth- and nineteenth-century magazines, see Frank Luther Mott, *A History of American Magazines: 1741–1850*, vol. 1.

2. See Grubb, "Growth of Literacy in Colonial America"; and *Columbian Phenix and the Boston Review*, both cited by Jack Lynch in his essay, "Every Man Able to Read: Literacy in Early America." On the factors responsible for the increase in literacy, see Stevens Jr., "Mass Literacy in Nineteenth-Century United States."

3. Webster to Converse, May 23, 1828 (see Collectible Auctions, http://icollector.com, for the letter put up by Nate D. Sanders, Inc.); Converse to Goodrich, November 11, 1830, GFP, box 1, folder 9.

4. Webster to Howe, Kinglsey, and Woodward, December 8, 1829, and Converse to Goodrich, November 11, 1830, GFP, box 1, folder 9.

5. *Phillips Bulletin* 19 (July 8, 1918). For a sketch of Worcester's years in Salem, Massachusetts, see Margaret B. Moore, *The Salem World of Nathaniel Hawthorne*, 79–84.

6. Moore, *The Salem World of Nathaniel Hawthorne*, chap. 4, "A Salem Education."

7. See Higgins, *A Distinguished and Gracious New England Lexicographer*, chap. 1.

8. Newell, "Memoir of J. E. Worcester, LL.D."; Higginson, *Old Cambridge*, 51–52. On Higginson's friendship with Dickinson, see Wineapple, *White Heat*; and Cristanne Miller on Webster's influence on Dickinson, in *Emily Dickinson: A Poet's Grammar* (reprinted as a chapter in Farr, ed., *New Century Views of Emily Dickinson*; and in Miller, *Reading in Time*).

9. *American Monthly Review* 1 (January–June 1832): 95–96.

10. Worcester edition of *Todd-Johnson* (London, 1827), preface, ix–x.

11. Webster to William Fowler, September 29, 1830, Webster Letter-Book.

12. Converse's much later account is taken from Worcester, *A Gross Literary Fraud Exposed, Relating to the Publication of Worcester's Dictionary*, 13.

13. Worcester, *A Gross Literary Fraud Exposed, Relating to the Publication of Worcester's Dictionary*, 13.

14. Woolsey, "A Discourse in Commemoration of the Life and Service of Chauncey Allen Goodrich."

15. Webster to Worcester, July 27, 1828, Webster Letter-Book; Goodrich to Worcester, July 28, 1828, GFP, box 1, folder 7. Both references are included in Worcester, *A Gross Literary Fraud Exposed, Relating to the Publication of Worcester's Dictionary*, 13.

16. *An American Dictionary of the English Language* (revised octavo, 3rd ed., 1830), preface, iii.

17. "Webster's Octavo Dictionary," *Methodist Quarterly Review* 30 (January 1848): 106 (quoted by Cmiel, *Democratic Eloquence*, 88; see also 84–85); Woolsey, "A Discourse in Commemoration of the Life and Service of Chauncey Allen Goodrich," 22–23.

18. Worcester, *A Gross Literary Fraud Exposed, Relating to the Publication of Worcester's Dictionary*, 13.

19. Goodrich to George and Charles Merriam, October 27, 1853, Merriam Papers, box 10, folder 127.

20. Worcester to Goodrich, October 28, 1828, GFP, box 1, folder 7.

21. Worcester to Goodrich, October 28 and 31, 1828, GFP, box 1, folder 7.

22. Worcester to Goodrich, December 9, 1828, GFP, box 1, folder 7; preface, 1830 octavo abridgment of the quarto, iii.

23. On Worcester's methods in the revisions, see Burkett, *American Dictionaries of the English Language before 1861*, 174–75; and on aspects of Goodrich's strategy, see Micklethwait, *Noah Webster and the American Dictionary*, 201–2.

24. Worcester to Goodrich, April 9, 1829, GFP, box 1, folder 8.

Chapter 6

1. Webster to Fowler, April 11, 1843, Webster Letter-Book.

2. Converse to Webster, May 20, 1828, Ellsworth Letters, CHS. See also E. Jennifer Monaghan, *A Common Heritage*, 140–41, on the rift between Webster and Converse.

3. *A Dictionary of the English Language, for the Use of Primary Schools and the Counting-House* (1829), ii.

4. Webster to Fowler, December 28, 1829, Webster Letter-Book.

5. Webster to Fowler, December 28, 1829, Webster Letter-Book; Goodrich to Fowler, April 11, 1843, Webster Letter-Book; and Fowler's recollections, *Printed, but Not Published*, 6–7.

6. Goodrich to Ellsworth, October 18, 1843, GFP, box 2, folder 17.
7. Webster affidavit, May 7, 1833, GFP, box 1, folder 11.
8. Webster signed his second agreement on July 12, 1833 (GFP, box 1, folder 11).
9. Webster to J. L. Kingsley, Hezekiah Howe, and Thomas G. Woodward, December 28, 1829, GFP, box 1, folder 9; to Fowler, September 29, 1830, Webster Letter-Book; to Rebecca Webster, January 26, 1831, Ford Notes, 2:324.
10. Converse to Goodrich, November 11, 1830, GFP, box 1, folder 9.
11. Goodrich to Ellsworth, October 18, 1843, GFP, box 2, folder 17; Goodrich to the Merriams, December 19, 1844, Merriam Papers, box 19, folder 119.
12. Goodrich to Converse, May 29, 1833, GFP, box 1, folder 11.

Chapter 7

1. The most exhaustive study on Lyman Cobb and the spelling wars, on which this chapter draws heavily, is by Charles Monaghan, "Lyman Cobb and the British Elocutionary Tradition." I am indebted to him for background information on Cobb that he has shared with me. On spellers, see E. Jennifer Monaghan, *A Common Heritage*, 31–34.
2. E. Jennifer Monaghan, *A Common Heritage*, 152–57.
3. Cobb, *To the Teachers, School Committees or Inspectors, Clergymen, and to the Friends of Correct Elementary Instruction*. Reprinted in Burkett, *American Dictionaries of the English Language before 1861*, 165–66.
4. "To the Editor of the *Albany Argus*," December 1827, Webster Letters, 421–23.
5. *New York Evening Post*, June 27, 1829; Cobb's lists in the July 4, 1829, *Morning Herald* are summarized by Burkett, *American Dictionaries of the English Language before 1861*, 167–73, from which I have taken examples.
6. Barnes is cited by Burkett, *American Dictionaries of the English Language before 1861*, 169–70; and Read, "The Development of Faith in the Dictionary in America," 7.
7. Cobb cites Converse's involvement in this dispute in his *Critical Review of the Orthography of Dr. Webster's Series of Books for Systematick Instruction in the English Language Including His Former Spelling-Book and the Elementary Spelling-Book*, iii note. See Charles Monaghan, "Lyman Cobb and the British Elocutionary Tradition"; and Burkett, *American Dictionaries of the English Language before 1861*, 170–71, on the Cobb-Converse squabble.
8. Cobb, *A Critical Review*.
9. Webster, "To the Public," November 15, 1831, Webster Letters, 428–31.
10. Webster's letter to Henrick has been for sale by the New York City bookseller James Cummings, inventory no. 26005. Its present location is unknown.
11. Webster to McGuffey, March 3, 1837, Merriam Papers, box 14, folder 311. It is cited by Micklethwait, *Noah Webster and the American Dictionary*, 222.
12. Webster to Harriet Fowler, December 29, 1830, Webster Letter-Book.
13. Webster to Fowler, January 29, 1831, Webster Letters, 425; the self-advertisement is cited later in the 1839 edition, *The Elementary Spelling Book, Being an Improvement of the American Spelling Book*, advertisement, 4.
14. Harte, *The Works of Bret Harte*, Argonaut ed., vol. 8.

Chapter 8

1. Dunglison, *American Monthly Review* 1 (1832): 101–2; "Words Often Mispronounced," *Common School Journal* 1 (1839): 361; Webster to Fowler, November 24, 1830, Webster Letter-Book.

2. Webster to Fowler, April 20, 1831, Webster Letter-Book. For a detailed account of Worcester's *Comprehensive Dictionary*, see Higgins, *A Distinguished and Gracious New England Lexicographer*, 18–25. Higgins's book is a close study of how Worcester navigated through these tempestuous lexicographical waters. See also Burkett, *Dictionaries of the English Language before 1861*, 203–7.

3. Webster to Fowler, April 20, 1831, Webster Letter-Book; Higgins, *A Distinguished and Gracious New England Lexicographer*, 20–23; Worcester, *A Comprehensive Pronouncing and Explanatory Dictionary of the English Language* (Boston, 1830), xiii.

4. The word was coined by John Algeo, "Dictionaries as Seen by the Educated Public in Great Britain and the U.S.A.," 1:29.

5. Mugglestone, *Lost for Words*, xvi; McArthur, *Living Words*, 91. See also Béjoint, *The Lexicography of English*, 232.

6. Webster to Fowler, November 24, 1830, Webster Letter-Book. See also Joseph W. Reed, "Webster's Debt to Samuel Johnson."

7. Webster to Fowler, April 20, 1831, Webster Letter-Book.

8. *Worcester Palladium*, November 26, 1834; Burkett, *Dictionaries of the English Language before 1861*, 223.

9. *Worcester Palladium*, November 26, 1834.

10. Johnson's remark is in *Rambler*, no. 68, quoted in Warfel, *Noah Webster: Schoolmaster to America*, 35.

11. Willard, *North American Review* 64 (1817): 190. Worcester's remark on Willard's defense is quoted by Swan, "Worcester's Dictionaries," 10.

12. Worcester, *Worcester Palladium*, December 10, 1834. Worcester had been collecting dictionary editions for many years and continued to do so on his trip to Europe in 1831, where he bought many philological works.

13. Webster, *Worcester Palladium*, December 17, 1834.

14. *Worcester Palladium*, December 24, 1834.

15. Worcester, *Worcester Palladium*, February 6, 1835.

16. Webster, *Worcester Palladium*, February 13, 1835.

17. Worcester, *Worcester Palladium*, March 11, 1835.

18. Webster, *Worcester Palladium*, March 14, 1835. See Micklethwait, *Noah Webster and the American Dictionary*, 231–33, and Higgins, *A Distinguished and Gracious New England Lexicographer*, 36–41.

19. Prior, *A Life of the Right Honourable Edmund Burke*, 191.

20. Worcester, *Elementary Dictionary for the Common Schools with Pronouncing Vocabularies of Classical, Scripture, and Modern Geographical Names* (Boston, 1835), preface, 3.

21. Longfellow, "Craigie House," 23–26 (handwritten booklet, Craigie-Longfellow House, Cambridge, MA); Longfellow, "Dame Craigie," in Higginson, *Outdoor Studies Poems*,

355–56. For a history of the house, see Catherine Evans, *Cultural Landscape Report for Longfellow National Historic Site*, vol. 1 (Boston: National Park Service, 1993); and *New England Historical and Genealogical Register* 25 (July 1871): 237–38. I am grateful to Anita Israel, archives specialist at the house, for her help with the history of the Craigie house.

22. Longfellow to Stephen Longfellow, April 1, 1841, *The Letters of Henry Wadsworth Longfellow*, ed. Hilen, 293–94.

23. Tharp, *The Appletons of Beacon Hill*, 244.

Chapter 9

1. Webster to Harriet Fowler, November 5, 1835, Webster Letter-Book; Ford Notes, 1:375–76 (for the family friend [from an article on Noah Webster in *Mother's Magazine* by Mrs. Whitlesey, one of the Goodrich family, which was knit to him by friendship for years, and later by marriage] and for Webster's statement); Joshua Kendall, "Noah Webster: The Definition of Yankee Know-How," *Los Angeles Times*, October 15, 2008.

2. Webster to Fowler, August 31, 1835, Webster Letter-Book; Webster to Fowler, September 10, 1836, "Reasons for Adopting One Dictionary as a Standard of English Orthography, September 1836," Webster Letter-Book.

3. Webster to Dawes, August 5, 1809, Webster Letters, 330. On attitudes toward Johnson's style, see Ley, *The Critic in the Modern World*, 21–23.

4. "Reasons for Adopting One Dictionary as a Standard of English Orthography, September 1836," Webster Letter-Book.

5. *The Panoplist; Or, the Christian's Armory* 3, no. 3 (August 1807): 125; Elisa Tamarkin, *Anglophilia*, 290–92. Everett is cited in Andresen, *Linguistics in America, 1769–1924*. See also Lynch, *The Lexicographer's Dilemma*, for a comprehensive study of this tangled subject of prescriptiveness.

6. Webster to Fowler, July 9, 1836, Webster Letter-Book,

7. Webster to Fowler, July 9, 1836, December 8, 1837, January 9, 1838, March 10, 1838, Webster Letter-Book.

8. White to Goodrich, September 11, 1837, GFP, box 2, folder 14.

9. Webster to Fowler, February 27 and March 14, 1839, Webster Letter-Book.

10. Webster to Fowler, July 4, 1839, Webster Letter-Book.

11. Webster to Fowler, February 25, 1841, Webster Letter-Book.

12. Webster to Fowler, July 9, 1840, Webster Letter-Book.

13. See Mencken, "The Influence of Webster," *The American Language* (1937 ed.), 379–88, for several examples of Webster's orthographical retrenchment that I have cited.

14. Webster, *An American Dictionary of the English Language* (1841), appendix, 941–1008.

15. Webster to Fowler, July 7 and December 3, 1841, Webster Letter-Book. See Green, *Chasing the Sun*, 329. Fowler recorded his last conversation with Webster in his pamphlet, *Printed, but Not Published*. See Burkett, *American Dictionaries of the English Language before 1861*, 179–80, for additional details regarding the 1841 royal octavo.

16. "Account by Eliza Webster Jones 'For my Little Boy,'" in Ford Notes, 2:362–371.

17. Unger, *Noah Webster: The Life and Times of An American Patriot*, 338–40; Silliman is cited in Warfel, *Noah Webster: Schoolmaster to America*, 436–37.

Chapter 10

1. Harriet Fowler to Noah Webster, February 13, 1837, Noah Webster Papers, Manuscripts and Archives Division, New York Public Library, box 6.

2. Goodrich to Ellsworth, October 18, 1843, GFP, box 2, folder 17.

3. Webster to William Webster, November 9, 1835, Noah Webster Papers, Manuscripts and Archives Division, New York Public Library, box 1.

4. Ellsworth to William Webster, July 6, 1843, cited in Micklethwait, *Noah Webster and the American Dictionary*, 258. Micklethwait, a London lawyer, has unraveled the legal contractual complexity involving the Webster family and the several Webster editions, 256–71.

5. Ellsworth to William Webster, December 10, 1844, cited in Micklethwait, *Noah Webster and the American Dictionary*, 263; Ellsworth to J. S. and C. Adams, May 21, 1845, Merriam Papers, box 9, folder 95.

6. Ellsworth to Merriams, March 4, 1844, GFP, box 2, folder 17.

7. Merriams to Ellsworth, December 3, 1847, Merriam Papers, box 9, folder 122. For histories of the G. & C. Merriam Company, see Leavitt, *Noah's Ark, New England Yankees and The Endless Quest*, 41–53; and Leavitt, *100th Anniversary of the Establishment of the G. and C. Merriam Company, 1831–1931*.

8. Goodrich to Fowler, January 16, 1854, GFP, box 3, folder 28.

9. Goodrich to Ellsworth, January 1844, Merriam Papers, box 9, folder 119; and Goodrich to Ellsworth, January 20 and 21, 1845, GFP, box 2, folder 18.

10. Goodrich to Merriams, December 19, 1844, Merriam Papers, box 9, folder 119; Merriams to Goodrich, December 26, 1844, Merriam Papers, box 9, folder 119.

11. Goodrich to Merriams, December 19, 1844, Merriam Papers, box 9, folder 119

12. Goodrich to Merriams, December 19, 1844, Merriam Papers, box 9, folder 119.

13. Goodrich contract with the Merriams, January 30, 1845, GFP, box 2, folder 18.

14. Webster to William Webster, July 7, 1836, cited by Micklethwait, *Noah Webster and the American Dictionary*, 241; Fowler, *Printed, but Not Published*, cited by Micklethwait, *Noah Webster and the American Dictionary*, 242.

15. Huntington also owned the publishing rights to the High School, Primary, and Pocket school dictionaries.

16. Warfel, *Noah Webster: Schoolmaster to America*, 418; Fowler, *Printed, but Not Published*, quoted in Micklethwait, *Noah Webster and the American Dictionary*, 265–66.

17. Goodrich diary, October 1845, GFP, box 8, folder 90.

18. Fowler, *Printed, but Not Published*, quoted in Micklethwait, *Noah Webster and the American Dictionary*, 242.

19. Fowler, *Printed, but Not Published*, quoted in Micklethwait, *Noah Webster and the American Dictionary*, 264. Goodrich to Fowler, January 16, 1854, GFP, box 3, folder 28. Goodrich's January 1854 letter to Fowler was precipitated by a sour letter of Fowler's to Goodrich in January 1854 (GFP, box 3, folder 29) in which he told Goodrich that years earlier he had received deep injuries from him and that the latter had never repaired their personal relations, but that if Goodrich were to agree to new financial agreements in the family, he would take that as a movement toward improving their relationship. Goodrich replied

promptly that it was he who had been injured, not Fowler. Fowler's recollections are extensively quoted in Micklethwait, *Noah Webster and the American Dictionary*, 264–66.

20. Ellsworth to Goodrich, January 14, 1845, GFP, box 2, folder 18; Goodrich to Ellsworth, February 6, 1845, GFP, box 2, folder 18. See Burkett, *American Dictionaries of the English Language before 1861*, 182–86, for details of the innovations in the 1847 edition.

21. Goodrich to Merriams, June 9, 1845, Merriam Papers, box 9, folder 120.

22. Goodrich to Merriams, September 1845, Merriam Papers, box 9, folder 120.

23. Goodrich to Fowler, GFP, box 3, folder 28.

24. Fowler cited in Micklethwait, *Noah Webster and the American Dictionary*, 266; Goodrich to Fowler, January 16, 1854, GFP, box 3, folder 28.

25. Goodrich to Fowler, January 16, 1854, GFP, box 3, folder 28; Fowler to Goodrich, January 18, 1854, GFP, box 3, folder 28; Goodrich to Fowler, January 1854, GFP, box 3, folder 28.

26. Ellsworth to William Webster, February 1847, GFP, box 3, folder 28. See Micklethwait, *Noah Webster and the American Dictionary*, 268–69 on Fowler's last gasps of protest.

Chapter 11

1. Charles Merriam, "Recollections of Various Particulars in the History of Webster's Dictionaries," 1883, Merriam Papers, box 101, folder 696.

2. Charles Merriam to Ellsworth, March 2, 1846, Merriam Papers, box 9, folder 98.

3. Charles Merriam to Ellsworth, March 2, 1846, Merriam Papers, box 9, folder 98.

4. Charles Merriam to Ellsworth, March 2, 1846, Merriam Papers, box 9, folder 98; Goodrich to Merriams, June 9, 1845, Merriam Papers, box 9, folder 120.

5. Charles Merriam to Ellsworth, March 2, 1846, Merriam Papers, box 9, folder 98.

6. Worcester, *A Universal and Critical Dictionary of the English Language* (Boston: Wilkens, Carter and Co., 1846), iv–v; Charles Merriam, "Recollections," Merriam Papers, box 101, folder 696.

7. On the transformation of the English language in the nineteenth century, see a fascinating book by Richard W. Bailey, *Nineteenth-Century English*; also Cmiel, *Democratic Eloquence*.

8. *North American Review* 64 (1847): 194–95.

9. Worcester, *A Universal and Critical Dictionary*, v, lxv; *North American Review* 64, no. 134 (January 1847): 191 (for "judicious moderation").

10. Worcester, *A Universal and Critical Dictionary*, xxii, lxv; Cmiel, *Democratic Eloquence*, 88. For a detailed description of Worcester's dictionary, see Joseph Harold Friend, *The Development of American Lexicography 1798–1864*, 90–95.

11. Worcester, *A Universal and Critical Dictionary*, iii–v.

12. Worcester, *A Universal and Critical Dictionary*, v–vi.

13. Worcester, *A Universal and Critical Dictionary*, iv.

14. Merriams to William Webster, September 15, 1846, GFP, box 1, folder 20.

15. Worcester, *A Universal and Critical Dictionary*, 512.

16. Noah Porter, review of Worcester's *A Universal and Critical Dictionary of the English Language*, *American Review* 5 (May 1847): 508–13.

17. *The American Dictionary of the English Language*, ed. Chauncey Allen Goodrich (Springfield, MA: G. and C. Merriam, 1847), iii. See Burkett, *American Dictionaries of the English Language before 1861*, 176–77, for a summary of the characteristics of the 1847 royal octavo.

18. *The American Dictionary of the English Language*, preface, v.

19. *The American Dictionary of the English Language*, preface, iii–iv.

20. *The American Dictionary of the English Language*, preface, vii.

21. Goodrich, *Morning Courier and New York Enquirer* (1849); *The American Dictionary of the English Language*, preface, v–vi. On Webster's role in determining much of American spelling, see Micklethwait's summary, *Noah Webster and the American Dictionary*, 295 (Goodrich is cited here); Mencken, *The American Language*, 1937 ed., chap. 8, 379–88; and Logan, "Noah Webster's Influence on American Spelling."

22. "Webster's International Dictionary—Especially Its Pronunciation," *New Englander* 53 (1890): 423, cited in Burkett, *American Dictionaries of the English Language before 1861*, 177.

23. The memoir, which Webster himself wrote, appeared originally in 1834 in *The National Portrait Gallery of Distinguished Americans*, ed. Longacre and Herring, 2:10; it appears in the 1847 Merriam edition with Goodrich's additions on xv–xxii.

24. Twain, *Roughing It* (1872), *The Complete Works of Mark Twain* (New York: Harper and Brothers, 1913), 5, 19, 20. See also Twain's letter to the Merriam Company, March 1891, Merriam Papers, box 8, folder 70.

25. Goodrich to Merriams, December 1, 1847, Merriam Papers, box 9, folder 122; Worcester, *A Gross Literary Fraud Exposed* (1853), 15.

26. Worcester, *A Gross Literary Fraud Exposed*, 16–17.

27. Charles Merriam to Ellsworth, March 2, 1846, Merriam Papers, box 9, folder 98.

Chapter 12

1. Merriam, advertisement in the *Boston Daily Advertiser*, August 5, 1853, cited in Worcester, *A Gross Literary Fraud Exposed*, 5; Worcester to Wilkins, August 23, 1853, cited in Worcester, *A Gross Literary Fraud Exposed*, 6. For accounts of the London fraud and the subsequent turmoil that erupted, see Higgins, *A Distinguished and Gracious New England Lexicographer*, 94–96; and Micklethwait, *Noah Webster and the American Dictionary*, 283–85.

2. Micklethwait, *Noah Webster and the American Dictionary*, 284, surmises that Bohn's motivation for the fraudulent edition could be traced to his frustrated desire to publish an edition of the Goodrich/Worcester abridgment. Since Goodrich had his own London publisher for the abridgment (Ingram, Cooke, and Co.), the next best thing for Bohn was to publish Worcester's book in what looked like a pretty good facsimile of that abridgment, the same size but stamped "Webster's Dictionary" in gold on the spine. That way he could pass it off as the abridgment and claim it had been made from Webster's materials.

3. Worcester to Wilkins, August 24, 1853, cited in Worcester, *A Gross Literary Fraud Exposed*, 7.

4. Wilkins to Worcester, August 31, 1853, cited in *A Gross Literary Fraud Exposed*, 8–9.

5. *London Illustrated News*, February 12, 1853.

6. Lowndes, *The Bibliographer's Manual of English Literature*.

7. Micklethwait, *Noah Webster and the American Dictionary*, 283.

8. Merriam, *The English Dictionaries of Webster and Worcester*; Worcester to Wilkins, August 23, 1853, cited in Worcester, *A Gross Literary Fraud Exposed*, 7; Worcester to Jenks, Hickling, and Swan, September 30, 1853, cited in Worcester, *A Gross Literary Fraud Exposed*, 3.

9. For a good account of the publishers' interaction with Worcester, see Leach, "A Stabilizing Influence," 41–48. His summary sheds light on the Merriams' aggressive strategy for capitalizing on the Bohn scandal.

10. Worcester, *A Gross Literary Fraud Exposed*, 10.

11. Charles and George Merriam, *The English Dictionaries of Webster and Worcester*, 12; Charles and George Merriam, *Worcester's Dictionary Published in England under the Guise of Webster's Dictionary*, 3, 5. In order to take advantage of their marketing advantage in the western parts of the country, the Merriams decided to do their advertising there first and only later in New England.

12. Worcester, *A Gross Literary Fraud Exposed*, 11.

13. Worcester, *A Gross Literary Fraud Exposed*, 13.

14. Worcester to Goodrich, October 26, 1853, cited in *A Gross Literary Fraud Exposed*, 25.

15. Goodrich to Worcester, November 2, 1853, Merriam Papers, box 10, folder 127.

16. Worcester to Goodrich, November 21, 1853, cited in Worcester, *A Gross Literary Fraud Exposed*, 26.

17. Merriam pamphlet, early December, *A Gross Literary Forgery Exposed*, 26; Worcester on the pamphlet, Worcester, *A Gross Literary Forgery Exposed*, 26.

18. Worcester to Converse, December 13, 1853, and Converse to Worcester, December 19, 1853: Merriam and both of them cited in Worcester, *A Gross Literary Fraud Exposed*, 26–27.

19. Merriams quoted in Worcester, *A Gross Literary Fraud Exposed*, 14.

20. Worcester, *A Gross Literary Fraud Exposed*, 14–15, 28, 30.

21. Worcester to Goodrich, January 31, 1854, appendix 2, *A Gross Literary Fraud Exposed*, 30.

22. Goodrich to Merriams, October 27, 1853, Merriam Papers, box 10, folder 127; Goodrich to Merriams, November 4, 1853, Merriam Papers, box 10, folder 127.

23. Goodrich to Merriams, February 17, 1854, Merriam Papers, box 10, folder 129. See Charles and George Merriam, *Worcester's Dictionary Published in England under the Guise of Webster's Dictionary*, 6.

24. Goodrich to Merriams, February 4, 1854, Merriam Papers, box 10, folder 129.

25. Goodrich to Merriams, February 4, 1854, Merriam Papers, box 10, folder 129.

26. Goodrich to Merriams, March 31, 1854, Merriam Papers, box 10, folder 129.

27. Goodrich to Merriams, May 3, 1854, Merriam Papers, box 10, folder 129; Worcester, *A Gross Literary Fraud Exposed*, "Postscript," 34.

28. Worcester to Goodrich, April 14, 1854, in *A Gross Literary Fraud Exposed*, appendix 3, 31–33.

29. Worcester, *A Gross Literary Fraud Exposed*, 34.

30. In the preceding three years, Worcester had also come out with *An Elementary Dictionary for Common Schools, with Pronouncing Vocabularies of Classical, Scripture, and Modern Geographical Names* (1850) and his "little manual" *A Primary Pronouncing Dictionary of the English Language* (1851). Both sold well.

Chapter 13

1. Sherman Converse to his son George, March 3, 1851 (found at a blog, *Spared and Shared*, belonging to "Griff," who bought the letter at an unidentified auction, http://sparedshared4 .wordpress.com/1851).

2. Converse to Worcester, December 19, 1853, in *A Gross Literary Forgery Exposed*, appendix 3, 3–4. (Worcester tacked on Converse's "Answer" at the end of appendix 3, with its own separate pagination.)

3. *A Gross Literary Fraud Exposed*, appendix 3, 33–34.

4. Converse, "Answer," 4–5.

5. For an idea of the scale of public censure of Webster up through the publication of his *Compendious Dictionary*, see Cassedy, "'A Dictionary Which We Do Not Want.'"

6. Converse, "Answer," 5–6.

7. Converse, "Answer," 6–7.

8. Converse, "Answer," 10.

9. Converse, "Answer," 10.

10. Converse to Worcester, August 30, 1854, postscript to the "Answer," *A Gross Literary Fraud Exposed*, appendix 3, 11–12. Converse's allusion to the Merriams' "dark insinuations" is in "Answer," 11.

11. Converse to Worcester, August 30, 1854, postscript to the "Answer", *A Gross Literary Fraud Exposed*, appendix 3, 12.

12. Converse to Goodrich, April 3, 1854, GFP, box 1, folder 29.

13. Goodrich to the Merriams, May 3, 1854, Merriam Papers, Box 10, folder 129.

14. G. and C. Merriam, *A Summary of the Charges with Their Refutations in Attacks upon Noah Webster, LL.D., His Dictionaries, or His Publishers, Made by Mr. Joseph Worcester, Mr. Sherman Converse, and Messrs. Jenks, Hickling, and Swan* (1854), 20. Converse to Worcester, August 30, 1854, "Answer," 12.

Chapter 14

1. Swan, *A Reply to Messrs. G. and C. Merriam's Attack on the Character of Dr. Worcester and His Dictionaries*, 14.

2. A vast amount of scholarship has been published on child development in America, but especially useful here has been Smith, *Theories of Education in Early America, 1655–1819*, chap. 13; and Volo and Volo, *Family Life in 19th-Century America*.

3. Swan, *A Reply to Messrs. G. and C. Merriam's Attack*, 16–19, 25.

4. These sales figures are drawn from tables prepared by Burkett, *American Dictionaries of the English Language before 1861*, 263–69; she compiled her figures from an appendix to the Merriams' advertising volume, *Have We a National Standard of Lexicography?*, 17–20. The sales figures reported by seventy-four book dealers across the country from March to May 1854, the same year in which Swan published his pamphlet, was bad news for Worcester and his supporters. It showed that the overwhelming majority of sales were of Webster: 2,422 to 425 in New York City (a ratio of almost six-to-one); in Philadelphia, 123 to 4 (a ratio of thirty-to-one); in Chicago, 1,650 to zero (reported); in Vicksburg, Mississippi, 55 to 1.

5. In his *Reply* to the Merriams in 1854, Swan cited their remark, "In the Empire State of New York, and at the West, Worcester is almost wholly unknown" (32).

6. Charles Merriam to Goodrich, September 5, 1853, Merriam Papers, box 10, folder 125. See Bhaskar, *The Content Machine*, 27.

7. Charles Merriam to Goodrich, September 5, 1853, Merriam Papers, box 10, folder 125.

8. Charles Merriam to Goodrich, September 5, 1853, Merriam Papers, box 10, folder 125.

9. Charles Merriam to Goodrich, September 5, 1853, Merriam Papers, box 10, folder 125.

10. See Cmiel, *Democratic Eloquence*, 86–87.

11. Swan, *A Reply to Messrs. G. and C. Merriam's Attack*, 21; Swan cited Irving's comment in this *Reply*, 30.

12. Irving to Beekman, reprinted in *A Reply to Messrs. G. and C. Merriam's Attack*, 30. See Kime, *Pierre M. Irving and Washington Irving*, 152.

13. *Daily Advertiser*, July 29 and August 5, 1853 (cited in Burkett, *American Dictionaries of the English Language before 1861*, 228–29 and 229–31, respectively).

14. *Daily Advertiser*, August 5, 1853.

15. Beekman, cited in Swan, *A Reply to Messrs. G. and C. Merriam's Attack*, 29–30.

16. Swan, *A Reply to Messrs. G. and C. Merriam's Attack*, 32.

17. Holmes, *The Professor at the Breakfast-Table*, 45.

18. Holmes, *The Autocrat of the Breakfast-Table*, 145.

19. Holmes, *The Autocrat of the Breakfast-Table*, 145; Holmes to Worcester, July 5, 1852, Massachusetts Historical Society, microfilm P-347, reel 52, p. 134.

20. Holmes, *The Professor at the Breakfast-Table*, 40–44.

21. Holmes, *The Poet at the Breakfast-Table* (reprint, Boston, 1887), 9.

22. Holmes, "To George Peabody," in *Parnassus*, ed. Ralph Waldo Emerson (Boston: Houghton, Osgood, and Co., 1880).

Chapter 15

1. Tocqueville, *Democracy in America*, 2:296. For some of the information regarding newspapers, see "American Newspapers, 1800–1860: City Newspapers," University of Illinois Library (Urbana-Champaign), video (2015).

2. *New York Times*, April 15, 1868; Gould, *Good English*; "Mr. Beecher on Newspapers," *New York Tribune*, May 19, 1879. Cmiel provides an excellent account of the social trends affecting language in mid-nineteenth-century America in *Democratic Eloquence*, chaps. 2 and 4.

3. Reprinted in Swan, *A Reply to Messrs. G. and C. Merriam's Attack*, 31.

4. Worcester, "Introduction," *Universal and Critical Dictionary*, lvii.

5. G. and C. Merriam, *Have We a National Standard of Lexicography?*, 5–16; about this pamphlet, see Higgins, *A Distinguished and Gracious New England Lexicographer*, 99–101, on which I have drawn. Friend has an account of the 1846 and 1860 Worcester editions in *The Development of American Lexicography*, 90–95, 95–103. I have referred to several examples mentioned in those pages.

6. On Stowe and the Merriams' defense of him, see Higgins, *A Distinguished and Gracious New England Lexicographer*, 101–2.

7. *Boston Post*, March 22, 1855.

8. Poole, "Battle of the Dictionaries." See also Burkett, *American Dictionaries of the English Language before 1861*, 245; and especially Higgins's summary in *A Distinguished and Gracious New England Lexicographer*, 103ff. On the growth of mercantile libraries, see Augst, "The Business of Reading in Nineteenth-Century America."

9. G. and C. Merriam, *A Summary Summing of the Charges, with Their Refutations*; *Glances at the Metropolis: A Hundred Illustrated Gems* (New York, 1854), 1—printed as a foreword

to *Dictionaries in the Boston Mercantile Library and Boston Athenaeum*, reprinted with that new title from the *Mercantile Library Reporter*. The Abigail Adams citation is taken from Jill Lepore, *The Story of America*, 132. See also Williamson, *William Frederick Poole and the Modern Library Movement*; and Poole, *Dictionaries in the Boston Mercantile Library Association and Boston Athenaeum*.

10. Worcester, *A Pronouncing, Explanatory and Synonymous Dictionary of the English Language*, 3.

11. Worcester, *Pronouncing . . . Dictionary*, 4.

12. Worcester, *Pronouncing . . . Dictionary*, 4.

13. Landau, *Dictionaries: The Art and Craft of Lexicography*, 104, 105–6. Landau notes that synonym discriminations are more difficult to prepare than thesauruses, which is why they have not been as popular as the latter. Two important books on synonyms that followed Worcester's in the late nineteenth century were Charles John Smith's *Synonyms Discriminated* and James C. Fernald's *English Synonyms and Antonyms*. Worcester's new dictionary was published just two years before—and may even have influenced—Dean Richard Chevenix Trench's game-changing call to the London Philological Society in 1857 for a dictionary (eventually named the *Oxford English Dictionary*) that paid far more attention than even Worcester's to "the distinguishing of synonymous words." For sales statistics of Worcester's dictionary, see Allibone, *A Critical Dictionary of English Literature and British and American Authors*, vol. 1.

14. Worcester, *Pronouncing . . . Dictionary*, 2, 23, 5. See also Higgins, *A Distinguished and Gracious New England Lexicographer*, 105.

15. Worcester, *Pronouncing . . . Dictionary*, 5.

16. Worcester, *Pronouncing . . . Dictionary*, 21.

17. Smart to Worcester, December 26, 1856 (letter headed, Athenaeum Club, Pall-Mall, London), Worcester Letters.

18. Gould, *Good English; or Popular Errors in Language*; Swan, *A Reply to Messrs. G. and C. Merriam's Attack upon the Character of Dr. Worcester and His Dictionaries*, 30–31.

19. Gould, "A Review of Webster's Orthography," reprinted in Swan, *Recommendations of Worcester's Dictionaries; to which is Prefixed a Review of Webster's System of Orthography from the United States Democratic Review, for March 1856*, 2.

20. Cobb to the Merriams, September 11 and 30, 1856, Merriam Papers, box 8, folder 72.

21. Higgins provides the best detailed account of Gould's attacks on Webster and Sargent's counterattacks in *A Distinguished and Gracious New England Lexicographer*, 107–16. See also Swan, *The Critic Criticized*.

22. *Vanity Fair*, March 24, 1860, 210; *Old Guard* 7 (November 1869): 876; *Knickerbocker* 60 (August 1862): 185; Bryant, *New York Evening Post*, March 22, 1856.

23. Worcester to Samuel T. Worcester, January 24, May 1, and October 17, 1859, Worcester Letters.

24. Goodrich to the Merriams, March 18, 1857, Merriam Papers, box 10, folder 131.

25. Goodrich to the Merriams, March 18, 1857, Merriam Papers, box 10, folder 131.

26. Goodrich to Charles Merriam, May 6, 1857, Merriam Papers, box 10, folder 13.

27. Charles Merriam to Goodrich, October 27, 1858, Merriam Papers, box 10, folder 132.

Chapter 16

1. Goodrich to William Webster, December 17, 1858, GFP, box 9, folder 34.
2. Gould, "Webster's Dictionary," *Home Journal* (March 1859), cited in Micklethwait, *Noah Webster and the American Dictionary*, 291–92 (also cited in Higgins, *A Distinguished and Gracious New England Lexicographer*, 121–23). "Jonathan's" letter in the *Home Journal* commending Gould's article is cited by Micklethwait, *Noah Webster and the American Dictionary*, 293.
3. Poole, *Orthographical Hobgoblin*, 5, 4.
4. Poole, *Orthographical Hobgoblin*, 7–14.
5. *Atlantic Monthly* (1859), cited by Burkett, *American Dictionaries of the English Language before 1861*, 250; Swan, *A Comparison of Worcester's and Webster's Quarto Dictionaries*, quoted by Burkett, 250; Charles Merriam, "Recollections," Merriam Papers, box 1, folder 696; B. H. Smart, August 1860, and Herbert Coleridge August 7, 1860, in "The Rival Dictionaries," *New York Times*, September 5, 1860.
6. Bosworth to Worcester, March 27, 1860, Massachusetts Historical Society, microfilm P347, reel 55. For analyses of Worcester's 1860 edition, see especially Higgins, *A Distinguished and Gracious New England Lexicographer*, 123–30; Friend, *The Development of American Lexicography 1798–1864*, 95–102; and Burkett, *American Dictionaries of the English Language before 1861*, 212–18.
7. Worcester, *Dictionary of the English Language* (1860), preface, 3; "Principles of Pronunciation," xi–xxiv.
8. *New York Times*, May 26, 1860, 9.
9. *New York Times*, May 26, 1860, 9.
10. *North American Review* 90, no. 187 (April 1860): 305, 565–66; Worcester, *Dictionary of the English Language* (1860), preface, vii.
11. Holmes to Worcester, January 10, 1860, Massachusetts Historical Society, microfilm P347, reel 55, p. 524; Quincy to Worcester, cited in Newell, "Memoir of J. E. Worcester, LL.D." Horace says of his own poetry, "I have reared (for myself) a monument (or memorial) more enduring than bronze."
12. Hawthorne to Worcester, April 14, 1861, *Select Letters of Nathaniel Hawthorne*, ed. Myerson, 236–37.
13. Carlyle, Dickens, and Thackeray to Worcester, all cited in Newell, "Memoir of J. E. Worcester, LL.D.," 173.
14. Worcester to his brother Samuel, January 24 and 28, 1859, Worcester Letters.
15. Worcester to Samuel T. Worcester, February 16 and June 26, 1862, Worcester Letters.
16. For a detailed account of this new round of attacks and counterattacks following Worcester's 1860 edition, see Higgins, *A Distinguished and Gracious New England Lexicographer*, 132–44, on which I have drawn for portions of my own briefer account.
17. Marsh, "The Two Dictionaries," *New York World*, June 15, 1860.
18. "Equal Justice" responded to Marsh in the *New York World*, September 1860; the article was reprinted by the Merriams in *Two Dictionaries: or The Reviewer Reviewed* and quoted by them, 3–4, 5–6, 7, 13, 15.
19. Worcester to Samuel T. Worcester, August 6, 1860, Worcester Letters.

20. Swan, *The Critic Criticized and Worcester Vindicated*. Swan's essay is discussed in Higgins, *A Distinguished and Gracious New England Lexicographer*, 133–41.

21. Agassiz quoted in Swan, *A Comparison of Worcester's and Webster's Quarto Dictionaries*, 22.

22. *Atlantic Monthly* 5 (May 1860): 631; Wheatley, "Chronological Notices of Dictionaries of the English Language"; *Athenaeum*, October 1873, 48.

23. Green, *Chasing the Sun*, 275.

24. For sales figures, see Burkett, *American Dictionaries of the English Language before 1861*, 263–72.

25. Worcester to Samuel T. Worcester, April 16, 1865, Worcester Letters. See also Faust, *The Republic of Suffering*.

26. Worcester's dictionaries, largely unrevised, were left to make their lonely way in the world and pretty well disappeared except for editions of his *Comprehensive Dictionary* in 1871; *The Universal and Critical Dictionary* in 1874; his magnum opus, *A Dictionary of the English Language*, in 1881, 1886, 1908; more recently (with supplement) his *Academic Dictionary: A New Etymological Dictionary of the English Language* in 1888 and 1910; and his *New School Dictionary* in 1926.

27. Lippincott to Stewart Archer Steger, quoted in Steger's book, *American Dictionaries*, 82.

28. Abbot, "Joseph Emerson Worcester," 114–15.

29. "President's Remarks on Dr. Worcester," *Proceedings of the Massachusetts Historical Society* 8 (November 1864–65): 467–68.

Chapter 17

1. Goodrich to the Merriams, January 1860, Merriam Papers, box 10, folder 134.

2. Porter to the Merriams, February 3, 1860, Merriam Papers, box 13, folder 249.

3. Goodrich to the Merriams, January 26, 1860, Merriam Papers, box 10, folder 133.

4. Dexter is quoted in "Chauncey Allen Goodrich: Yale's Professor of Compassion and Revival," *Yale Standard*, February 26, 2012, 7; Woolsey, "A Discourse Commemorative of the Life and Service of the Rev. Chauncey Allen Goodrich."

5. William Adolpus Wheeler to the Merriams, November 29, 1860, Merriam Papers, box 17, folder 349.

6. Merriams to Wheeler, February 20, 1862, Merriam Papers, box 17, folder 357.

7. See Winchester, *The Professor and the Madman*; Kendall, "A Minor Exception"; and Kendall, "Redefining Webster's" (mainly on Gilbert).

8. Charles Merriam, "Recollections," Merriam Papers, box 101, folder 696. For details regarding the stereotyping and publication process of the 1864 edition, see Madeline Kripke, "Guest Post: 'Get the Best': Bringing a Dictionary to Market in 1864," Merriam-Webster Unabridged, November 20, 2014, http://unabridged.merriam-webster.com/blog/2014/11/guest-post-get-the-best-bringing-a-dictionary-to-market-in-1864. Madeline Kripke owns a vast personal collection of nineteenth-century archives and private papers of the G. & C. Merriam Company, as well as one of the largest collections of dictionaries of English in the world.

9. "Thank God for Worcester": see Merriam Papers, box 95, folder 681; Porter, preface, *An American Dictionary of the English Language* (1864; rev. and enlarged ed., 1874), v.

10. Porter, preface, *An American Dictionary of the English Language*, iii, v, iii, viii.

11. Leavitt, *Noah's Ark, New England Yankees, and the Endless Quest*, 54. See also Deppman, *Trying to Think with Emily Dickinson*, 113. Deppman's book is an insightful look at how the definitions of words were at the center of much of Dickinson's poetry, and (more specifically) how the 1844 edition of Webster's dictionary, like the King James Bible, is "an important source for reading Emily Dickinson's life and work."

12. Emerson to the Merriams, August 21, 1864, Merriam Papers, box 9, folder 102; Longfellow to the Merriams, August 17, 1878, Merriam Papers, box 12, folder 202; Whittier to the Merriams, November 10, 1878 (quoted in Leavitt, *Noah's Ark, New England Yankees, and the Endless Quest*, 66).

13. Twain (Samuel Clemens) to the Merriams, March 1891, Merriam Papers, box 8, folder 70.

14. Whitman, *An American Primer*, 30.

15. Grant, quoted in Leavitt, *Noah's Ark, New England Yankees, and the Endless Quest*, 65.

16. "English Dictionaries," *London Quarterly Review*, October 1873, quoted in *Noah's Ark, New England Yankees, and the Endless Quest*, 69.

17. George Merriam to Charles Merriam, November 19, 1844, Merriam Papers, box 12, folder 219.

Appendix A

1. Quoted by Micklethwait, *Noah Webster and the American Dictionary*, 305. For a brief but clear account of the complicated legislation relating to the Merriam brand, see 307.

2. On the Webster name, see Micklethwait, *Noah Webster and the American Dictionary*, 299–308.

3. Foreword, *Webster's New World Dictionary of the American Language*, vii.

Bibliography

Note: A chronological selection of dictionaries of English may be found in appendix B.

I. Works Cited and Consulted

Abbot, Ezra. "Joseph Emerson Worcester." *Proceedings of the American Academy of Arts and Sciences* 7 (May 1865–May 1868): 112–16.

Adams, John. *The Works of John Adams*. 10 vols. Edited by Charles F. Adams. Vol. 9, *Letters and State Papers, 1799–1811*. Boston: Little, Brown and Co., 1856.

Andresen, Julie Tetel. *Linguistics in America 1769–1924: A Critical History*. London: Routledge, 2006.

Bailey, Richard W. *Nineteenth-Century English*. Ann Arbor: University of Michigan Press, 1997.

Basker, James. "Samuel Johnson and the American Common Reader." *Age of Johnson: A Scholarly Annual* 6 (1994): 3–30.

———. *Samuel Johnson in the Mind of Thomas Jefferson*. Charlottesville: University of Virginia Press, 1999.

Béjoint, Henri. *The Lexicography of English: From Origins to Present*. Oxford: Oxford University Press, 2010.

Belknap, Jeremy. *Correspondence between Jeremy Belknap and Ebenezer Hazard*. Massachusetts Historical Society Collections: Jeremy Belknap Papers. Boston: The Society, 1877.

Boorstin, Daniel J. *The Americans: The National Experience*. New York: Random House, 1965. Reprint, New York: History Book Club, 2002.

Boswell, James. *The Life of Samuel Johnson* (1791). Edited by George Birkbell Hill. Revised and enlarged by L. F. Powell. Vol. 3, *1776–1780*. Oxford: Oxford University Press, 1979.

Boucher, Jonathan. *Boucher's Glossary of Archaic and Provincial Words: A Supplement to the Dictionaries of the English Language, Particularly Those of Dr. Johnson and Dr. White*. Edited by Joseph Hunter and Joseph Stevens. London: Black, Young, and Young, 1832–33.

Bracha, Oren. "The Ideology of Authorship Revisited: Authors, Markets, and Liberal Values in Early American Copyright." *Yale Law Review* 118, no. 2 (November 2008): 186–271.

Brackenridge, Hugh Henry. *Modern Chivalry, Containing the Adventures of Captain Farrago and Teague O'Regan*. Pittsburgh, PA, 1819.

Bristed, John. *The Resources of the United States of America; or, A View of the Agricultural, Commercial, Financial, Political, Literary, Moral and Religious Capacity and Character of the American People*. New York: James Eastburn and Co., 1818.

Buinicki, Martin T. *Negotiating Copyright: Authorship and the Discourse of Literary Rights in Nineteenth-Century America.* New York: Routledge, 2003.

Burkett, Eva Mae. *American Dictionaries of the English Language before 1861.* Metuchen, NJ: Scarecrow Press, 1979.

Butler, Marilyn. *John Horne Tooke, Burke, Paine, Godwin, and the Revolution Controversy.* Cambridge: Cambridge University Press, 1984.

Bynack, Vincent P. "Noah Webster's Linguistic Thought and the Idea of an American National Culture." *Journal of the History of Ideas* 45 (1984): 99–114.

Cassedy, Tim. "'A Dictionary Which We Do Not Want': Defining America against Noah Webster, 1783–1810." *William and Mary Quarterly*, 3rd ser., 71, no. 2 (April 2014): 229–54.

Channing, William Ellery. *The Importance and Means of a National Literature.* London: Edward Rainford, 1830.

Cheever, Susan. *American Bloomsbury: Louisa May Alcott, Ralph Waldo Emerson, Margaret Fuller, Nathaniel Hawthorne, and Henry David Thoreau: Their Lives, Their Loves, Their Work.* Detroit, MI: Thorndike Press, 2006.

Cmiel, Kenneth. "'A Broad Fluid Language of Democracy': Discovering the American Idiom." *Journal of American History* 79, no. 3 (December 1992): 913–36.

———. *Democratic Eloquence: The Fight over Popular Speech in Nineteenth-Century America.* New York: William Morrow, 1990.

Cobb, Lyman. *A Critical Review of the Orthography of Dr. Webster's Series of Books for Systematick Instruction in the English Language Including His Former Spelling-Book and the Elementary Spelling-Book.* New York: Collins and Hannay, 1831.

Cooper, James Fenimore. *The American Democrat* (1838). Edited by George Dekker and Larry D. Johnston. Baltimore, MD: Penguin Books, 1969.

———. *Notions of the Americans, Picked up by a Travelling Bachelor* (1828). 2 vols. Philadelphia: Carey, Lea, and Blanchard, 1835.

———. *Satanstoe; or, The Littlepage Manuscripts: A Tale of the Colony.* Albany: State University of New York Press, 1990.

Cresswell, Nicholas. *The Journal of Nicholas Cresswell 1774–77, with a Preface by S. Thornely.* New York: Dial Press, 1924.

DeMaria, Robert, Jr., and Gwin Kolb, eds. *Johnson on the English Language.* Vol. 18 of *The Yale Edition of the Works of Samuel Johnson.* New Haven, CT: Yale University Press, 2005.

Dexter, Franklin B. "Chauncey Allen Goodrich: Yale's Professor of Compassion and Revival." *Yale Standard*, February 26, 2012.

Dexter, Henry M. Editorial. *Congregationalist*, January 27, 1860.

Draper, L. C., ed. "Eulogies on James Gates Percival." *Collections of the Historical Society of Wisconsin* 3 (1904): 66–80.

Dwight, Timothy. *Remarks on the Review of Inchiquin's Letters.* Boston: Samuel T. Armstrong, 1815.

Eaton, Joseph. *The Anglo-American Paper War: Debates about the New Republic.* New York: Palgrave Macmillan, 2012.

———. "From Anglophile to Nationalist: Robert Walsh's *An Appeal from the Judgments of Great Britain.*" *Pennsylvania Magazine of History and Biography* 132, no. 2 (April 2008): 141–71.

Edwards, Lester C. *Glances at the Metropolis: A Hundred Illustrated Gems*. New York: Isaac D. Guyer, 1854.

Emerson, Ralph Waldo. *The Collected Works of Ralph Waldo Emerson: Nature, Addresses, and Lectures*. Edited by Robert E. Spiller and Alfred R. Ferguson. Cambridge, MA: Harvard University Press, 1971.

"Equal Justice." *Two Dictionaries: or, The Reviewer Reviewed; A Reply to a Correspondent of the New York World*. Springfield, MA: G. and C. Merriam, 1860.

Everett, Edward. "England and America." *North American Review* 13 (1821).

———. "Mr. Walsh's Appeal." *North American Review* 10 (April 1820).

Fischer, Henry W. *Abroad with Mark Twain and Eugene Field: Tales They Told to a Fellow Correspondent*. New York: N. L. Brown, 1922.

Ford, Emily Ellsworth Fowler. *Notes on the Life of Noah Webster*. Edited by Emily Ellsworth Ford Skeel. 2 vols. New York: privately printed, 1912.

Fowler, William C. "American Dialects." In *The English Language in Its Elements and Forms*. New York: Harper and Bros., 1850.

———. *Printed, but Not Published*. Noah Webster Papers, New York Public Library, Mss Col. 3250, vol. 13, no. 7.

Franklin, Benjamin. *Papers of Benjamin Franklin*. Vol. 4. New Haven, CT: Yale University Press, 1961.

Friend, Joseph H. *The Development of American Lexicography, 1798–1864*. The Hague: Mouton, 1967.

Garnett, Richard. "English Lexicography." In *The Philological Essays of the Late Rev. Richard Garnett*, edited by his son. London: Williams and Norgate, 1859.

Goodrich, S. G. *Recollections of a Lifetime*. New York: Miller, Orton and Mulligan, 1856.

Gordon, Lord Adam. *Journal of an Officer Who Travelled in America and the West Indies in 1764 and 1765*. In *Travels in the American Colonies*, edited by Newton D. Mereness. New York: Macmillan, 1916.

Gould, Edward. *Good English; or Popular Errors in Language*. New York: W. J. Widdleton, 1867.

———. "A Review of Webster's Orthography." *Democratic Review* 39 (March 1856). Reprinted in Swan, *Recommendations of Worcester's Dictionaries; to Which Is Prefixed a Review of Webster's System of Orthography from the United States Democratic Review, for March 1856*. Boston: Hickling, Swan, and Brown, 1856.

———. "Webster's Dictionary," *Home Journal*, March 19, 1859.

———. "Worcester's Dictionaries." In *A Reply to Messrs. G. and C. Merriam's Attack upon the Character of Dr. Worcester and His Dictionaries*. Boston: Jenks, Hickling, and Swan, 1854.

Green, Jonathon. *Chasing the Sun: Dictionary-Makers and the Dictionaries They Made*. London: Jonathan Cape, 1996. Reprint, London: Random House, 1997.

Grugg, F. W. "Growth of Literacy in Colonial America: Longitudinal Patterns, Economic Models, and the Direction of Future Research." *Social Science History* 14, no. 4 (1990): 451–82.

Hall, Basil. *Travels in North America in the Years 1827 and 1828*. 3 vols. 2nd ed. Edinburgh: Cadell and Co.; London: Simkin and Marshall, 1830.

Hallen, Cynthia L., and Tray B. Spackman. "Biblical Citations as a Stylistic Standard in Johnson's and Webster's Dictionaries." *Lexis* 5 (2010): 1–56.

Hamilton, Thomas. *Men and Manners in America*. Philadelphia: Carey, Lea, and Blanchard, 1833.

Harte, Bret. *The Works of Bret Harte*. Argonaut ed., vol. 8. New York: P. F. Collier, 1914, by special arrangement with Houghton Mifflin.

Hawthorne, Nathaniel. *Passages from English Note-Books*. 2 vols. London: James R. Osgood and Co., 1876.

Hayashi, Tetsuro. *The Theory of English Lexicography 1530–1791*. Amsterdam: John Benjamins, 1978.

Higgins, Matthew. *A Distinguished and Gracious New England Lexicographer*. Concord, NH: Duncross Books, 2007.

Higginson, Thomas Wentworth. *Old Cambridge*. New York: Macmillan, 1899.

———. *Outdoor Studies Poems*. Cambridge, MA: Riverside Press, 1888, 1900.

Holmes, Oliver Wendell. *The Autocrat of the Breakfast-Table*. Boston: Phillips, Sampson and Co., 1858.

———. *The Poet at the Breakfast-Table*. Boston: James R. Osgood and Co., 1872. Reprint, Boston: Houghton-Mifflin, 1887.

———. *The Professor at the Breakfast-Table*. Boston: Ticknor and Fields, 1860.

Horne Tooke, John. *Diversions of Purley*. London: Thomas Tegg, 1786 (part 1), 1805 (part 2); first American ed., Philadelphia: William Duane, 1806–7.

Irving, Washington. *The Sketch Book of Geoffrey Crayon, Gent*. New York: C. S. Van Winkle, 1819–20.

Jefferson, Thomas. *The Adams-Jefferson Letters: The Complete Correspondence between Jefferson and Abigail and John Adams*. Edited by Lester J. Cappon. Chapel Hill: University of North Carolina Press, 1959 (later ed., 1988).

———. *The Papers of Thomas Jefferson*. Retirement Series. Edited by J. Jefferson Looney. Princeton, NJ: Princeton University Press, 2012.

———. *The Writings of Thomas Jefferson*. Vol. 6. Edited by Andrew A. Lipscomb and Albert Ellery Bergh. Washington, DC: Thomas Jefferson Memorial Association of the United States, 1903.

Johnson, Samuel. *The Dictionary of the English Language*. 2 vols. London: J. and P. Knapton et al., 1755.

———. "Review of Lewis Evans, *Analysis of a General Map of the Middle British Colonies in America*." *Literary Magazine* 1, no. 6 (September 15–October 15, 1756). Reprinted in Donald J. Greene, ed., *Political Writings*, vol. 10 of *The Yale Edition of the Works of Samuel Johnson*. New Haven, CT: Yale University Press, 1977.

Jones, Sir William. *The Works of Sir William Jones*. London: G. G. and J. Robinson, 1799.

Katula, Richard. *The Eloquence of Edward Everett: America's Greatest Orator*. New York: Peter Lang, 2010.

Kendall, Joshua. *The Forgotten Founding Father: Noah Webster's Obsession and the Creation of an American Culture*. New York: G. P. Putnam's Sons, 2011.

———. "A Minor Exception: On W. C. Minor and Noah Webster." *Nation*, April 4, 2011.

———. "Redefining Webster's." *Johns Hopkins Magazine*, March 2011.

Kent, James. "Anniversary Address to the Phi Beta Kappa Society Chapter of Connecticut," in *Dictionaries in the Boston Mercantile Library and Boston Athenaeum*, 1856.

Kime, Wayne R. *Pierre M. Irving and Washington Irving: A Collaboration in Life and Letters.* Waterloo, ON: Wilfred Laurier University Press, 1977.

Kirkman, Samuel. *English Grammar in Familiar Lessons.* Lecture 1. New York: Robert B. Collins, 1829.

Krapp, George Philip. *The English Language in America.* 2 vols. New York: Frederick Ungar, 1925.

Landau, Sidney I. *Dictionaries: The Art and Craft of Lexicography.* Cambridge: Cambridge University Press, 1989.

———. "Johnson's Influence on Webster and Worcester in Early American Lexicography." *International Journal of Lexicography* 18, no. 2 (June 2005): 217–29.

Lang, Andrew. "Americanisms." Letter (February 23, 1895) to *Academy*, March 2, 1895, 193.

Leach, James F. "A Stabilizing Influence: The 'War of the Dictionaries,' 1848–1861." Master's thesis, University of Massachusetts, 1996.

Leavitt, Robert Keith. *Noah's Ark, New England Yankees, and the Endless Quest: A Short History of the Original Webster Dictionaries, with Particular Reference to Their First Hundred Years as Publications of G. and C. Merriam Co.* Springfield, MA: G. and C. Merriam Co., 1947.

———. *100th Anniversary of the Establishment of the G. and C. Merriam Company, 1831–1931.* Springfield, MA: G. and C. Merriam, 1931.

Lepore, Jill. *A Is for American: Letters and Other Characters in the Newly United States.* New York: Alfred A. Knopf, 2002.

———. "Introduction." In Arthur Schulman, *Websterisms: A Collection of Words and Definitions Set Forth by the Founding Father of American English.* New York: Free Press, 2008.

———. "Noah's Mark: Webster and the Original Dictionary Wars." *New Yorker*, November 6, 2006.

———. *The Story of America.* Princeton, NJ: Princeton University Press, 2012.

Lodge, Henry Cabot. "Colonialism in the United States." In *Studies in History.* Boston: Houghton, Mifflin and Co., 1884.

Logan, Conrad T. "Noah Webster's Influence on American Spelling." *Elementary English Review* 14, no. 1 (January 1937): 18–21.

Long, Orie William. *Literary Pioneers: Early American Explorers of European Culture.* Cambridge, MA: Harvard University Press, 1935.

Long, Percy W. "English Dictionaries before Webster." *Bibliographical Society of America, Papers* 4 (1909): 25–43.

Longfellow, Henry Wadsworth. *The Letters of Henry Wadsworth Longfellow.* Edited by Andrew Hilen. Cambridge, MA: Harvard University Press, 1982.

Longmore, Paul K. "'They . . . Speak Better English Than the English Do': Colonialism and the Origins of National Linguistic Standardization in America." *Early American Literature* 40, no. 2 (2005): 279–314.

Lowndes, W. T. *The Bibliographer's Manual of English Literature.* Revised by Henry G. Bohn. London, 1864.

Lynch, Jack. "Every Man Able to Read: Literacy in Early America." *Colonial Williamsburg Foundation Journal* (Winter 2011): 24–29.

———. *The Lexicographer's Dilemma: The Evolution of "Proper" English from Shakespeare to South Park.* New York: Walker, 2009.

Mactaggart, John. *Three Years in Canada*. 2 vols. London: Henry Colburn, 1829.

Marryat, Frederick. *A Diary in America: With Remarks on Its Institutions*. New York: William H. Colyer, 1839.

Martineau, Harriet. *Society in America*. 2 vols. London: Saunders and Otley, 1837.

Mathews, M. M., ed. *The Beginnings of American English: Essays and Comments* (1931). Chicago: University of Chicago Press, 1963.

Matthews, James W. "Fallen Angel: Emerson and the Apostasy of Edward Everett." *Studies in the American Renaissance* (1990): 23–32.

McArthur, Tom. *Living Words: Language, Lexicography and the Knowledge Revolution*. Exeter, UK: University of Exeter Press, 1998.

Mencken, H. L. *The American Language: An Inquiry into the Development of English in the United States* (1919). 4th ed. New York: Alfred A. Knopf, 1937.

Merriam, G. and C. *The English Dictionaries of Webster and Worcester, May 1853*. Springfield, MA: G. and C. Merriam Co., 1853.

———. *A Gross Literary Fraud Exposed; Relating to the Publication of Worcester's Dictionary in London, as Webster's Dictionary*. Springfield, MA: G. and C. Merriam Co., 1854.

———. *Have We a National Standard of Lexicography? Or, Some Comparisons of the Claims of Webster's Dictionaries, and Worcester's Dictionaries*. Springfield, MA: G. and C. Merriam Co., 1854.

———. *A Summary Summing of the Charges, with Their Refutations, in Attacks upon Noah Webster, LL.D., His Dictionaries, or His Publishers, Made by Mr. Joseph Worcester, Mr. Sherman Converse, and Messrs. Jenks, Hickling, and Swan*. Springfield, MA: G. and C. Merriam Co., 1854.

———. *Worcester's Dictionary Published in England under the Guise of Webster's Dictionary*. Springfield, MA: G. and C. Merriam, 1853.

Merriam, Homer. "My Father's History and Family." Annals of the Merriam Family, Merriam Papers, Beinecke Rare Book and Manuscript Library, Yale University.

Mesick, Jane Louise. *The English Traveller in America 1785–1835*. New York: Columbia University Press, 1922.

Micklethwait, David. *Noah Webster and the American Dictionary*. Jefferson, NC: McFarland, 2000.

Miles, Edwin A. "William Allen and the Webster-Worcester Dictionary Wars." *Dictionaries: Journal of the Dictionary Society of North America* 13 (1991): 1–15.

Miyoshi, Kusujiro. *Johnson and Webster's Verbal Examples: With Special Reference to Exemplifying Usage in Dictionary Entries*. Tübingen: Max Niemeyer Verlag, 2007.

Monaghan, Charles. "Lyman Cobb and the British Elocutionary Tradition." *Paradigm: Journal of the British Text Book Colloquium* 2, no. 7 (December 2003).

———. *The Murrays of Murray Hill*. Brooklyn, NY: Urban History Press, 1998.

Monaghan, E. Jennifer. *A Common Heritage: Noah Webster's Blue-Back Speller*. Hamden, CT: Archon Books, 1983.

———. *Learning to Read and Write in Colonial America*. Amherst: University of Massachusetts Press, 2005.

Moore, Margaret M. *The Salem World of Nathaniel Hawthorne*. Columbia: University of Missouri Press, 1998.

Mott, Frank Luther. *A History of American Magazines: 1741–1850*. Vol. 1. Cambridge, MA: Harvard University Press, 1930.

Mugglestone, Lynda. *Lost for Words: The Hidden History of the Oxford English Dictionary*. New Haven, CT: Yale University Press, 2005.

Murray, K. M. Elisabeth. *Caught in the Web of Words: James Murray and the Oxford English Dictionary*. New Haven, CT: Yale University Press, 1977.

Myerson, Joel, ed. *Select Letters of Nathaniel Hawthorne*. Columbus: Ohio State University Press, 2002.

National Portrait Gallery of Distinguished Americans. Vol. 2 (containing "Noah Webster"). Edited by James B. Longacre and James Herring. Philadelphia: Henry Perkins, 1835.

Nevins, Allan. *American Social History as Recorded by British Travelers*. New York: Holt and Co., 1923.

Newell, William. "Memoir of J. E. Worcester, LL.D." *Proceedings of the Massachusetts Historical Society* 14 (1880–81): 173.

Paine, Thomas. "A Letter Addressed to the Abbe Raynal, on the Affairs of North-America." London: J. Ridgwauy, 1791.

Papers of the Continental Congress, 1774–1789. Washington, DC: National Archives.

Pelanda, Brian. "Declarations of Cultural Independence: The Nationalistic Imperative behind the Passage of Early American Copyright Laws, 1783–1787." *Journal of the Copyright Society of the U.S.A.* 58 (2011): 431–54.

Percy, Carol. "*Plane* English; or, The Orthography of Opposition in Mid-Eighteenth-Century Britain." *Age of Johnson: A Scholarly Annual* 15 (2004): 223–68.

———. "Political Perspectives on Linguistic Innovation in Independent America: Learning from the Libraries of Thomas Jefferson (1743–1826)." In *Transatlantic Perspectives on Late Modern English*, edited by Marina Dossena, 37–53. Amsterdam: John Benjamins, 2015.

Pickering, John. *Vocabulary: or, Collection of Words and Phrases, Which Have Been Supposed to Be Peculiar to the United States of America*. Boston: Cummings and Hilliard, 1816.

Pickering, Mary Orne. *Life of John Pickering*. Boston: privately printed, 1887.

Pickering, Octavius. *The Life of Timothy Pickering*. Boston: Little, Brown, and Co., 1867.

Poole, William F. "Battle of the Dictionaries." *Mercantile Library Reporter* (1855): 69–72.

———. *Dictionaries in the Boston Mercantile Library Association and Boston Athenaeum*. Boston: Damrell and Moore, 1850.

———. *The Orthographical Hobgoblin*. Springfield, MA: G. and C. Merriam, 1859.

Porter, Noah. "Lexicography." *Bibliotheca Sacra* 20, no. 77 (January 1863): 78–123.

Prior, Matthew. *A Life of the Right Honourable Edmund Burke*. 5th ed. London: H. G. Bohn, 1854.

Read, Allen Walker. "Amphi-Atlantic English." In *Milestones in the History of English in America*, edited by Richard W. Bailey, 55–82. Durham, NC: Duke University Press for the American Dialect Society, 2002.

———. "British Recognition of American Speech in the Eighteenth Century." In *Perspectives on American English*, edited by Joey Lee Dillard. The Hague: Mouton, 1980. Reprinted in Bailey, *Milestones in the History of English in America*, 37–54.

———. "The Development of Faith in the Dictionary in America." *Publications of the Modern Language Association of America* 49 (1934): 1295–336.

———. "Dictionaries." In *The New Encyclopedia Britannica*. 15th ed. Chicago: Encyclopaedia Britannica, Inc., 1974. Updated for the 2007 ed.

———. "Edward Everett's Attitude towards American English," *New England Quarterly* 12, no. 1 (March 1939): 112–29.

———. "Milestones in the Branching of British and American English." In Bailey, *Milestones in the History of English in America*, 4–21.

———. "The Spread of German Linguistic Learning in New England during the Lifetime of Noah Webster." *American Speech* 41 (1967): 163–81.

———. "Suggestions for an Academy in England in the Latter Half of the Eighteenth Century." *Modern Philology* 36, no. 2 (November 1938): 145–56.

———. "The War of the Dictionaries in the Middle West." In *Papers on Lexicography, in Honor of Warren N. Cordell*, edited by J. E. Congleton, J. Edward Gates, and Donald Hobar, 3–16. Terre Haute, IN: Dictionary Society of North America, 1979.

Reed, Joseph W. "Noah Webster's Debt to Samuel Johnson." *American Speech* 37, no. 2 (May 1962): 95–105.

Reef, Catherine. *Education and Learning in America*. New York: Facts on File, 2009.

———. *Noah Webster: Man of Many Words*. New York: Houghton Mifflin Harcourt/Clarion Books, 2015.

Reid, Ronald. *Edward Everett: Unionist Orator*. New York: Greenwood Press, 1990.

Richardson, Charles. *A New Dictionary of the English Language*. London: William Pickering, 1837.

———. Review, "An American Dictionary of the English Language." *Westminster Review* 27 (1831): 82.

Robinson, Fred C. "Noah Webster as Etymologist." *Neuphilologische Mitteilungen* 111, no. 2 (January 2010): 167–74.

Rollins, Richard M., ed. *The Autobiographies of Noah Webster: From the Letters and Essays, Memoir, and Diary*. Columbia: University of South Carolina Press, 1989.

———. *The Long Journey of Noah Webster*. Philadelphia: University of Pennsylvania Press, 1980.

Sargent, Epes. "The Critic Criticized: A Reply to a Review of Webster's System in the Democratic Review for March, 1856." *Democratic Review*, June 1856.

Schulman, Arthur. *Websterisms: A Collection of Words and Definitions Set Forth by the Founding Father of American English*. Introduction by Jill Lepore. New York: Simon and Schuster/ Free Press, 2008.

Schweiger, Beth Barton. "A Social History of English Grammar in the Early United States." *Journal of the Early Republic* 30, no. 4 (Winter 2010): 533–55.

Scudder, Horace E. *Noah Webster* (1881). 2nd ed. Cambridge, MA: Houghton, Mifflin, and Co., 1890.

Sheldon, Esther K. "Walker's Influence on the Pronunciation of English." *Publications of the Modern Language Association* 62, no. 1 (March 1947): 130–46.

Shoemaker, Ervin C. *Noah Webster: Pioneer of Learning*. New York: Columbia University Press, 1936.

Simpson, David. *The Politics of American English, 1776–1850*. New York: Oxford University Press, 1986.

Sledd, James H., and Gwin J. Kolb. *Dr. Johnson's Dictionary: Essays in the Biography of a Book.* Chicago: University of Chicago Press, 1955.

Smith, Wilson. *Theories of Education in Early America, 1655–1819.* New York: Bobbs-Merrill, 1973.

Snyder, Alan I. *Defining Noah Webster: A Spiritual Biography.* Washington DC: Allegiance Press, 2002.

Soltow, Lee, and Edward Stevens. *The Rise of Literacy and the Common School in the United States: A Socio-Economic Analysis to 1870.* Chicago: University of Chicago Press, 1991.

Starnes, De Witt T., and Gertrude E. Noyes. *The English Dictionary from Cawdrey to Johnson 1604–1755.* Chapel Hill: University of North Carolina Press, 1946. Republished in the series Studies in the History of the Language Sciences, no. 57. Amsterdam: John Benjamins, 1991.

Steger, Stewart Archer. *American Dictionaries.* Baltimore, MD: J. H. Furst Co., 1913.

Swan, William Draper. *A Comparison of Worcester's and Webster's Quarto Dictionaries, also Specimen Pages of Worcester's Quarto Dictionary, Recommendations from Eminent Scholars, and Reviews from Leading Periodicals, American and Foreign.* Boston: Swan, Brewer, and Tileson, n.d. [1860?].

———. *The Critic Criticized and Worcester Vindicated: Consisting of a Review in the "Congregationalist," upon the Comparative Merits of Worcester's and Webster's Quarto Dictionaries, Together with a Reply to the Attacks of Messrs. G. & C. Merriam upon the Character of Dr. Worcester and His Dictionaries.* Boston: Swan, Brewer, and Tileson, 1860.

———. *Recommendations of Worcester's Dictionaries; to Which Is Prefixed a Review of Webster's System of Orthography from the United States Democratic Review, for March 1856.* Boston: Hickling, Swan, and Brown, 1856.

———. *A Reply to Messrs. G. and C. Merriam's Attack upon the Character of Dr. Worcester and His Dictionaries.* Boston: Jenks, Hickling, and Swan, 1854.

———. "Worcester's Dictionaries." In *A Reply to Messrs. G. and C. Merriam's Attack upon the Character of Dr. Worcester and His Dictionaries.* Boston: Jenks, Hickling, and Swan, 1854.

Tamarkin, Elisa. *Anglophilia: Deference, Devotion, and Antebellum America.* Chicago: University of Chicago Press, 2008.

Taylor, Alan. *Writing Early American History.* Philadelphia: University of Pennsylvania Press, 2005.

Tharp, Louise Hall. *The Appletons of Beacon Hill.* Boston: Little Brown, 1973.

Ticknor, George. *Life, Letters, and Journals of George Ticknor.* Edited by George Stillman Hillard and Anna Eliot Ticknor. 2 vols. London: Samson, Low, Marston, Searle, and Rivington, 1876; Boston, 1881.

Tocqueville, Alexis de. *Democracy in America* (1840). Edited by Eduardo Nolla. Translated by James T. Schleifer. Vol. 2 of 4 vols. Indianapolis, IN: Liberty Fund, 2010.

Trench, Richard Chevenix. "On Some Deficiencies in Our English Dictionaries." Two lectures delivered to the London Philological Society, November 5 and 19, 1857, published as *Transactions of the Philological Society* (London, 1857; 2nd edition, 1860).

Trollope, Anthony. *North America* (1862). Reprint, New York: Harper and Brothers, 1962.

Trollope, Frances. *Domestic Manners of the Americans.* 2 vols. London: Whittaker, Treacher, and Co., 1832; 5th ed., 1839.

Unger, Harlow Giles. *Family Life in 19th-Century America.* Westport, CT: Greenwood Press, 2007.

———. *Noah Webster: The Life and Times of an American Patriot*. New York: John Wiley and Sons, 1998.

Ward, Julius H., *The Life and Letters of James Gates Percival*. Boston: Ticknor and Fields, 1866.

Warfel, Harry R., ed. *Letters of Noah Webster*. New York: Library Publishers, 1953; new ed., 1966.

———. *Noah Webster: Schoolmaster to America*. New York: Macmillan, 1936.

Webster, Noah. *The American Spelling Book*. Hartford, CT: Hudson and Goodwin, 1789.

———. *A Collection of Essays and Fugitiv Writings*. Boston: I. Thomas and E. T. Andrews, 1790.

———. *Dissertations on the English Language*. Boston: printed for author, 1789.

———. *The Elementary Spelling Book: Being An Improvement on the American Spelling Book*. Wells River, VT: White and Wilcox, 1831. Another ed., Portland, ME: Sanborn and Carter, ca. 1843.

———. *A Grammatical Institute of the English Language: . . . in Three Parts*. Parts 1 and 2: Hartford, CT: Hudson and Goodwin 1783, 1784; part 3: Hartford, CT: Barlow and Babcock, 1785.

———, ed. *The Holy Bible, Containing the Old and New Testaments, in the Common Version with Amendments of the Language*. New Haven, CT: Durrie & Peck, sold by Hezekiah Howe & Co., and by N. & J. White, 1833.

———. *Instructive and Entertaining Lessons for Youth*. New Haven, CT: Babcock and Durrie and Peck, 1835.

———. *A Letter to the Honorable John Pickering, on the Subject of His Vocabulary; or, Collection of Words and Phrases, Supposed to be Peculiar to the United States of America*. Privately circulated. Printed in Warfel, *Letters of Noah Webster*, 341–94.

———. *Mistakes and Corrections*. New Haven, CT: B. L. Hamlin, 1837.

———. *Observations on Language, Addressed to the Members of the Mercantile Library Association*. New Haven, CT: Babcock and Durrie and Peck, 1839.

———. "Revolution in France" (1794). Reprinted in *A Collection of Papers on Political, Literary, and Moral Subjects*. New York: Webster and Clark, 1843.

Wells, Ronald A. *Dictionaries and the Authoritarian Tradition: A Study in English Usage and Lexicography*. The Hague: Mouton, 1973.

White, Richard Grant. *England without and Within*. London: Samson, Low, Marston, Searle, and Rivington; Boston: Houghton Mifflin, 1881.

———. *Words and Their Uses, Past and Present: A Study of the English Language*. New York: Sheldon and Co., 1871.

Whitman, Walt. *An American Primer*. Edited by Horace Traubel. Boston: The University Press, 1904.

———. "American Slang." *North American Review*, November 1885.

———. *New York Dissected*. Edited by Emory Holloway and Ralph Adimari. New York: Rufus Rockwell Wilson, 1936.

———. *November Boughs*. Philadelphia: David Mackay, 1888.

Williamson, John H. *Casualties of War*. Master's thesis, Harvard University, 1999.

Williamson, William Landram. *William Frederick Poole and the Modern Library Movement*. Columbia University Studies in Library Service, no. 13. New York: Columbia University Press, 1963.

Willis, N. P. *Pencillings by the Way*. London: John Macrone, 1835.

Winchester, Simon. *The Professor and the Madman: A Tale of Murder, Insanity, and the Making of the* Oxford English Dictionary. New York: Harper Collins, 1998.

Witherspoon, John. "Druid." *Pennsylvania Journal and Weekly Advertiser*, nos. 5–7 (May 9, 16, 23, and 30, 1781). Reprinted in *The Beginnings of American English*, edited by Mitford M. Mathews, 13–30. Chicago: University of Chicago Press, 1963.

Woolsey, Thomas D. "A Discourse Commemorative of the Life and Service of the Rev. Chauncey Allen Goodrich" (1860). Funeral sermon, Yale Archives, New Haven, CT. Printed in the *New Englander*, May 5, 1860.

Worcester, Joseph Emerson. *A Gross Literary Fraud Exposed, Relating to the Publication of Worcester's Dictionary in London*. Boston: Jenks, Hickling, and Swan, 1853.

———. *A Gross Literary Fraud Exposed, Relating to the Publication of Worcester's Dictionary in London, Together with Three Appendixes Including the Answer of S. Converse to an Attack on Him by Messrs G. & C. Merriam*. Boston: Jenks, Hickling, and Swan, 1854.

Worcester, Samuel T. "Joseph Emerson Worcester, LL.D." *Granite Monthly* 3, no. 7 (April 1880): 245–72.

Zgusta, L. *Lexicography Then and Now*. Tübingen: Neimeyer, 2000.

II. Further Reading

Allen, Frederick Sturges. *Noah Webster's Place among English Lexicographers*. Springfield, MA: G. and C. Merriam Co., 1909.

Allibone, Samuel Austin. *A Critical Dictionary of English Literature and British and American Authors*. Vol. 1, 1854. Vols. 2–3, 1871. Reprint, Philadelphia: J. B. Lippincott, 1965.

Alston, R. C., ed. *Bibliography of the English Language*. Farnham, UK: Ashgate, 1965–73.

Arnove, Robert F., and Harvey J. Graff, eds. *National Literacy Campaigns and Historical Comparative Perspectives*. New York: Plenum Press, 1987.

Augst, Thomas. "American Libraries and Agencies of Culture." Introduction to *Print Culture History in Modern America*, edited by Thomas Augst and Wayne Wiegand. *American Studies* 42, no. 3 (Fall 2001): 5–22.

———. "The Business of Reading in Nineteenth-Century America: The New York Mercantile Library." *American Quarterly* 50, no. 2 (June 1998): 267–305.

Augst, Thomas, and Wayne Wiegand. *The Library as the Agency of Culture*. Madison: University of Wisconsin Press, 2003.

Baldasty, Gerald J. *The Commercialization of News in the Nineteenth Century*. Madison: University of Wisconsin Press, 1992.

Baron, Dennis E. *Grammar and Good Taste: Reforming the American Language*. New Haven, CT: Yale University Press, 1982.

Bartlett, John Russell. *Dictionary of Americanisms: A Glossary of Words and Phrases Usually Regarded as Peculiar to the United States*. Boston: Little, Brown, 1848; 2nd ed., 1859.

Bhaskar, Michael. *The Content Machine: Towards a Theory of Publishing from the Printing Press*. London: Anthem Press, 2013.

Bivens, Leslie. "Noah Webster's Etymological Principles." *Dictionaries: Journal of the Dictionary Society of North America* 4 (1982): 1–13.

Blakemore, Stephen. *Joel Barlow's "Columbiad": A Bicentennial Reading*. Knoxville: University of Tennessee Press, 2007.

Bragg, Melvyn. *The Adventure of English: The Biography of a Language*. London: Hodder and Stoughton, 2003.

Brown, Goold. *The Grammar of English Grammars*. 10th ed. New York: William Wood and Co., 1851.

Bryson, Bill. *The Mother Tongue: English and How It Got That Way*. New York: William Morrow, 1990. Published in England as *Mother Tongue: The Story of the English Language*. London: Penguin, 1990.

Burchfield, Robert W. *The English Language*. Oxford: Oxford University Press, 1985.

Bushman, Richard L. "The Genteel Republic." *Wilson Quarterly* 20, no. 4 (Autumn 1996): 13–23.

Cairns, William B. *British Criticisms of American Writings 1783–1815*. University of Wisconsin Studies in Language and Literature, no. 1. Madison: University of Wisconsin Press, 1918.

Chapman, Robert L. "A Working Lexicographer Appraises Webster's Third New International Dictionary." *American Speech* 42 (1967): 202–10.

Cmiel, Kenneth. "A Broad Fluid Language of Democracy: Discovering the American Idiom." In "Discovering America." Special issue, *Journal of American History* 79, no. 3 (December 1992): 913–36.

Cooper, Thomas. *Some Information Respecting America*. London: J. Johnson, 1794.

Cowie, A. P., ed. *The Oxford History of English Lexicography*. Oxford: Oxford University Press, 2008.

Crystal, David, ed. *Dr. Johnson's Dictionary: A Singularly Energetick Potpourri of some 4000 of the Most Entertaining and Historically Stimulating English Words and Definitions from Abactor to Zootomy Extracted from the World's Foremost Feat of Lexicography*. London: Penguin Classics, 2005.

———. *Spell It Out: The Singular Story of English Spelling*. London: Profile Books, 2012.

———. *The Stories of English*. London: Allen Lane, 2004.

DeMaria, Robert, Jr. *Johnson's Dictionary and the Language of Learning*. Chapel Hill: University of North Carolina Press, 1986.

Deppman, Jed. *Trying to Think with Emily Dickinson*. Amherst, MA: University of Massachusetts Press, 2008.

Dressman, Michael Rowan. "Walt Whitman's Plans for the Perfect Dictionary." In *Studies in the American Renaissance*, edited by Joel Myerson, 457–74. Boston: Twayne Publishers, 1980.

Edgerton, Franklin. "Notes on Early American Work in Linguistics." *Proceedings of the American Philosophical Society* 87, no. 1 (July 1943): 25–34.

Ellis, Joseph J. *After the Revolution: Profiles in Early American Culture*. New York: W. W. Norton, 1979.

Emerson, Ralph Waldo. *Selected Lectures*. Edited by Ronald A. Bosco and Joel Myerson. Athens: University of Georgia Press, 2005.

Farr, Judith, ed. *New Century Views of Emily Dickinson: A Collection of Critical Essays, 1830–1886*. Upper Saddle River, NJ: Prentice Hall, 1996.

Faust, Drew Gilpin. *The Republic of Suffering: Death and the American Civil War*. New York: Alfred A. Knopf, 2002.

Fernald, James C. *English Synonyms and Antonyms*. New York: Funk and Wagnalls, 1896.

Free, William J. "William Cullen Bryant on Nationalism, Imitation, and Originality." *Studies in Philology* 66, no. 4 (July 1969): 672–87.

Frothingham, Paul Revere. *Edward Everett: Orator and Statesman*. Boston: Houghton Mifflin, 1925.

Galtung, Johann. *Literacy and Social Development in the West*. Cambridge: Cambridge University Press, 1981.

Gove, Philip B. "Notes on Serialization and Competitive Publishing: Johnson and Bailey's Dictionaries, 1755," Oxford Bibliographical Society, *Proceedings and Papers* 5 (1940): 314–22.

———, ed. *Webster's Third New International Dictionary*. Springfield, MA: Merriam and Co., 1961.

Graff, Harvey J. *The Literacy Myth: Literacy and Social Structure in the Nineteenth-Century City*. New York: Academic Press, 1979. Reprint, New Brunswick, NJ: Transaction Publications, 1991.

Grubb, F. W. "Growth of Literacy in Colonial America." *Social Science History* 14, no. 4 (Winter 1990): 451–82.

Gura, Phillip F. "The Village Enlightenment in New England, 1760–1820." *William and Mary Quarterly*, 3rd ser., 47 (1990): 327–46.

Hartmann, R.R.K. *Lexicography: Reference Works across Time, Space, and Languages*. London: Taylor and Francis, 2003.

Hitchings, Henry. *Dr. Johnson's Dictionary: The Extraordinary Story of the Book That Defined the World*. London: John Murray, 2005.

———. *The Secret Life of Words: How English Became English*. New York: Farrar, Straus and Giroux, 2008.

Hodson, Jane. *Language and Revolution in Burke, Wollstonecraft, Paine, and Godwin*. Aldershot, UK: Ashgate, 2007.

Hudson, Frederic. *Journalism in the United States, from 1690 to 1872*. Vol. 1. London: Routledge/Thoemmes Press, 2000.

Huntzicker, William. *The Popular Press, 1833–1865*. Westport, CT: Greenwood Press, 1999.

Ikeda, Makoto. *Competing Grammars: Noah Webster's Vain Efforts to Defeat Lindley Murray*. Tokyo: Shinozaki Shorin, 1994.

Kennedy, J. Edgar, and Jerome McGann, eds. *Poe and the Remapping of Antebellum Print Culture*. Baton Rouge: Louisiana State University Press, 2012.

Kilbride, Daniel. *Being American in Europe 1750–1860*. Baltimore, MD: Johns Hopkins University Press, 2013.

Korshin, Paul. "Johnson and the Renaissance Dictionary." *Journal of the History of Ideas* 35 (1974): 300–312.

Ladd, Joseph Brown. *The Literary Remains of Joseph Brown Ladd, M.D.* New York: H. C. Sleight, 1832.

Laird, Charlton. "Etymology, Anglo-Saxon, and Noah Webster." *American Speech* 21, no. 1 (February 1946): 3–15.

Larkin, Jack. "The Merriams of Brookfield: Printing in the Economy and Culture of Rural Massachusetts in the Early Nineteenth Century." *Proceedings of the American Antiquarian Society* 96, pt. 1 (April 1986): 39–73.

Ley, James. *The Critic in the Modern World: Public Criticism from Samuel Johnson to James Wood*. London: Bloomsbury, 2014.

Littlejohn, David. *Dr. Johnson and Noah Webster: Two Men and Their Dictionaries*. San Francisco: Book Club of California, 1971.

Lockridge, Kenneth. *Literacy in Colonial New England*. Rev. ed. New York: W. W. Norton, 1974.

Longfellow, Ernest Wadsworth. *Random Memories*. Boston: Houghton Mifflin, 1922.

Lynch, Jack, ed. *Dr. Johnson's Dictionary*. Delray Beach, FL: Levenger Press, 2002; New York: Walker, 2003; London: Atlantic, 2004.

Lynch, Jack, and Anne McDermott, eds. *Anniversary Essays on Johnson's Dictionary*. Cambridge: Cambridge University Press, 2005.

Matthiesen, F. O. *American Renaissance: Art and Expression in the Age of Emerson and Whitman*. London: Oxford University Press, 1941.

McArthur, Tom, ed. *The Oxford Companion to the English Language*. Oxford: Oxford University Press, 1992.

McGill, Meredith. *American Literature and the Culture of Reprinting*. Philadelphia: University of Pennsylvania Press, 2003.

Miller, Cristanne. *Emily Dickinson: A Poet's Grammar*. Cambridge, MA: Harvard University Press, 1987.

———. *Reading in Time: Emily Dickinson and the Nineteenth Century*. Amherst: University of Massachusetts Press, 2012.

Mitchell, Linda. *Grammar Wars: Language as Cultural Battlefield in Seventeenth and Eighteenth Century England*. Aldershot, UK: Ashgate, 2001.

Morton, Herbert C. *The Story of* Webster's Third: *Phillip Gove's Controversial Dictionary and Its Critics*. Cambridge: Cambridge University Press, 1994.

Myers, Gustavus. *America Strikes Back: A Record of Contrasts*. New York: Ives, Washburn, 1935.

Nerone, John. *The Culture of the Press in the Early Republic: Cincinnati, 1793–1848*. New York: Garland, 1989.

Noyes, Gertrude. "The Critical Reception of Dr. Johnson's Dictionary." *Modern Philology* 52 (February 1955): 175–91.

Ostler, Rosemarie. *Founding Grammars: How Early America's War over Words Shaped Today's Language*. New York: St. Martin's Press, 2015.

Pachter, Mark, and Francis Wein, eds. *Abroad in America: Visitors to the New Nation 1776–1914*. Reading, MA: Addison-Wesley, 1976.

Pyles, Thomas. *Words and Ways of American English: An Authoritative Account of the Origins, Growth and Present State of the English Language in America*. London: Andrew Melrose, 1954.

Reddick, Allen. *The Making of Johnson's Dictionary 1746–1773*. Cambridge Studies in Publishing and Printing History. Cambridge: Cambridge University Press, 1990; rev. ed., 1996.

Roznicki, Michal Jan. "Between Private and Public Spheres: Liberty as Cultural Property in Eighteenth-Century British America." In *Cultures and Identities in Colonial British America*, edited by Robert Olwell and Alan Tully, 270–318. Baltimore, MD: Johns Hopkins University Press, 2006.

Rudolph, Frederick. *Essays on Education in the Early Republic*. Cambridge, MA: Harvard University Press, 1965.

Schele de Vere, Maximilian. *Americanisms: The English of the New World*. New York: Charles Scribner and Co., 1872.

———. *Studies in English*. New York: Charles Scribner and Co., 1867.

Schudson, Michael. *Discovering the News: A Social History of American Newspapers*. New York: Basic Books, 1998.

Smith, John Charles. *Synonyms Discriminated*. London: Bell and Daldy, 1871. 2nd ed., 1890.

Smith, Olivia. *The Politics of Language, 1791–1819*. Oxford: Oxford University Press, 1984.

Stevens, Edward, Jr. "Mass Literacy in Nineteenth-Century United States." In *National Literacy Campaigns: Historical and Comparative Perspectives*, edited by Robert F. Arnove and Harvey J. Graff, 99–122. New York: Plenum Press, 1987.

Todd, Charles Burr. *Life and Letters of Joel Barlow, LL.D.* New York: G. P. Putnam's Sons, 1886.

Venetsky, Richard L. "Spelling." In *The Cambridge History of the English Language*. Vol. 6, *English in North America*, edited by John Algeo, 340–57. Cambridge: Cambridge University Press, 2001.

Volo, James M., and Dorothy Denneen Volo. *The Antebellum Period*. Westport, CT: Greenwood Press, 2004.

———. *Family Life in 19th-Century America*. Westport, CT: Greenwood, 2007.

Weekley, Ernest. "On Dictionaries." *Atlantic Monthly*, June 1924, 782–91.

Wheatley, Henry B. "Chronological Notices of Dictionaries of the English Language." *Transactions of the Philological Society* 10, no. 1 (November 1865): 218–93.

Wineapple, Brenda, ed. *19th Century American Writers on Writing*. San Antonio, TX: Trinity University Press, 2010.

———. *White Heat: The Friendship of Emily Dickinson and Thomas Wentworth Higginson*. New York: Knopf, 2008.

Index